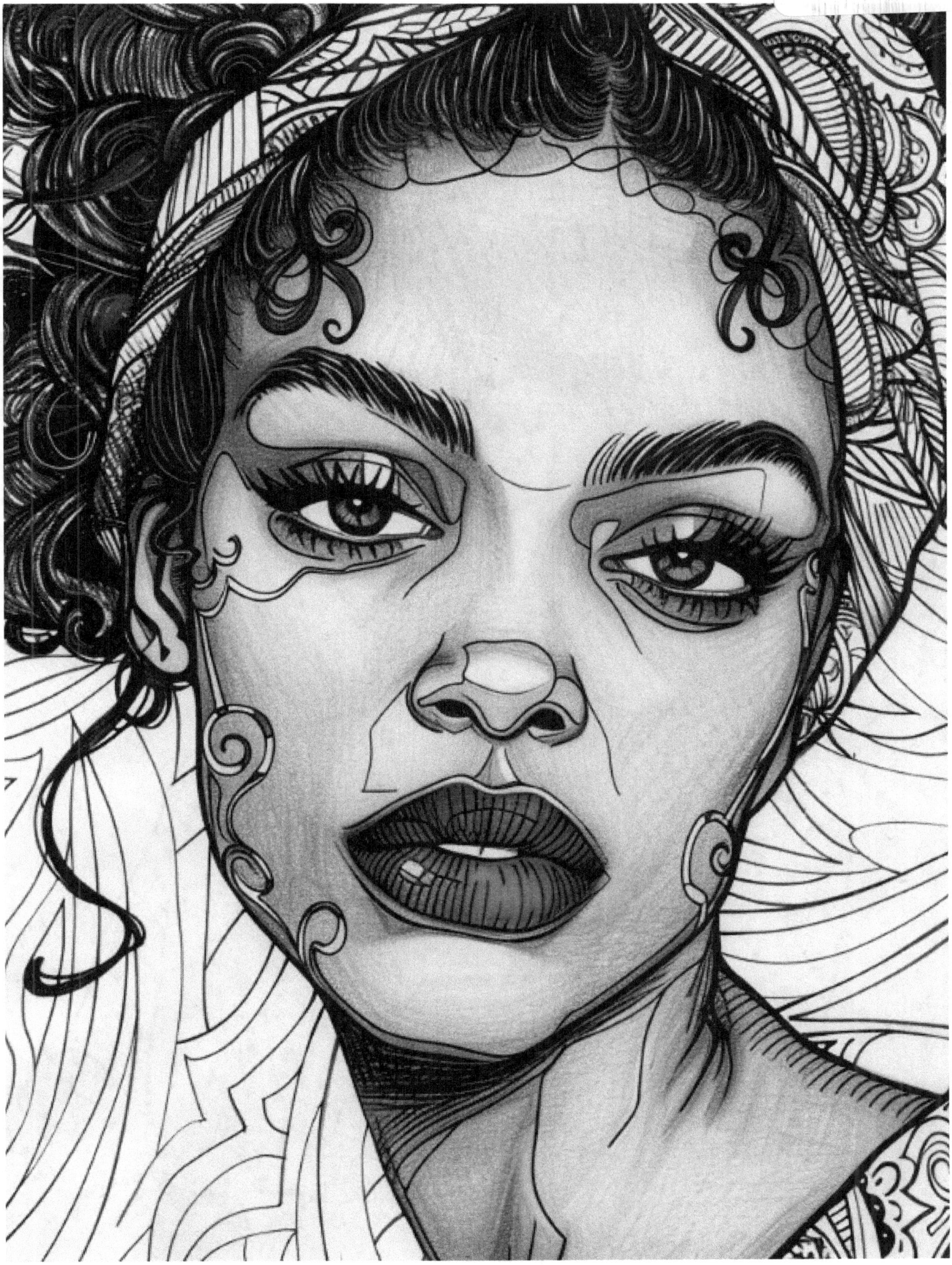

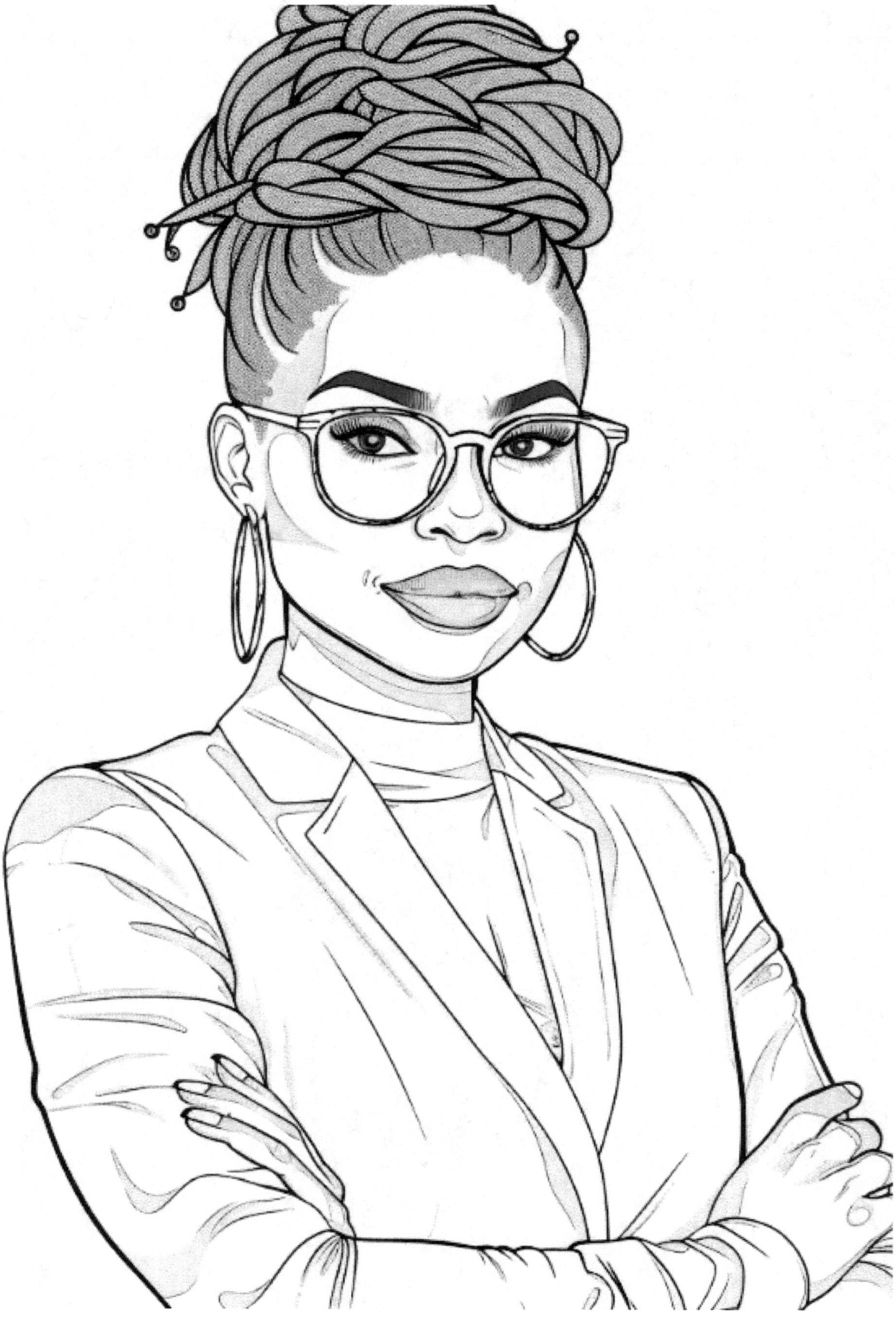

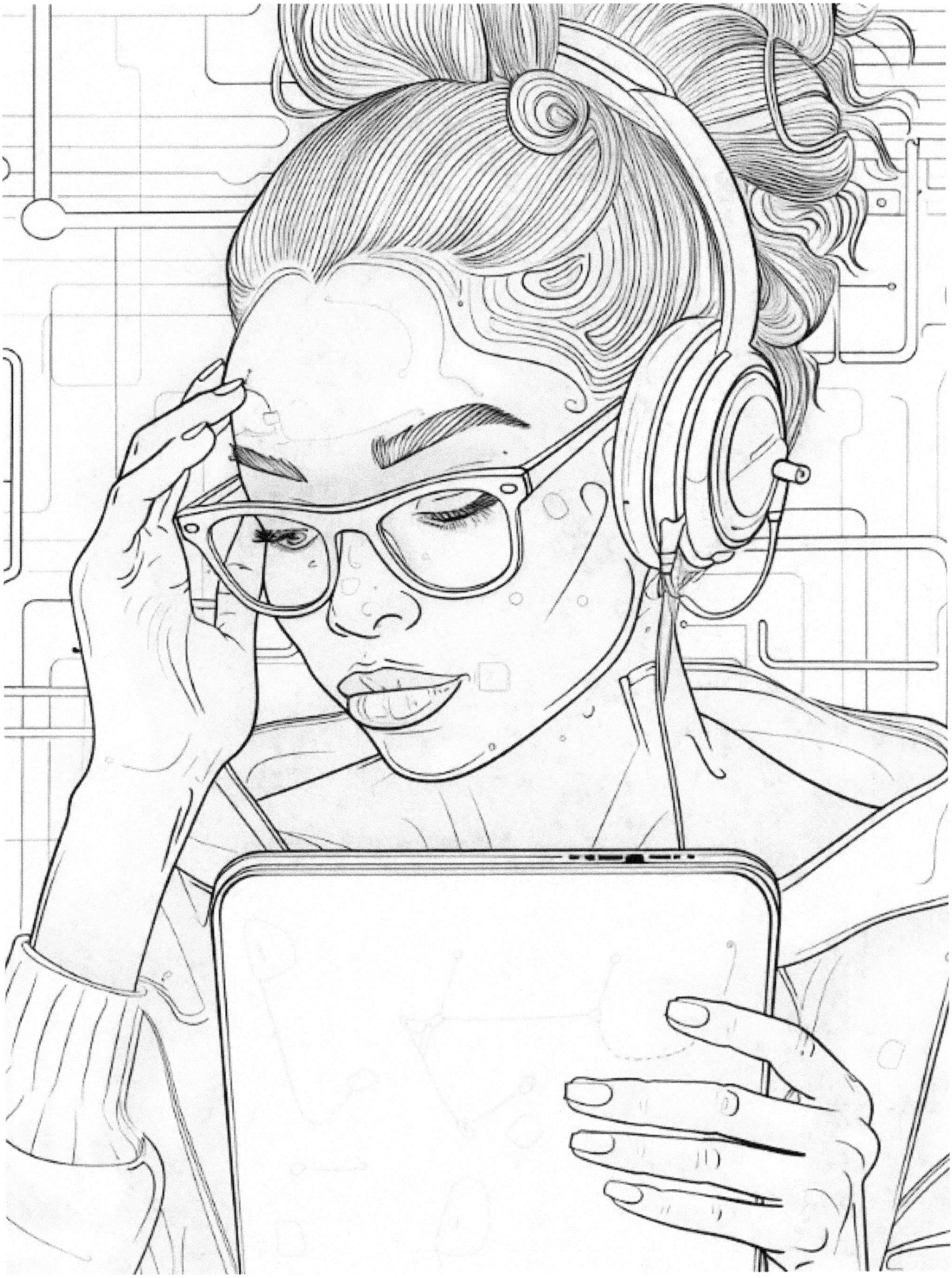

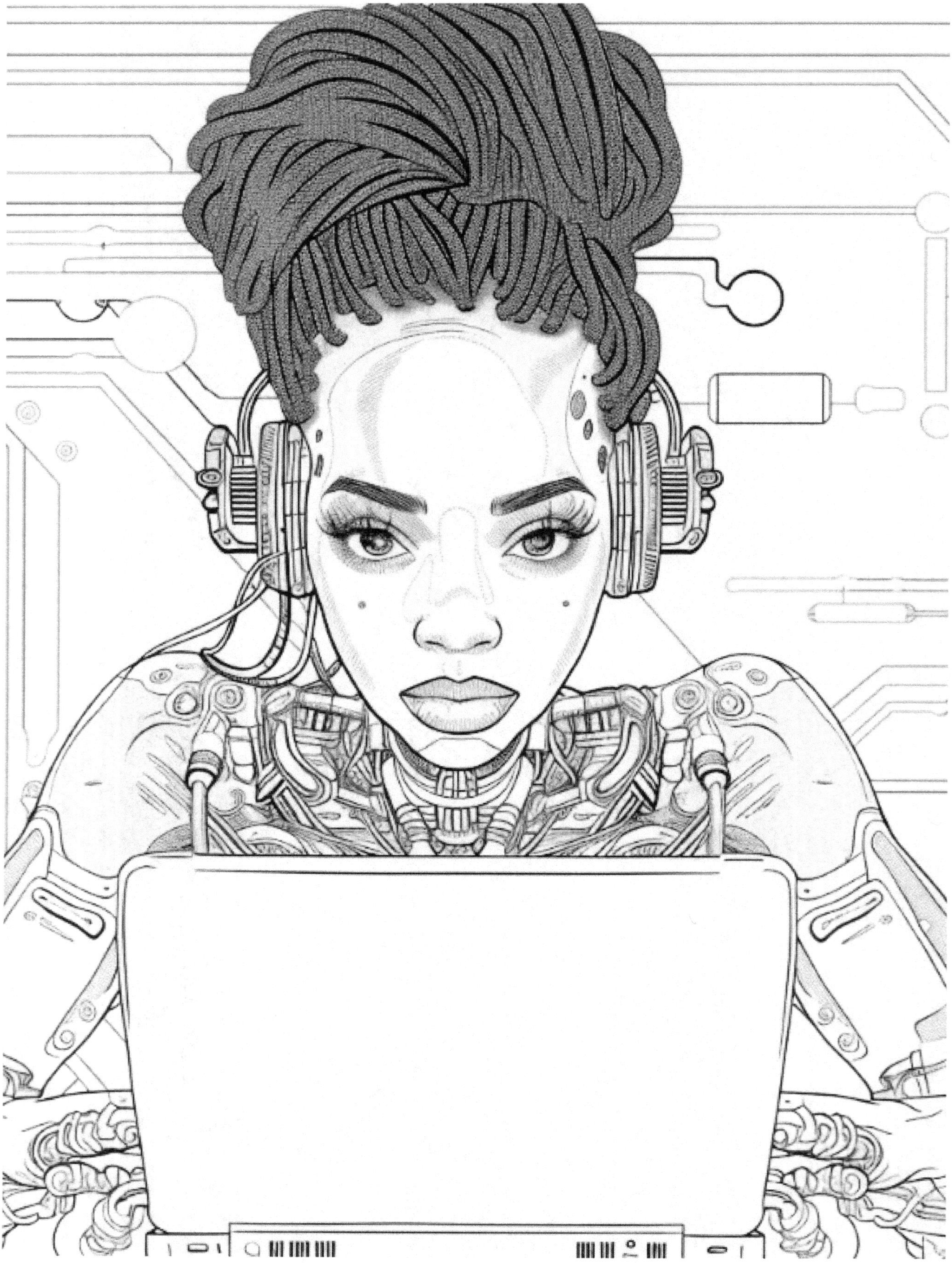

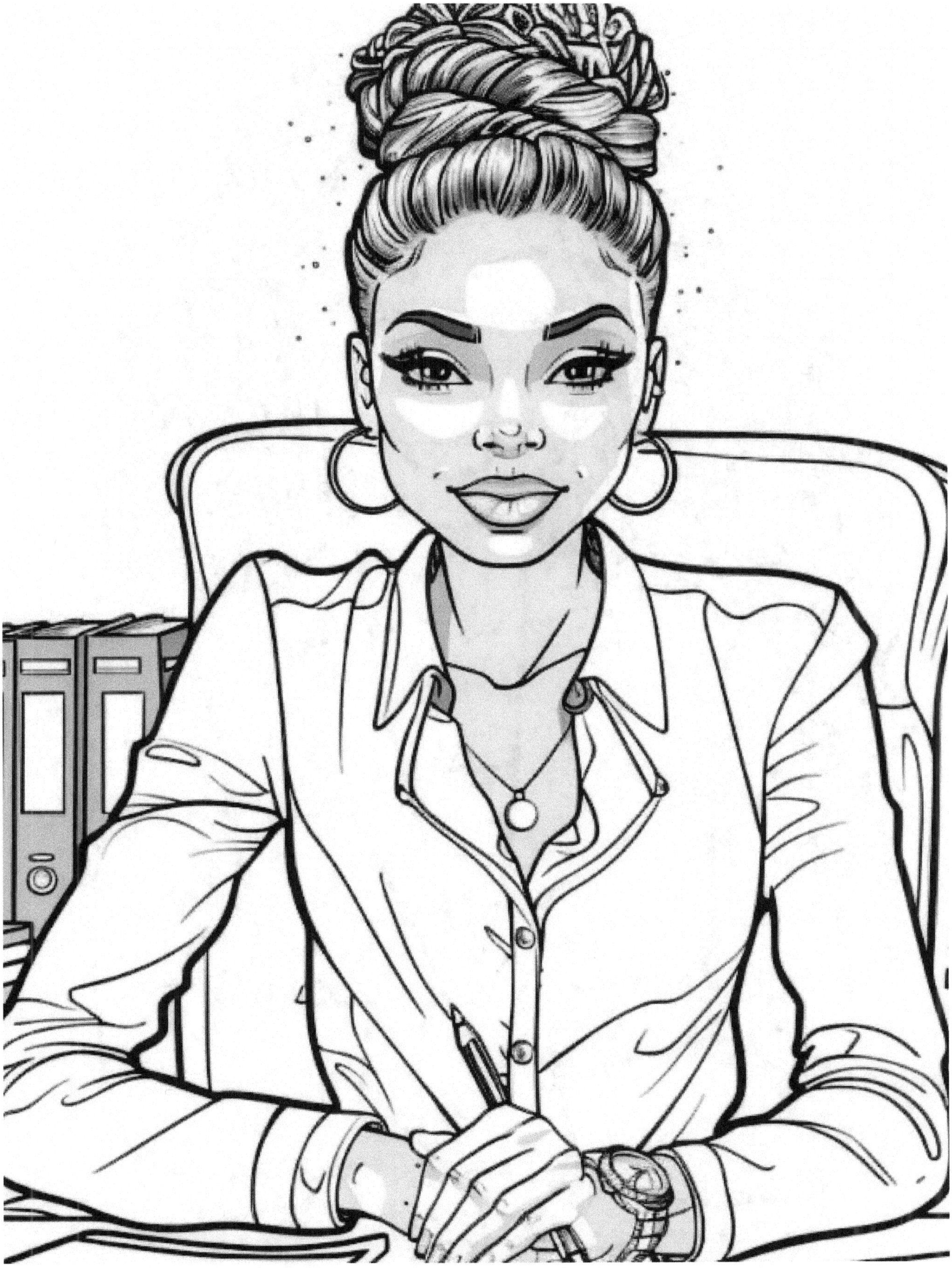

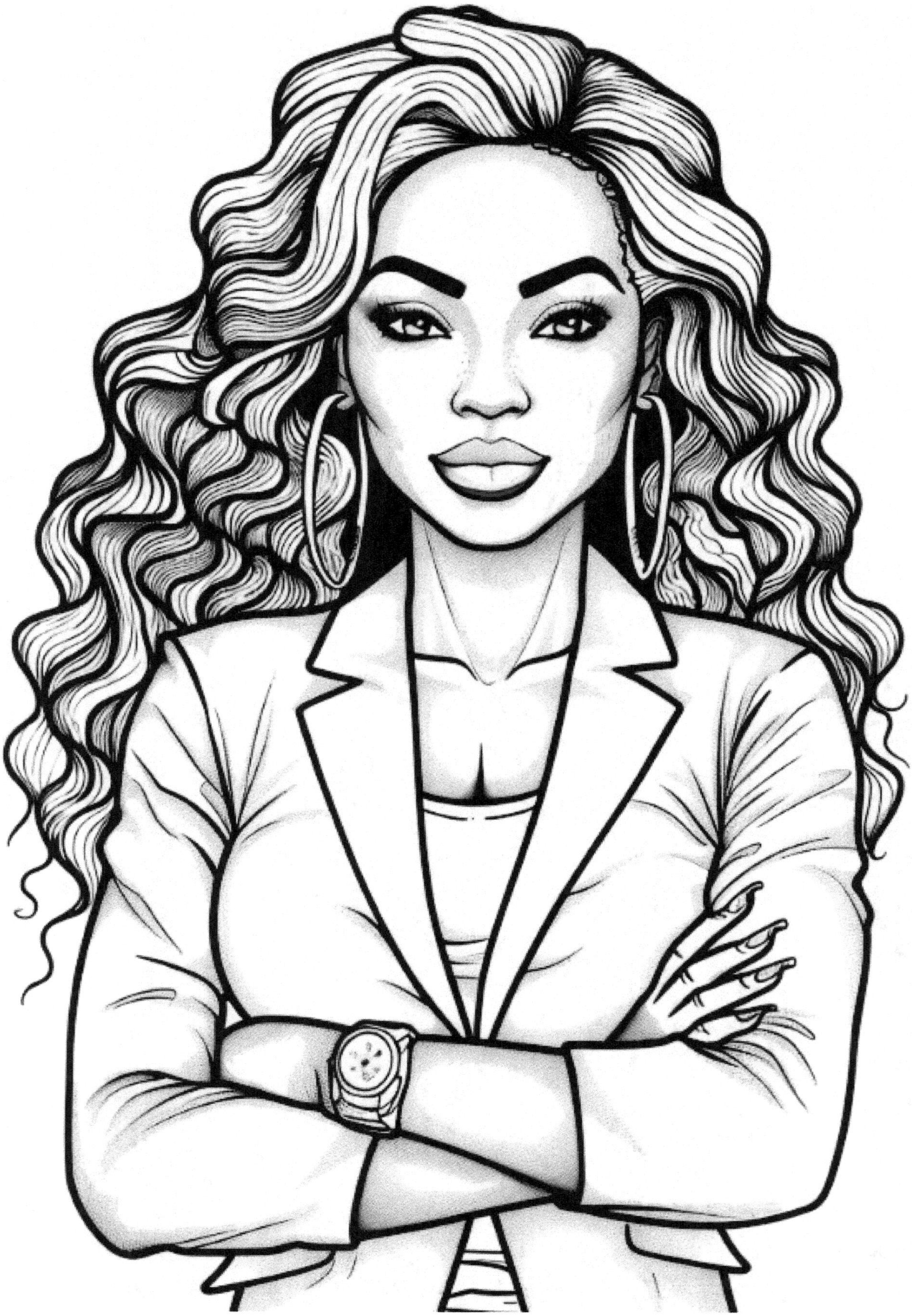

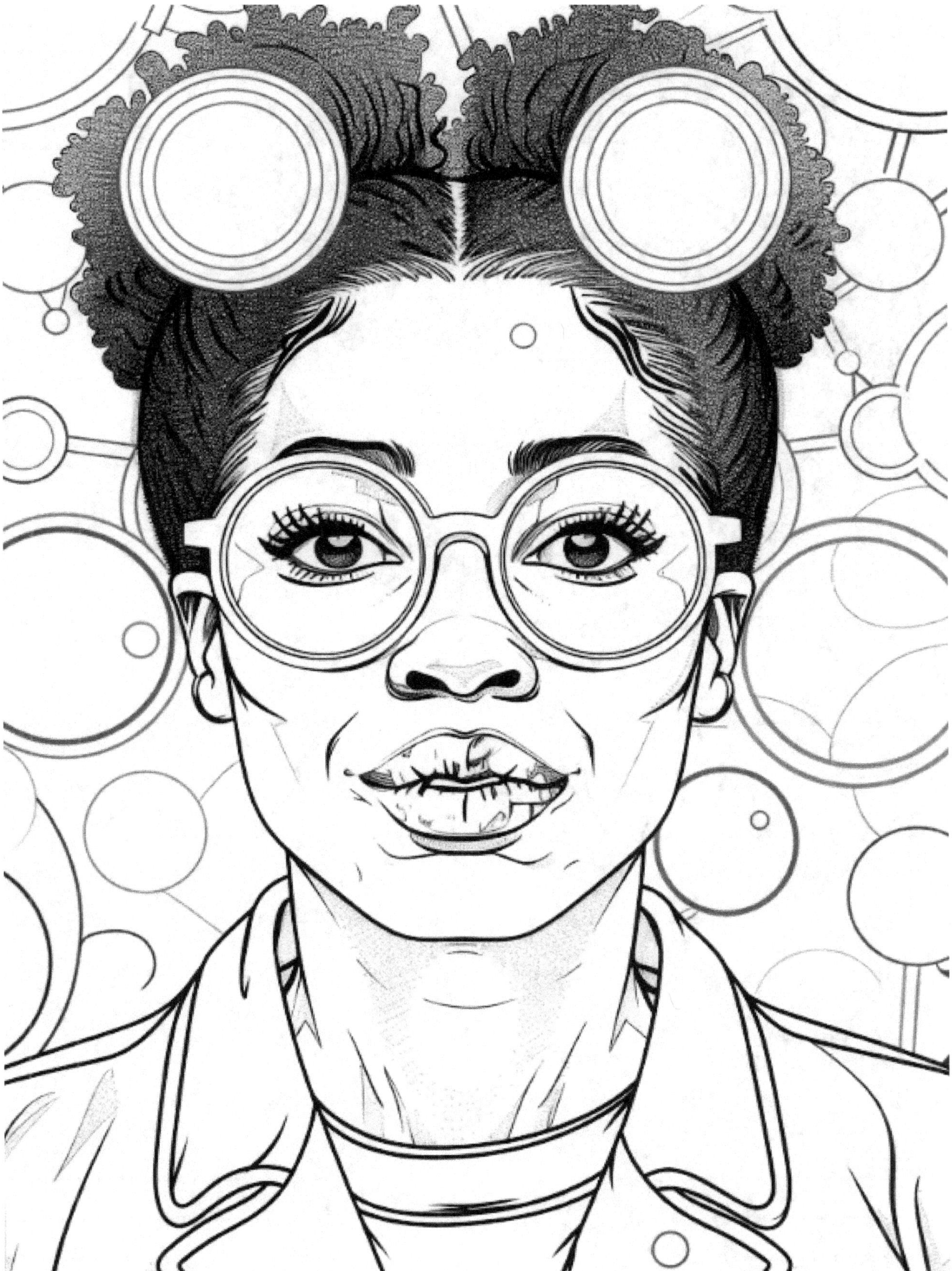

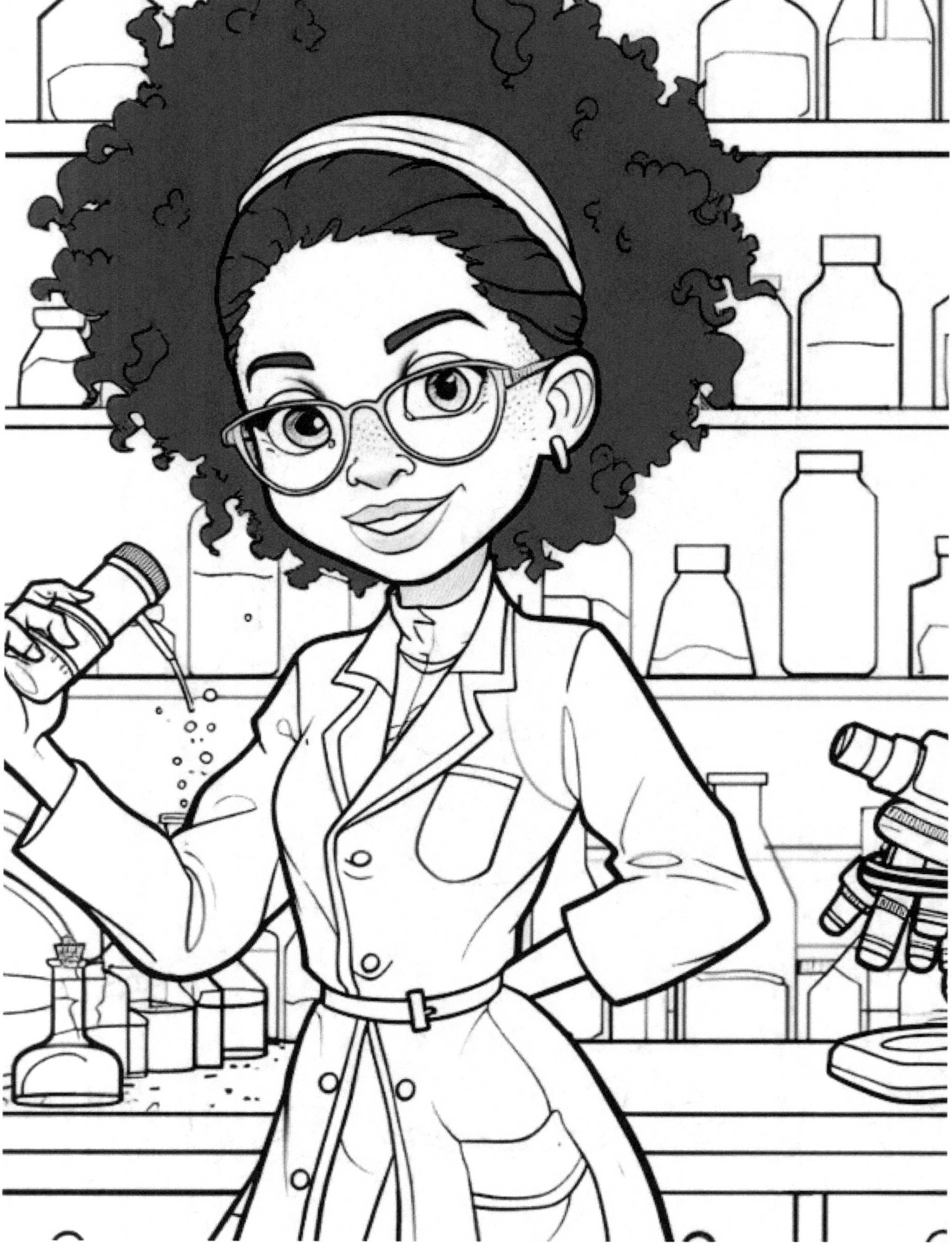

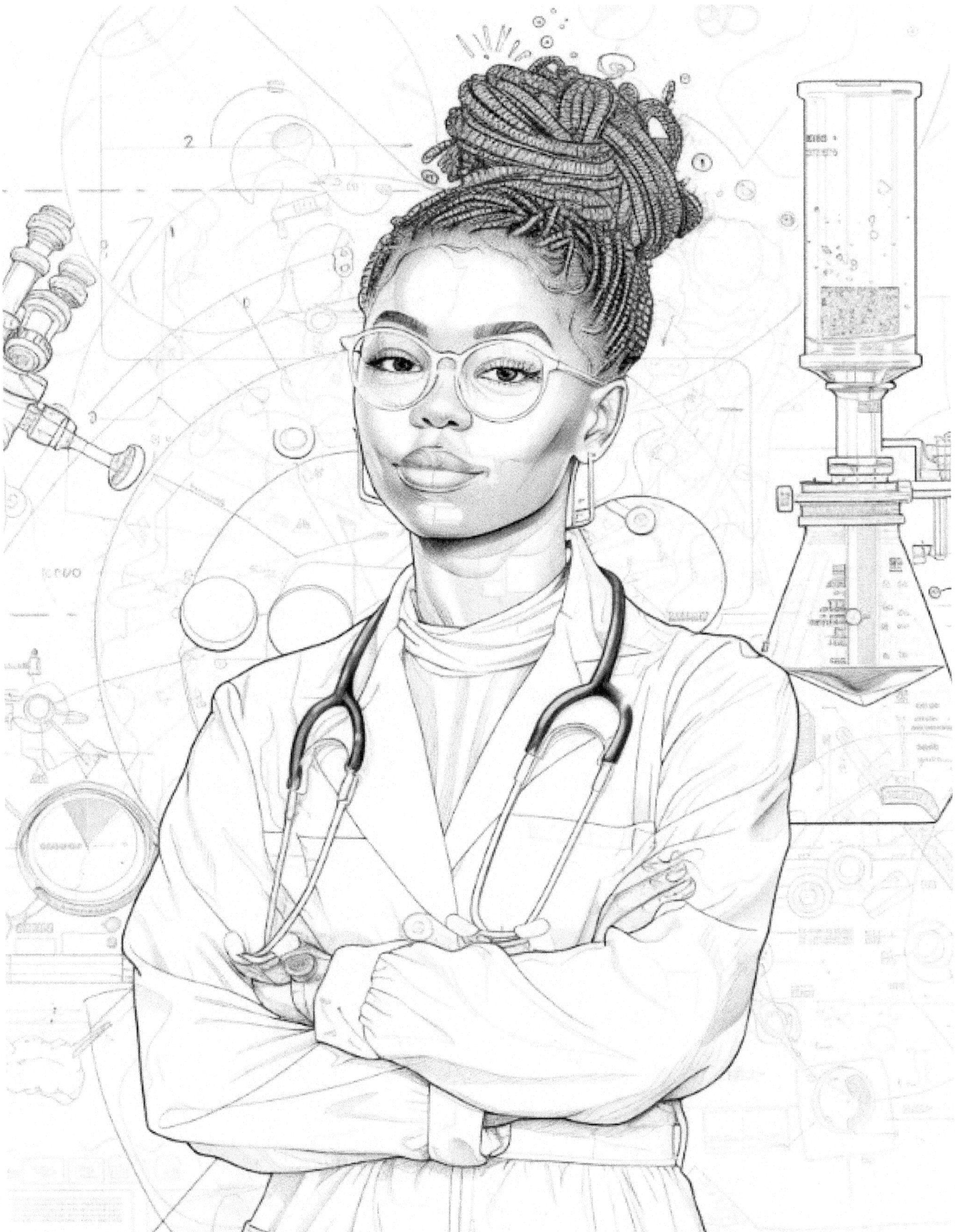

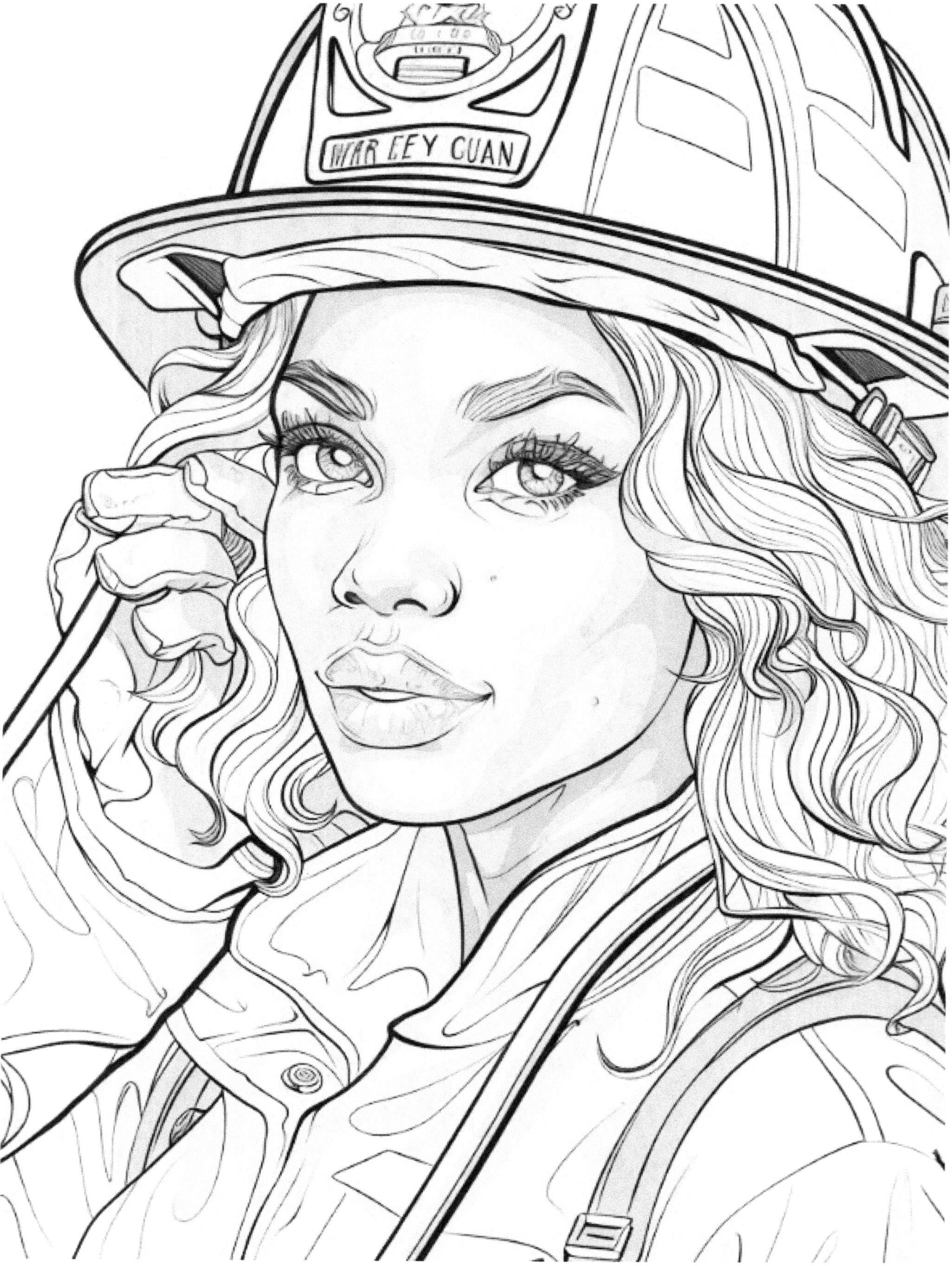

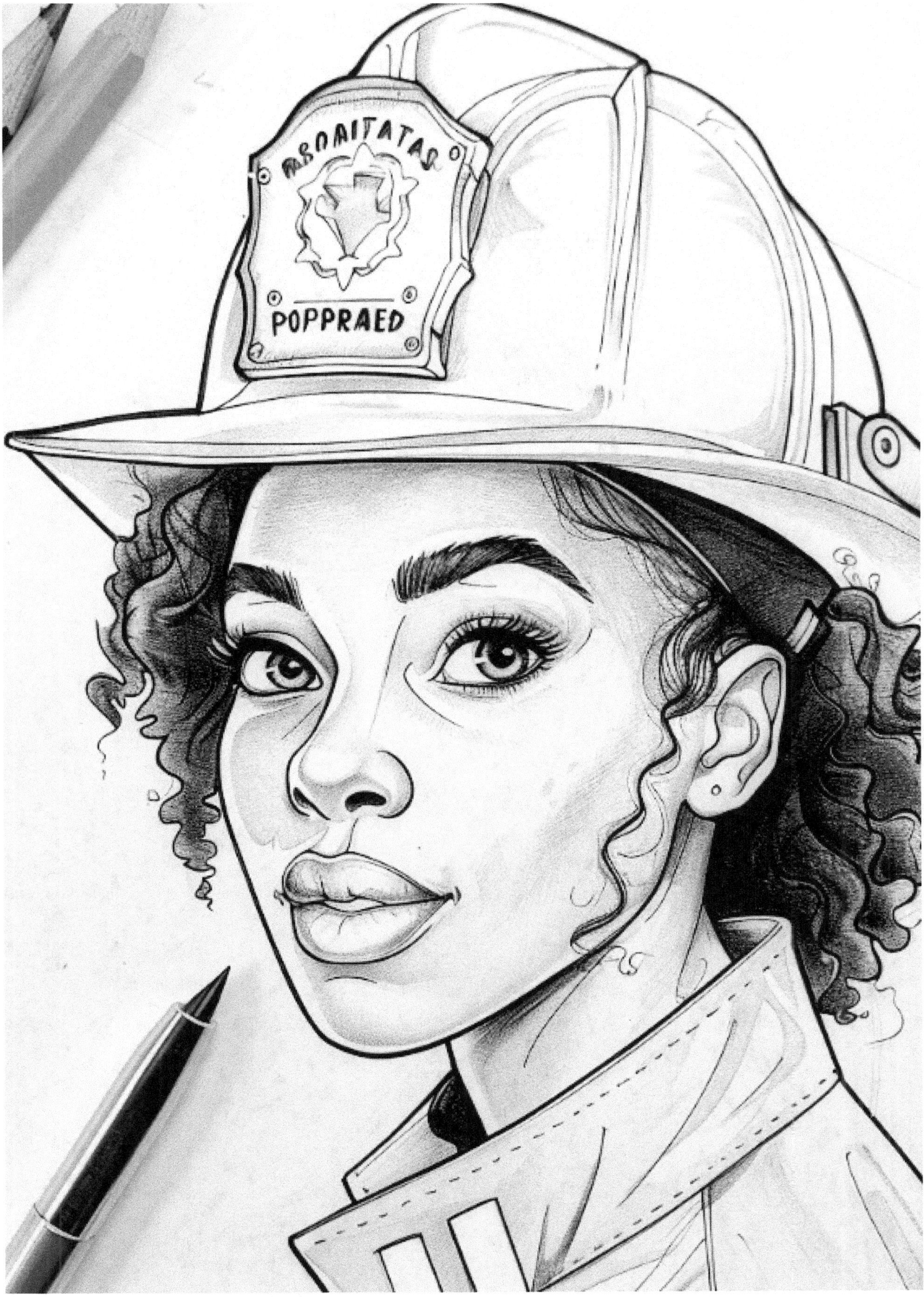
POPPRAED

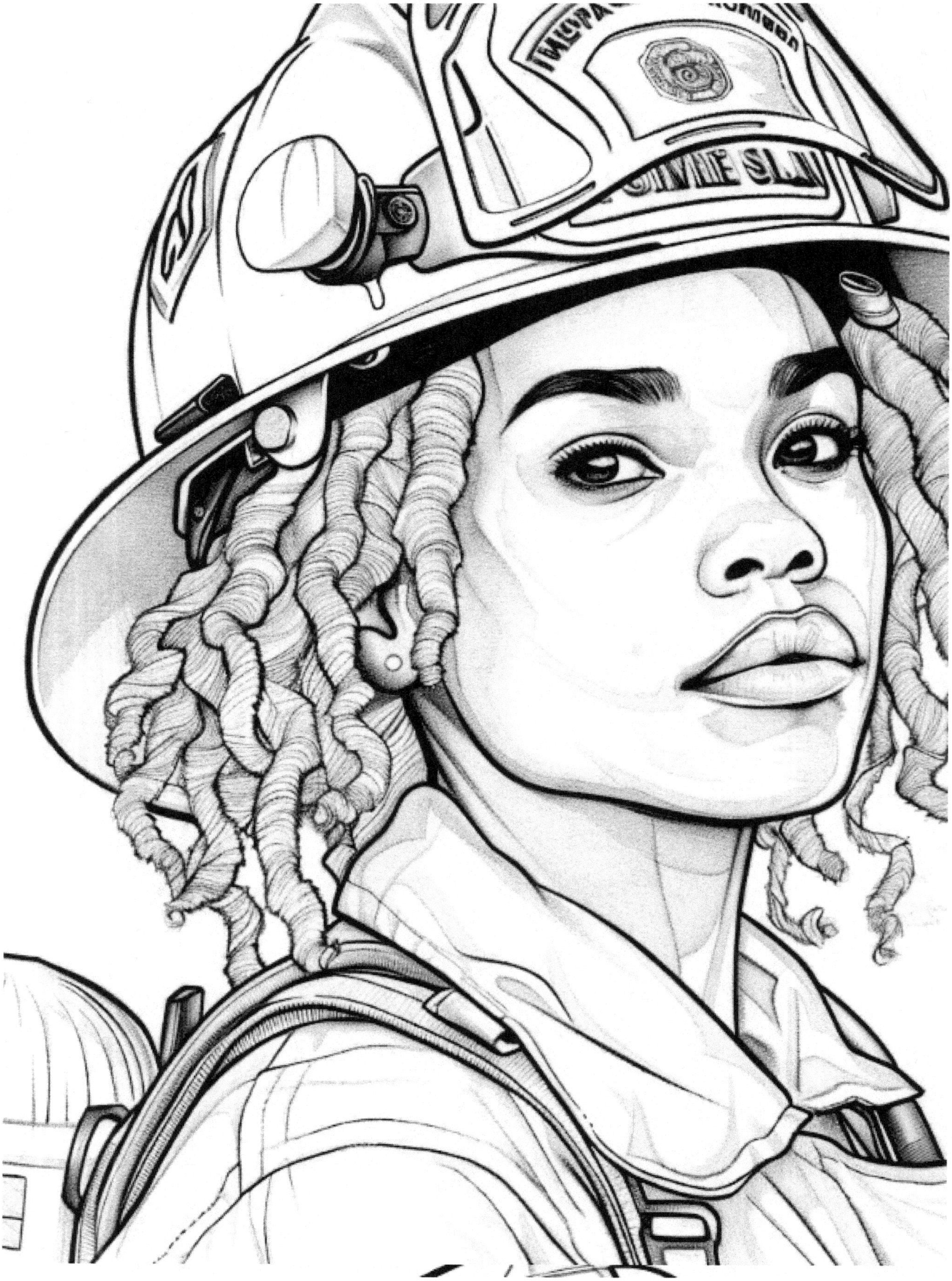

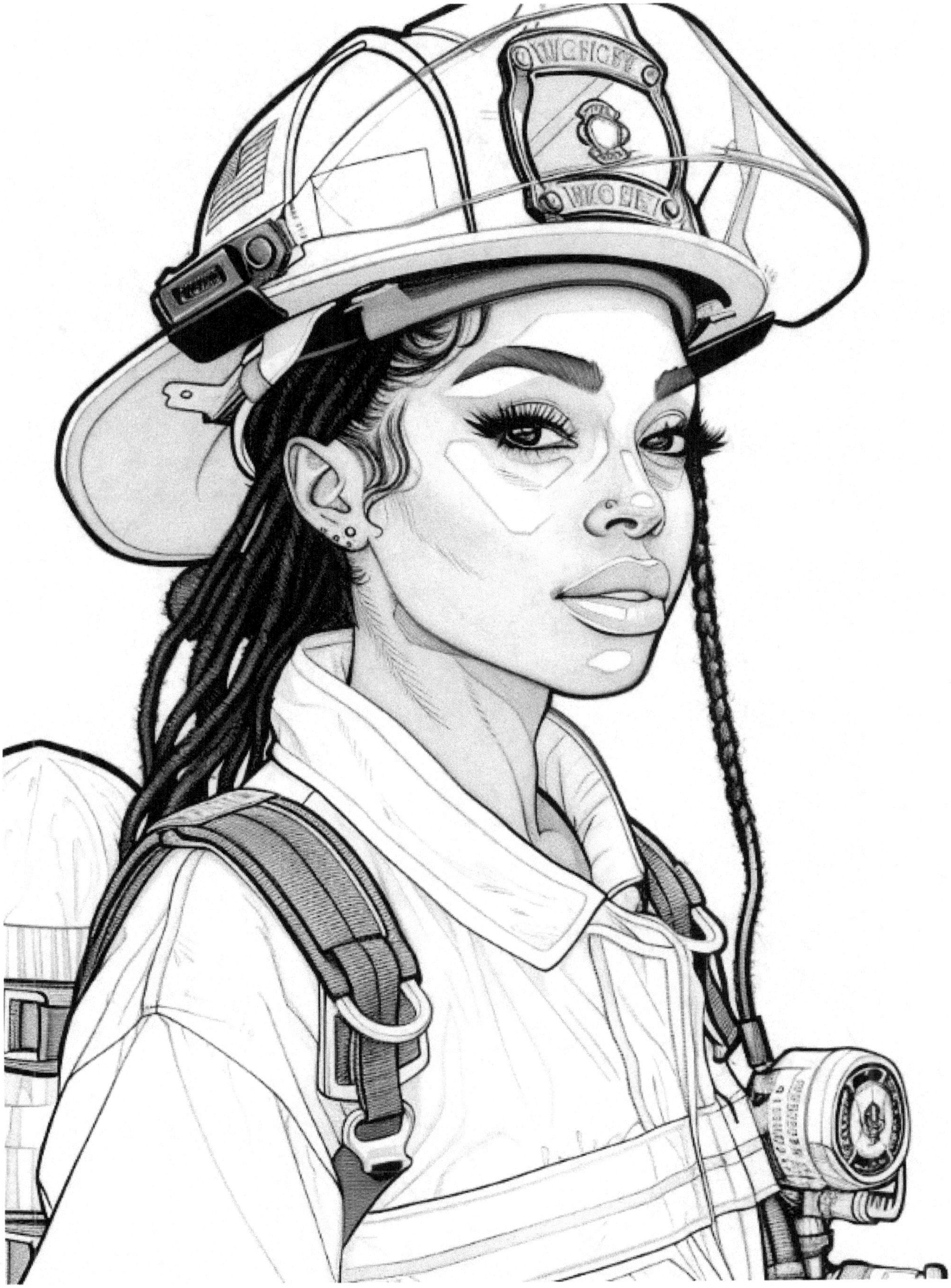

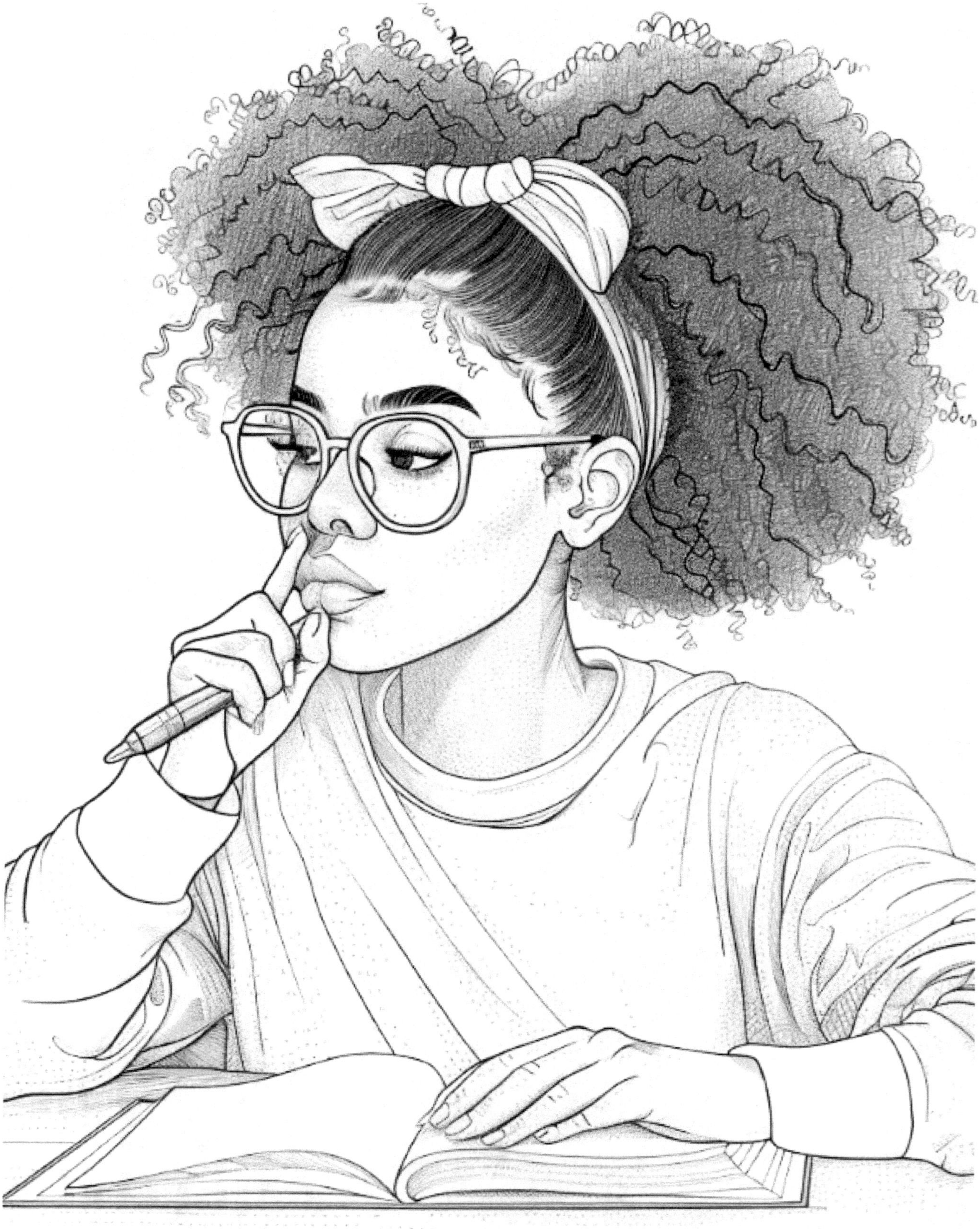

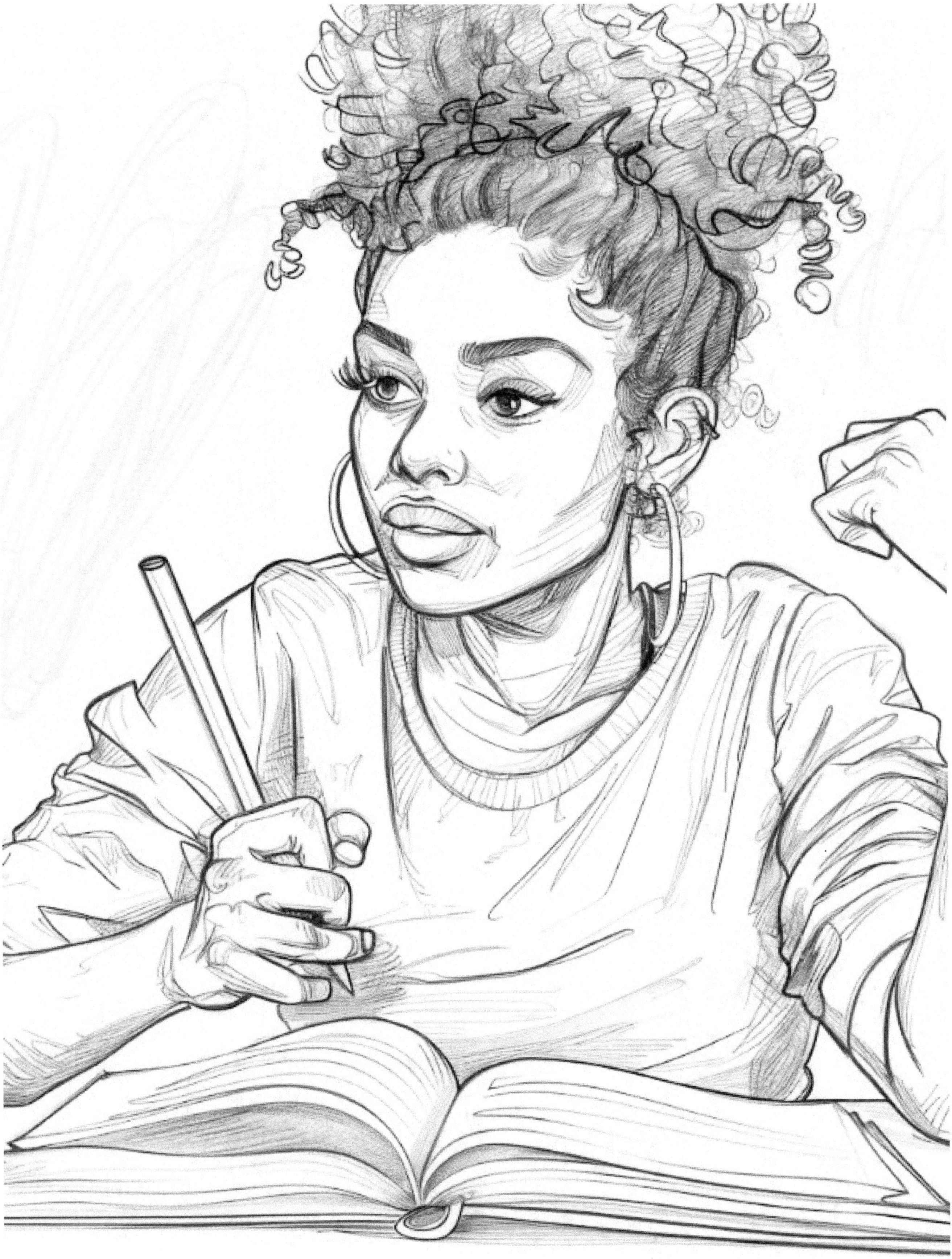

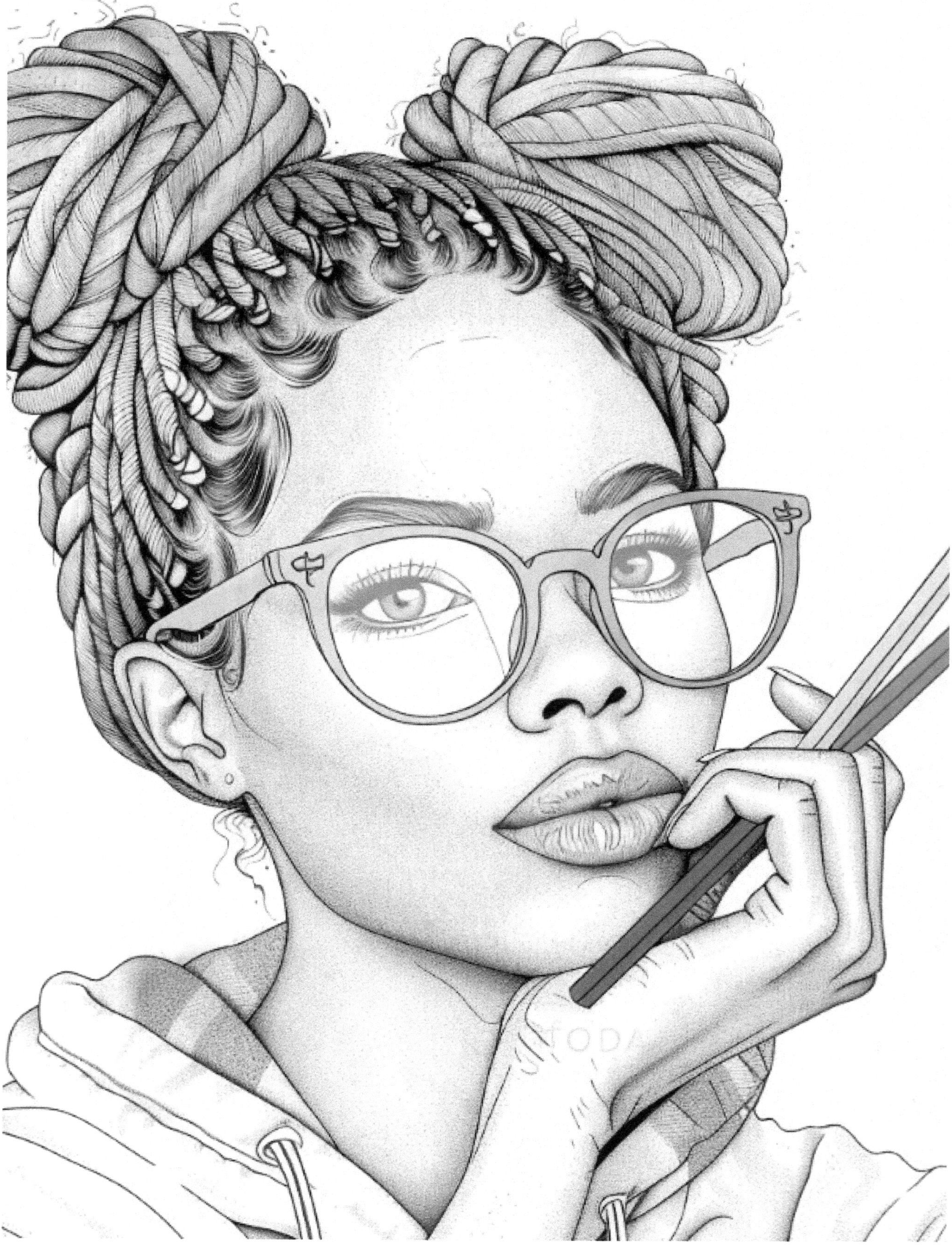

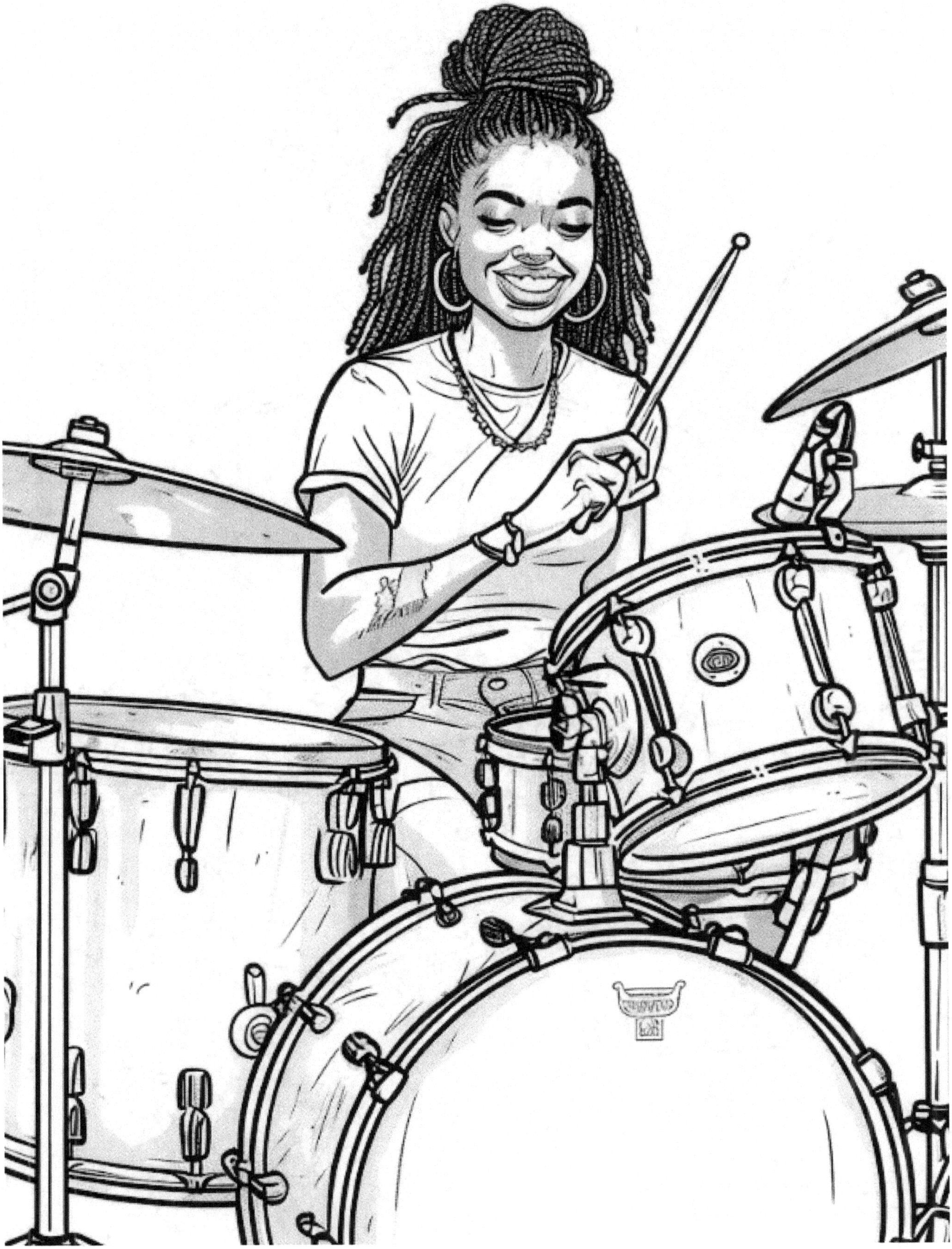

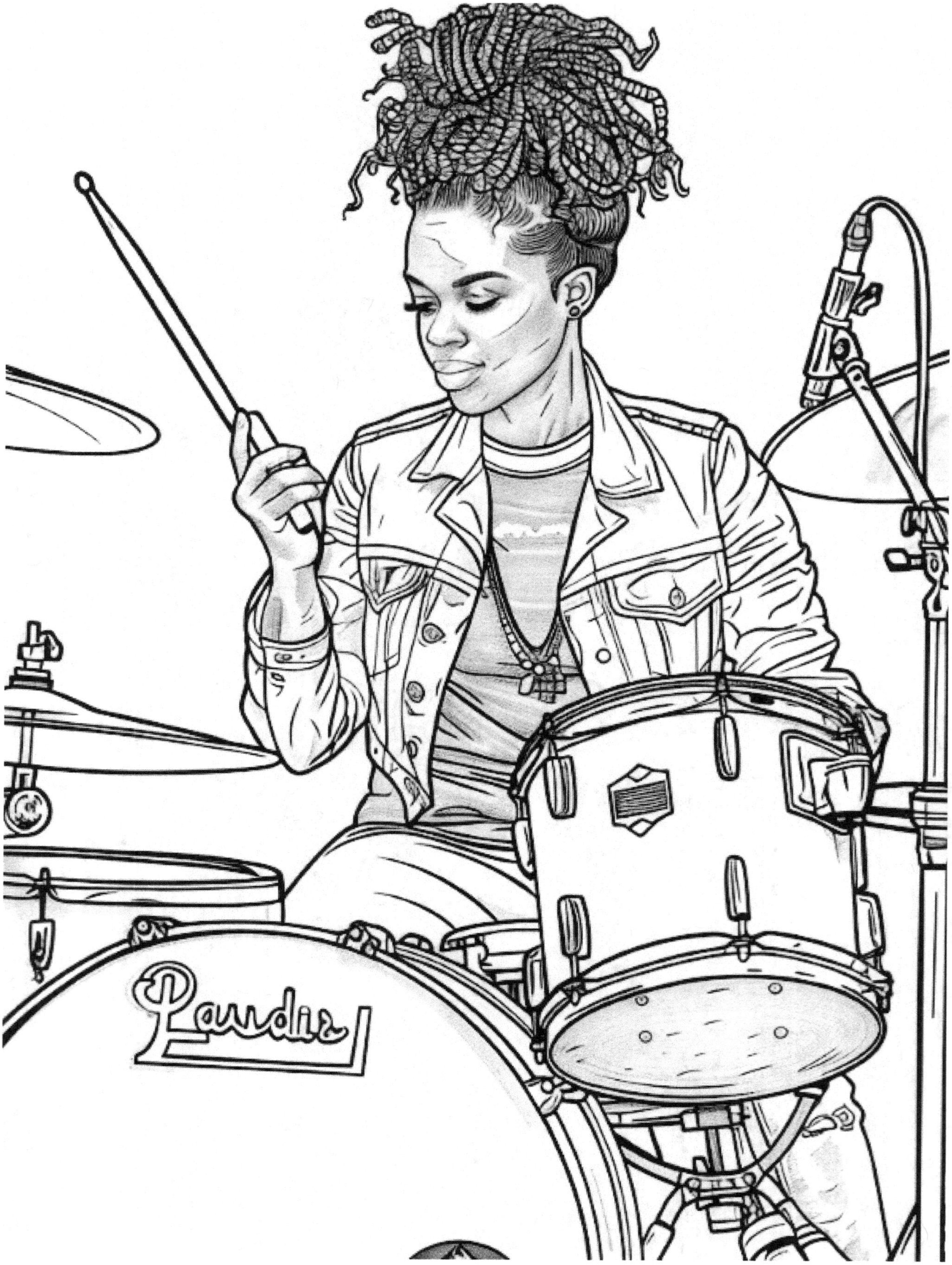

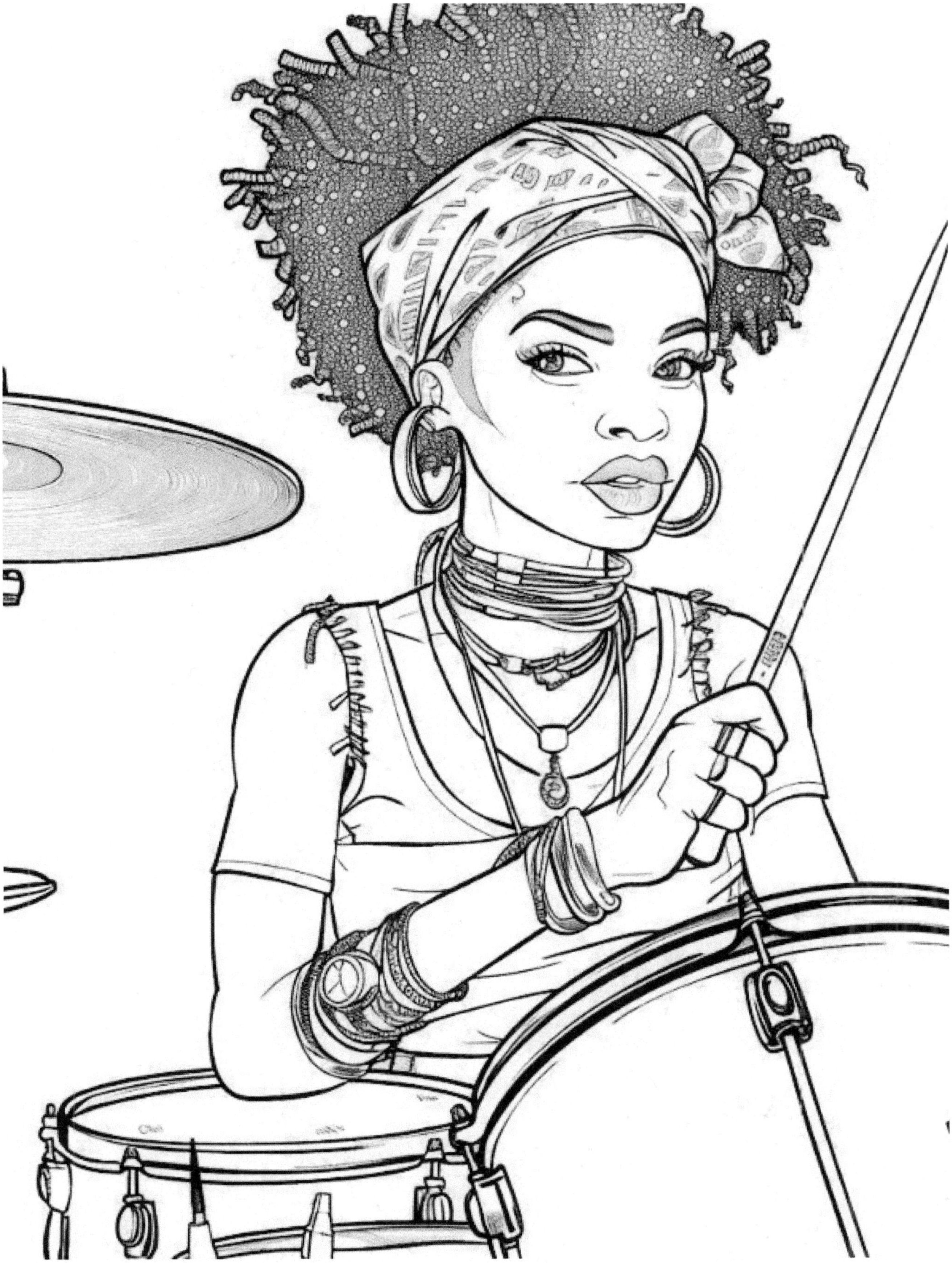

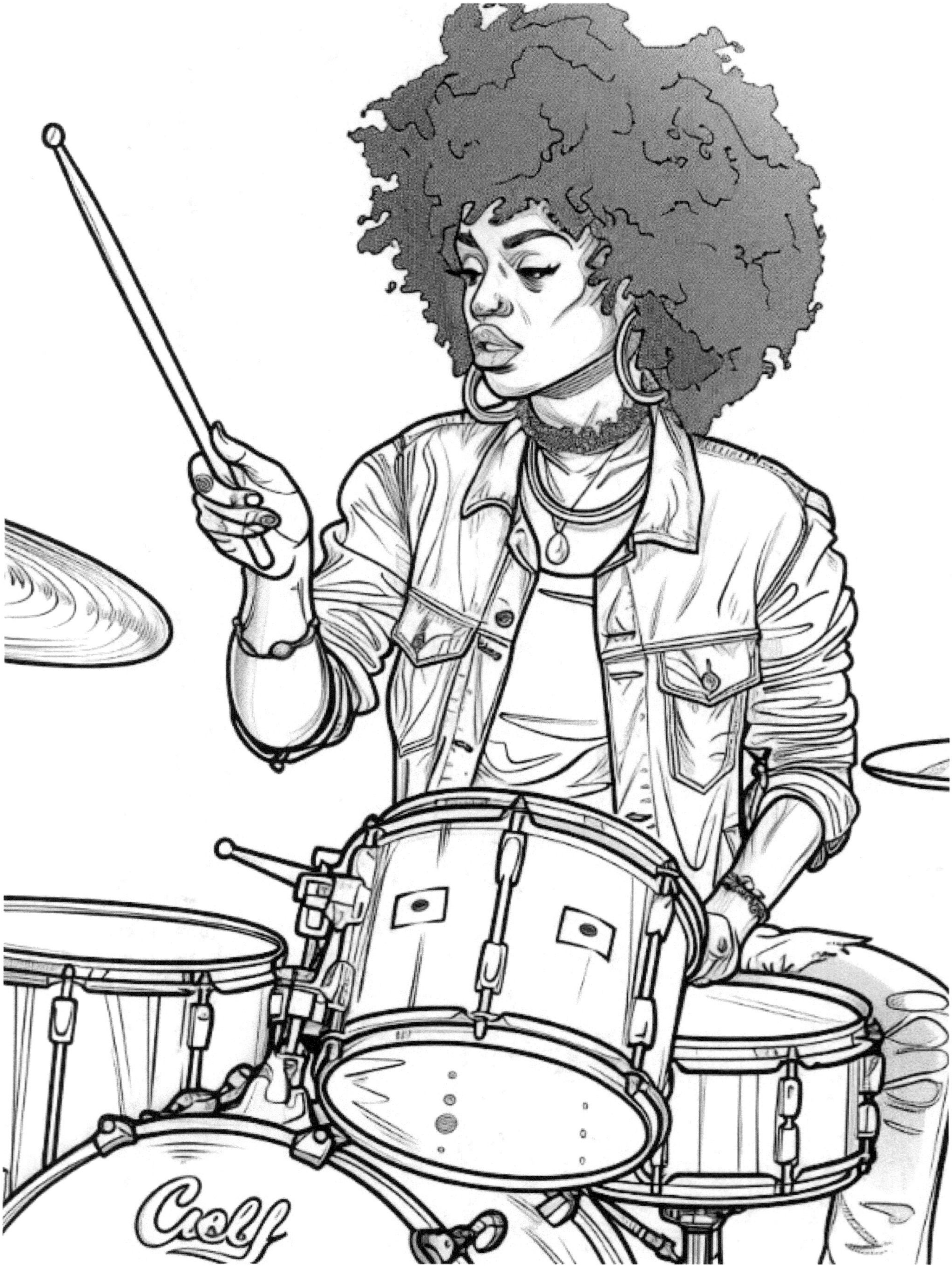

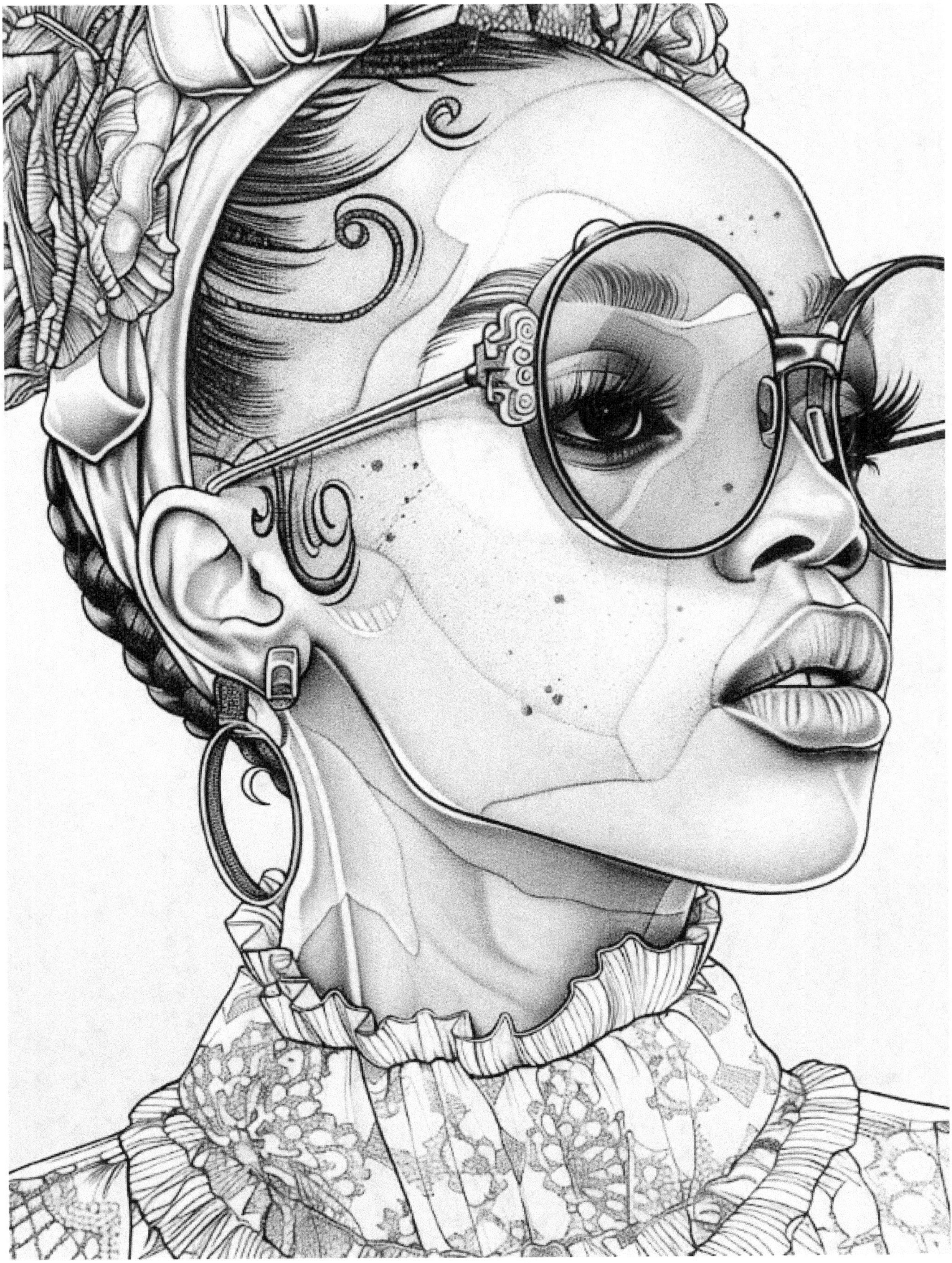

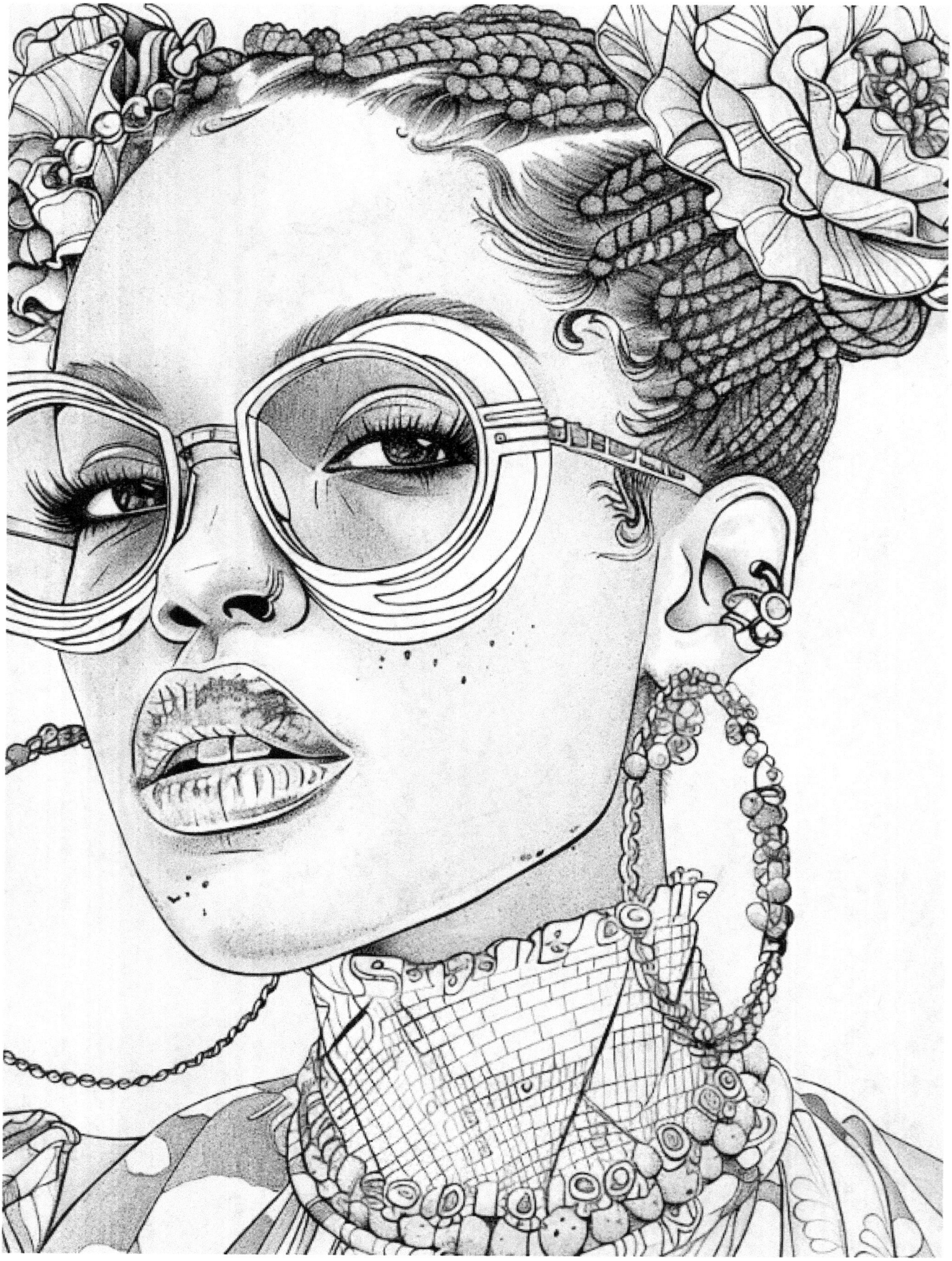

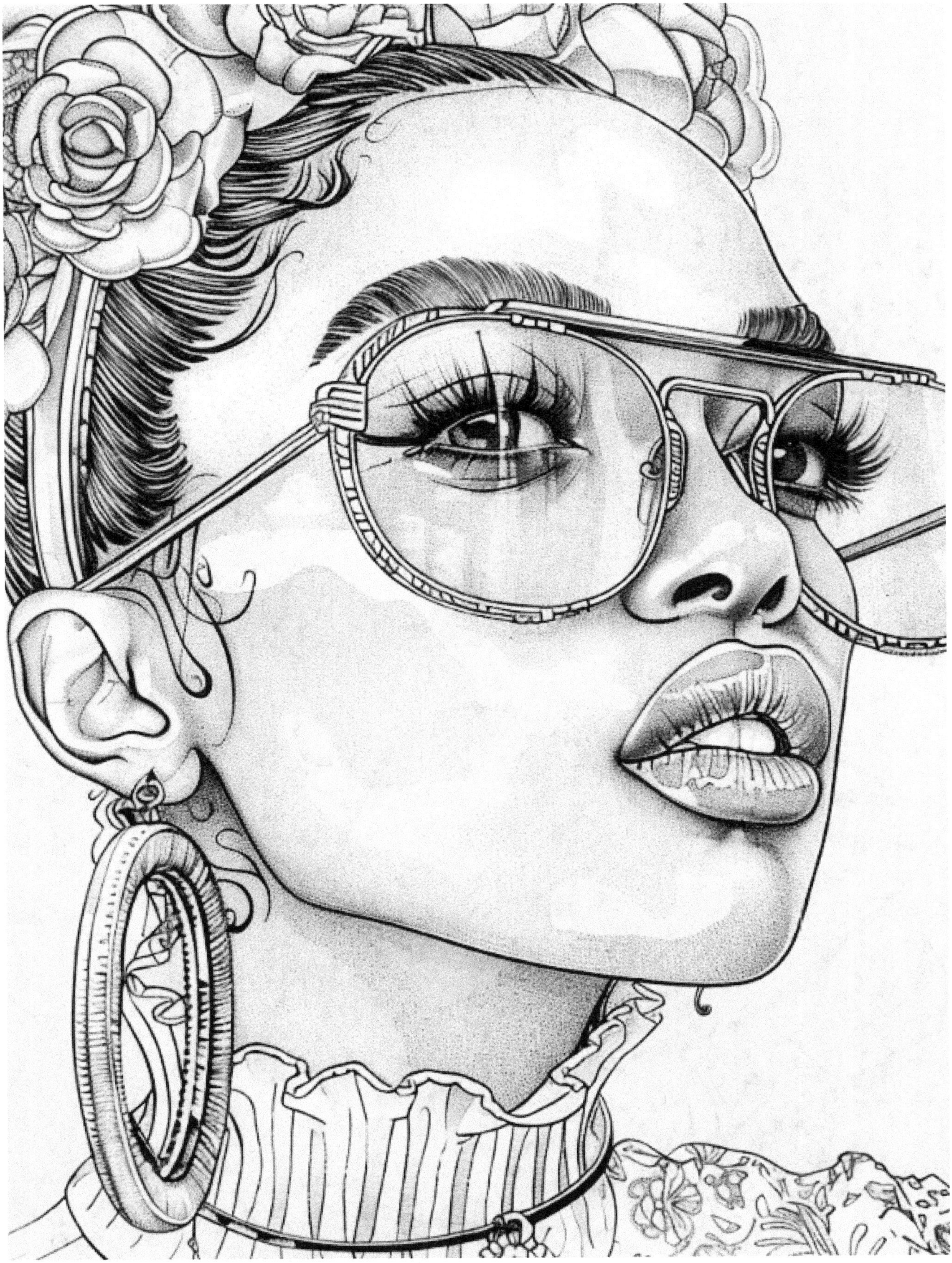

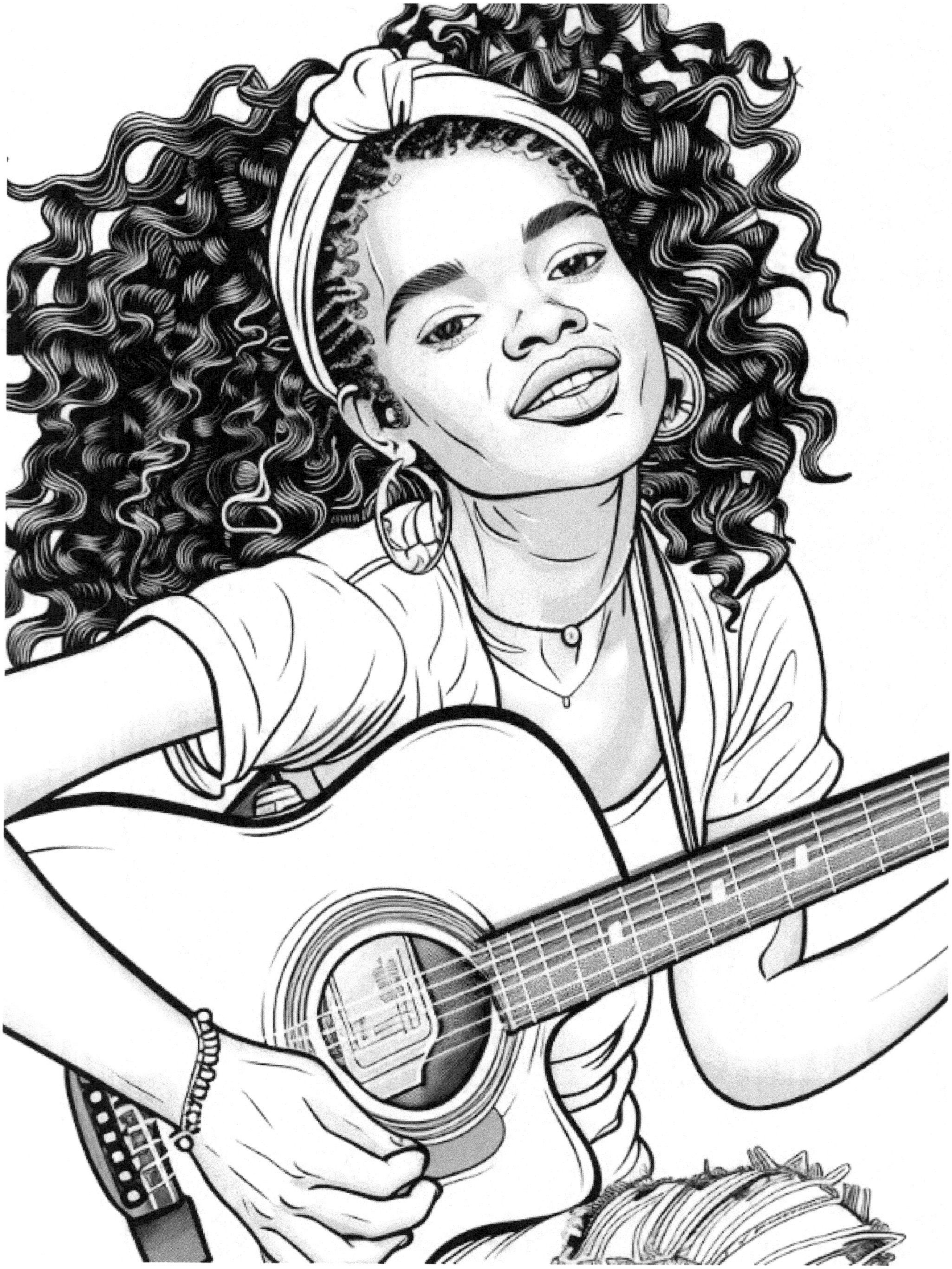

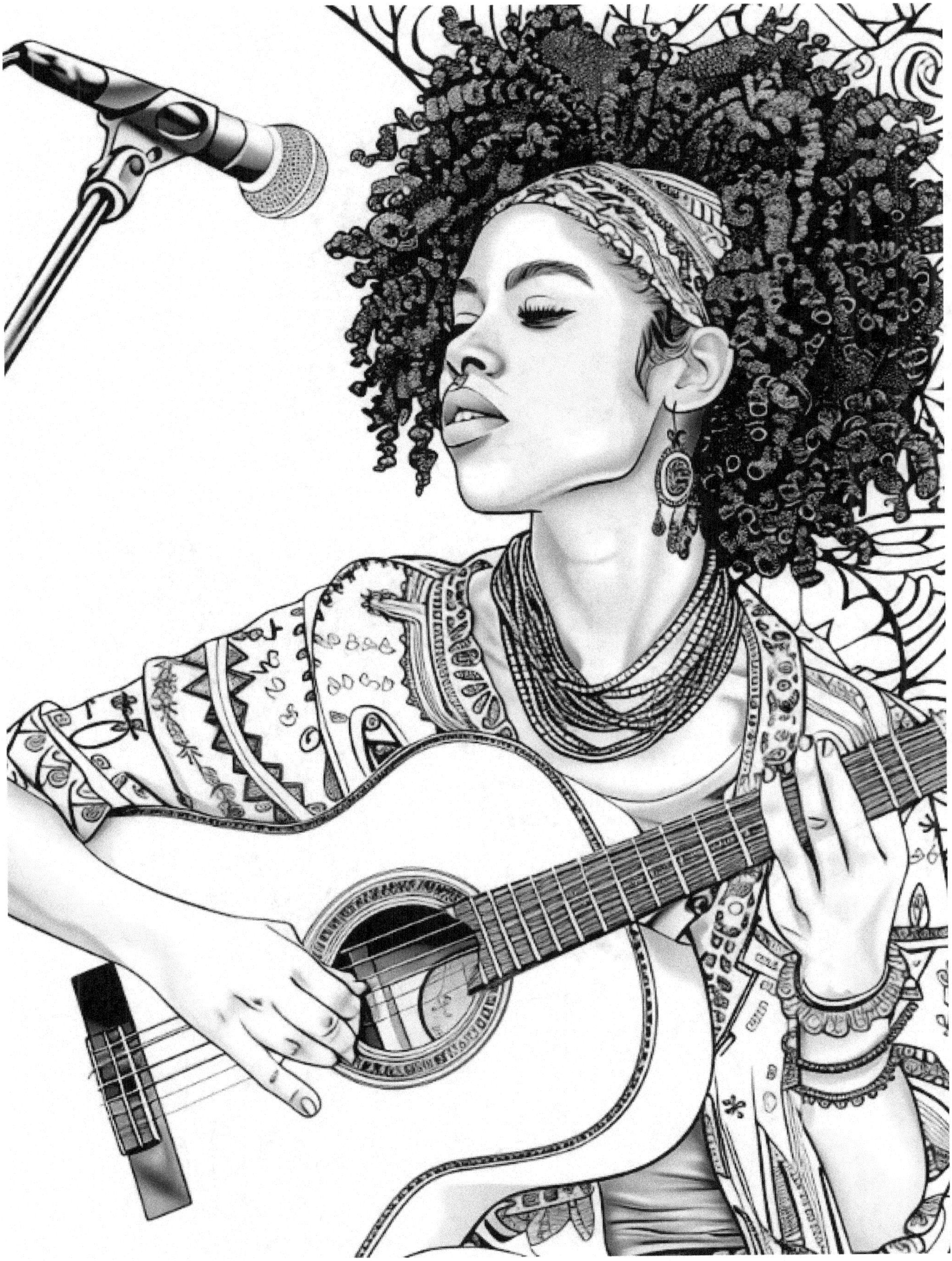

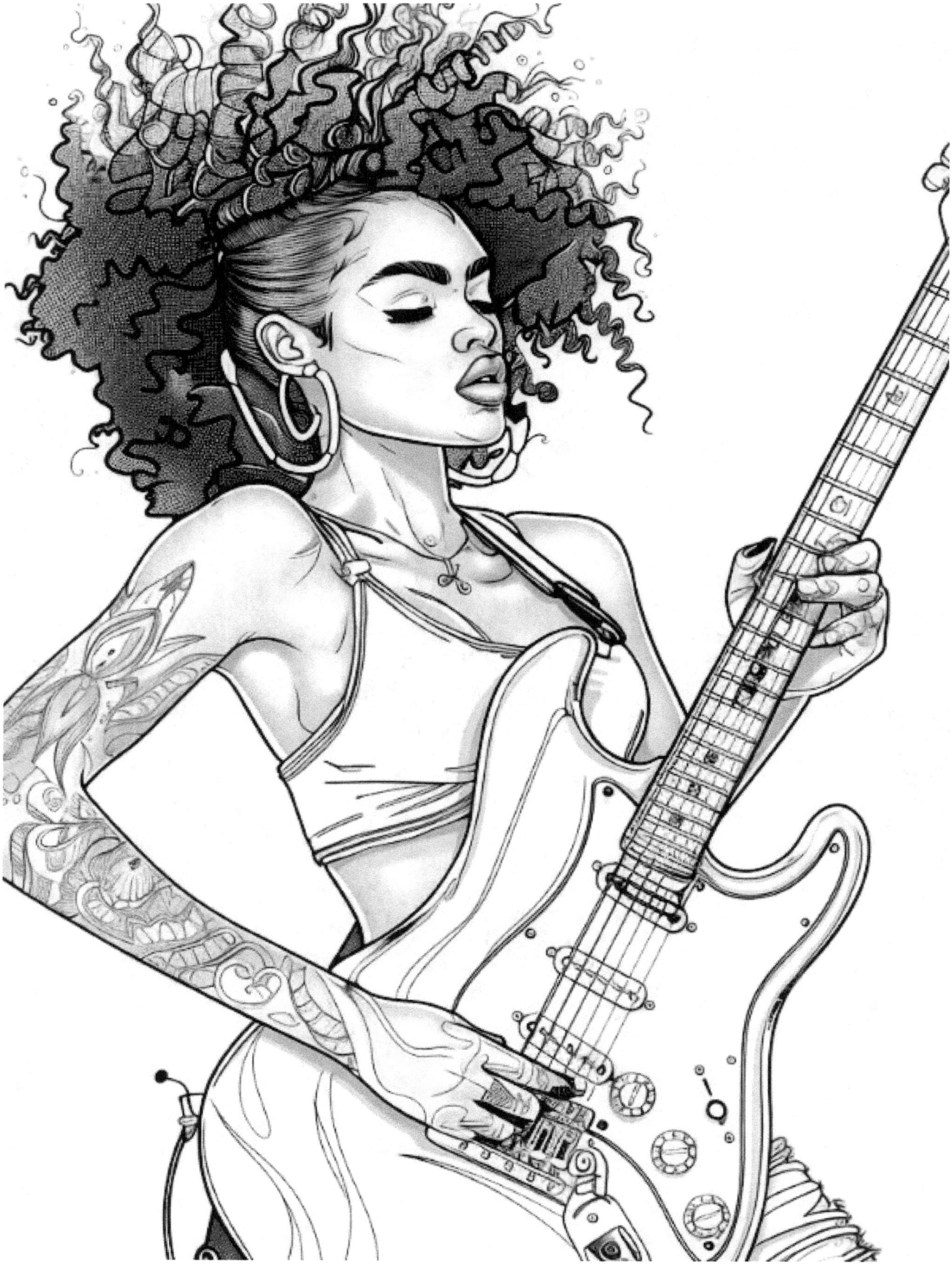

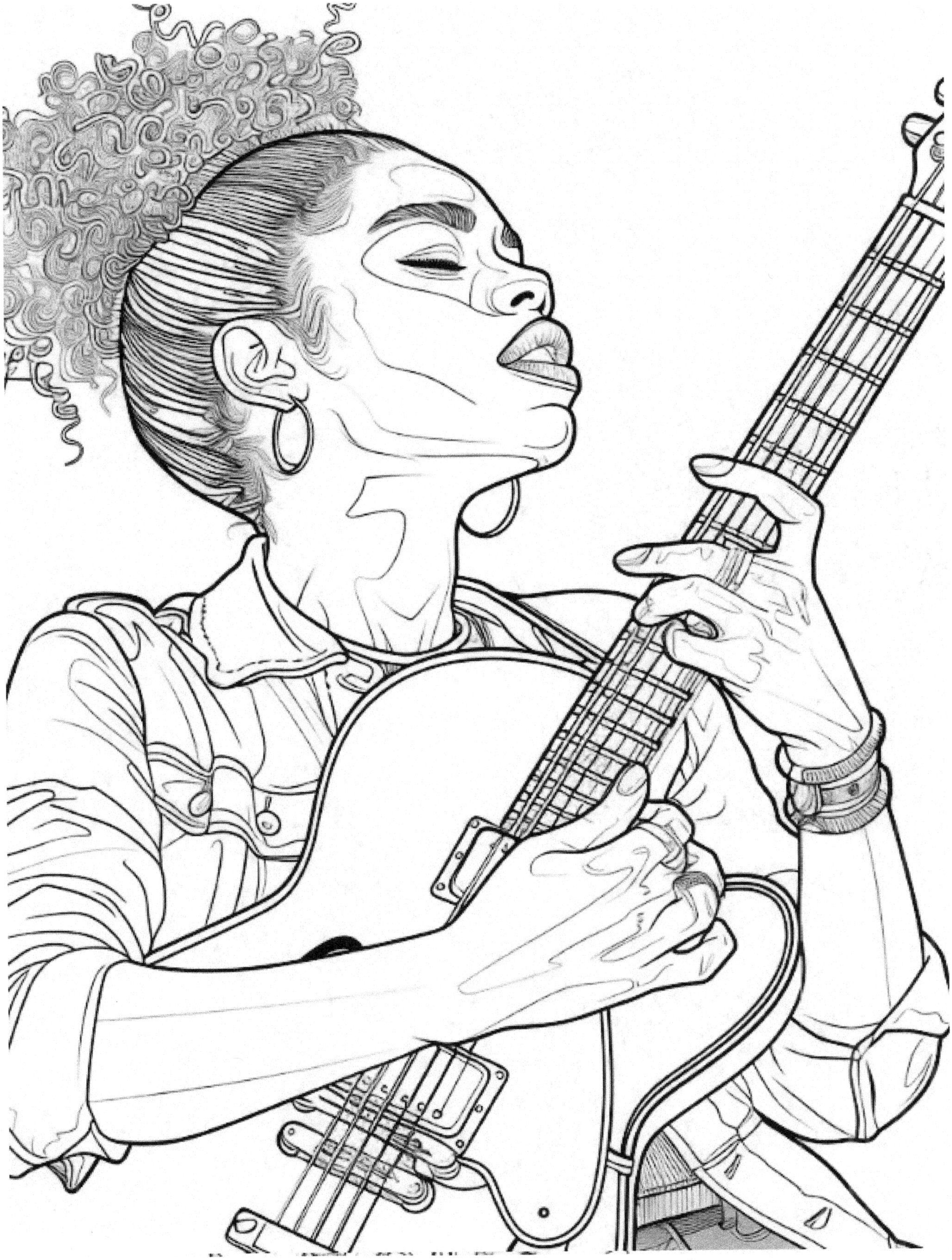

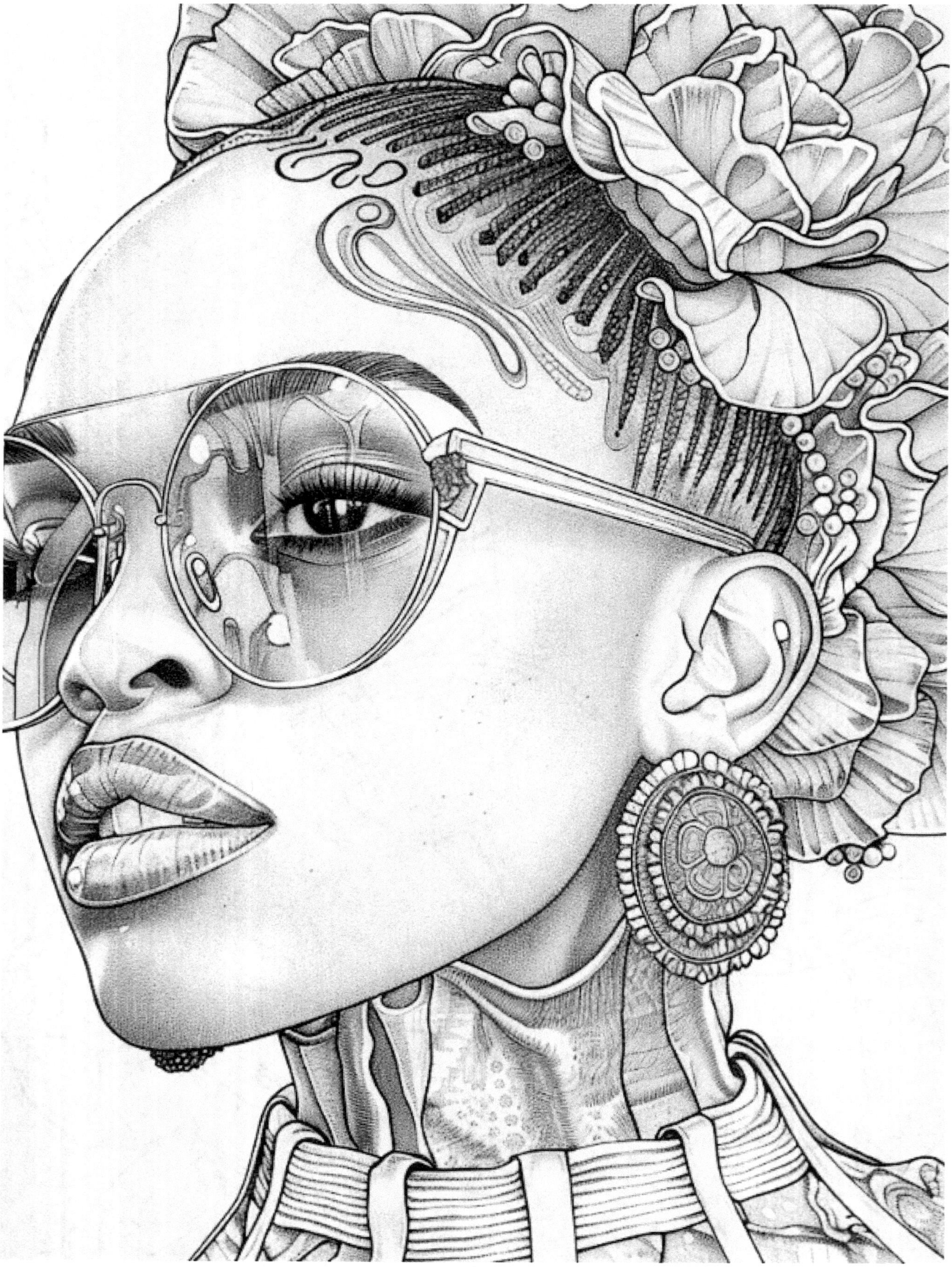

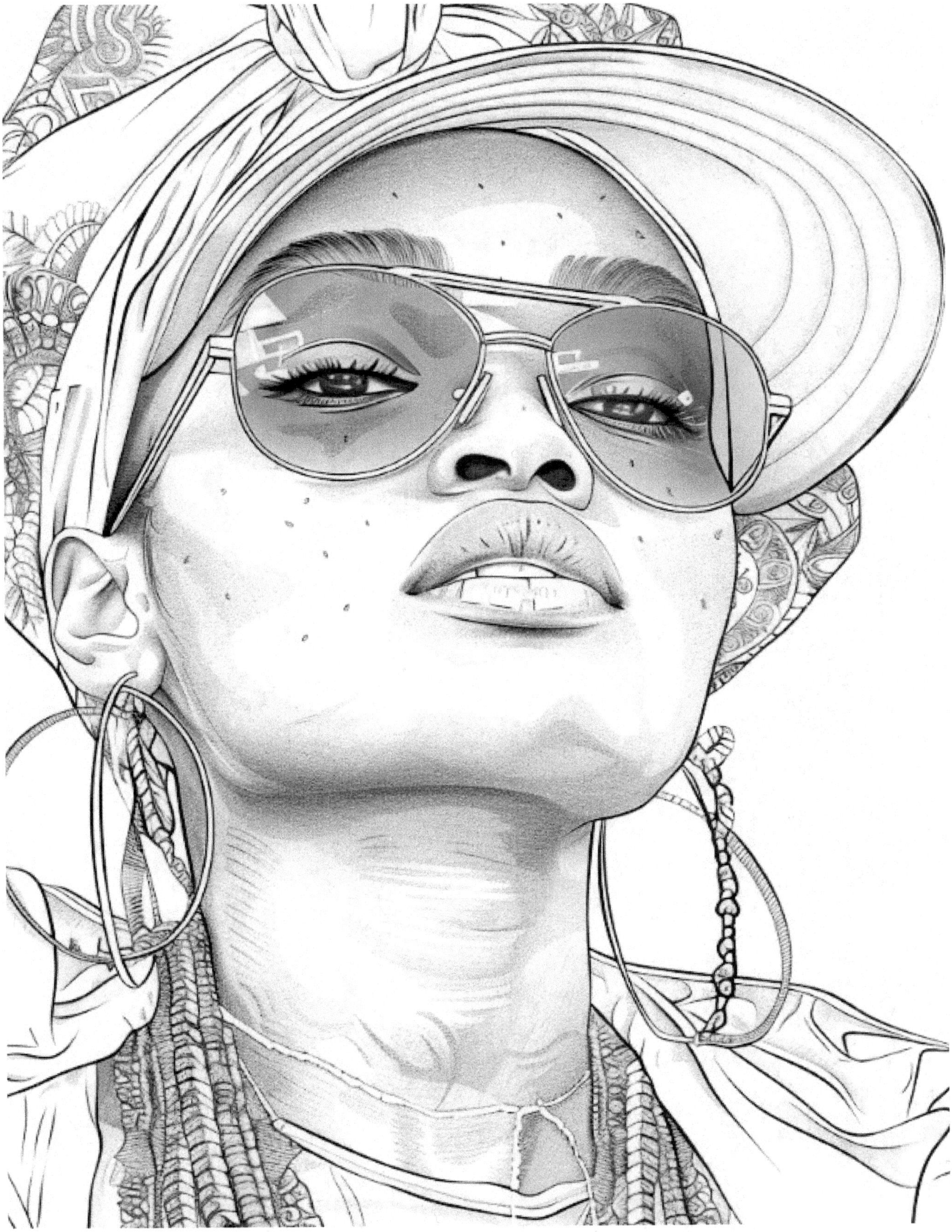

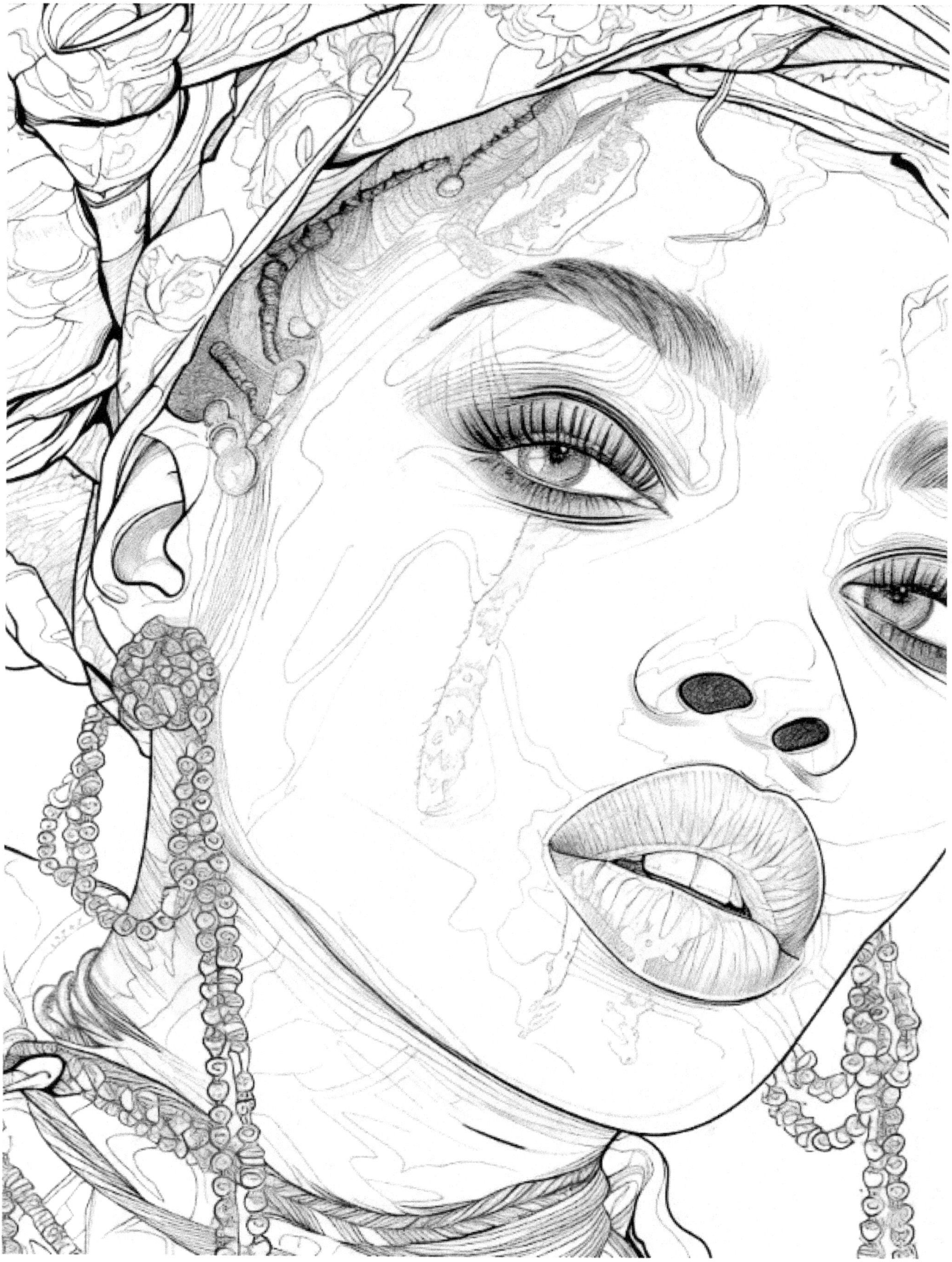

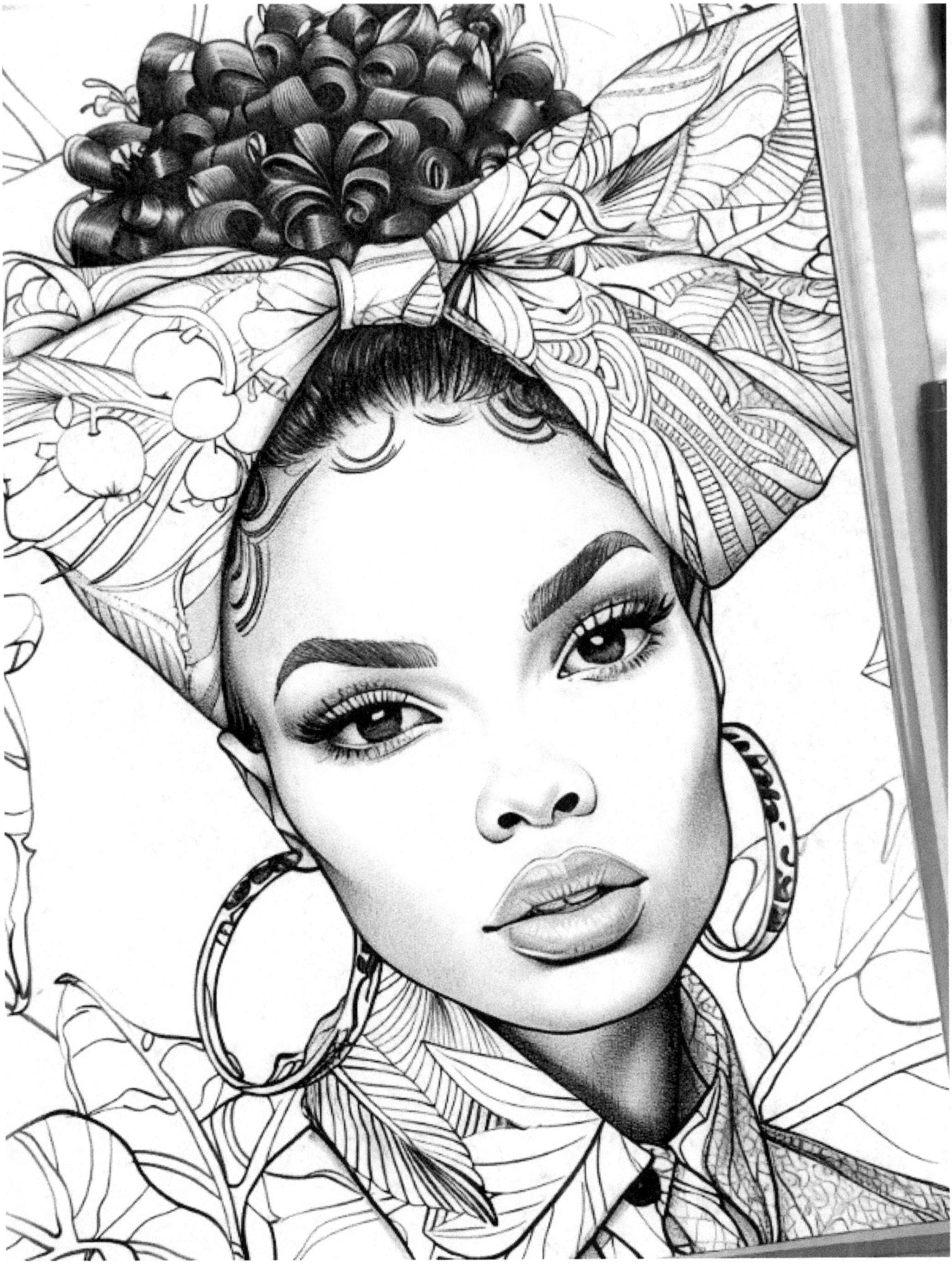

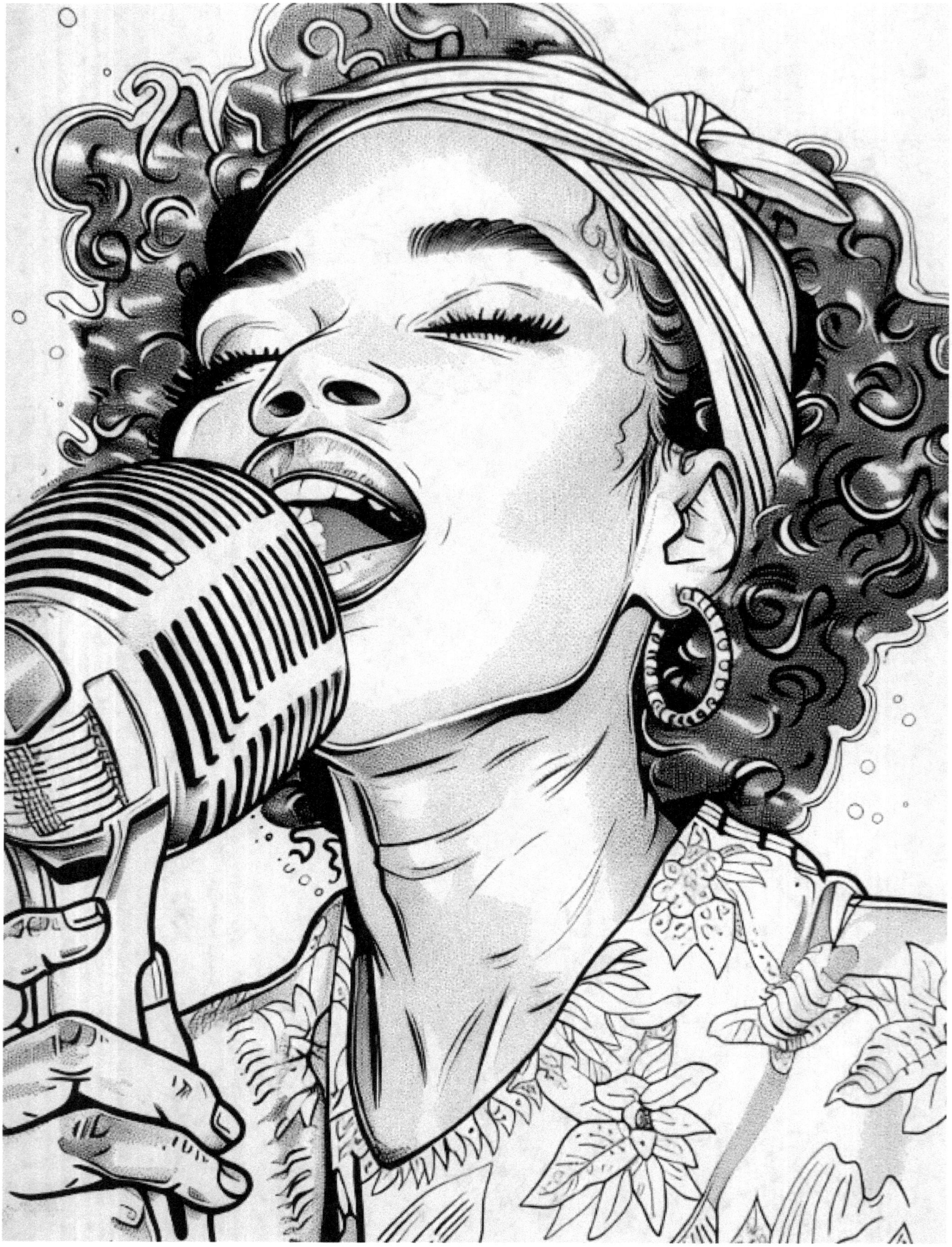

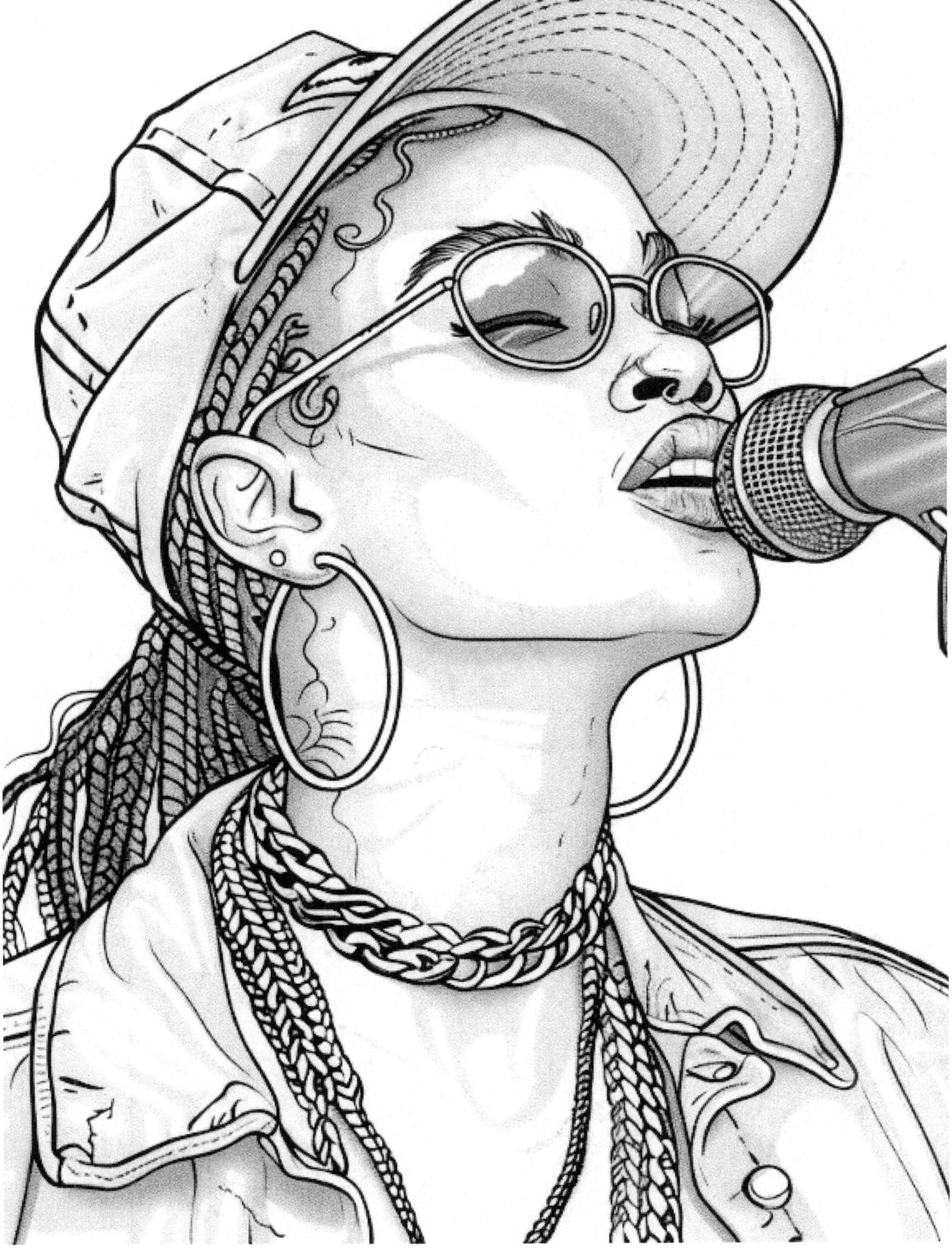

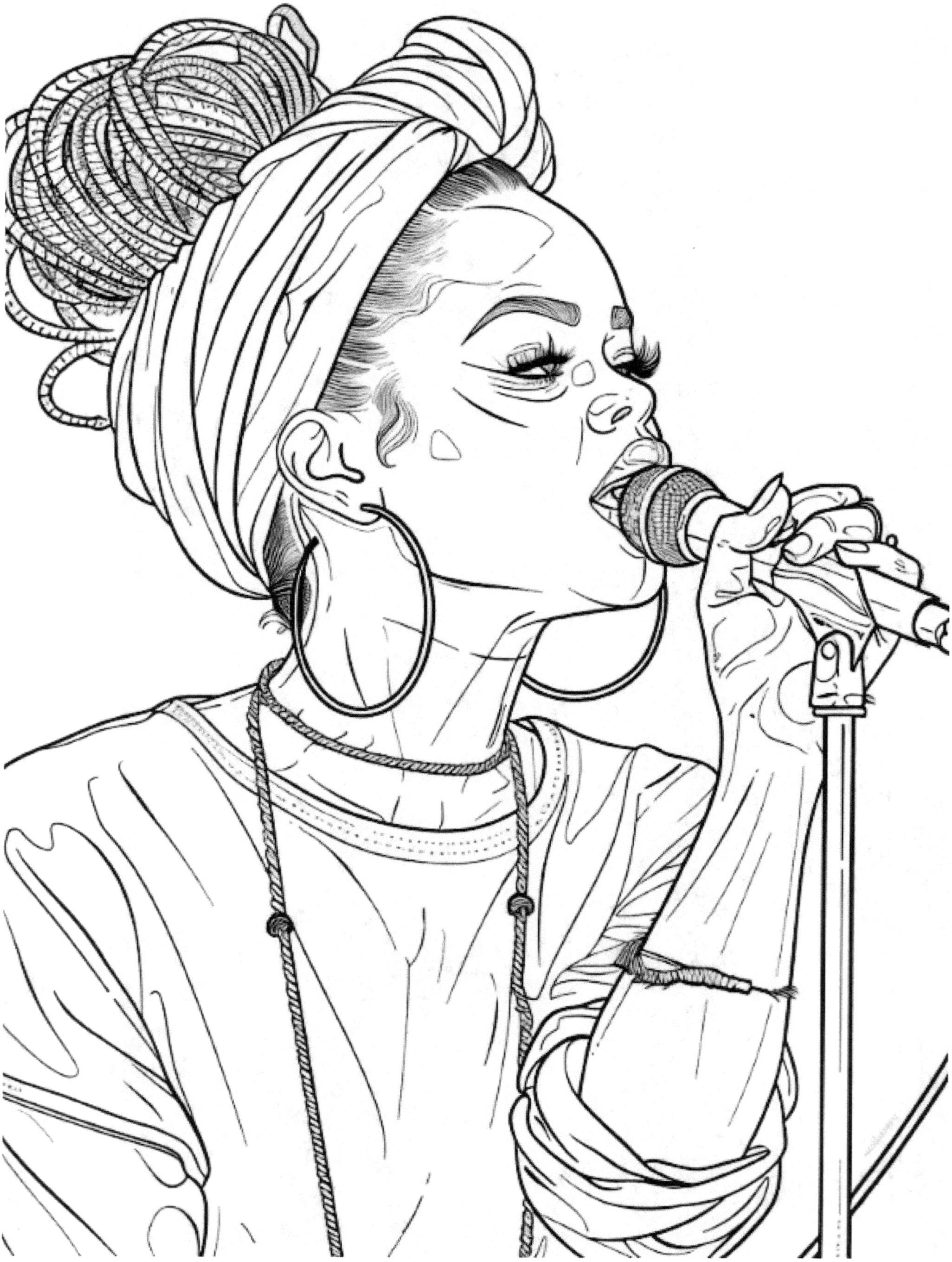

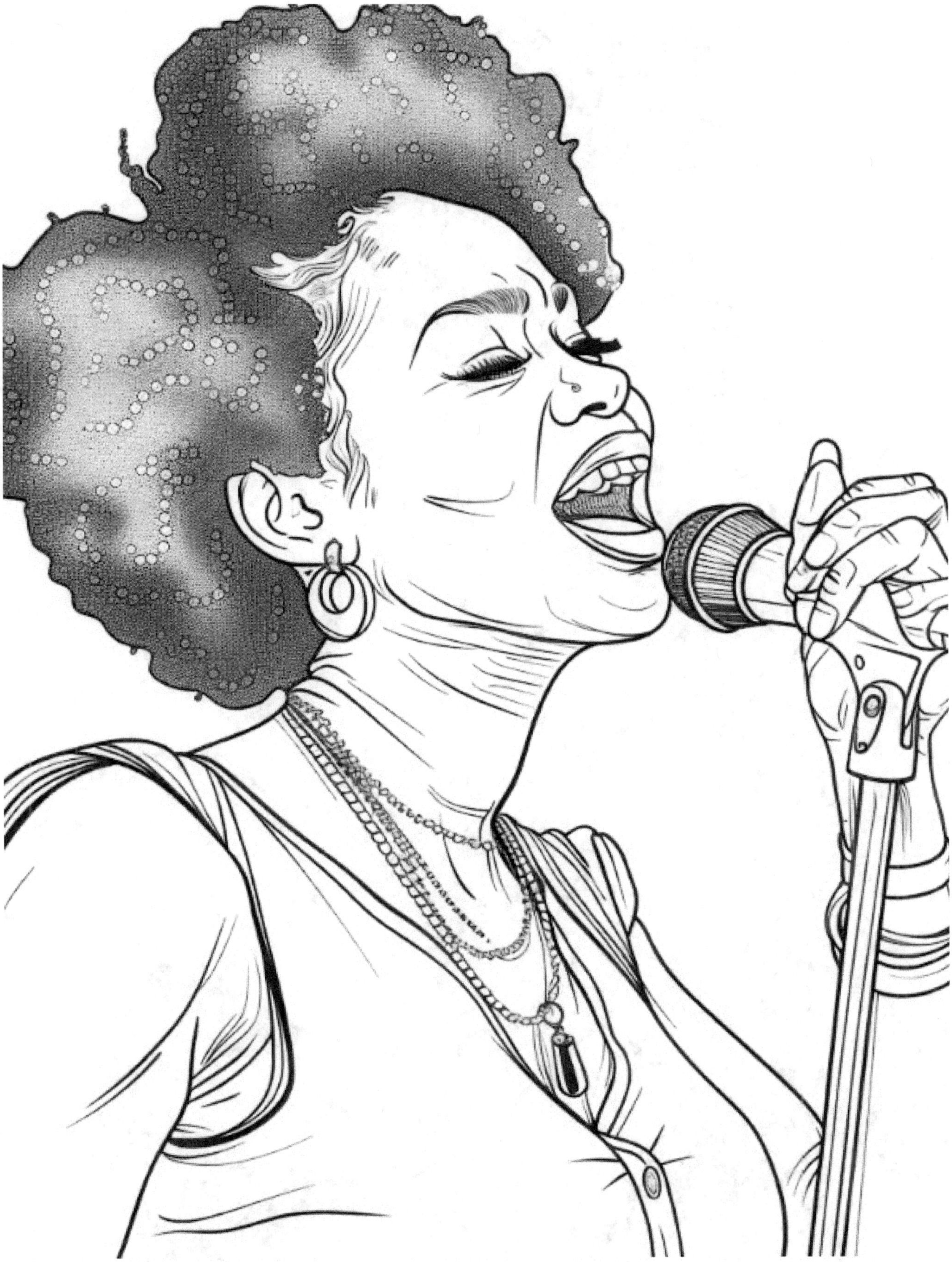

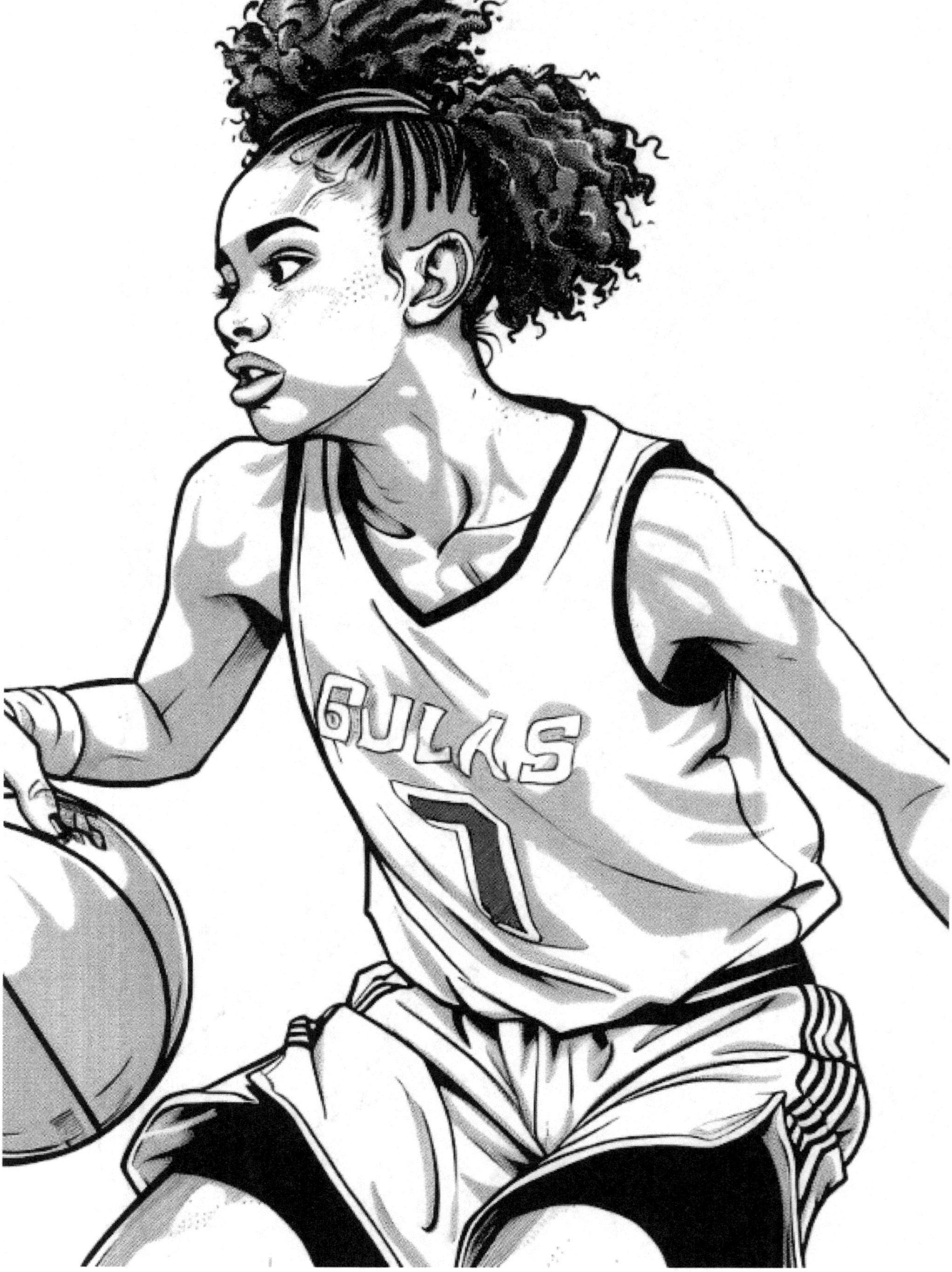
GULAS
1

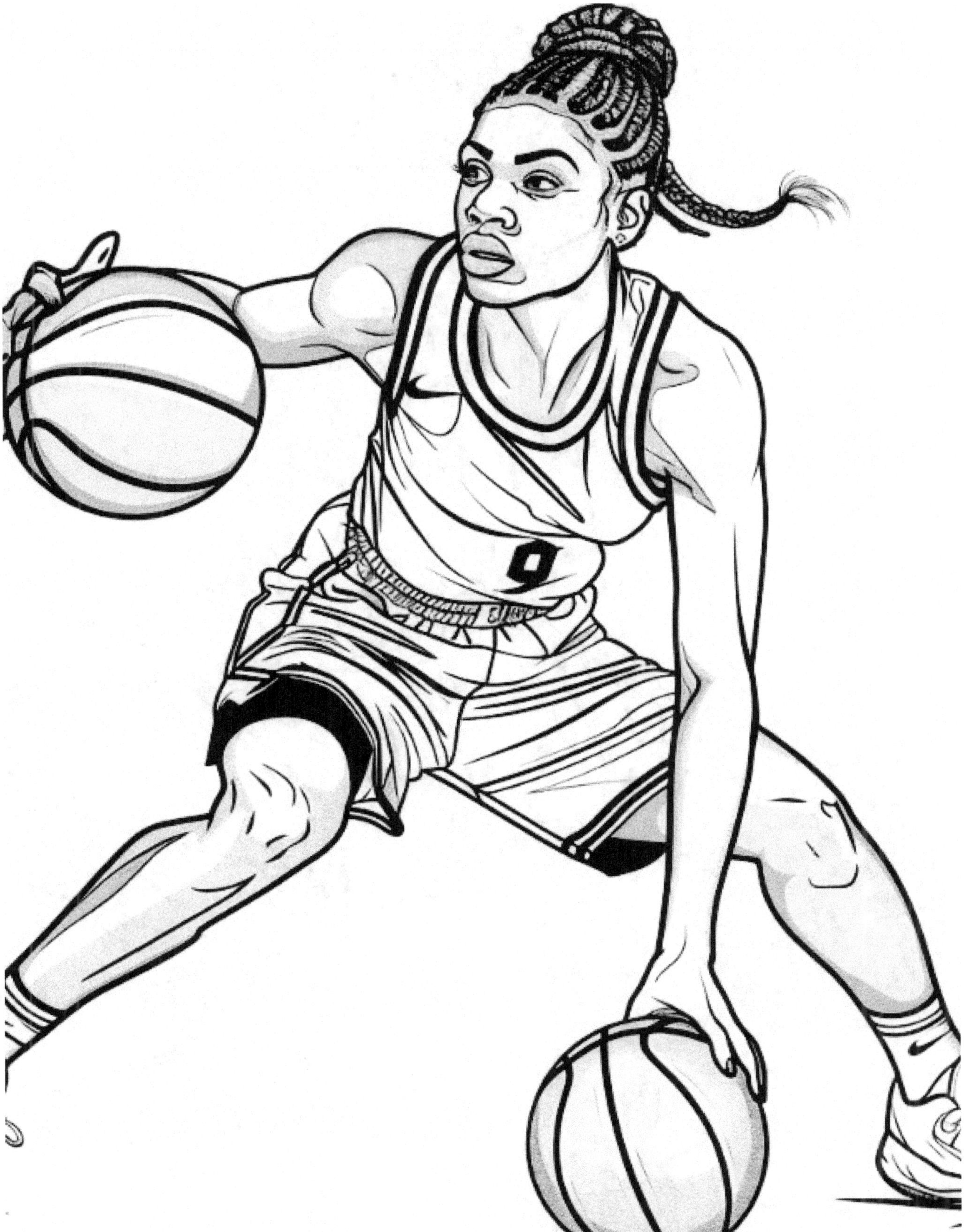
9

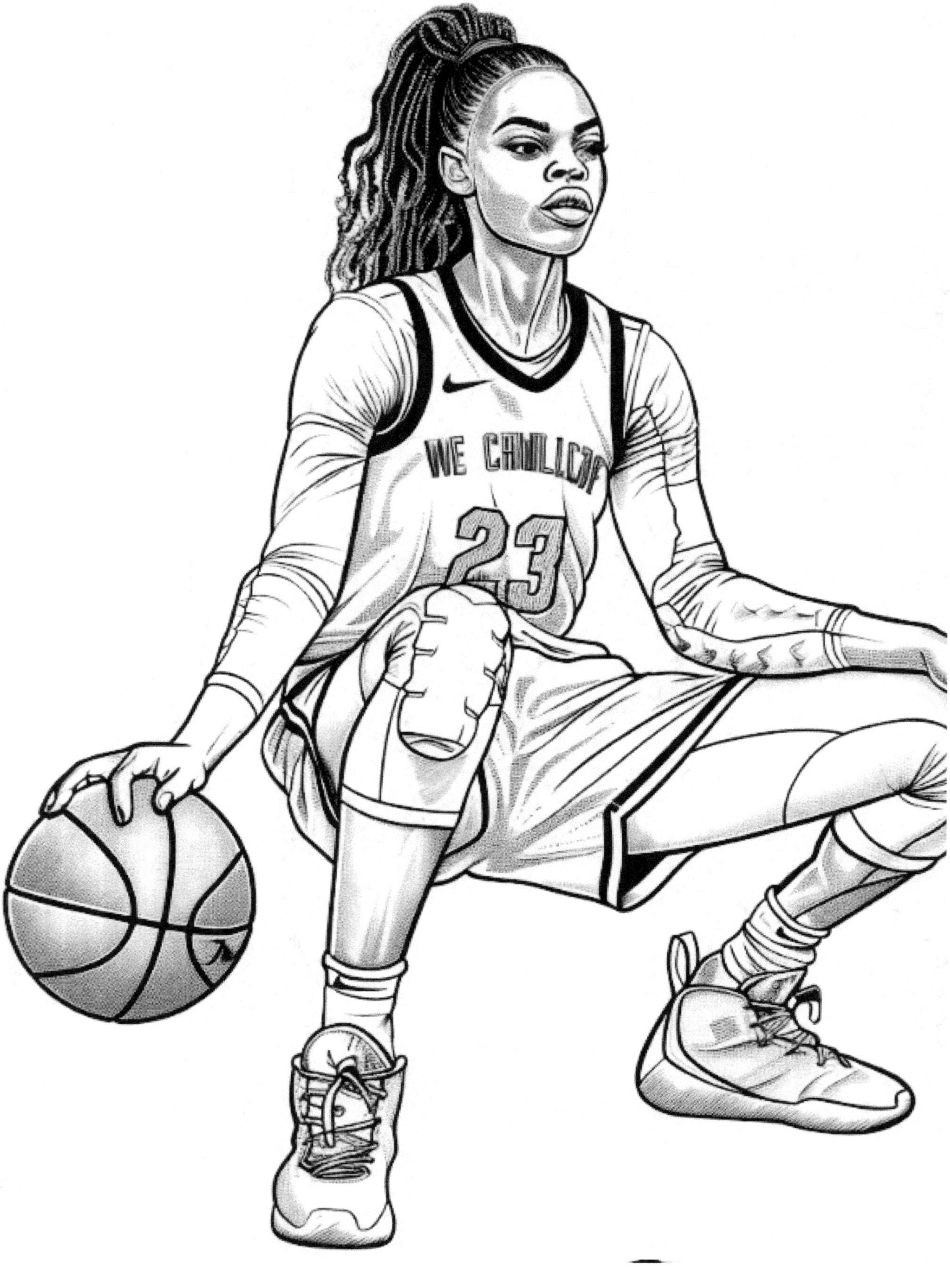
23

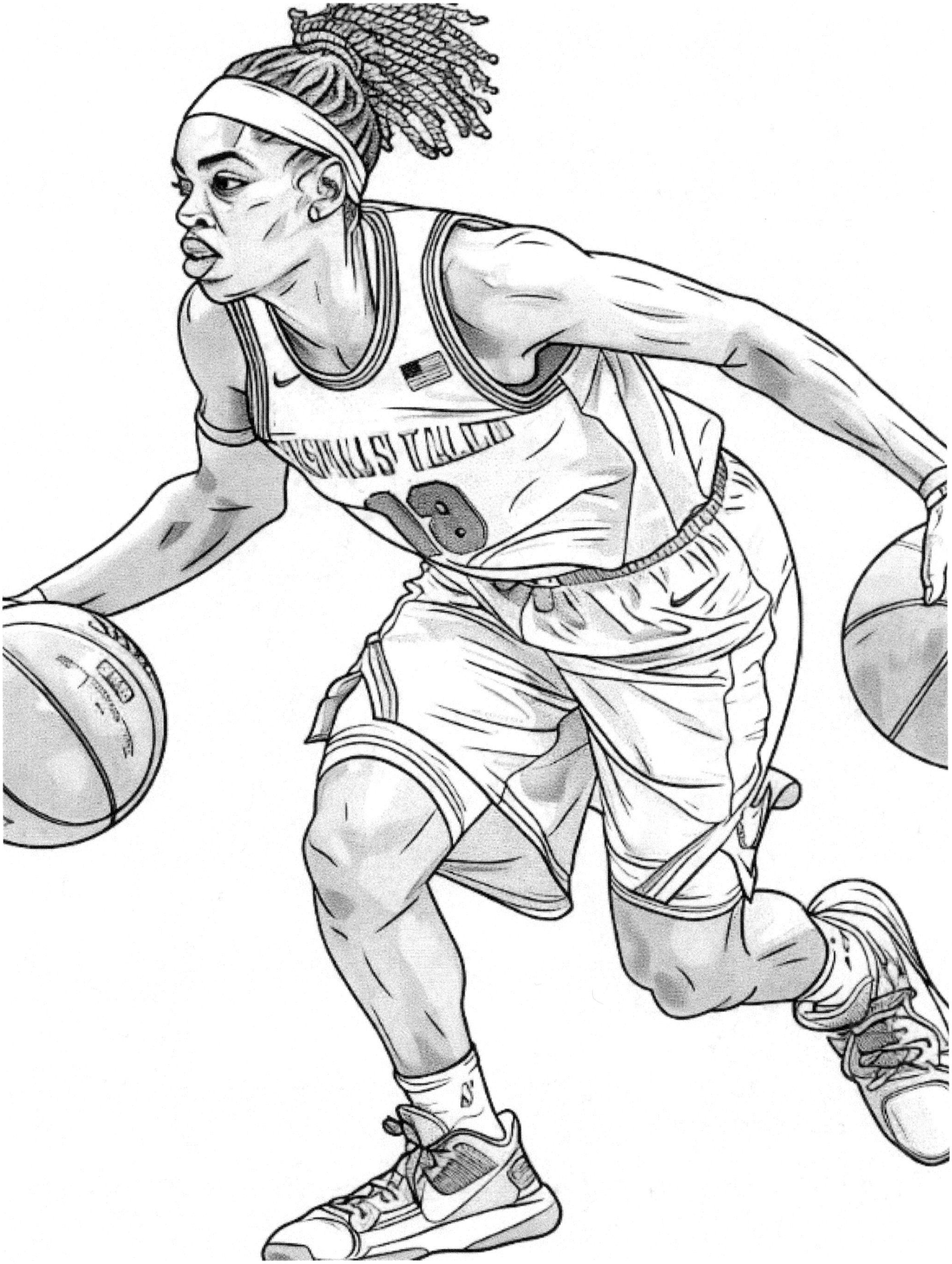

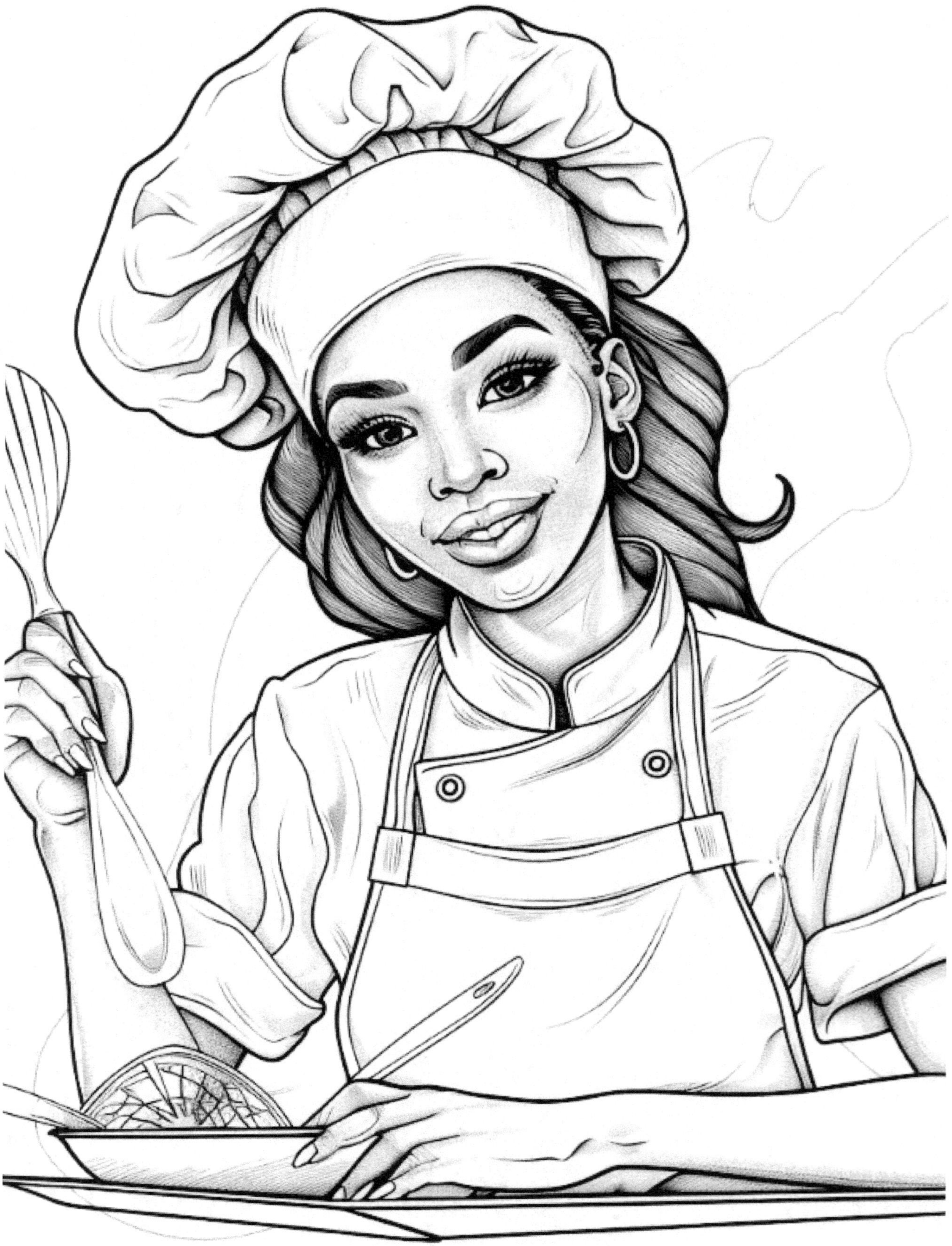

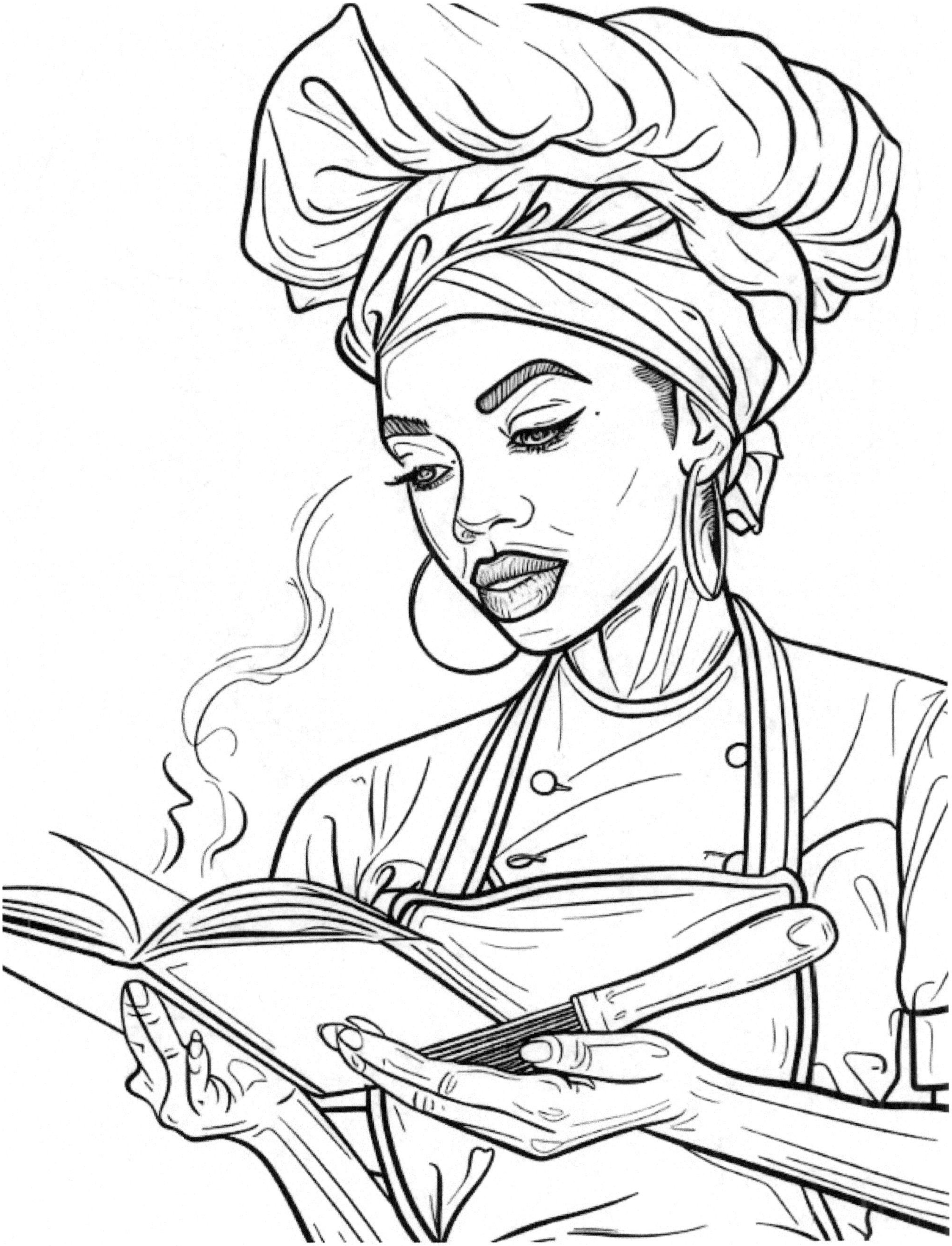

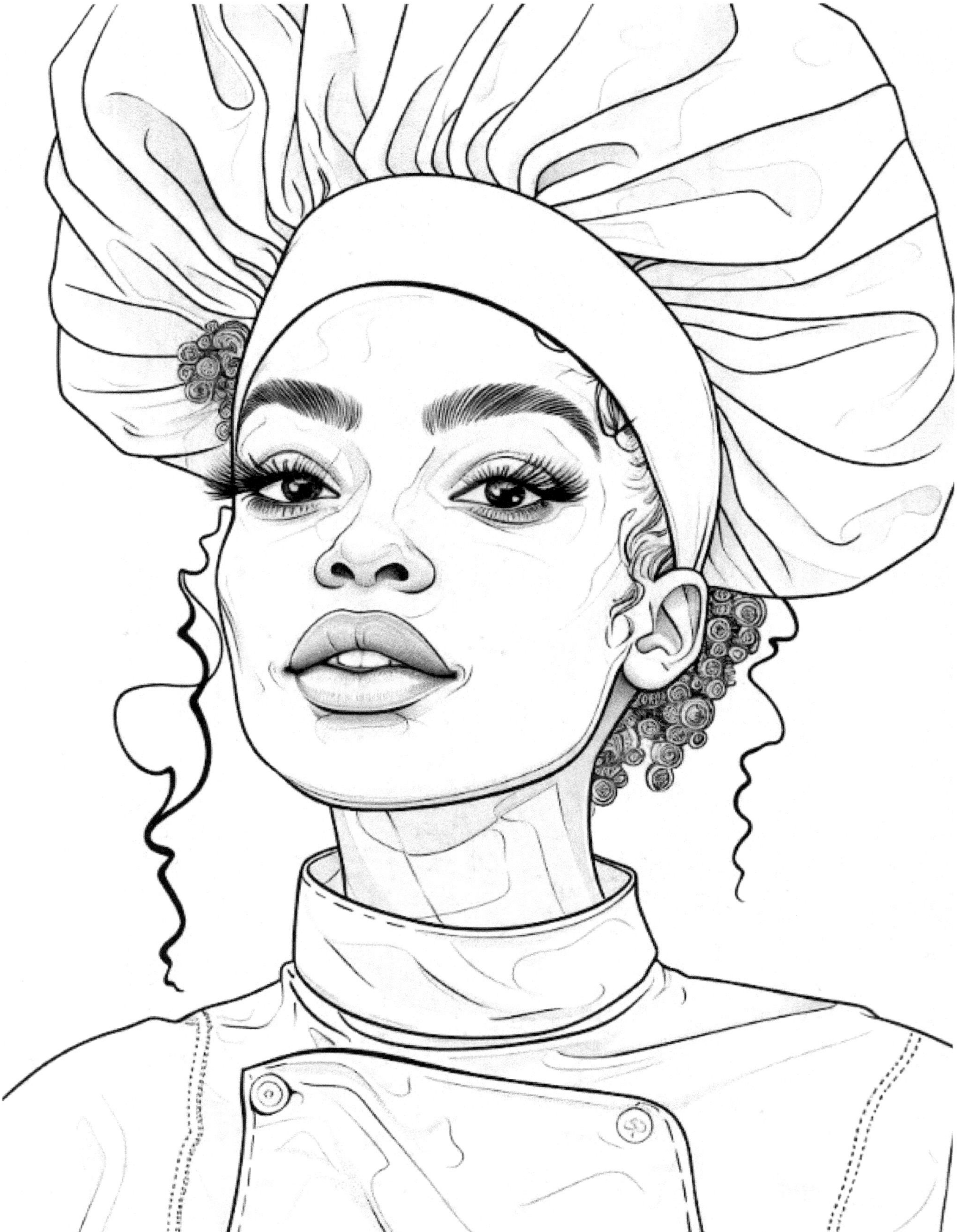

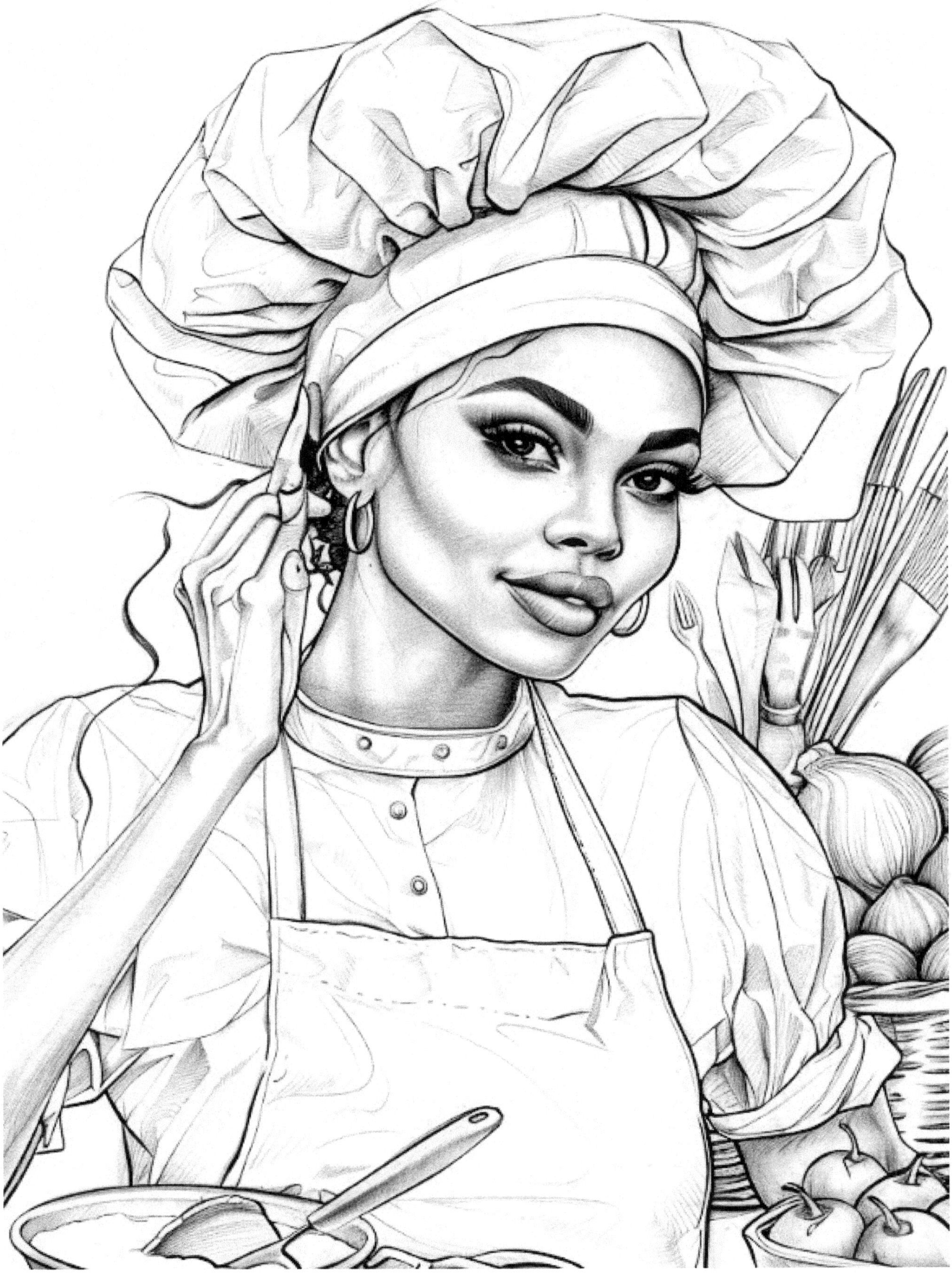

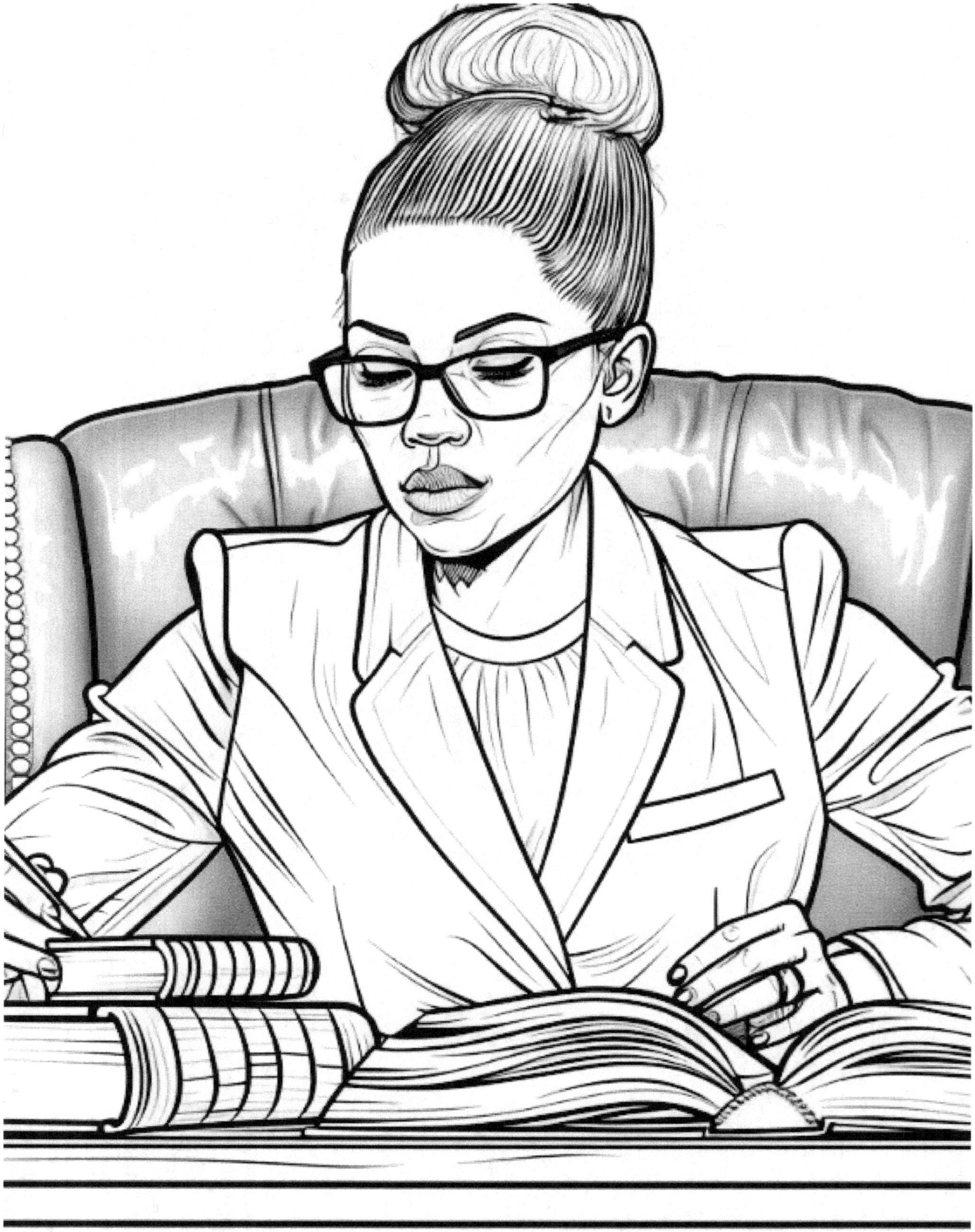

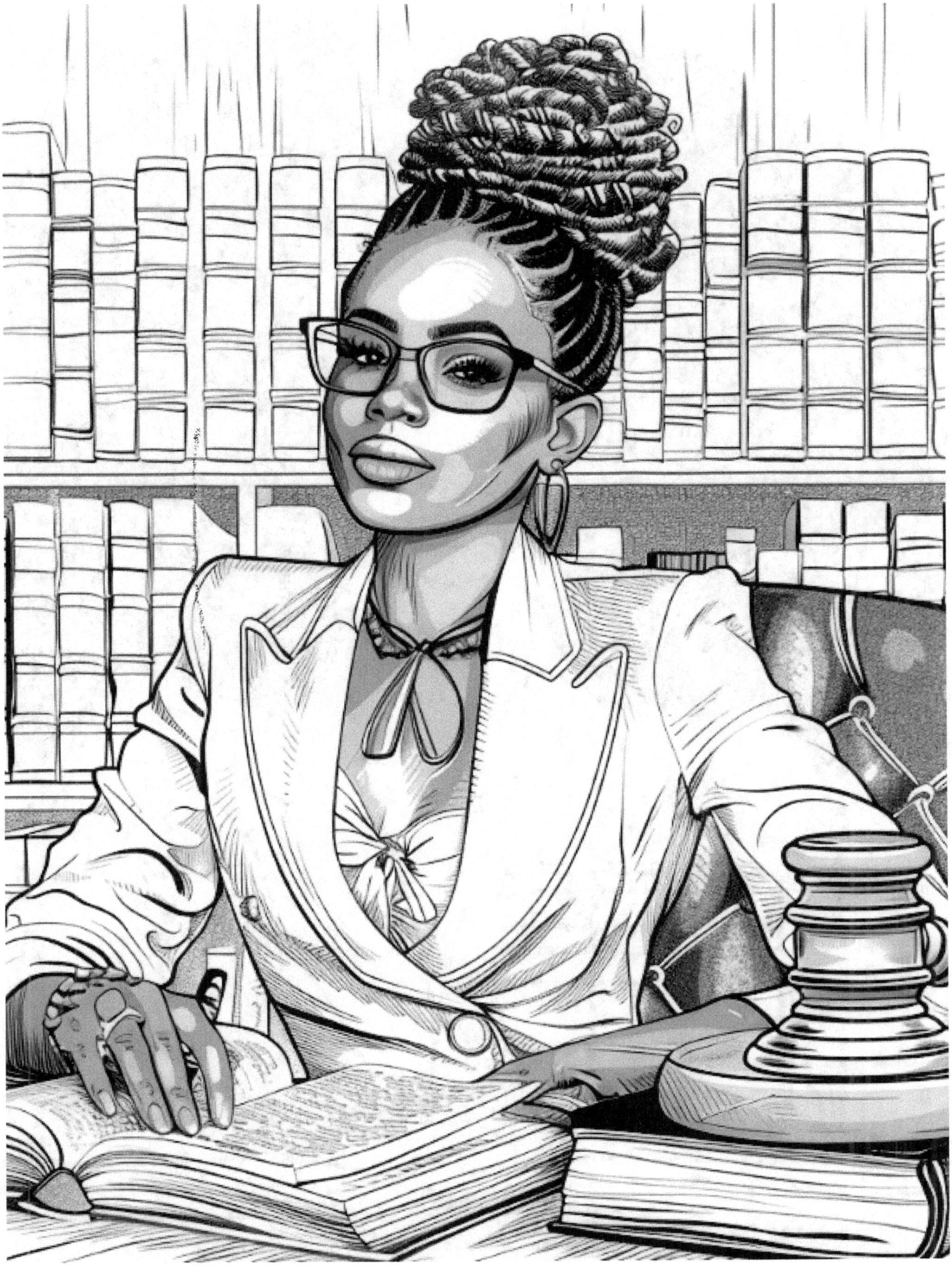

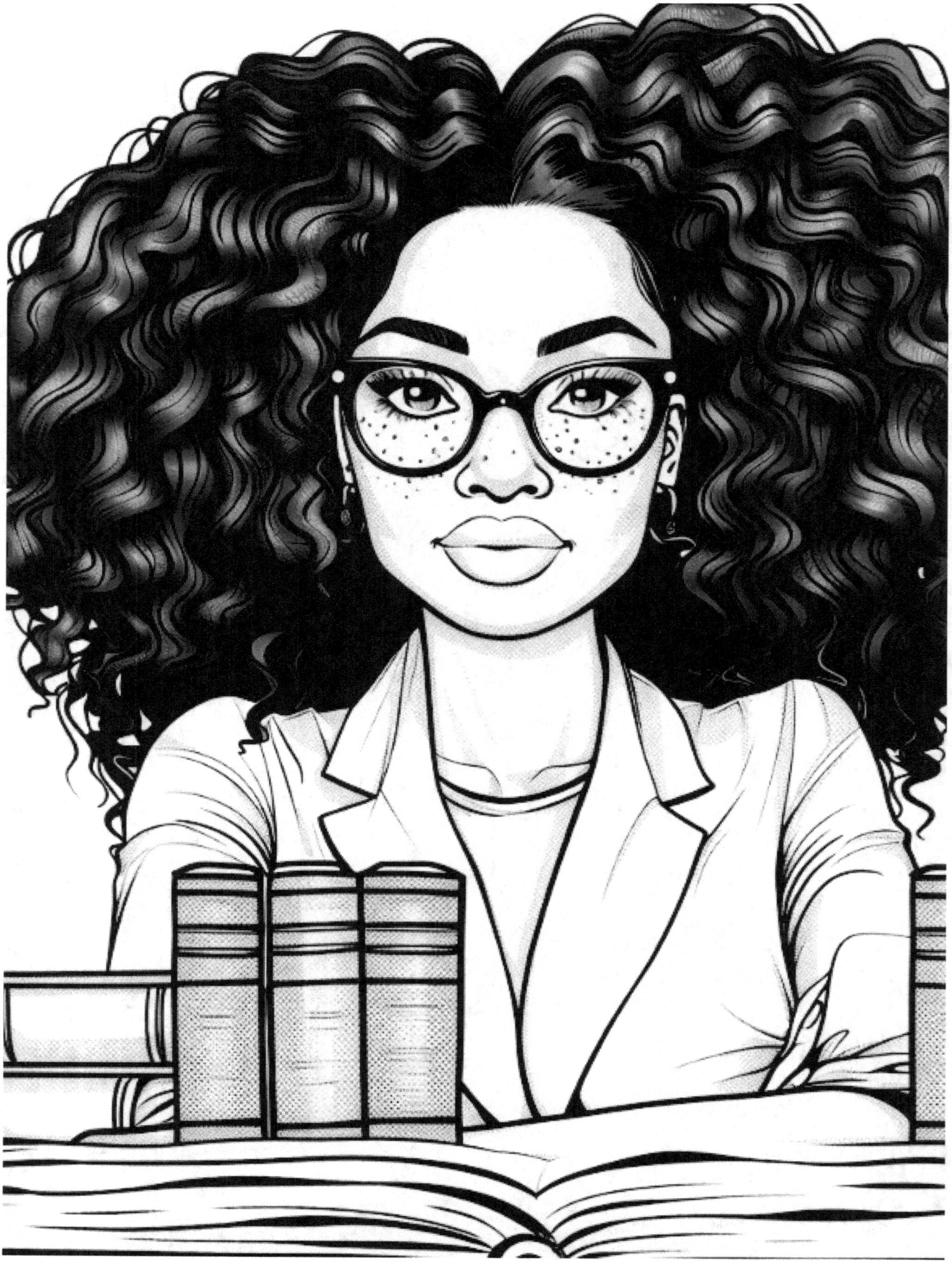

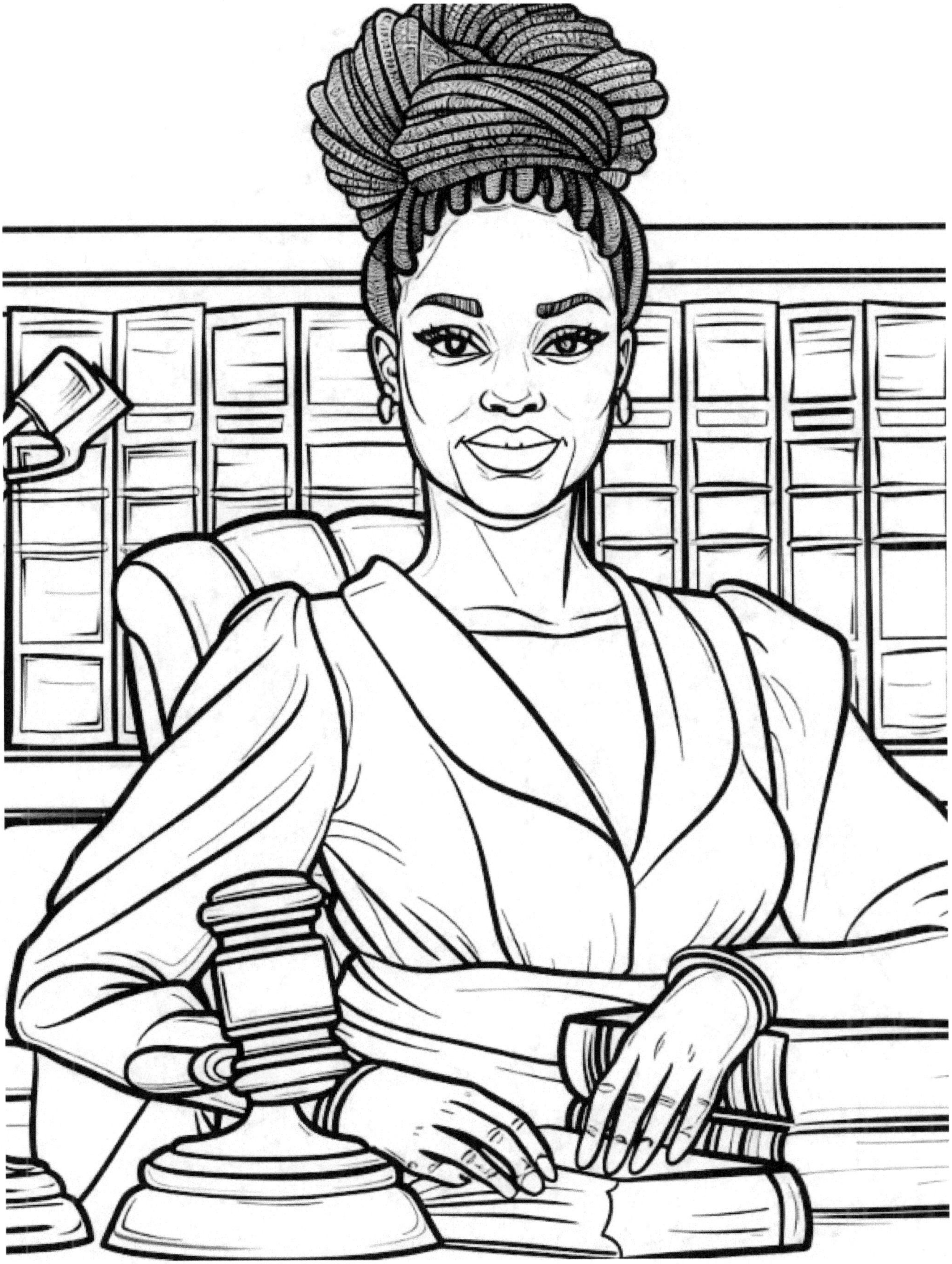

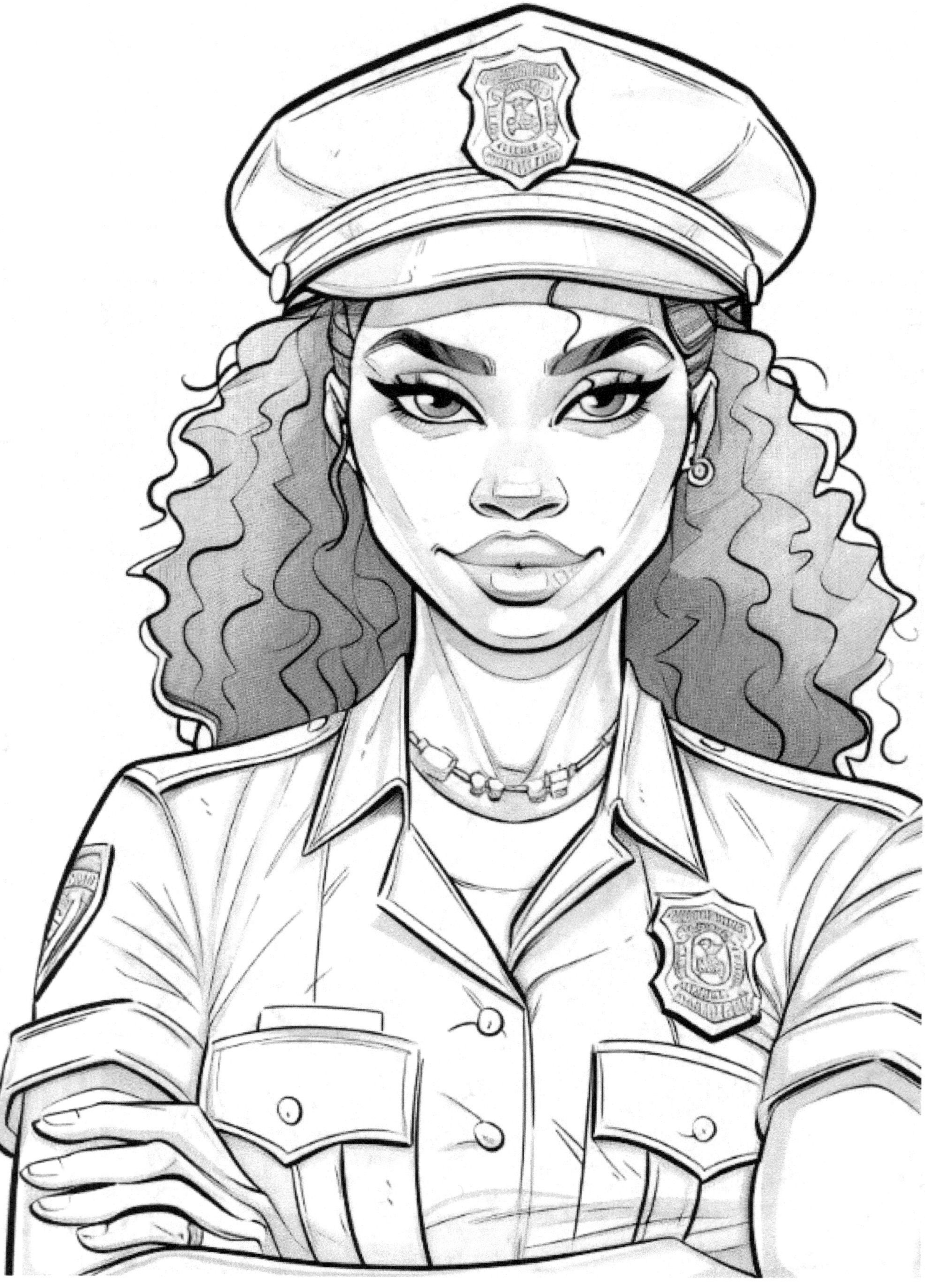

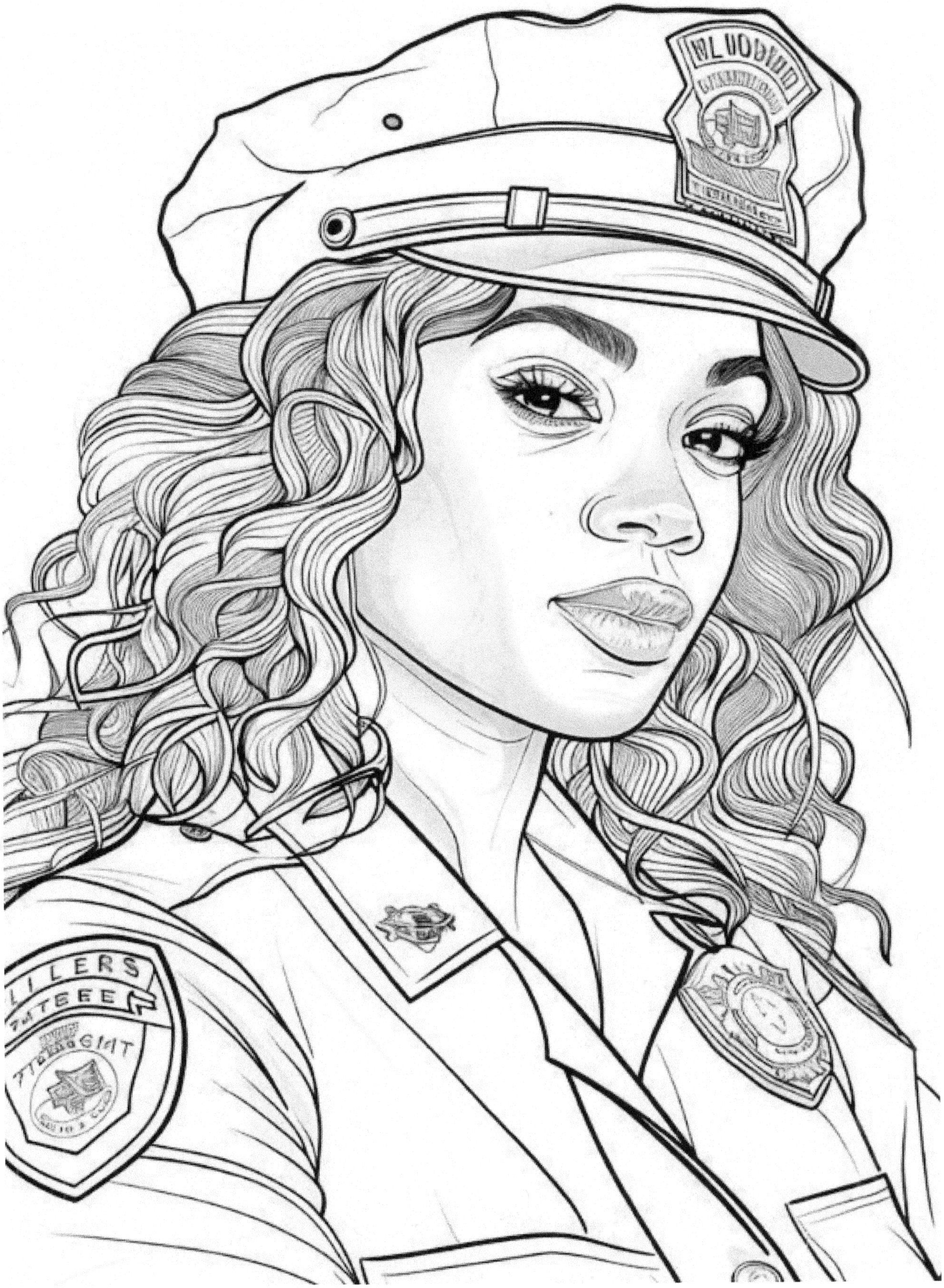

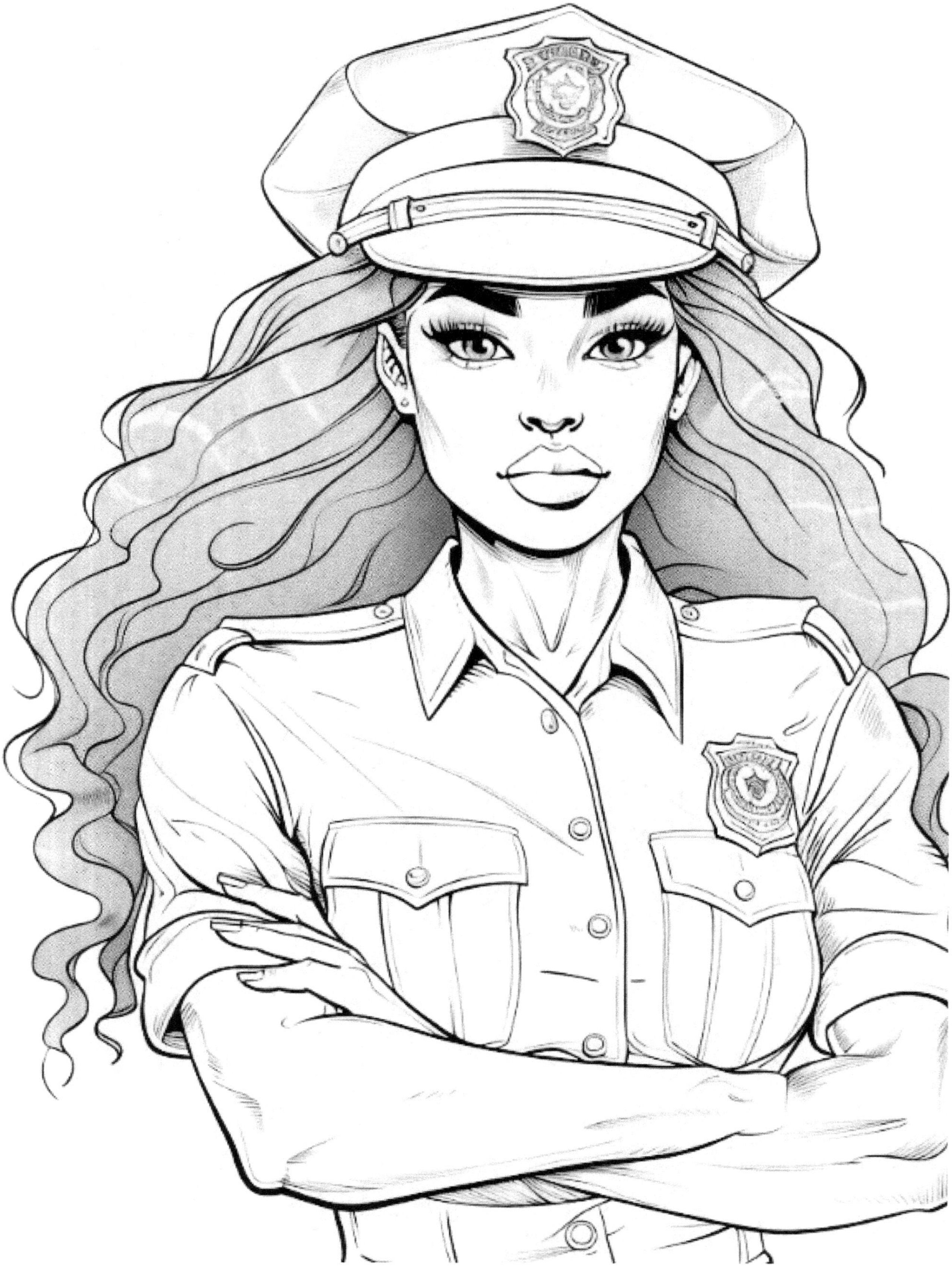

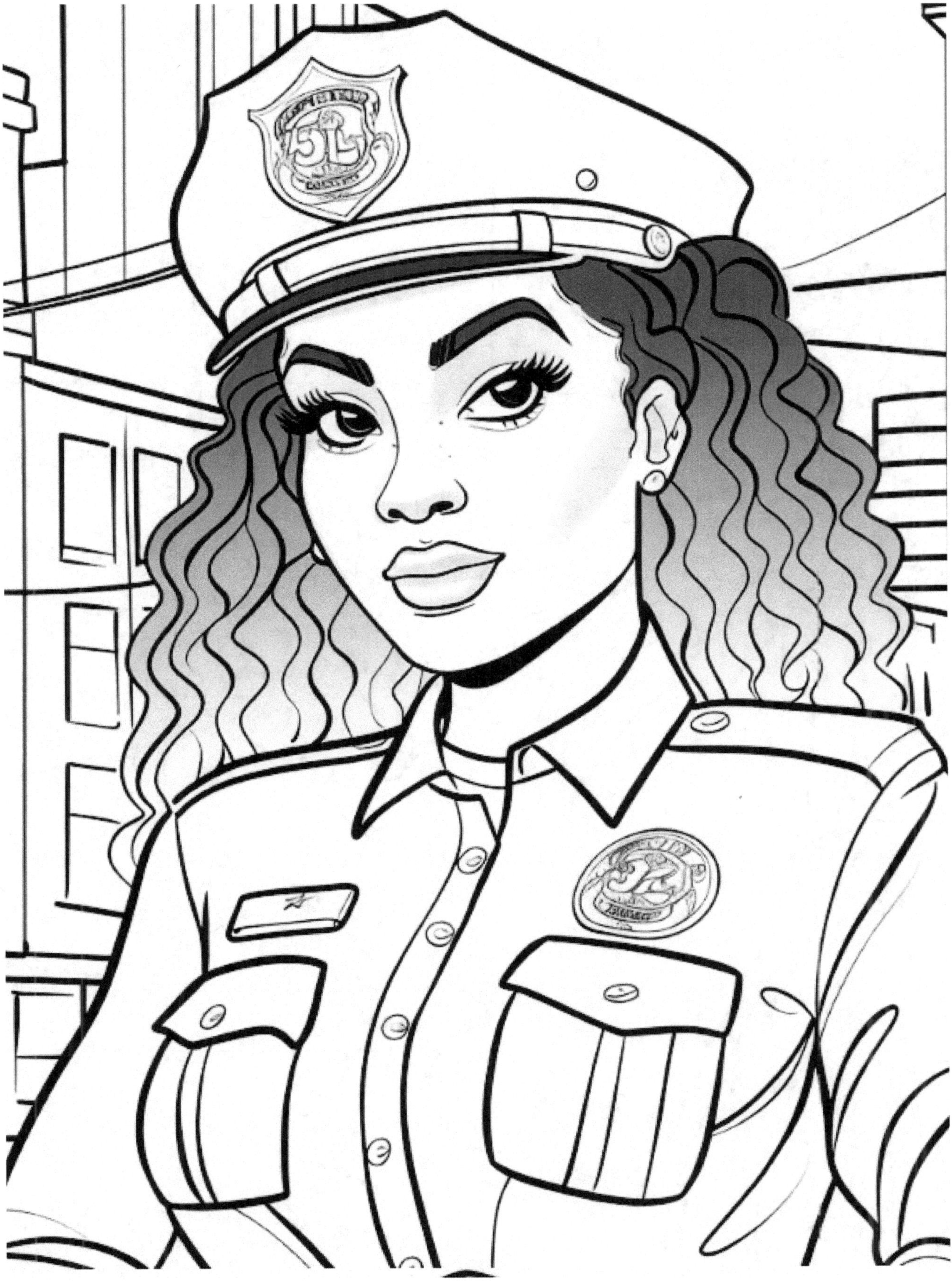

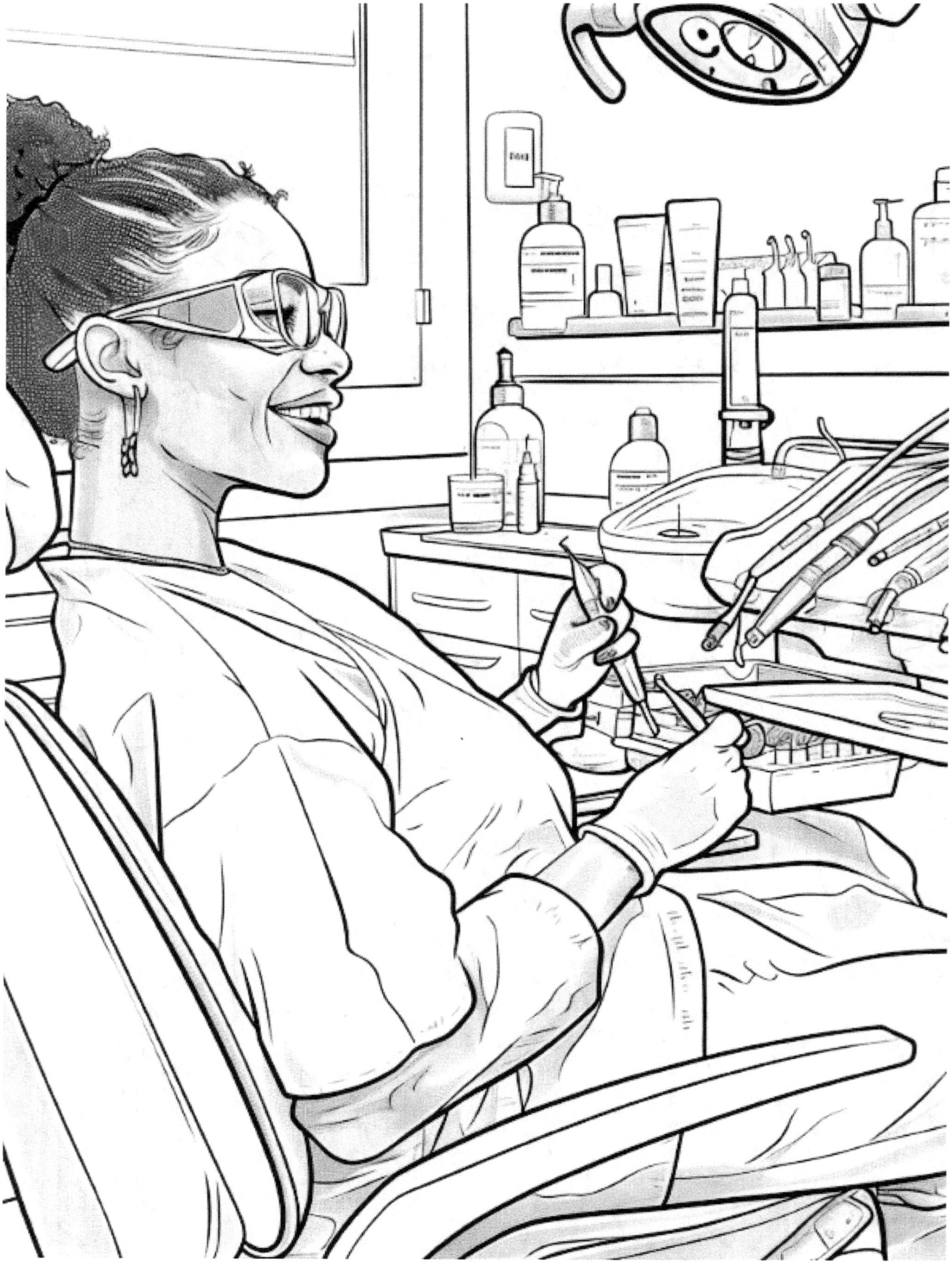

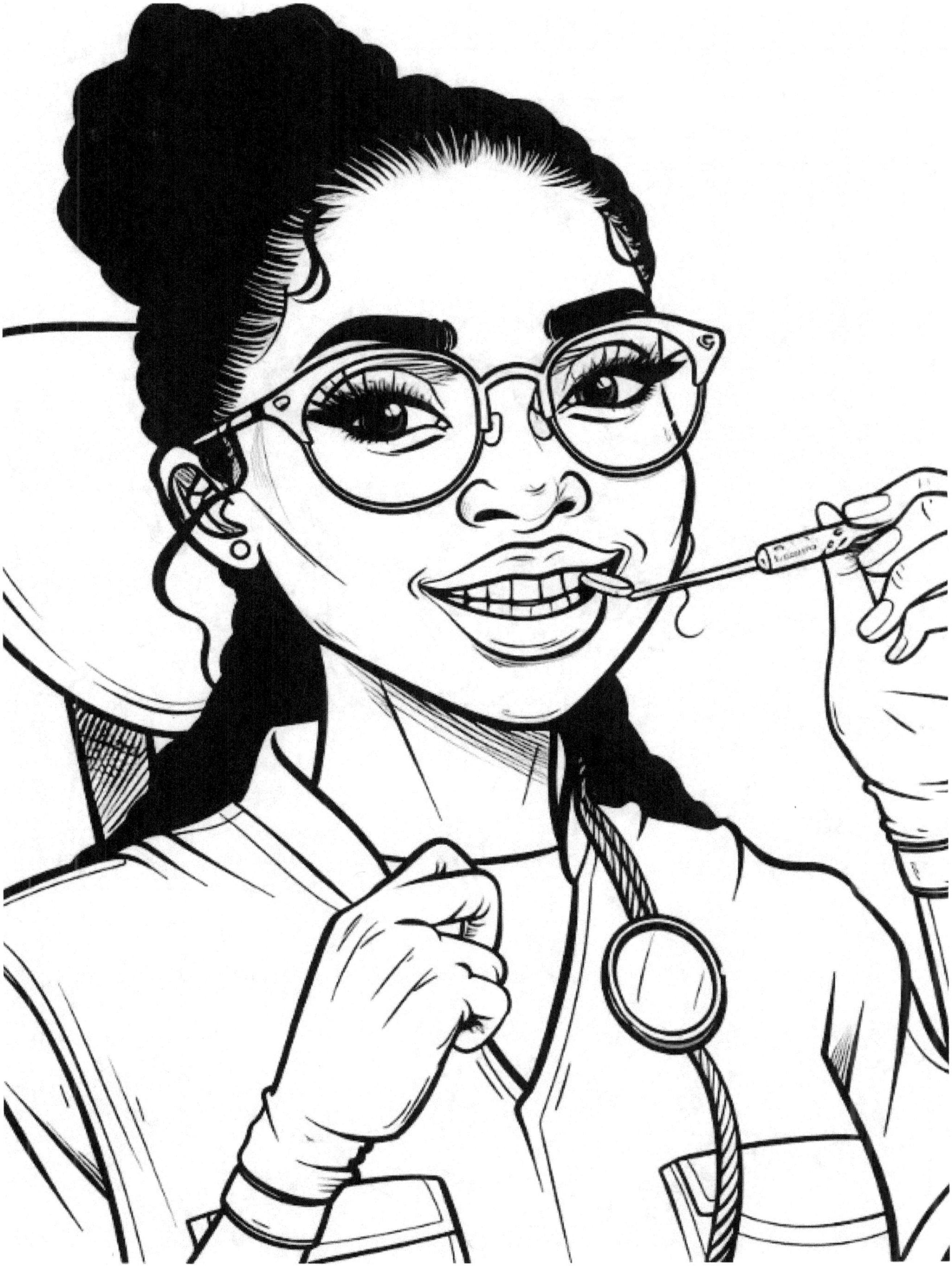

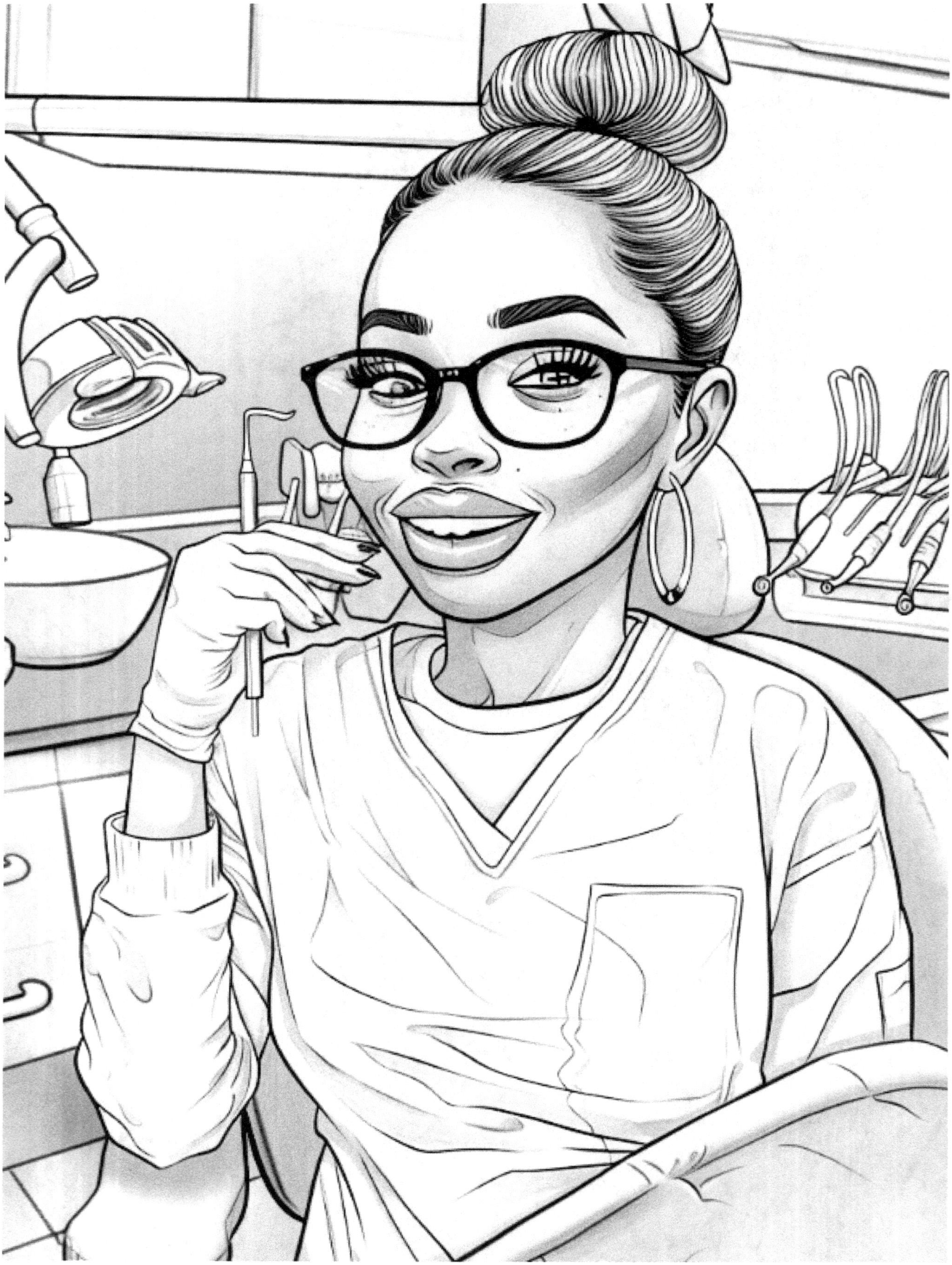

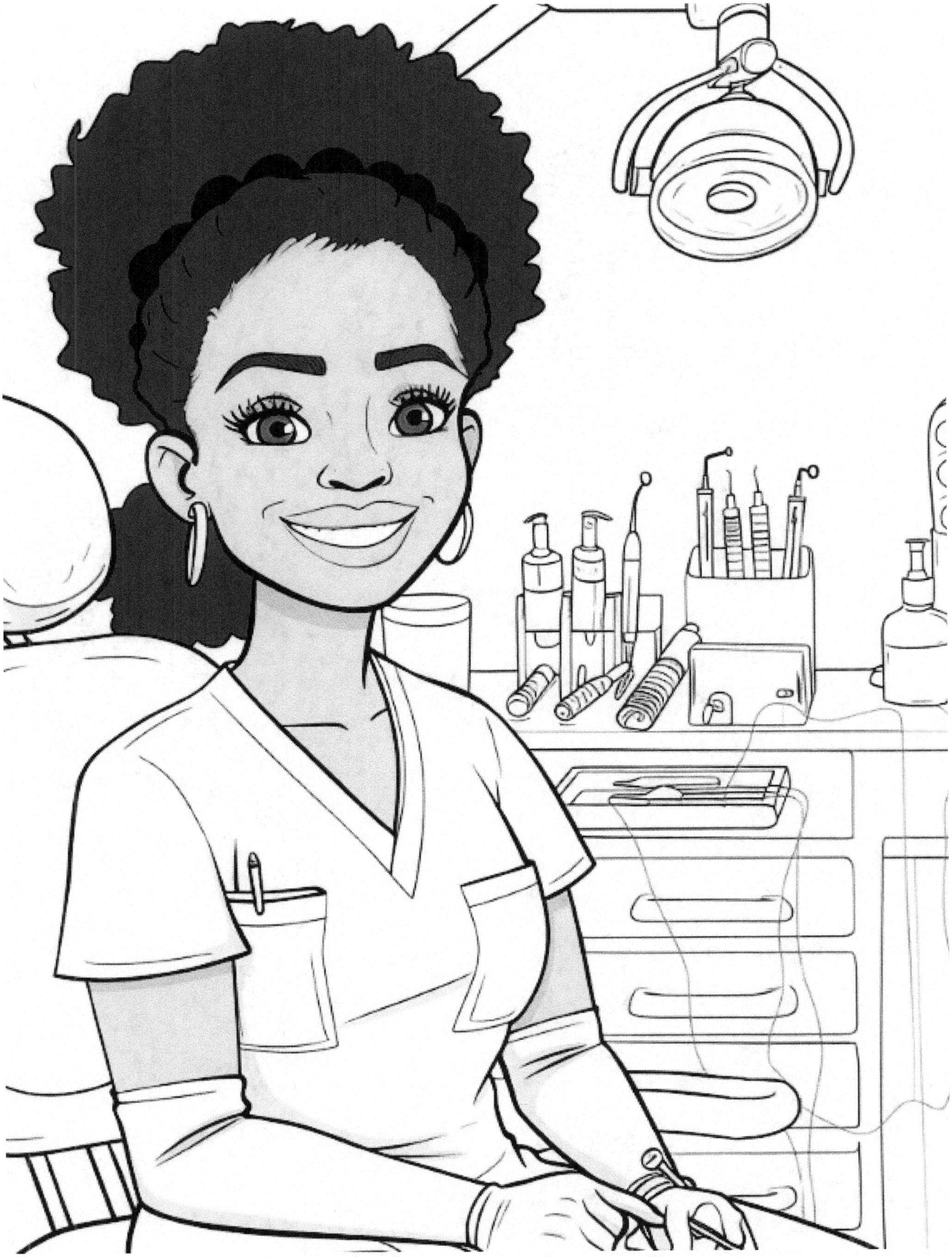

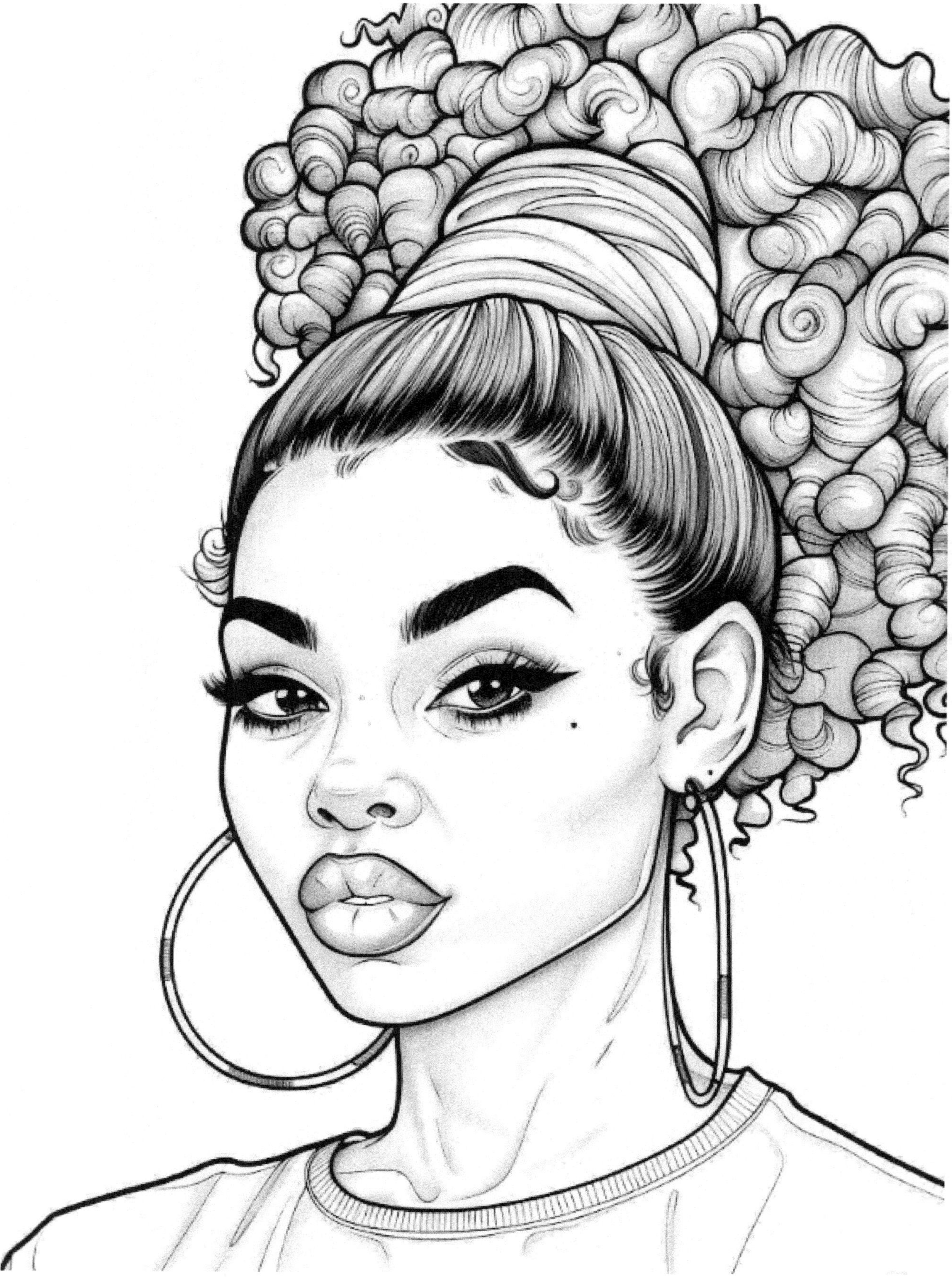

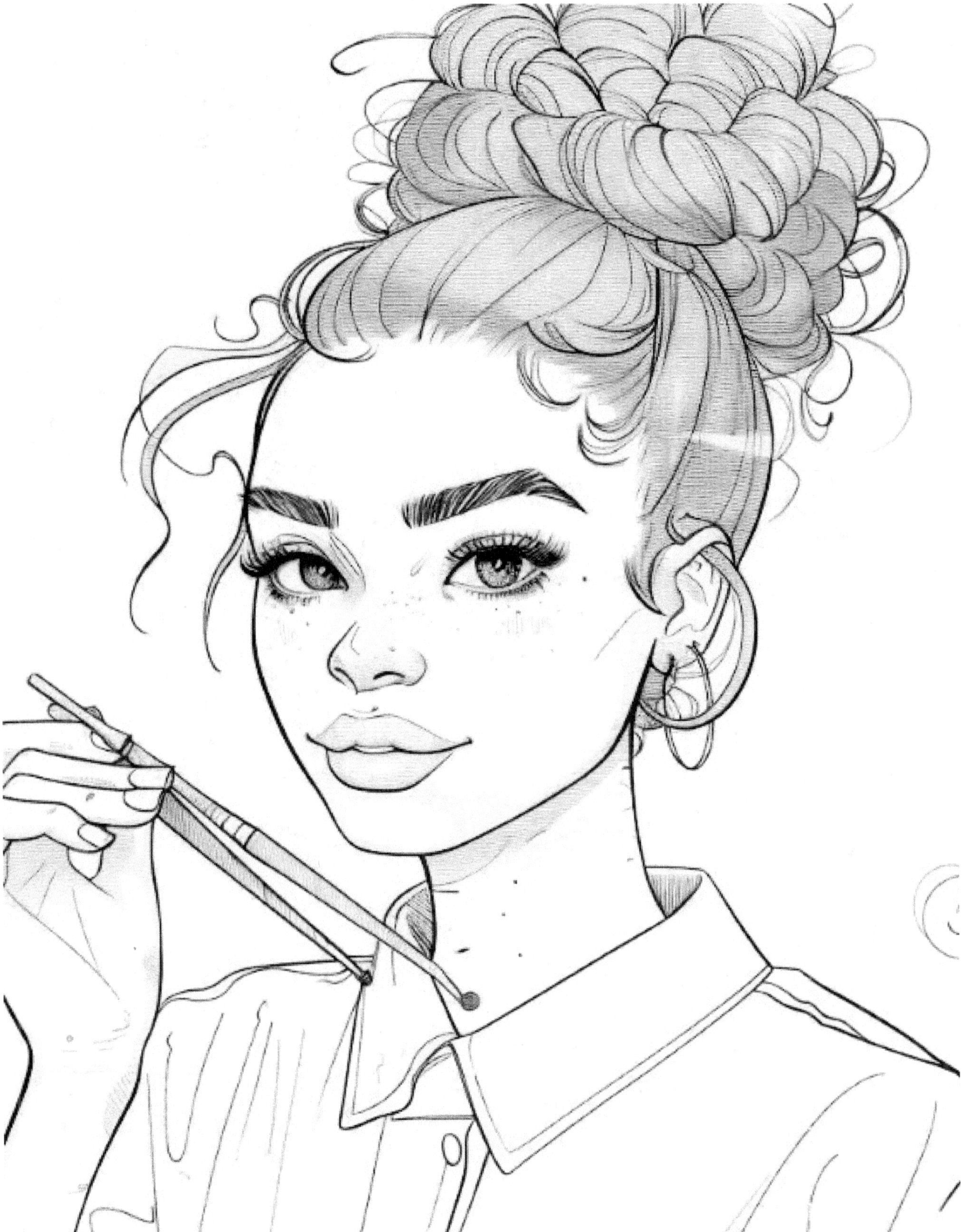

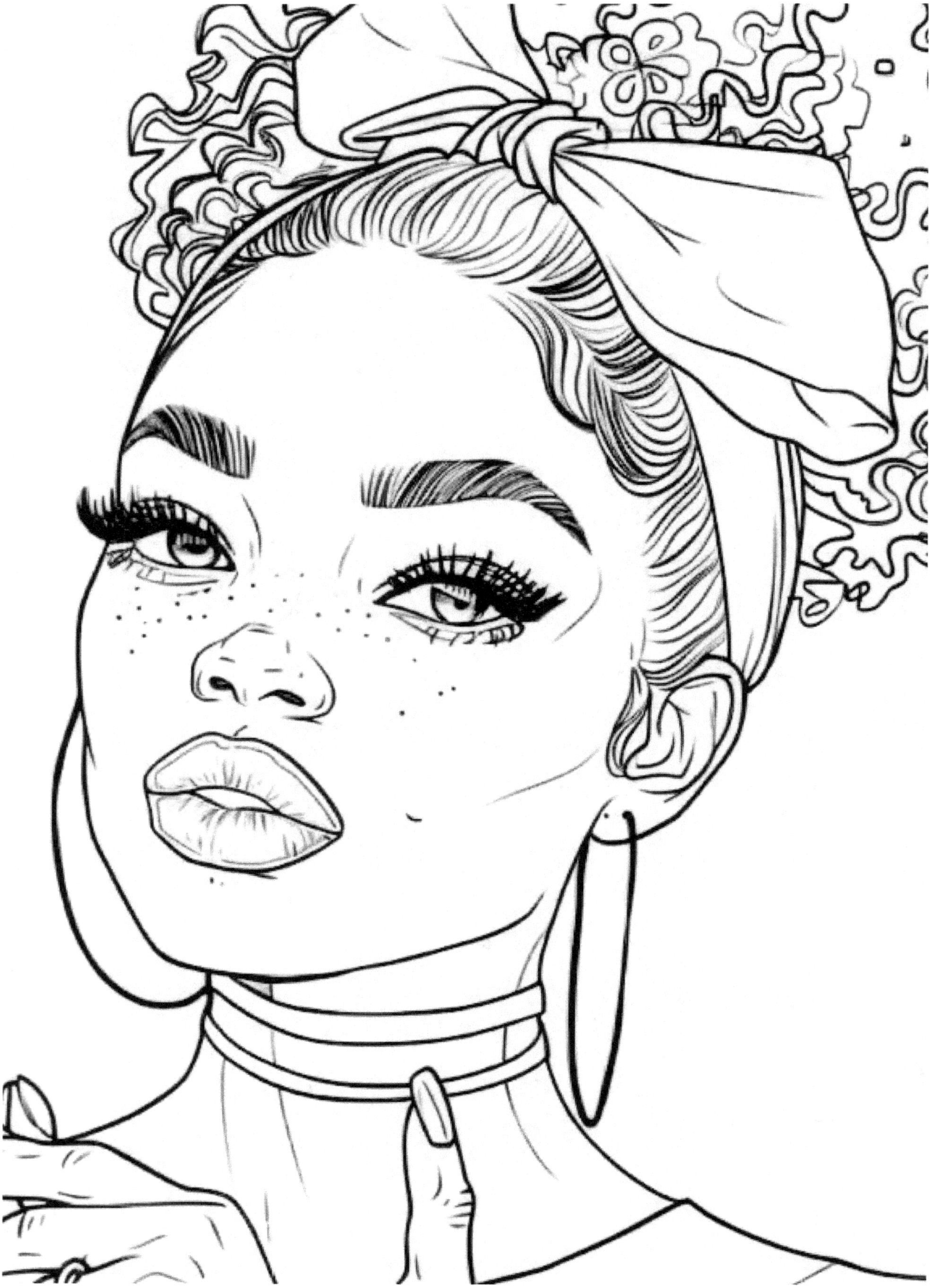

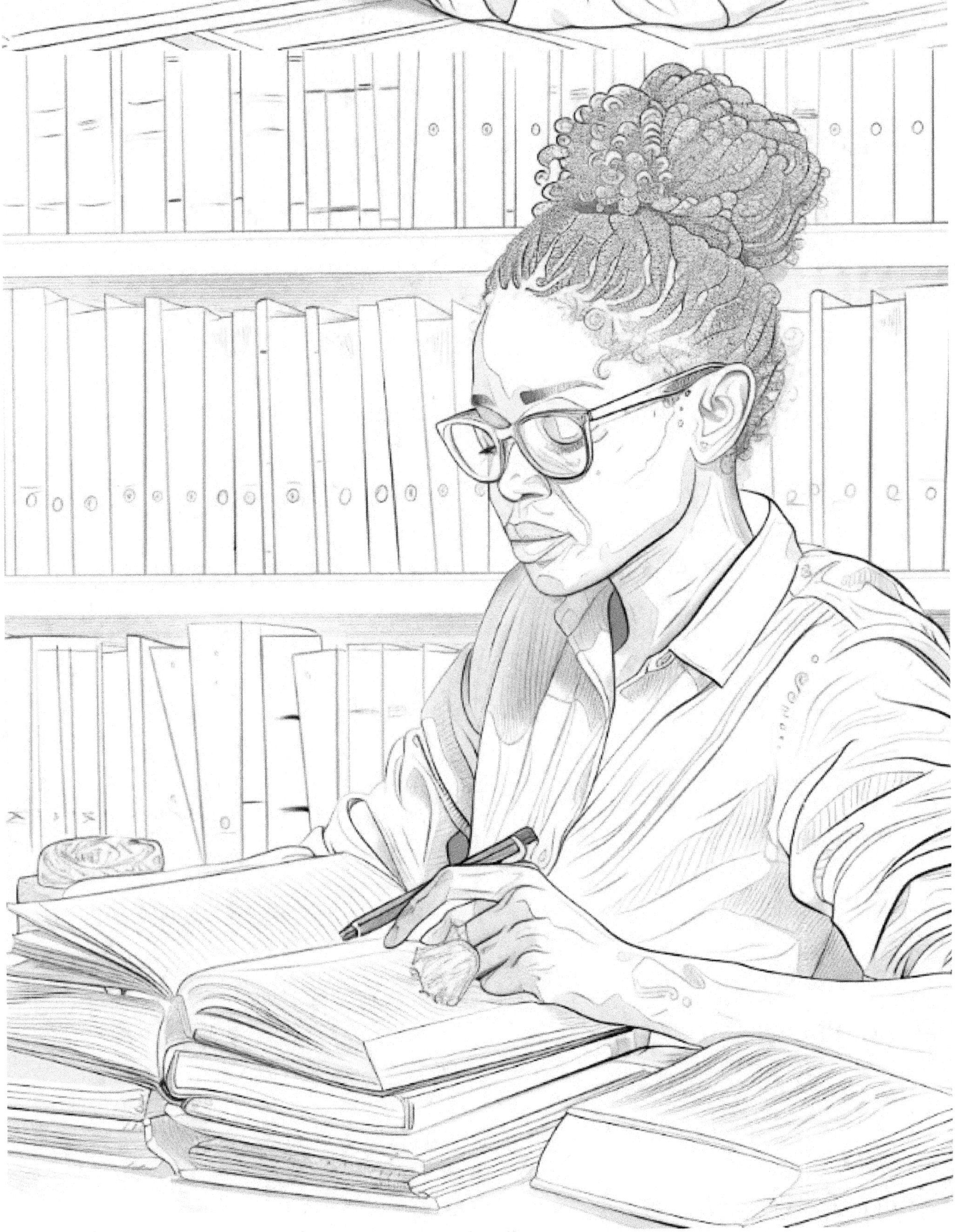

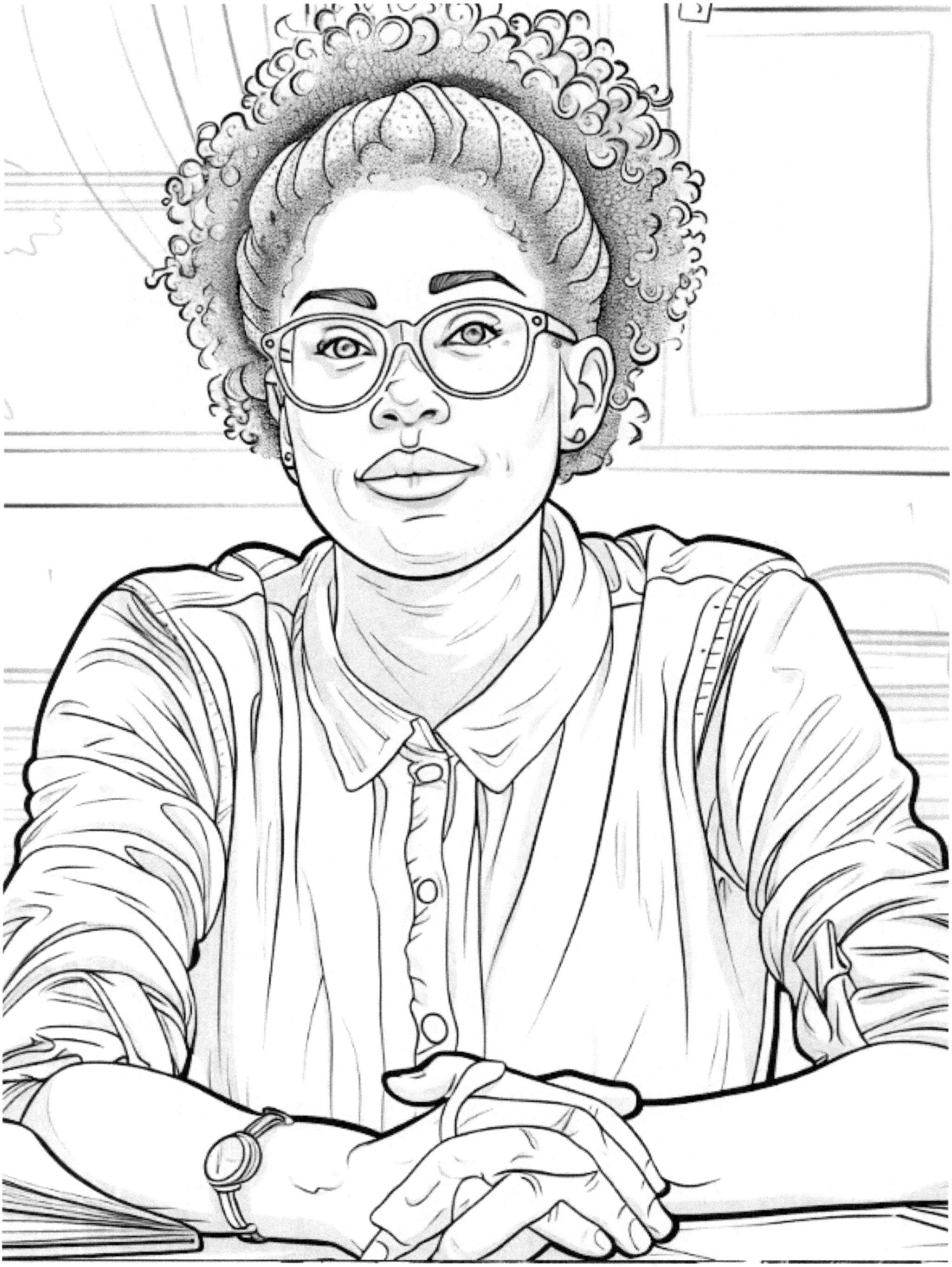

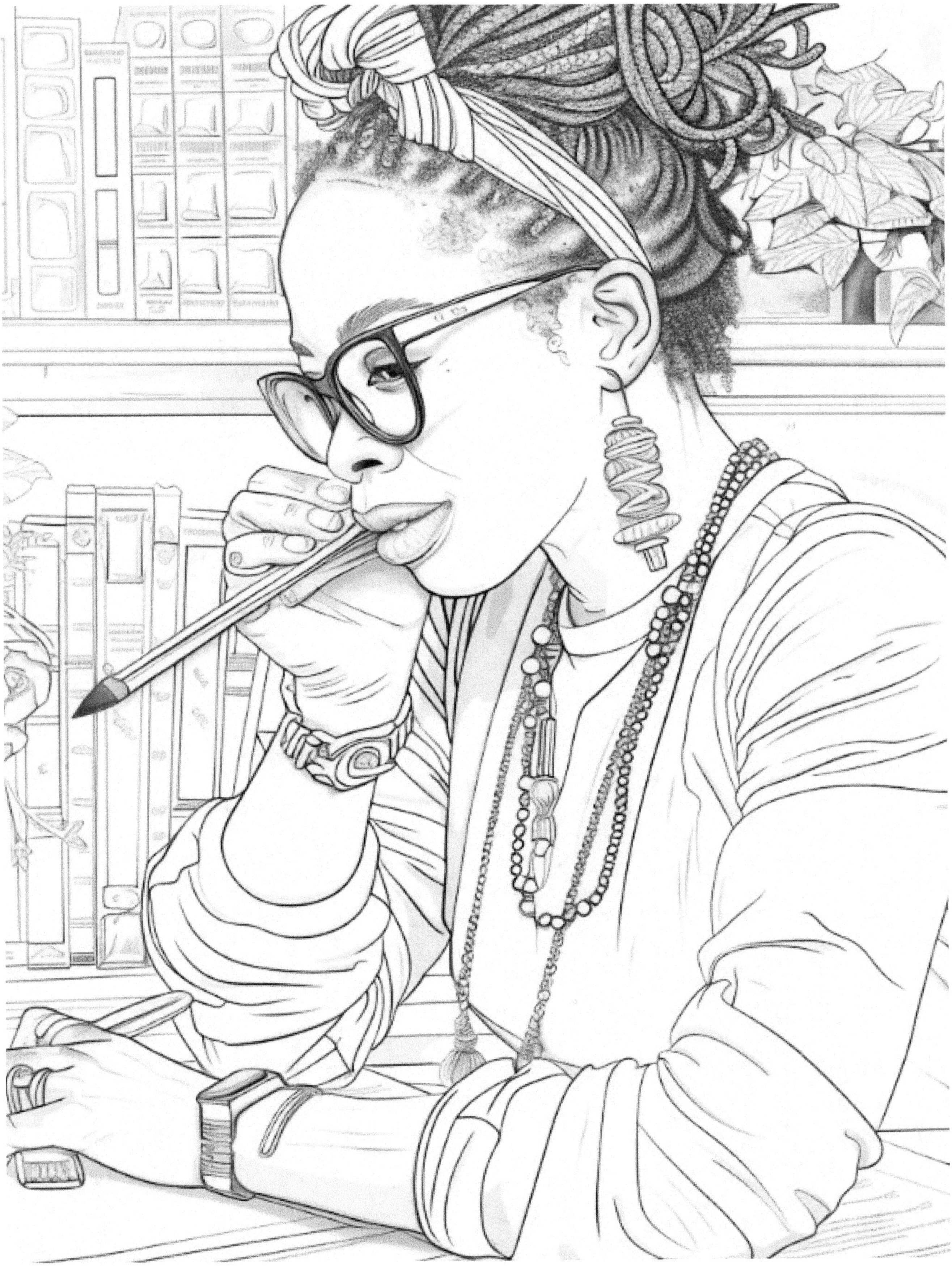

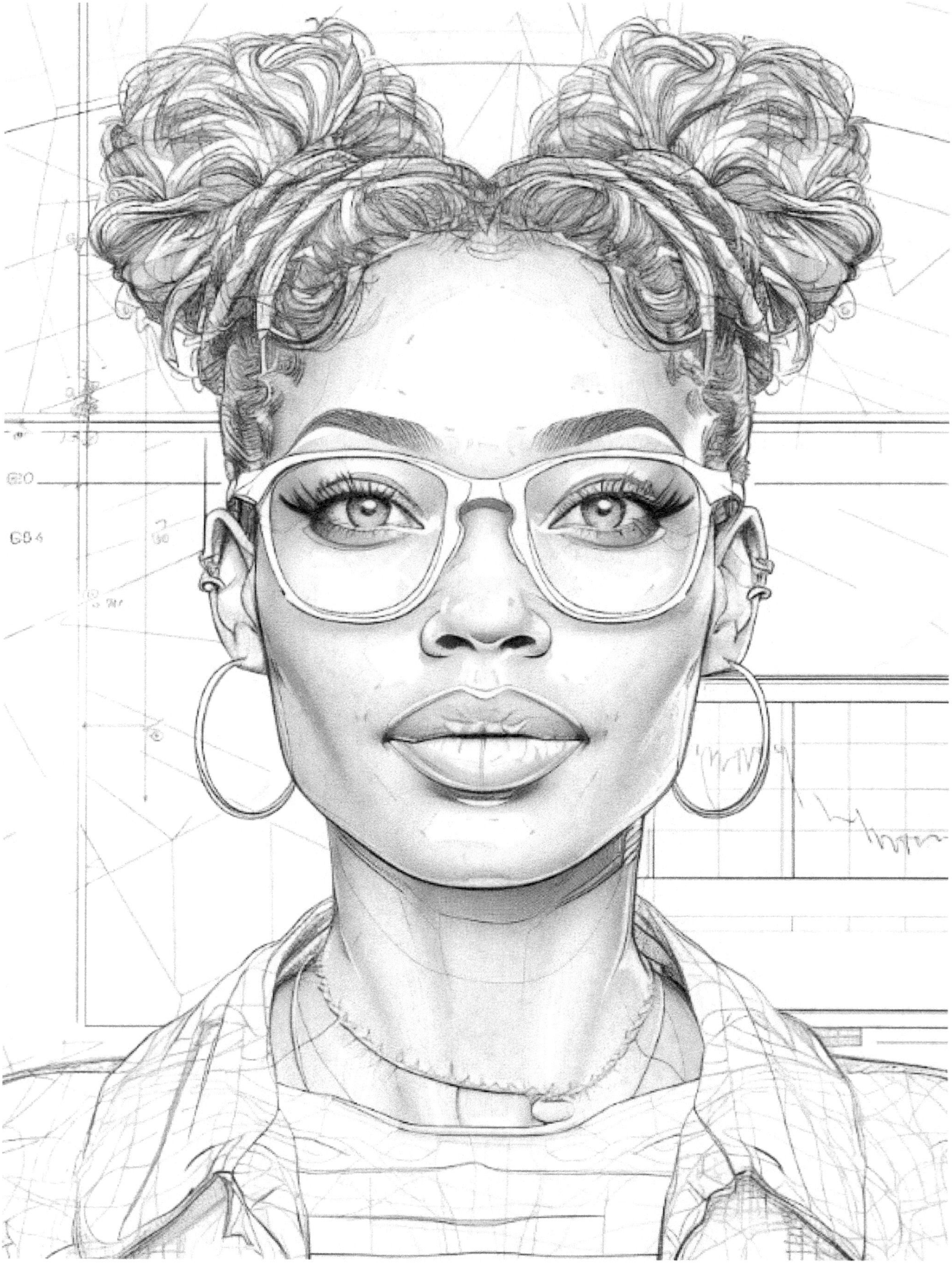

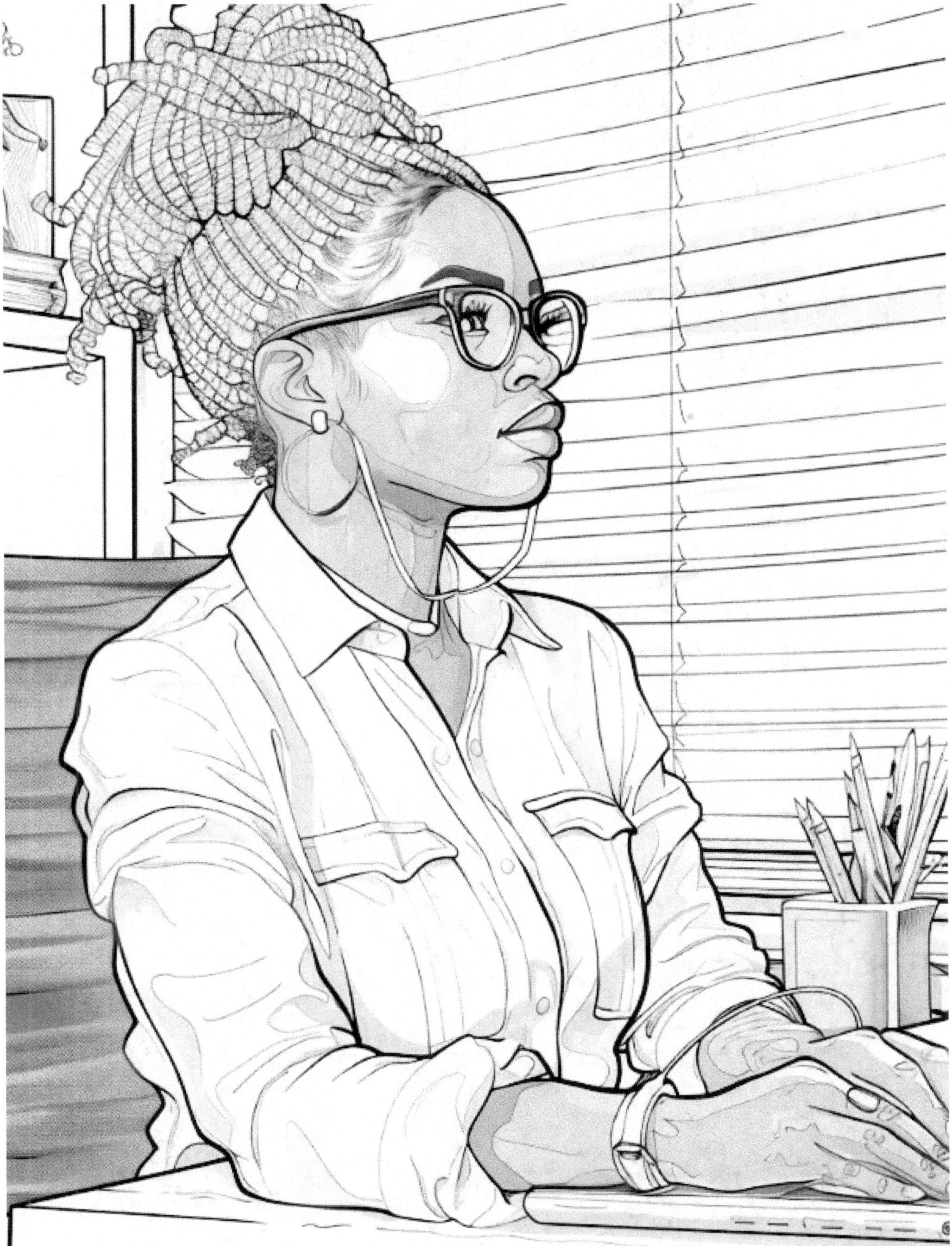

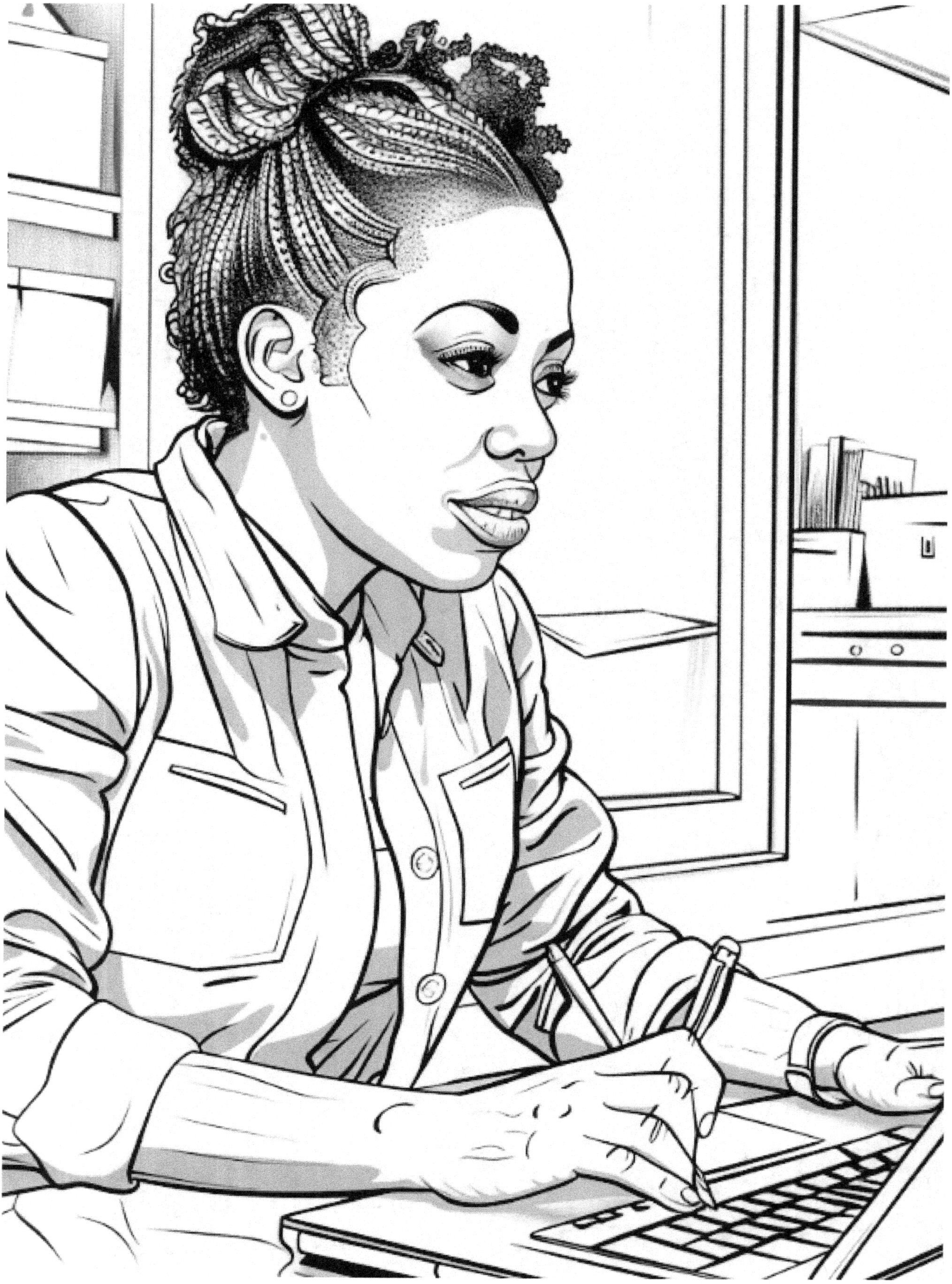

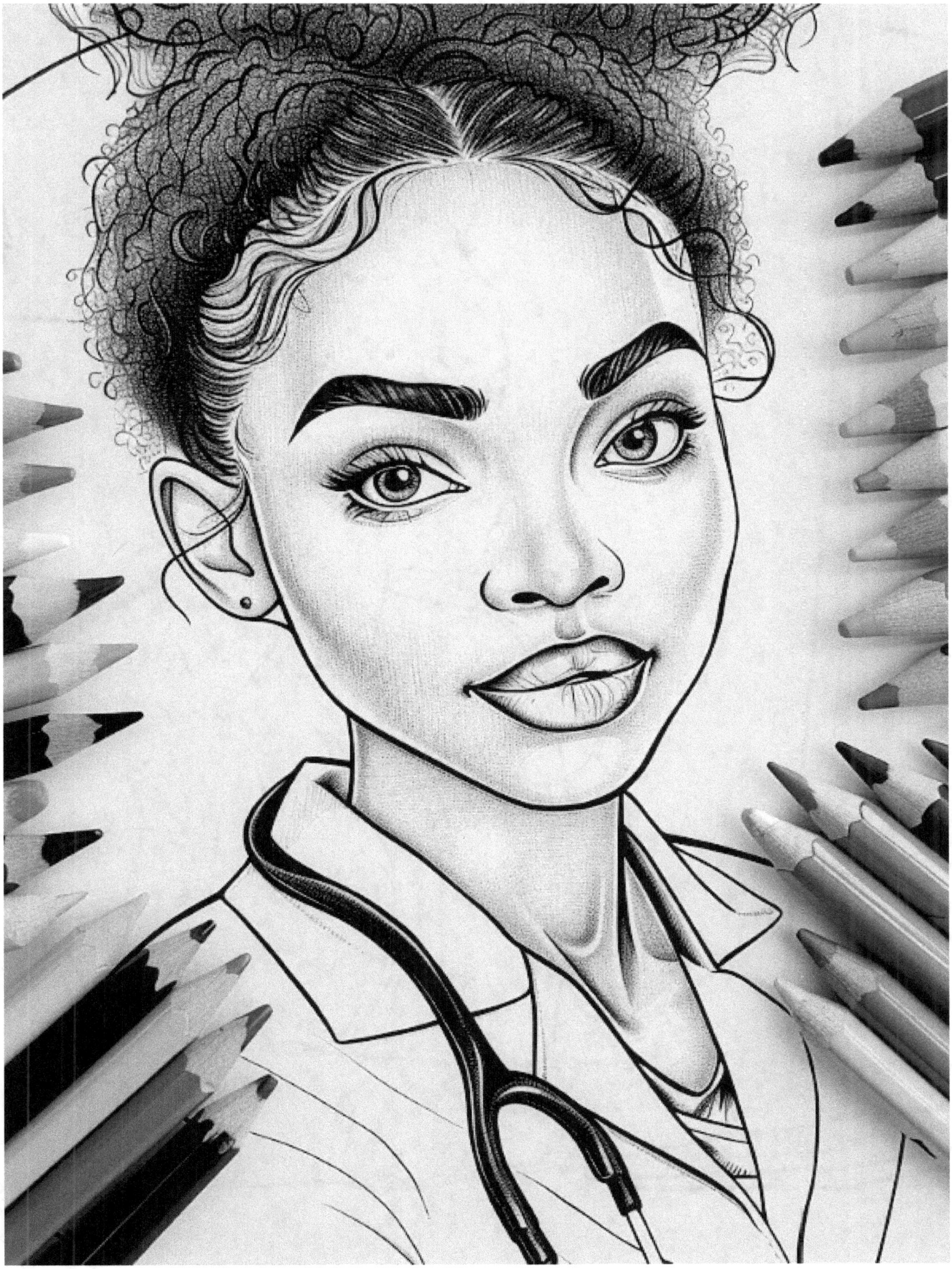

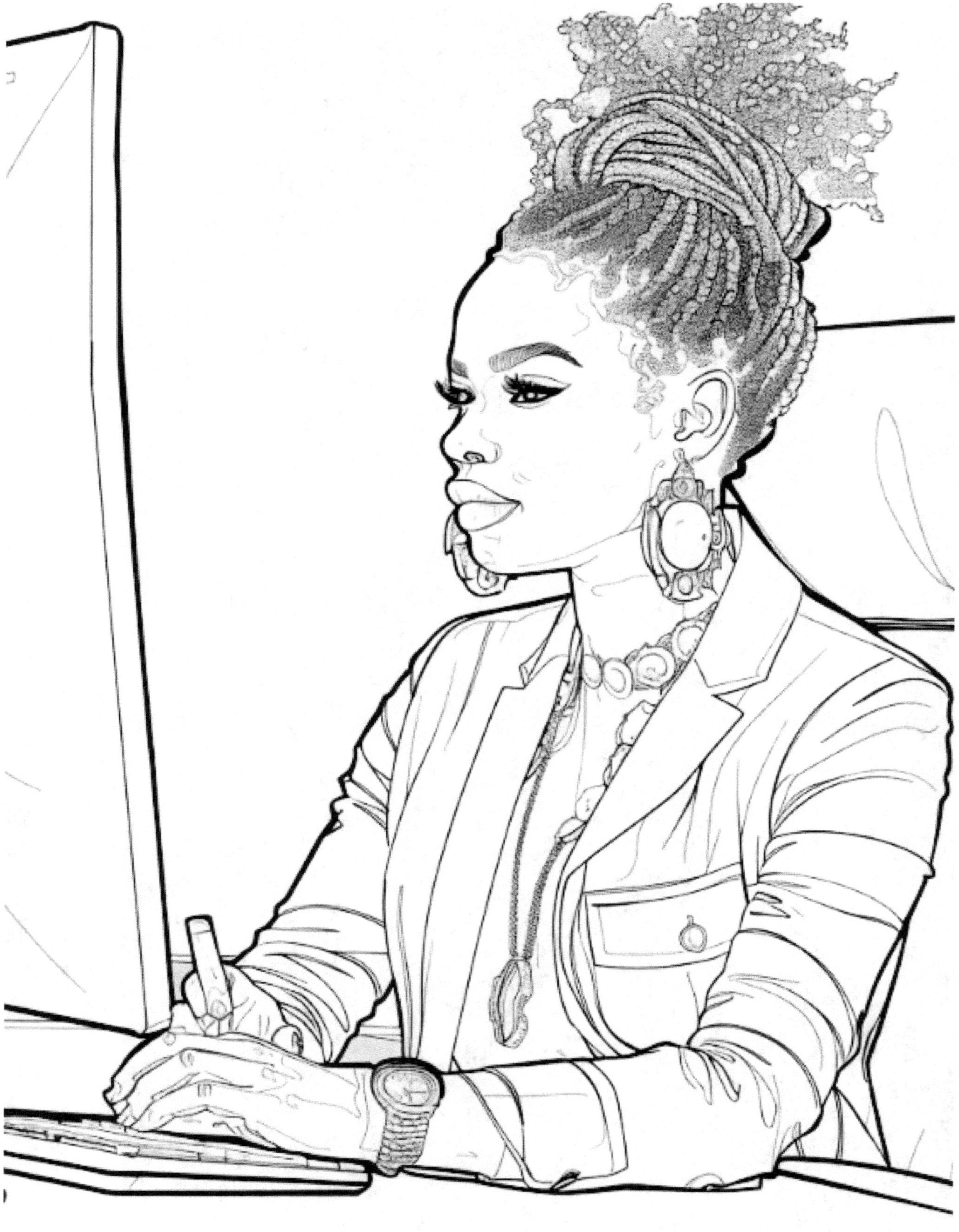

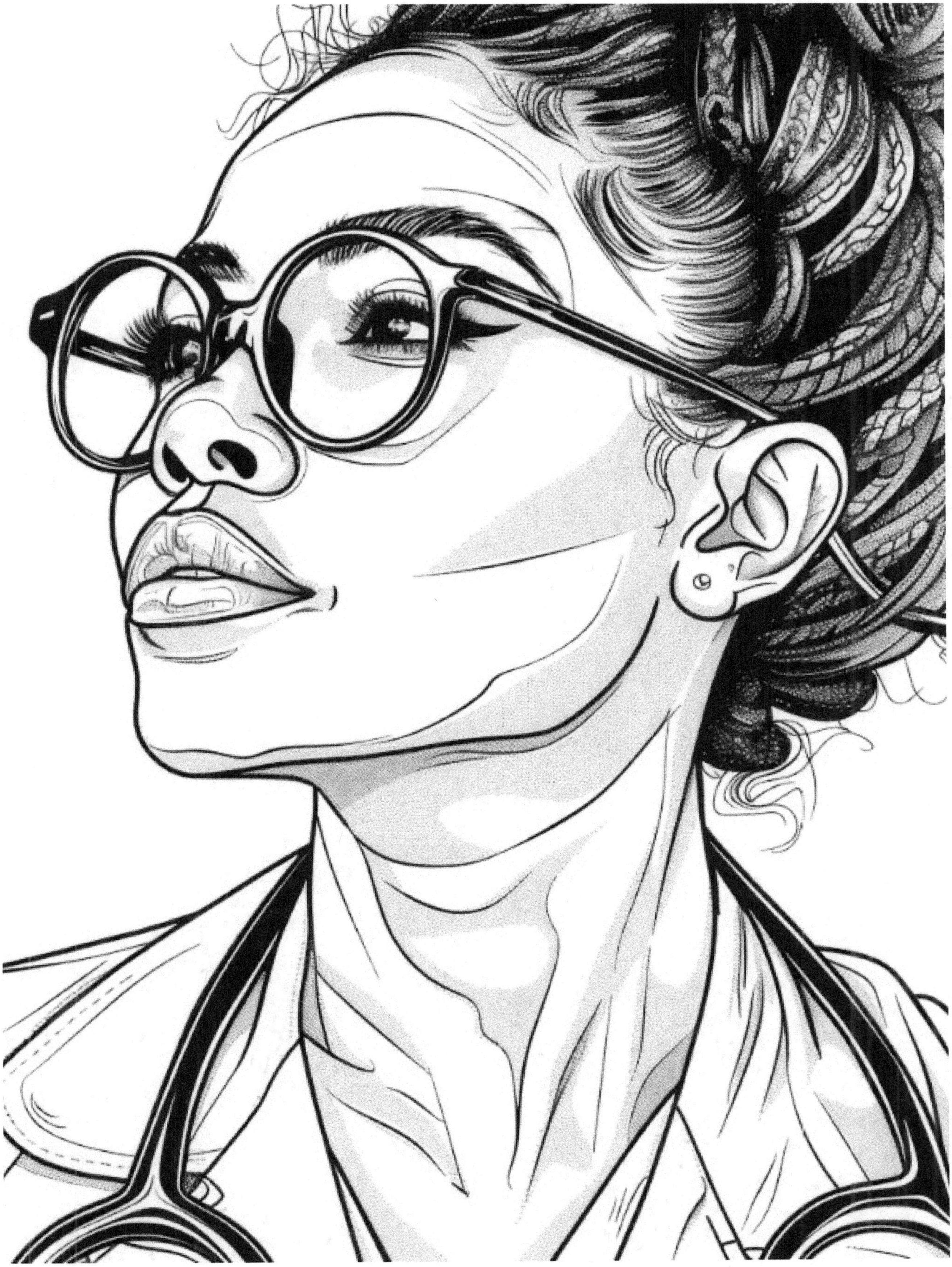

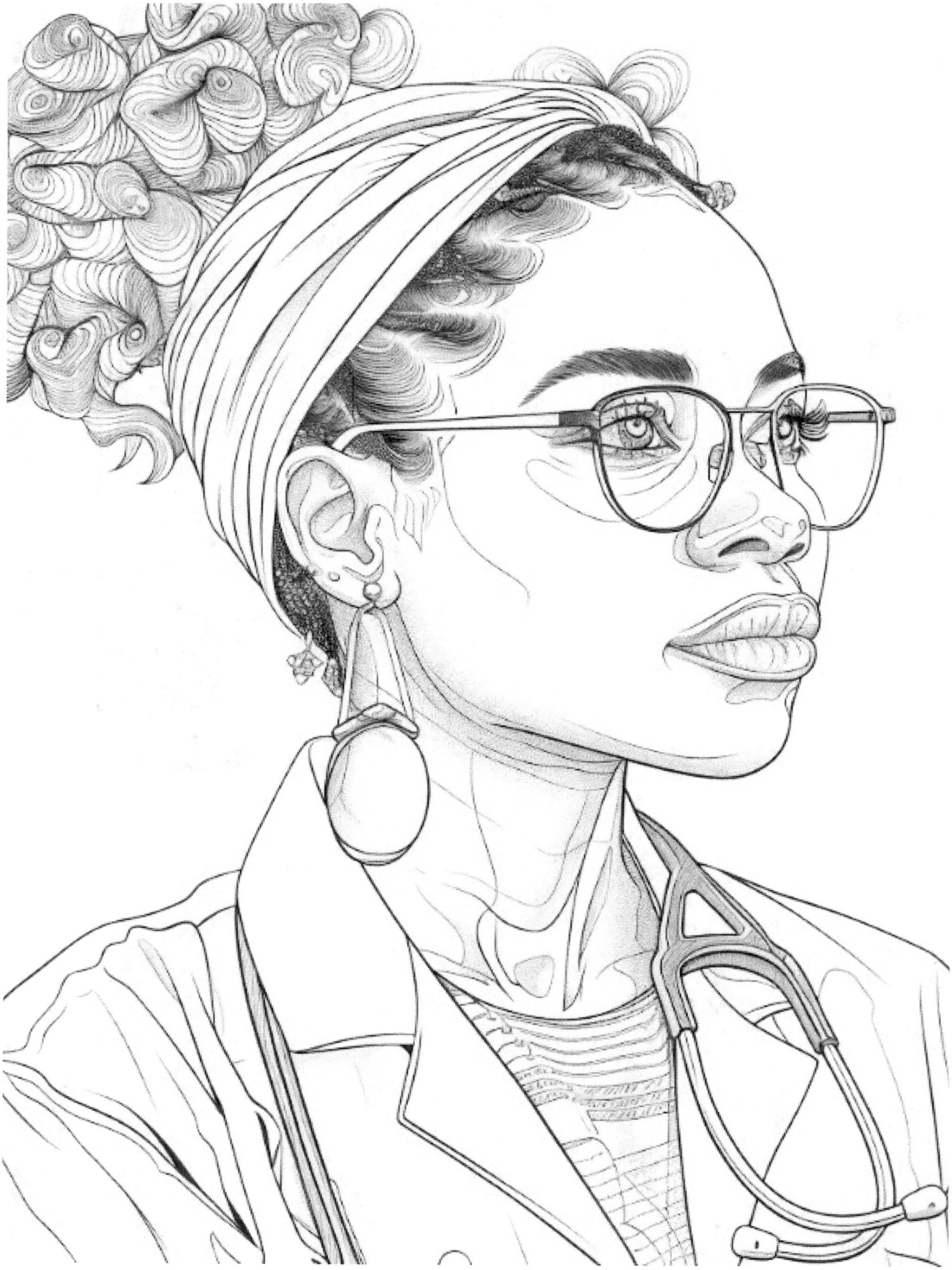

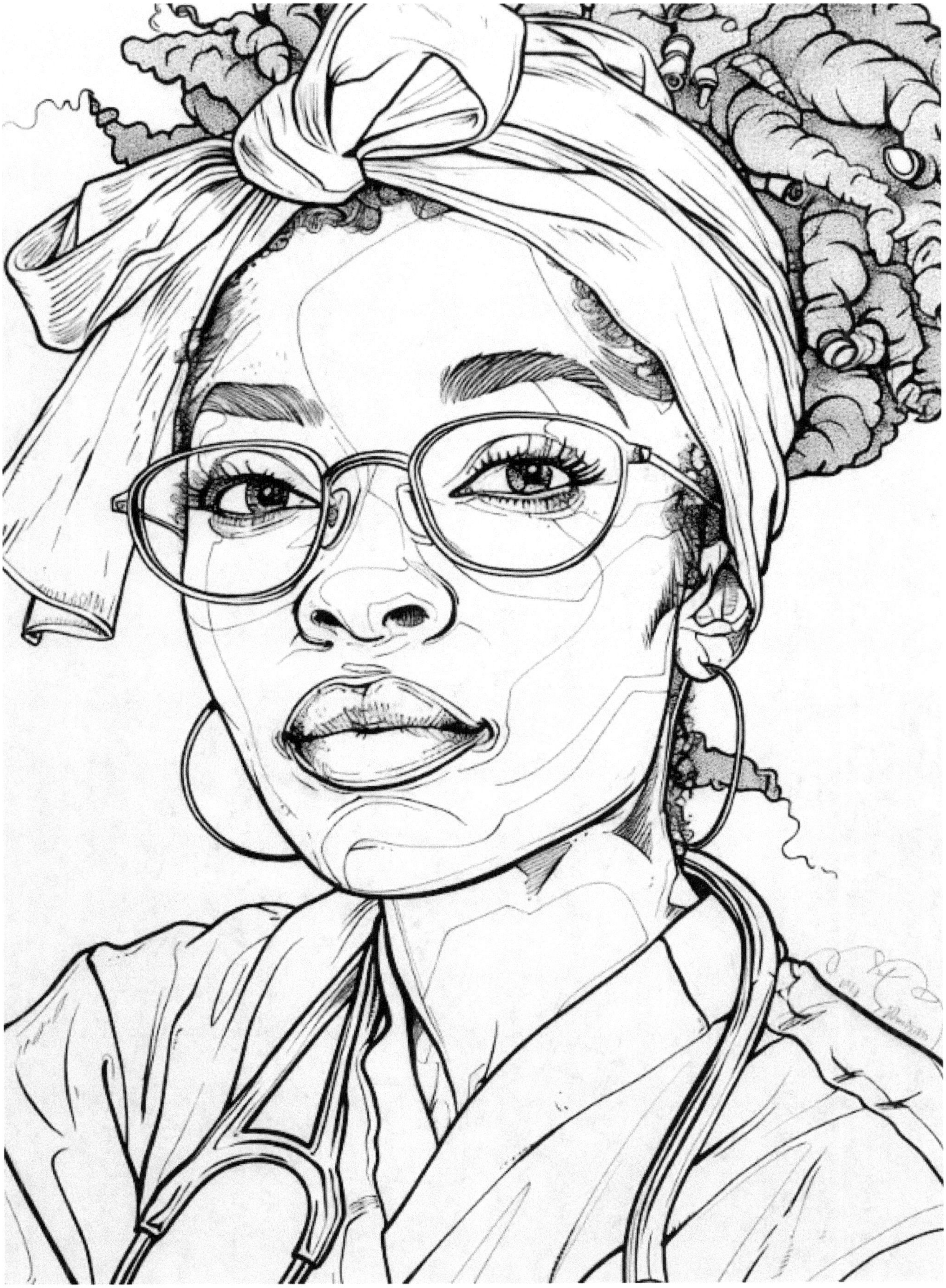

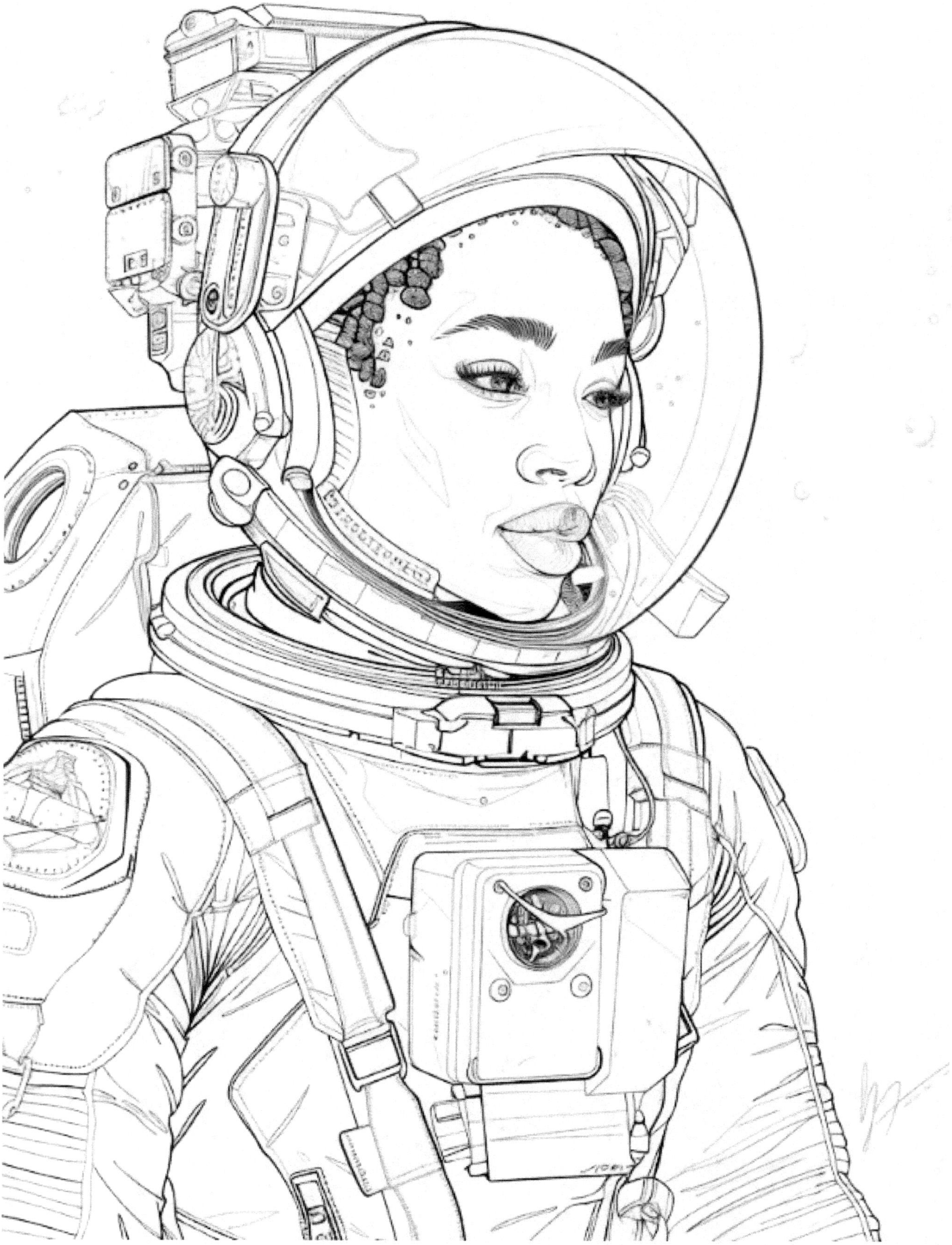

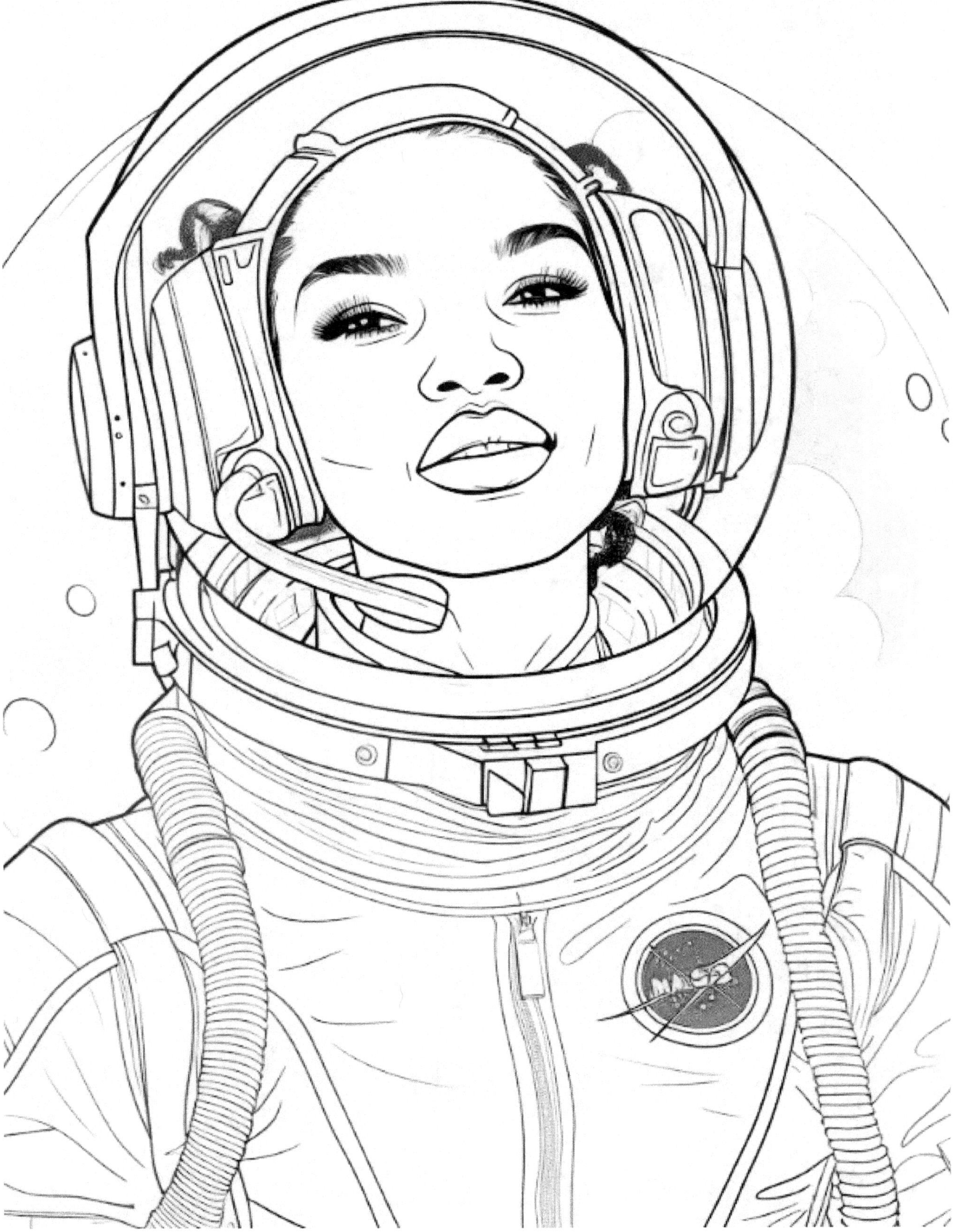

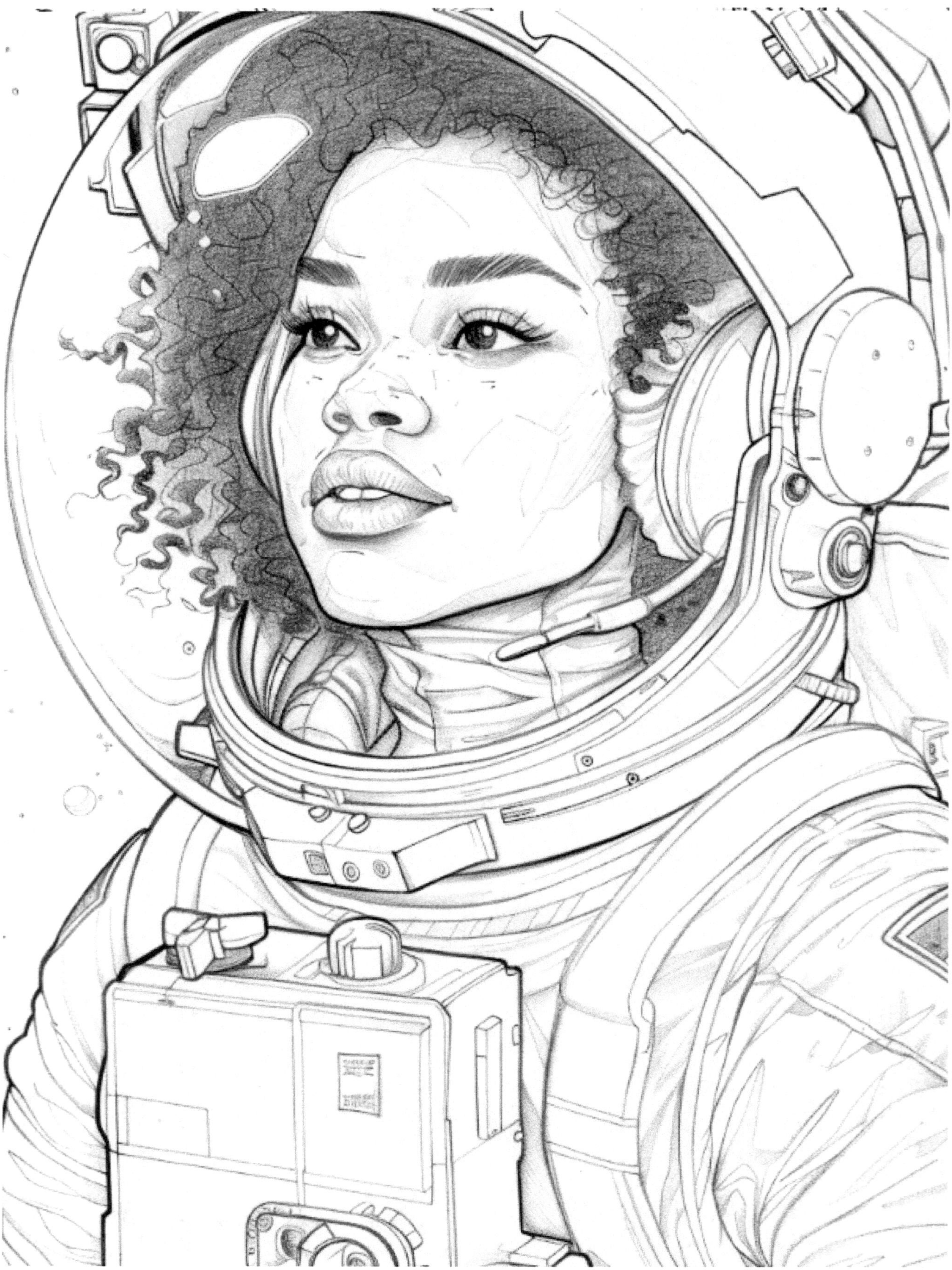

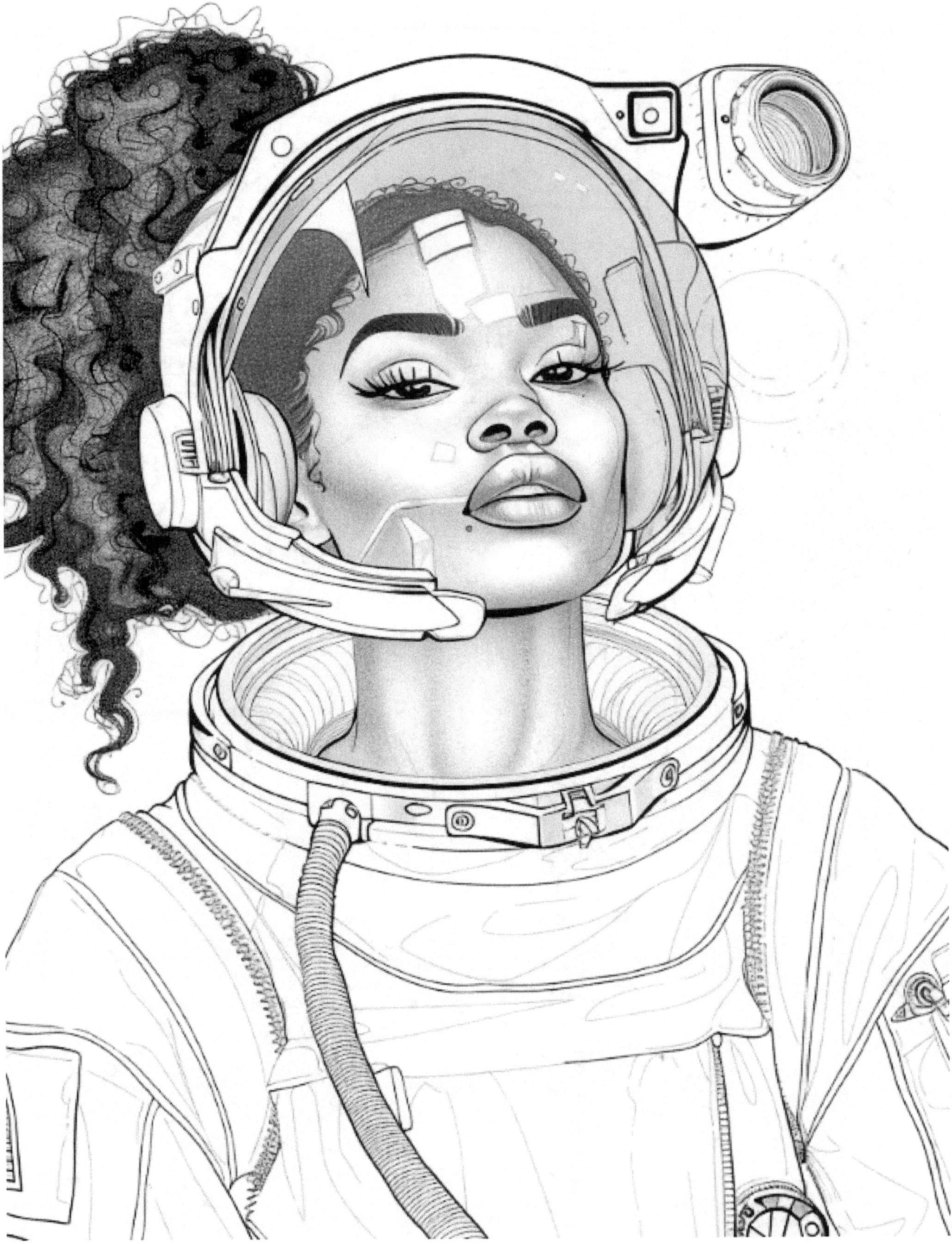

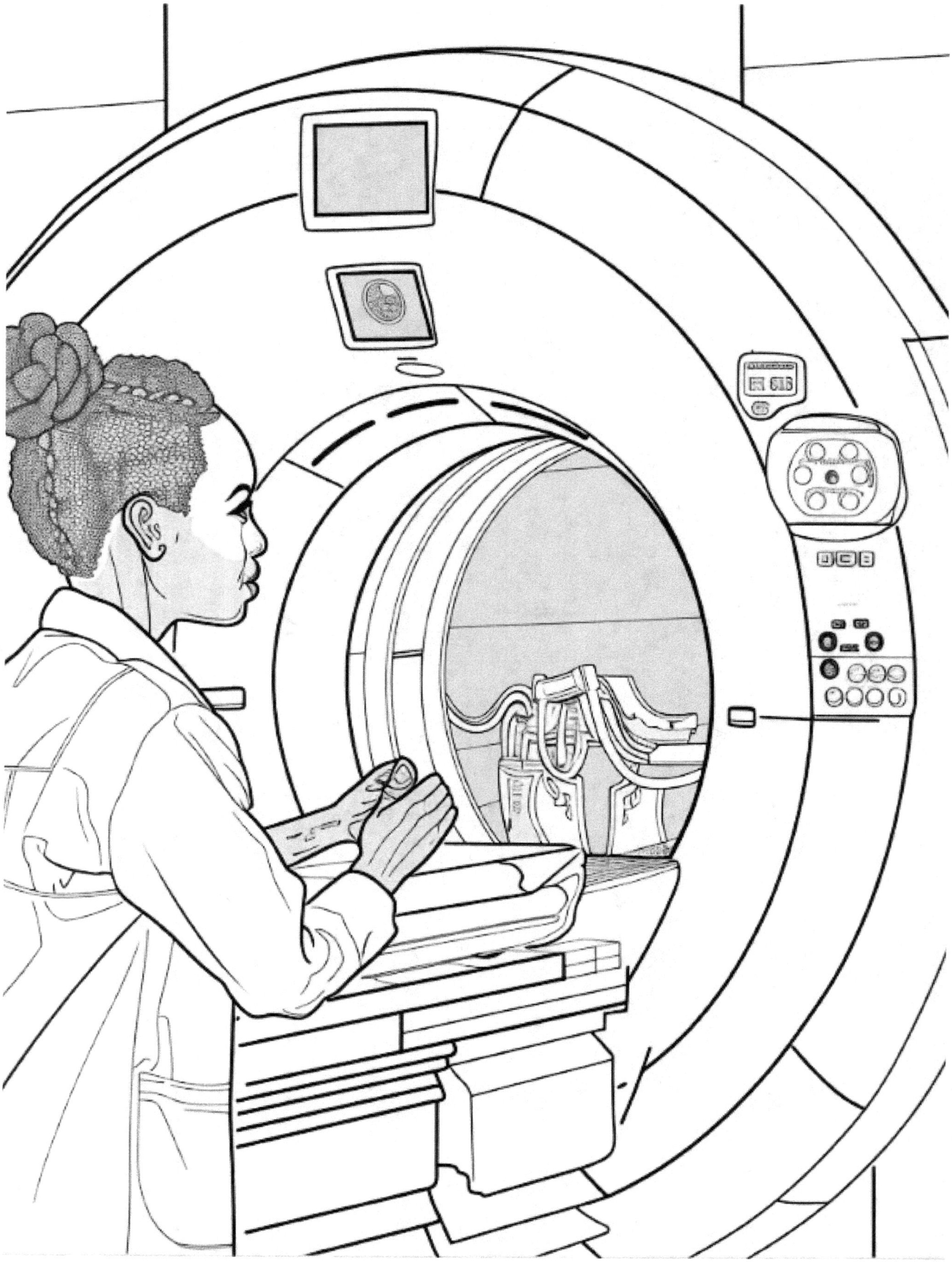

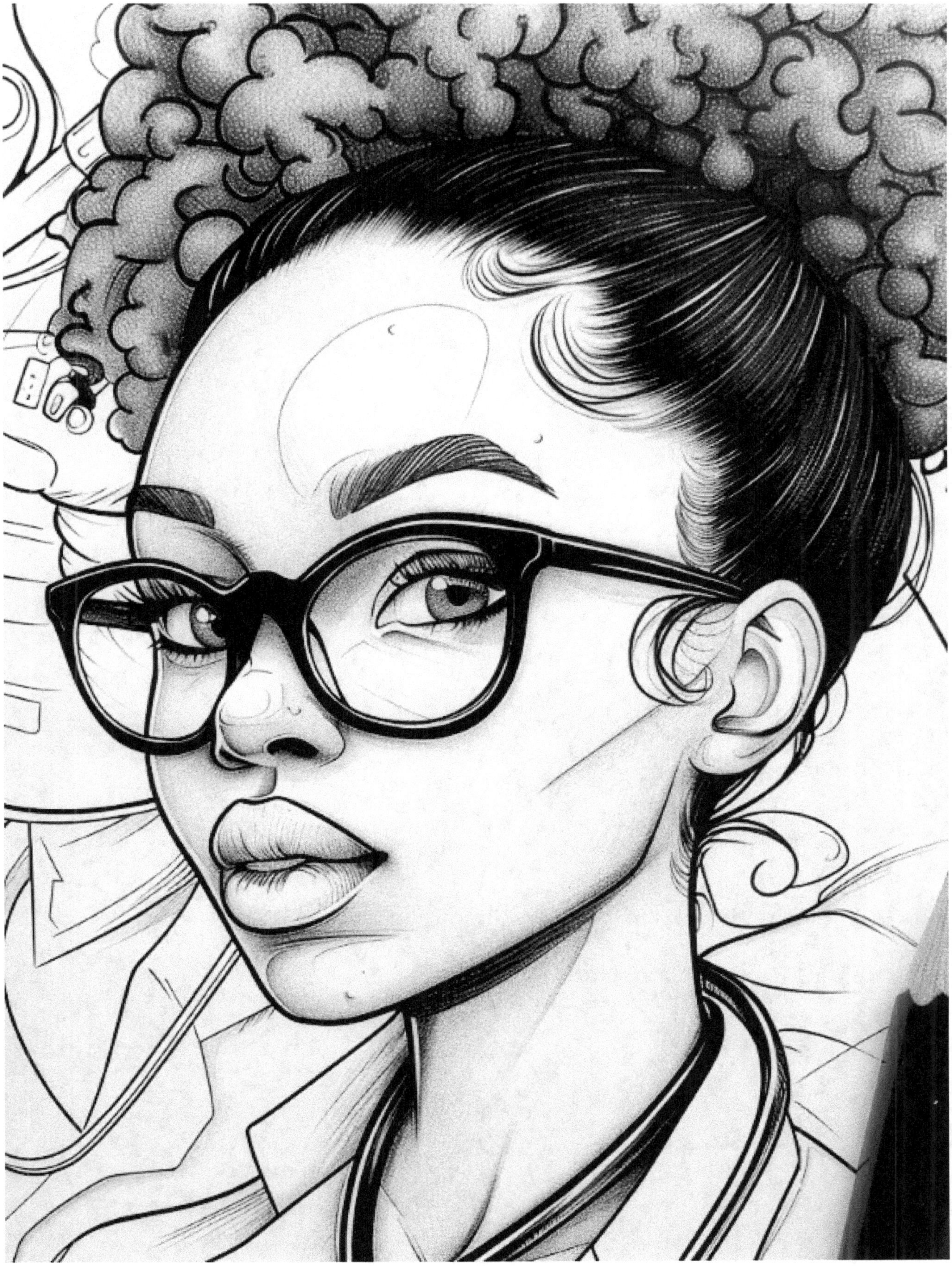

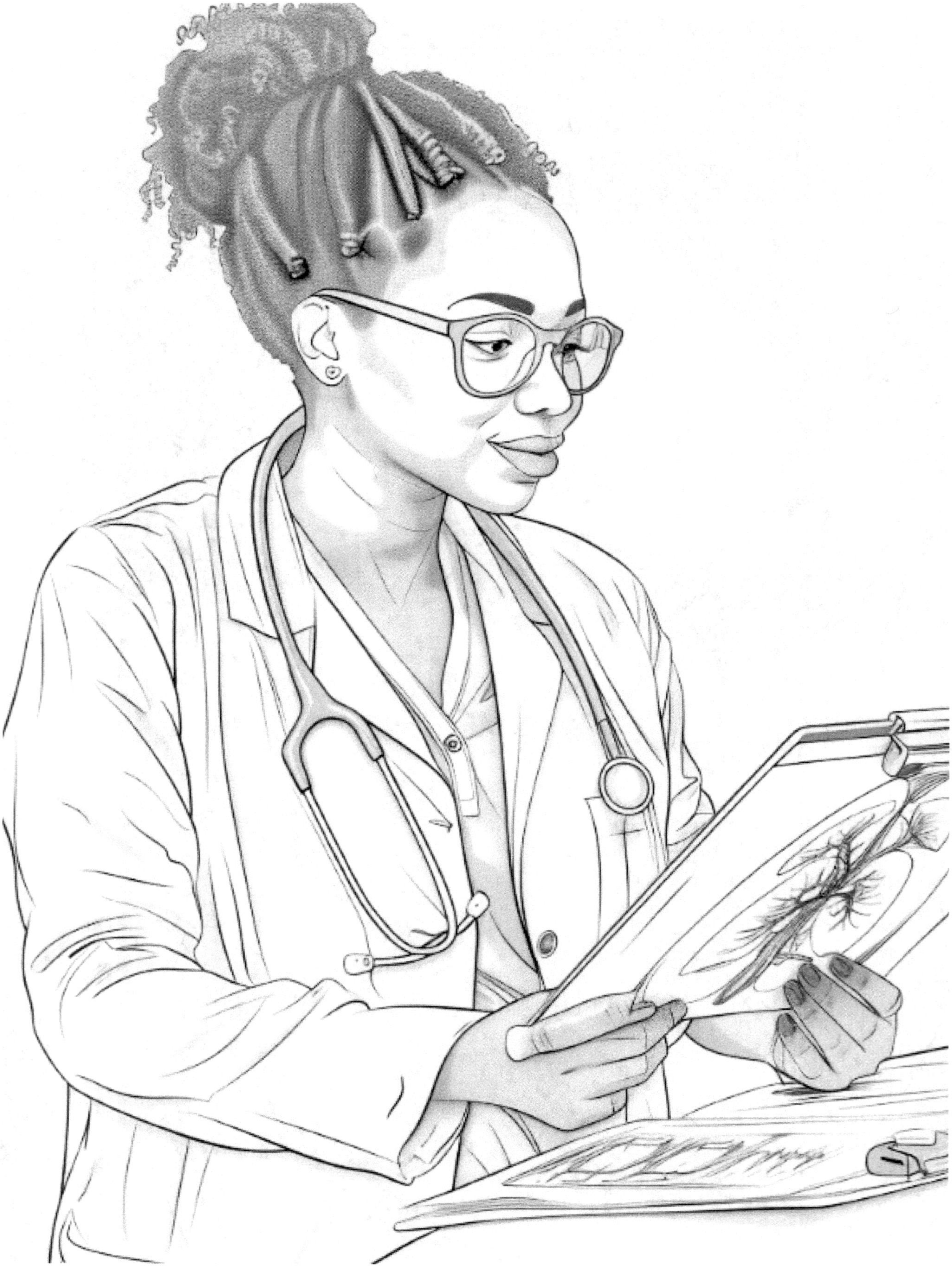

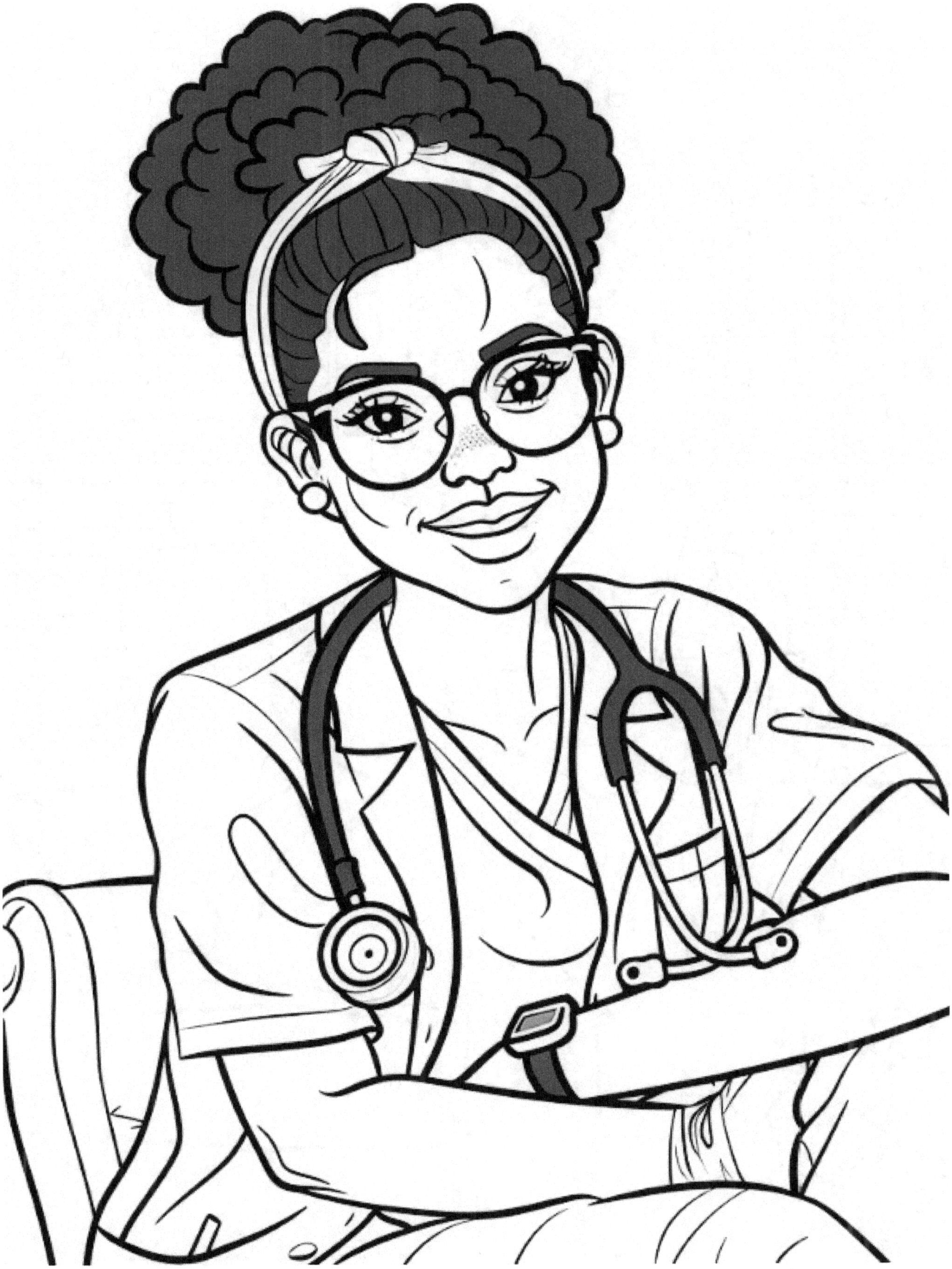

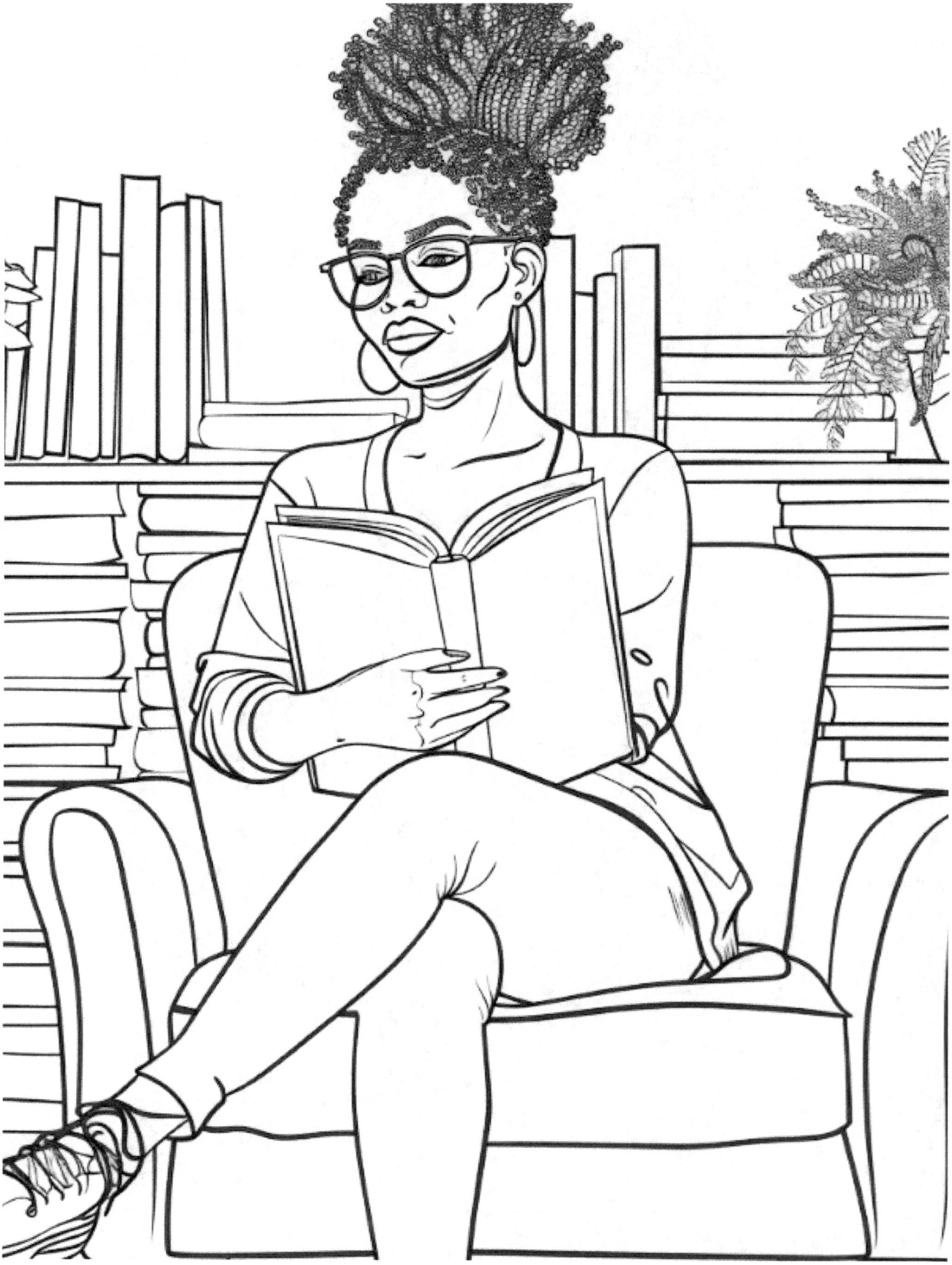

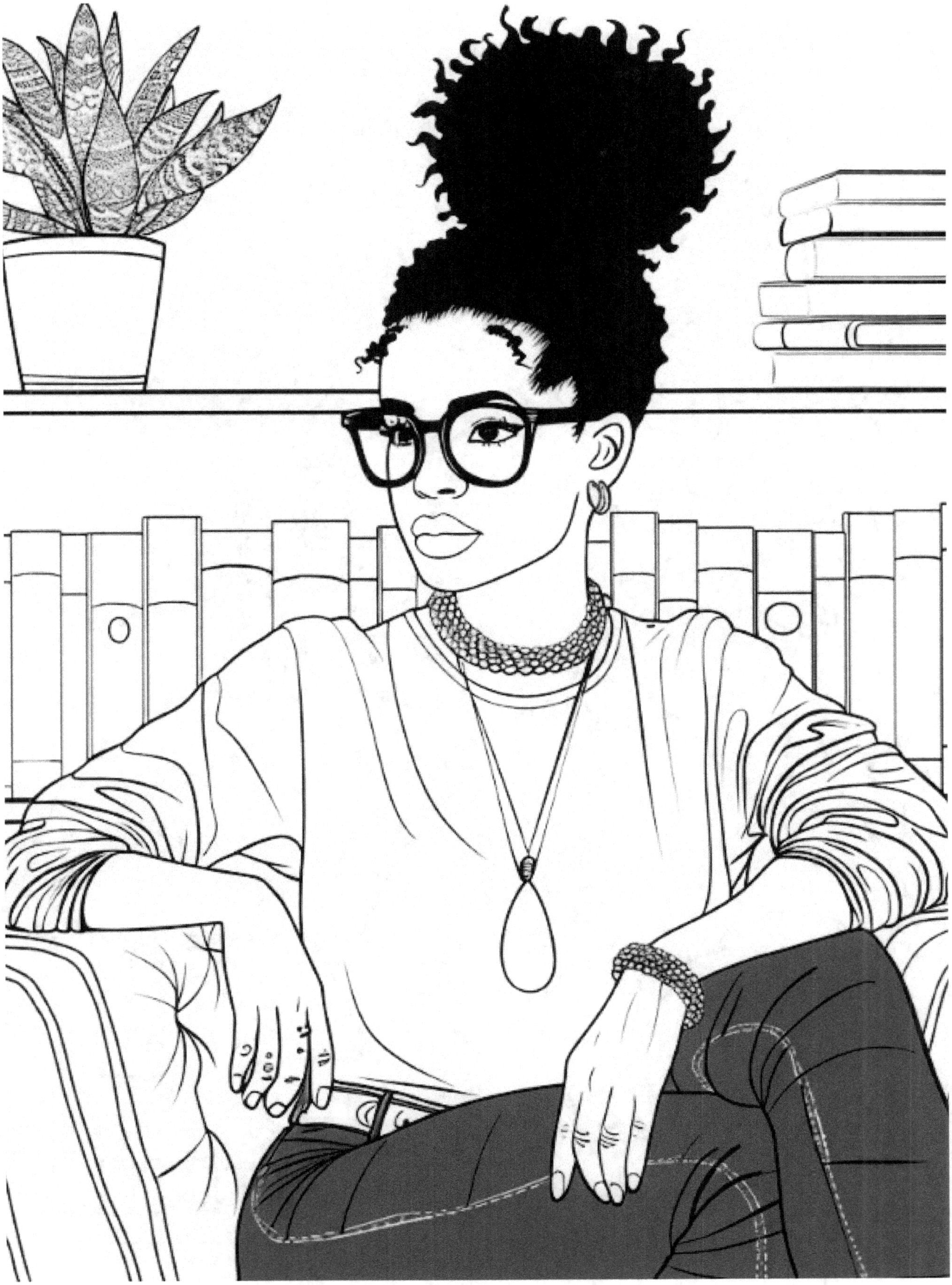

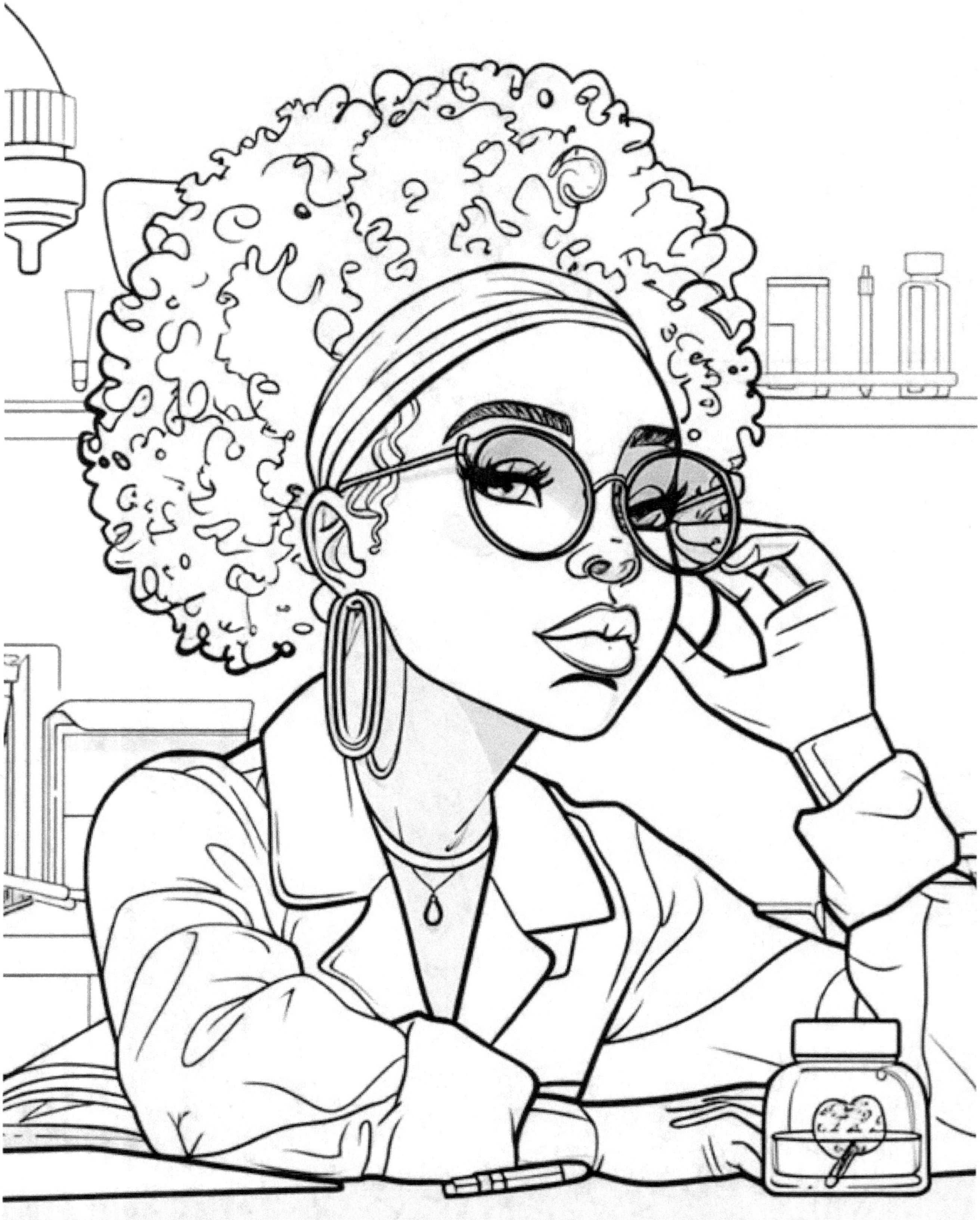

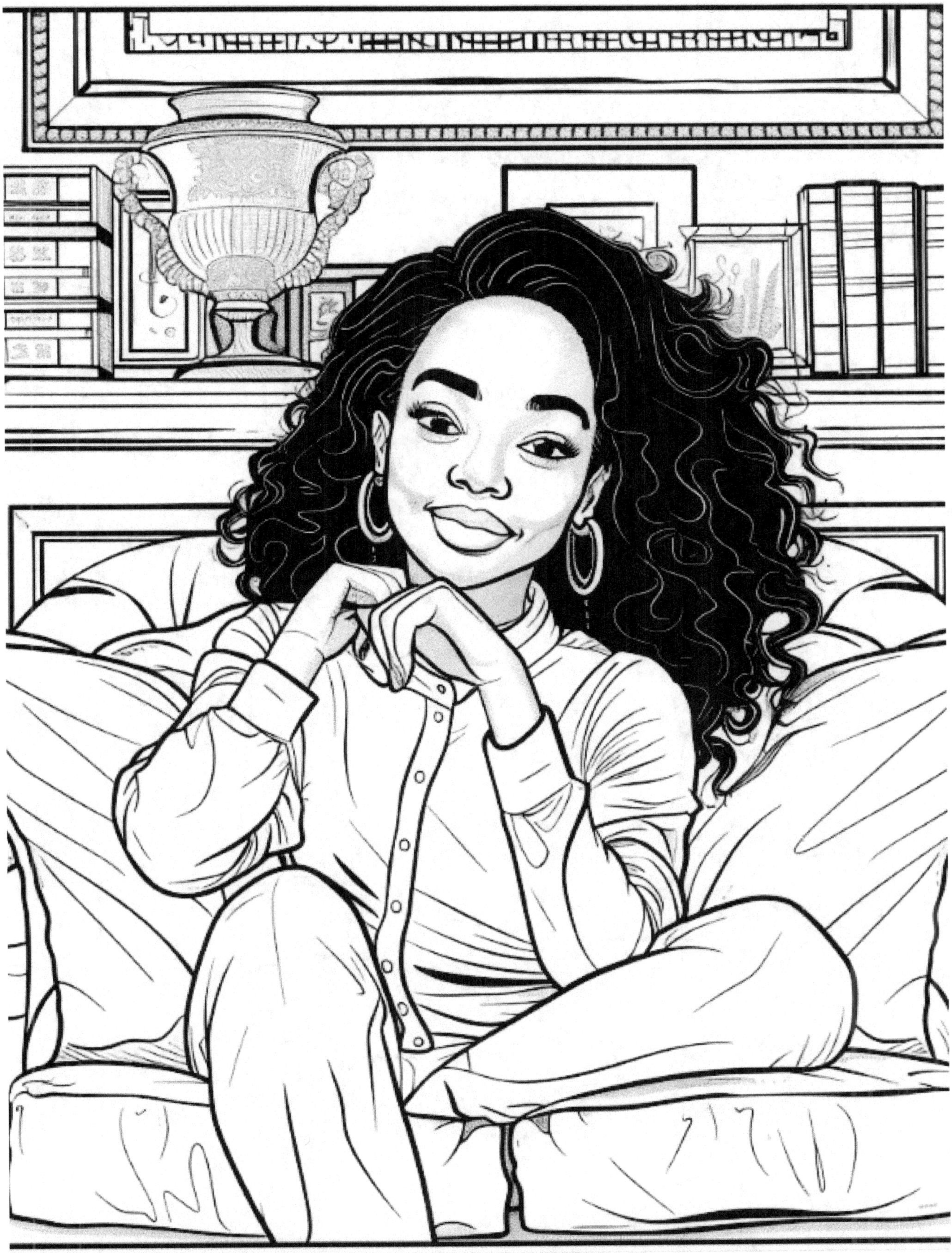

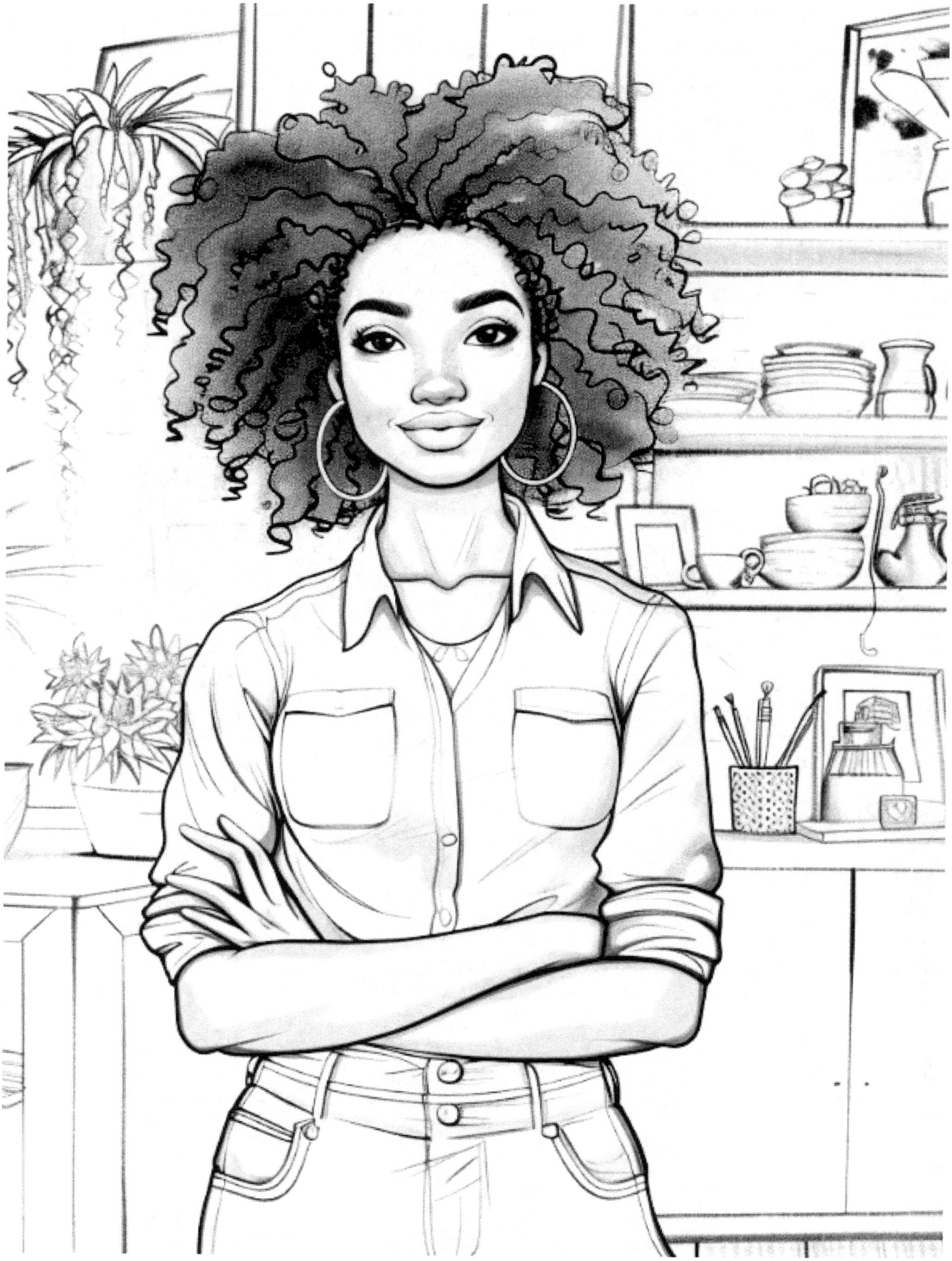

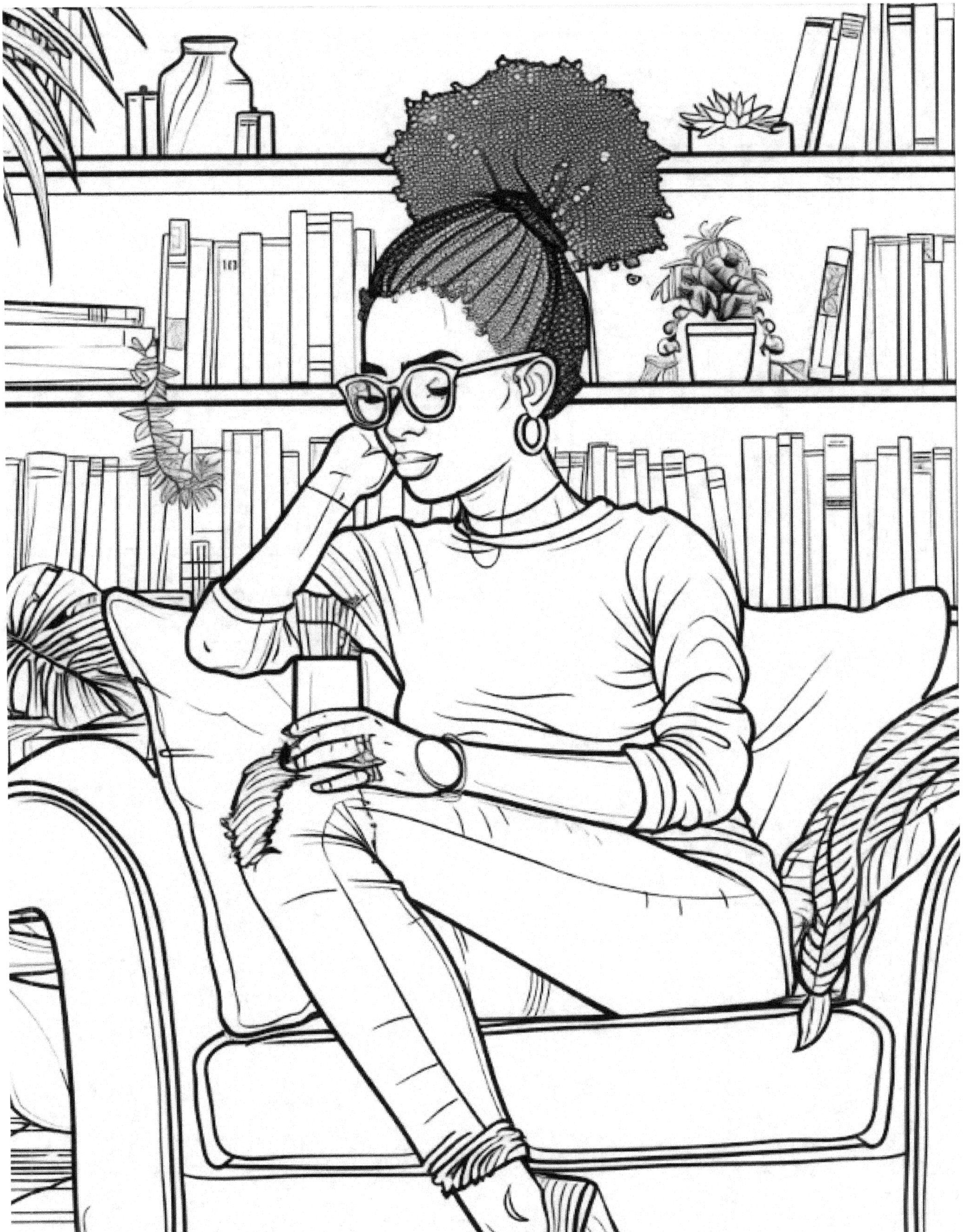

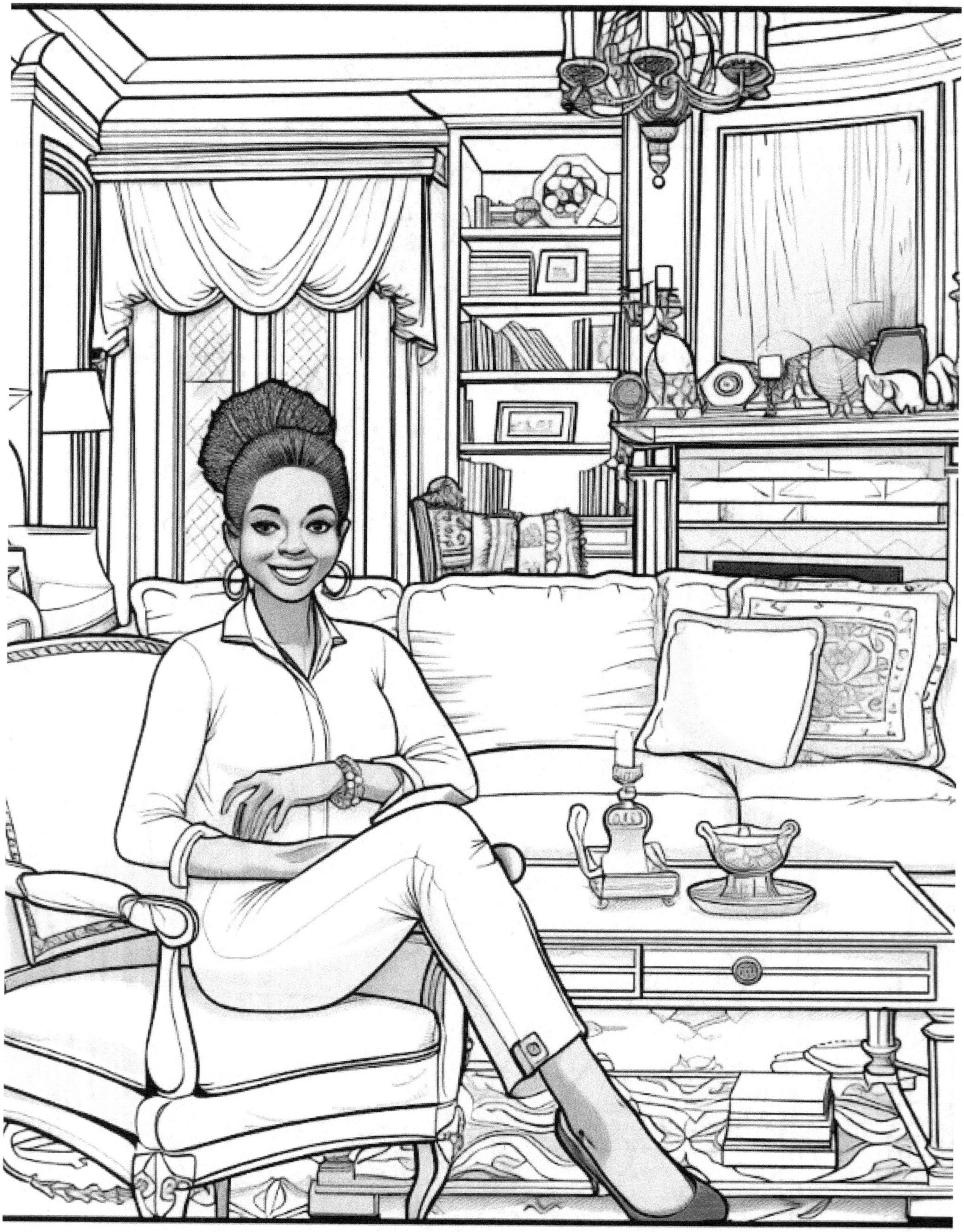

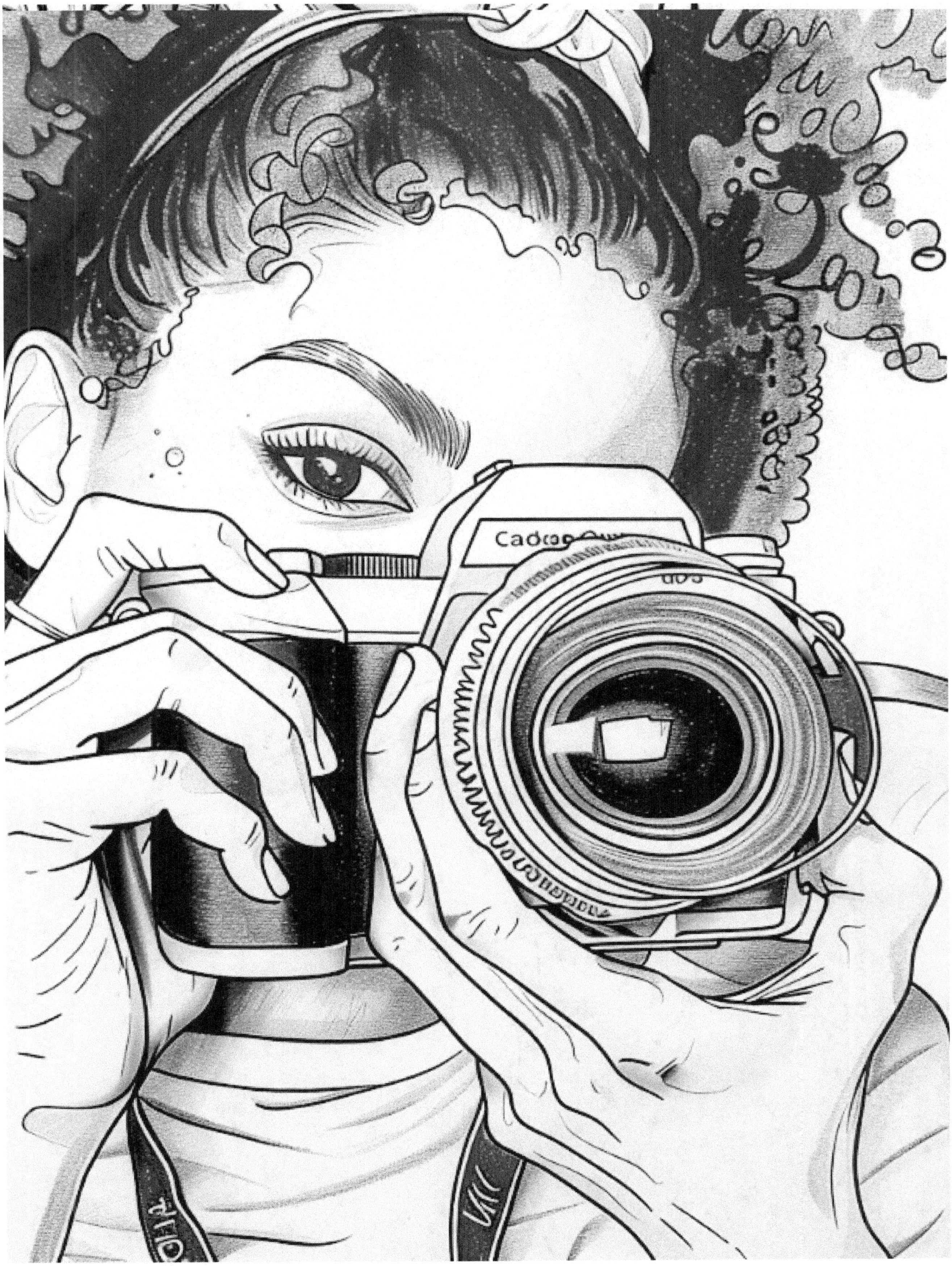

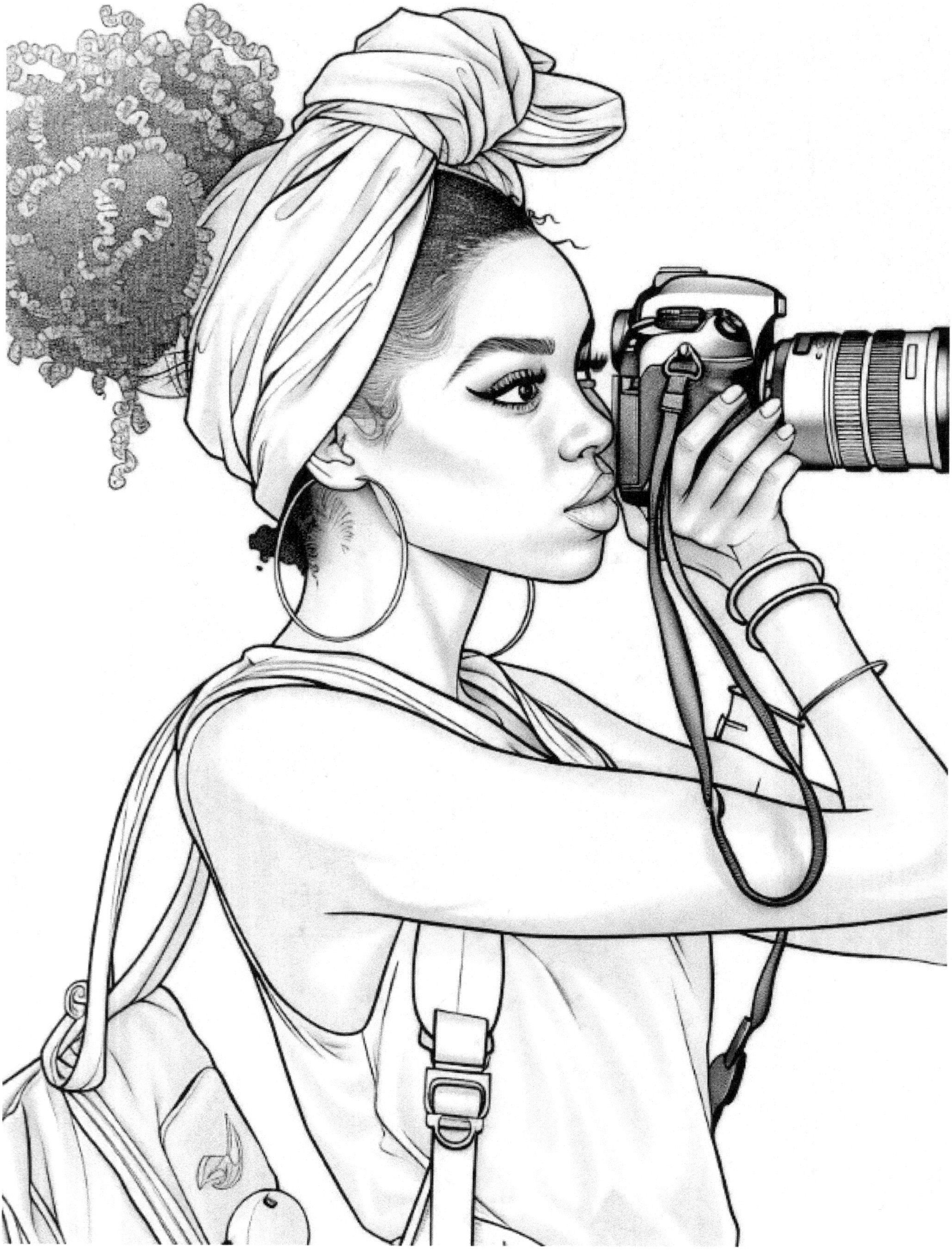

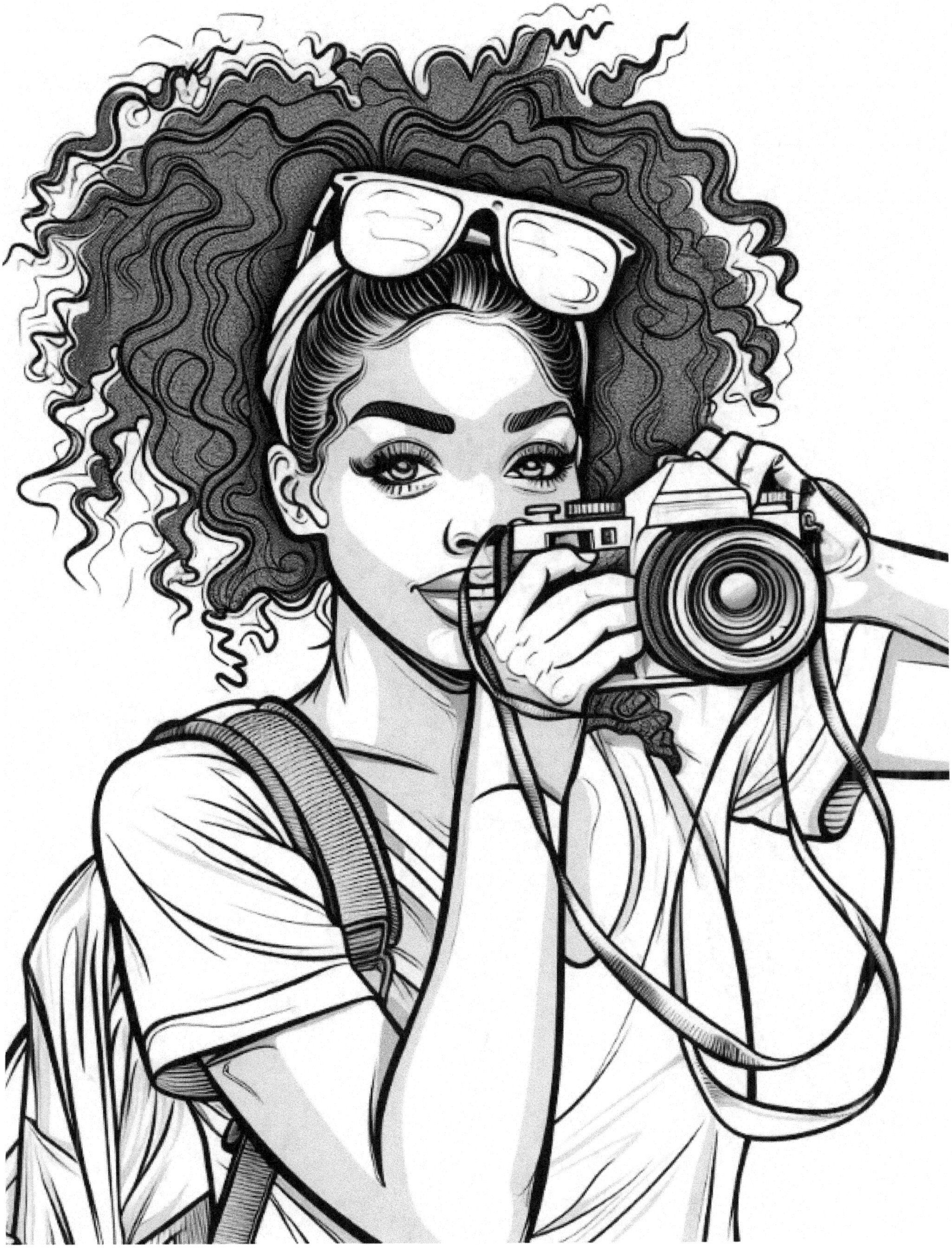

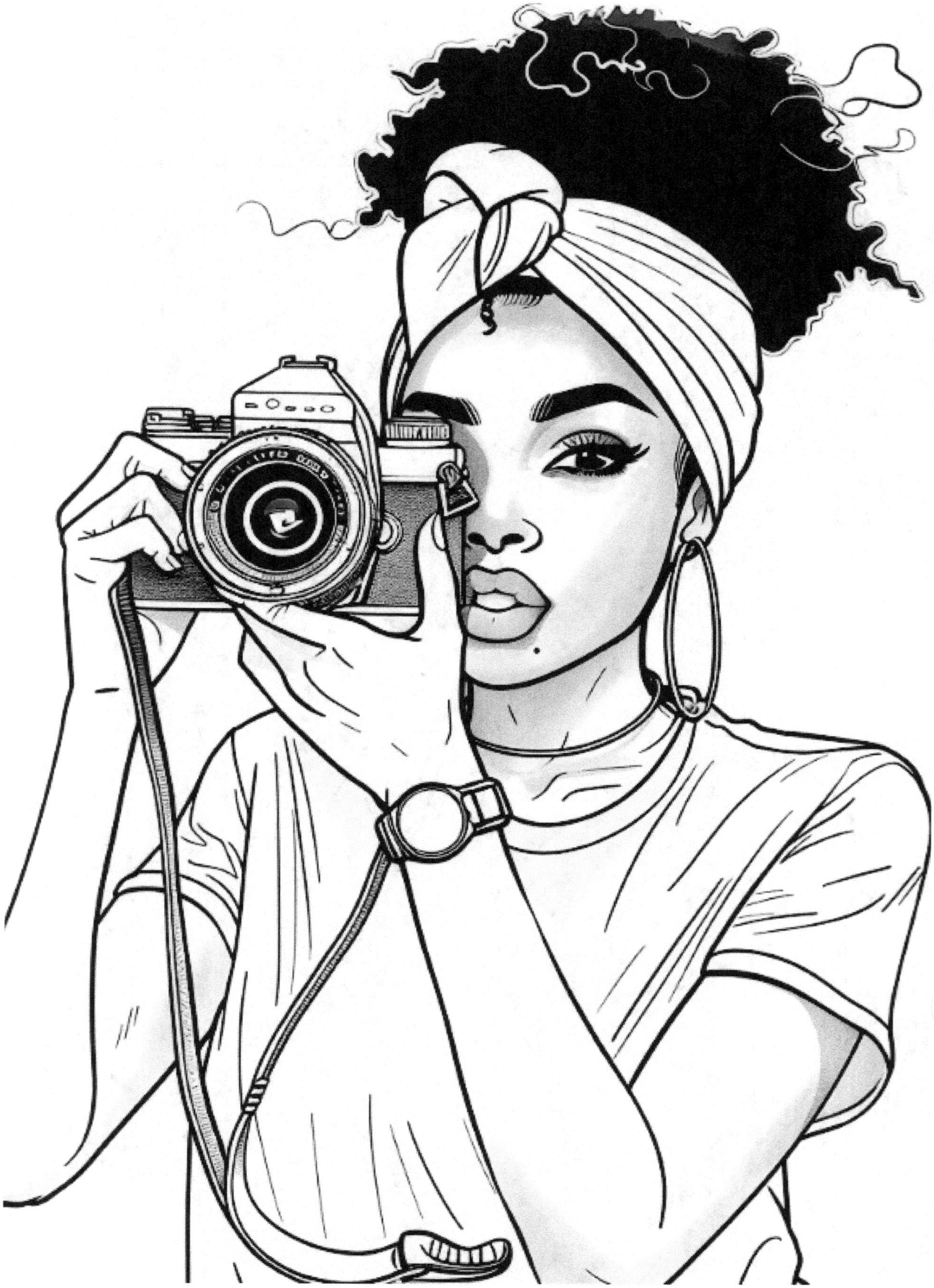

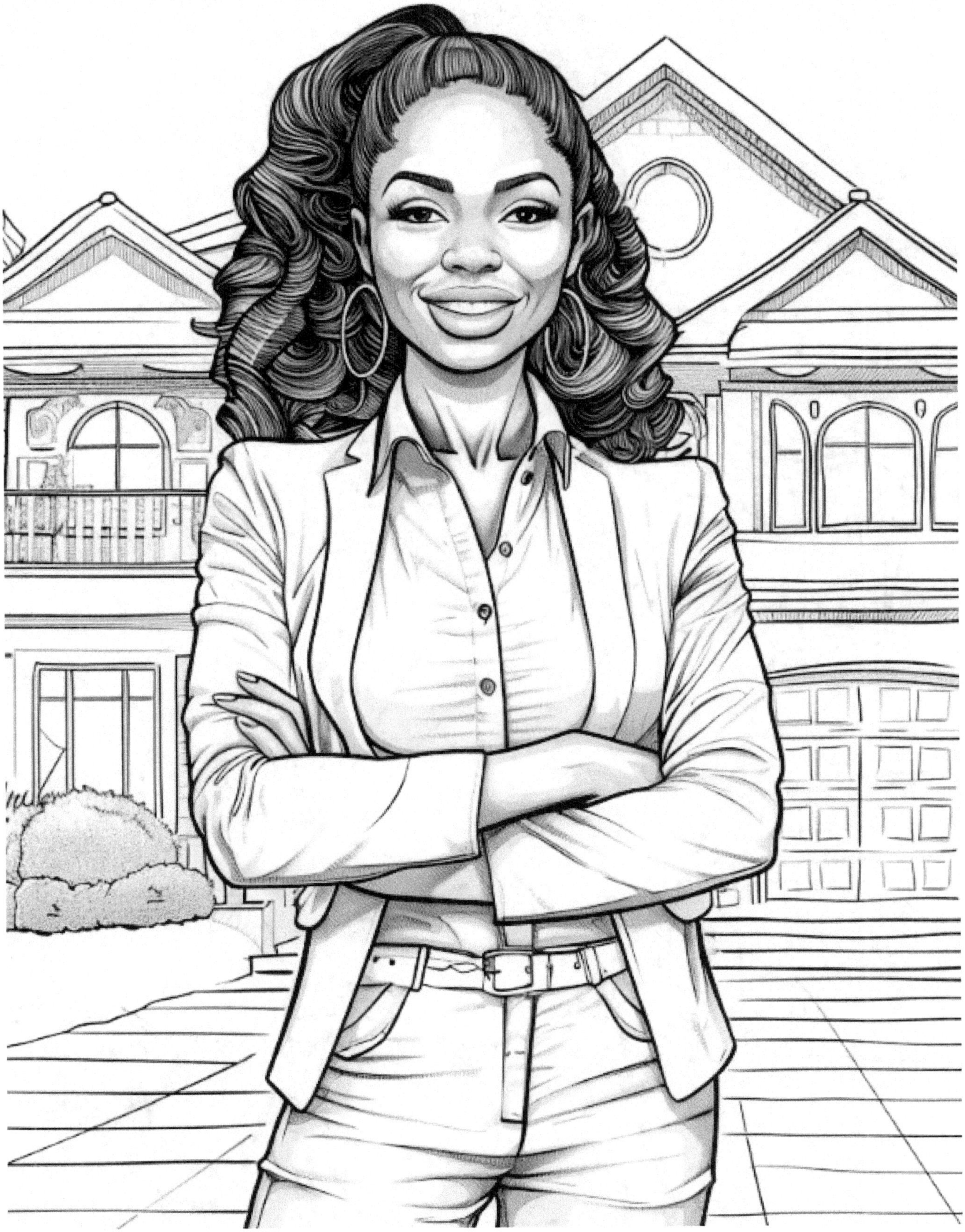

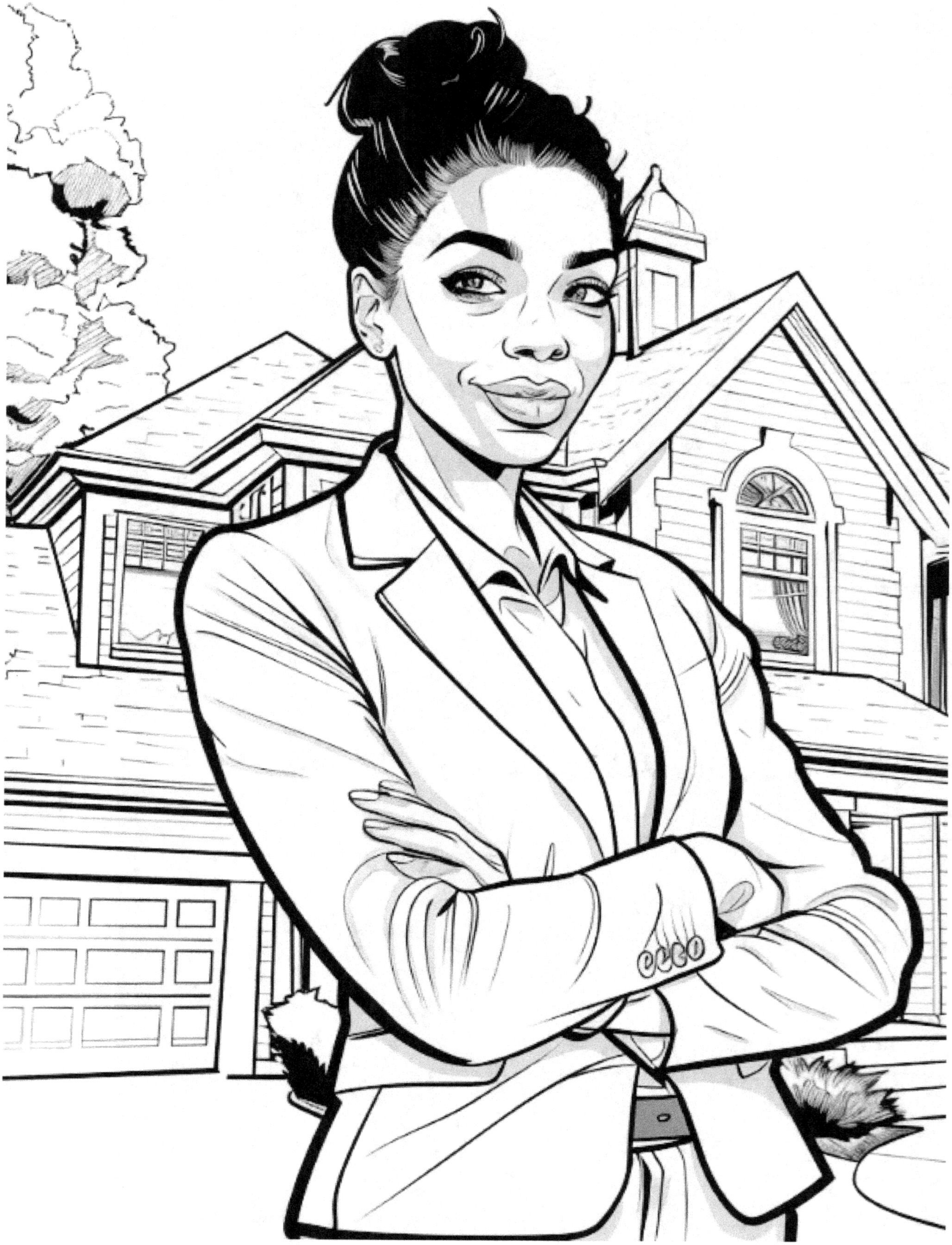

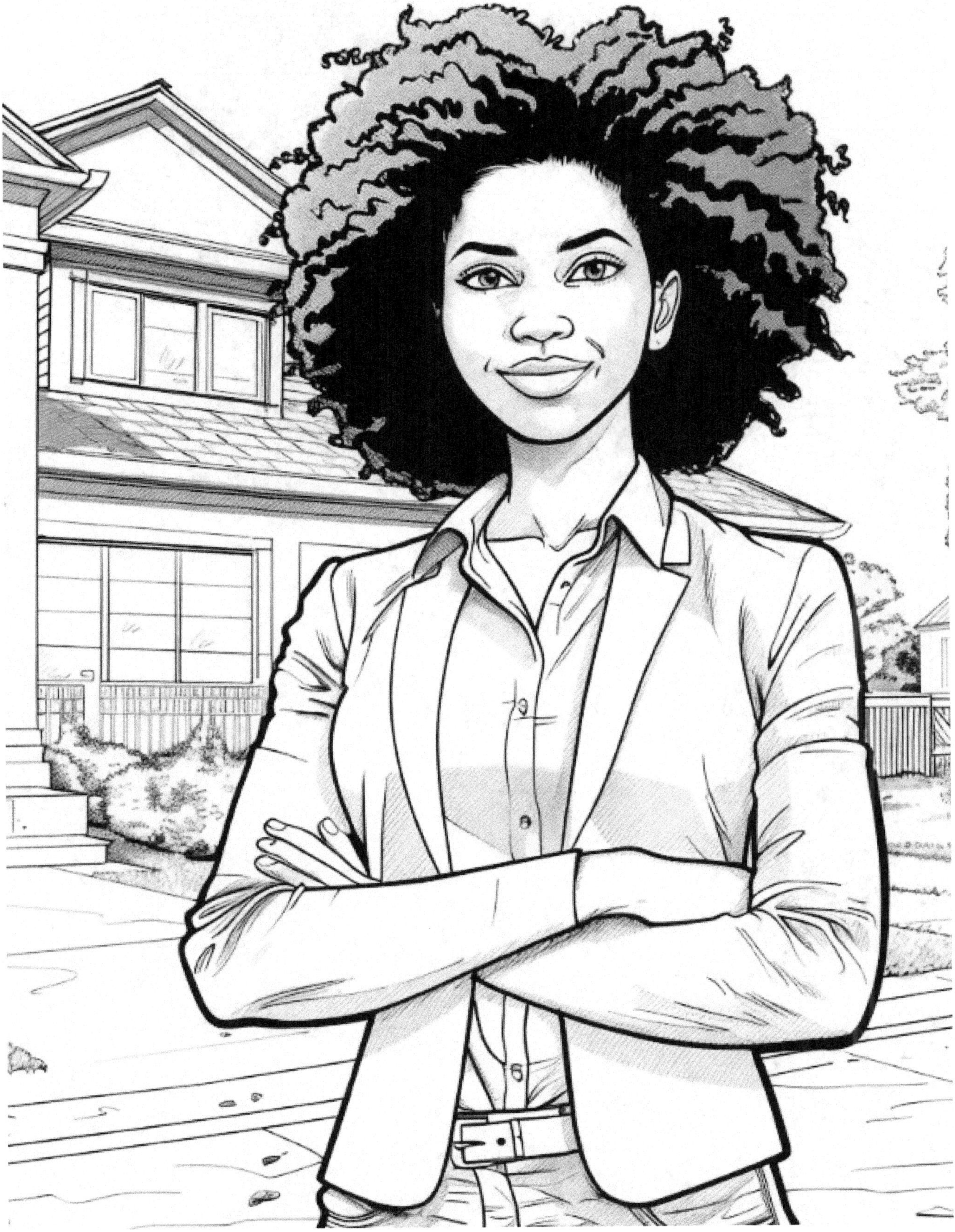

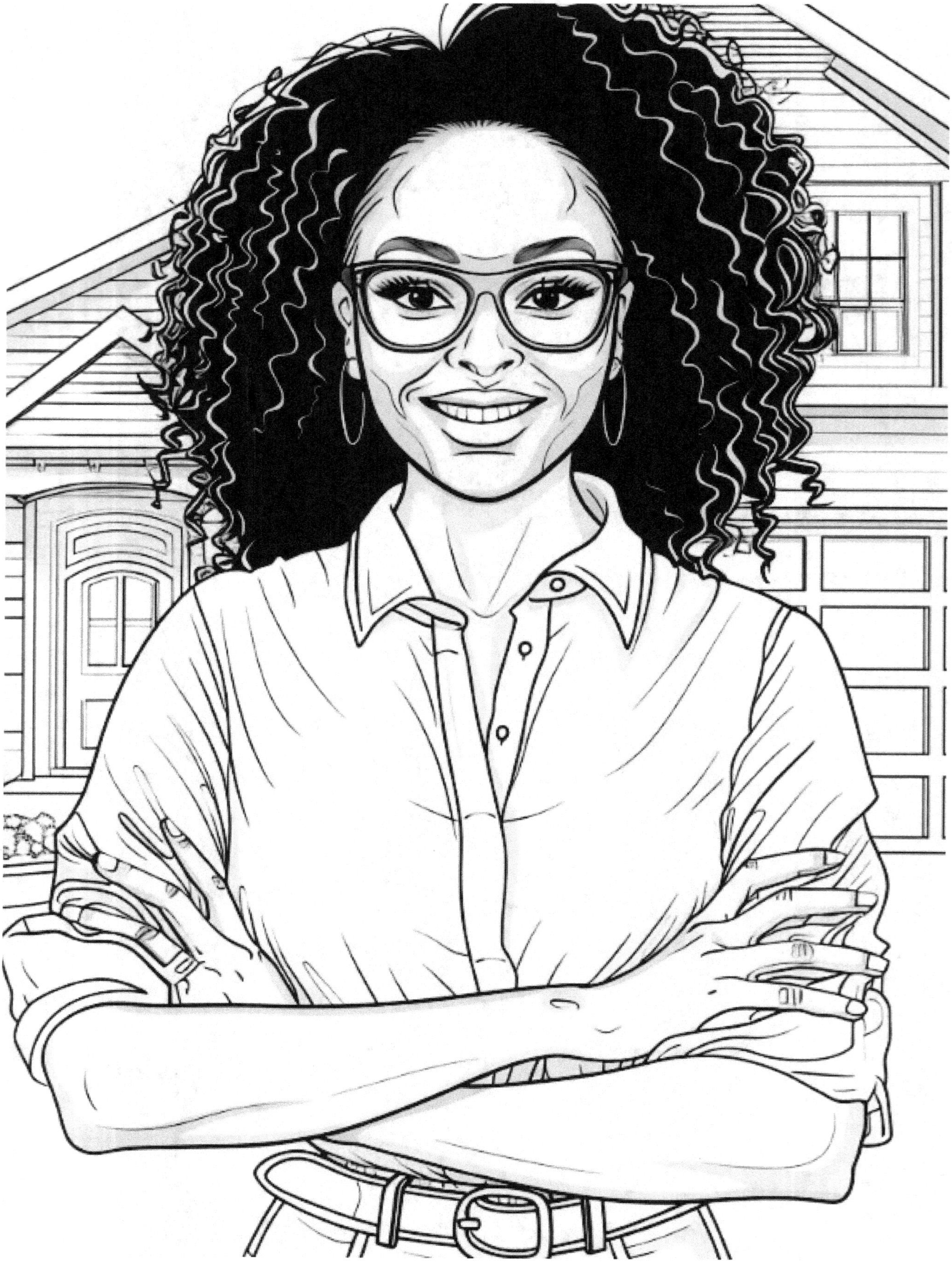

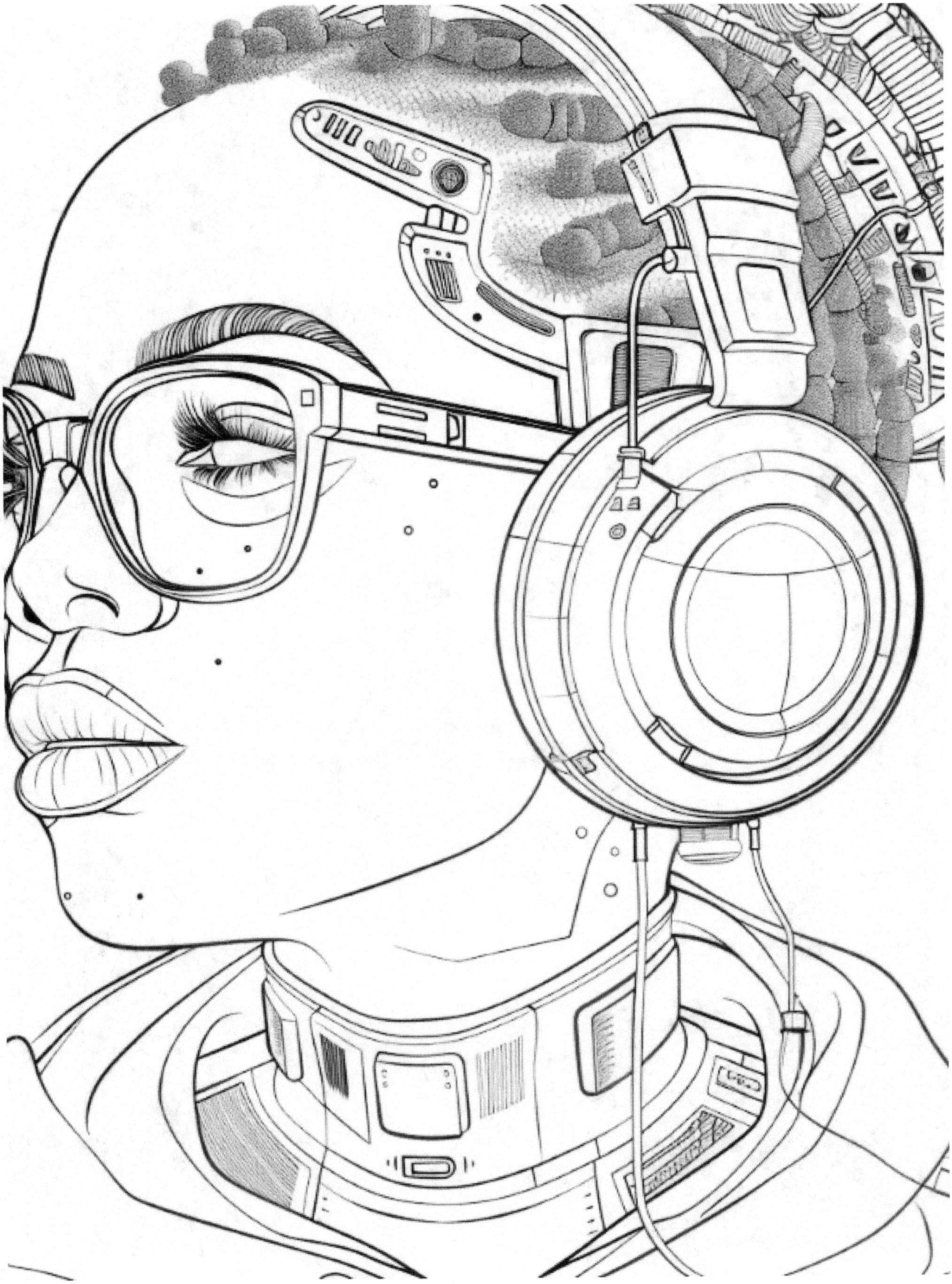

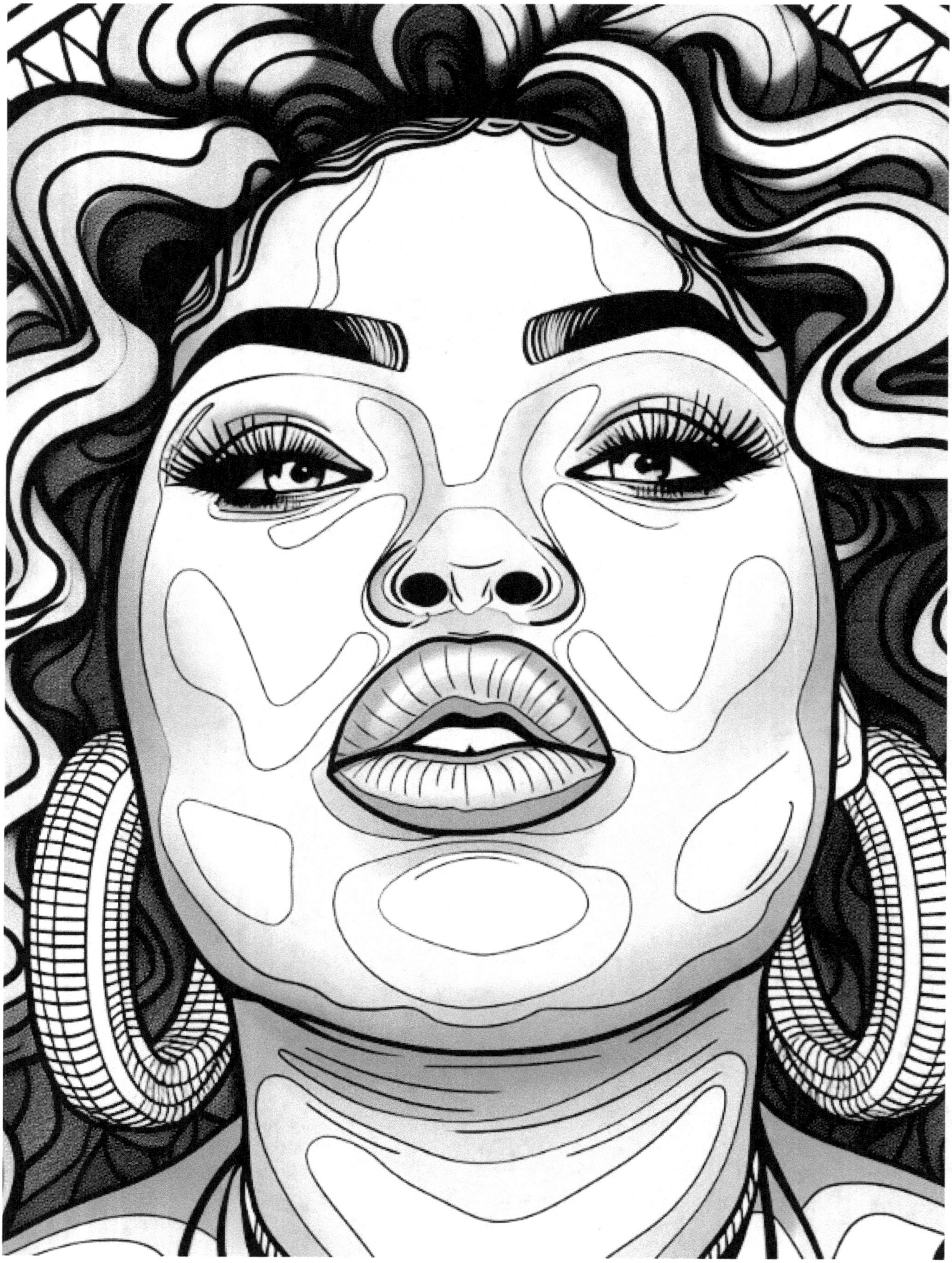

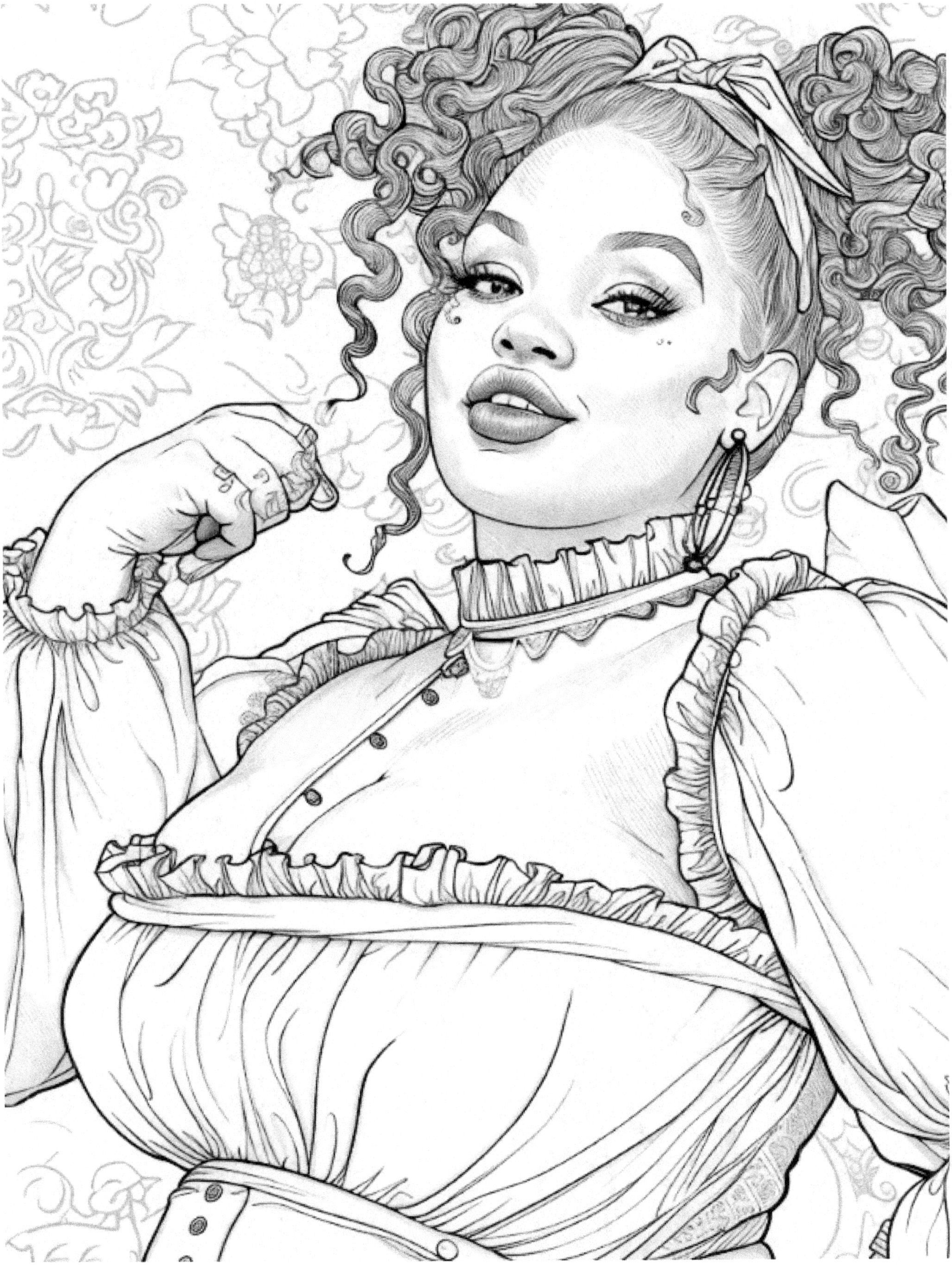

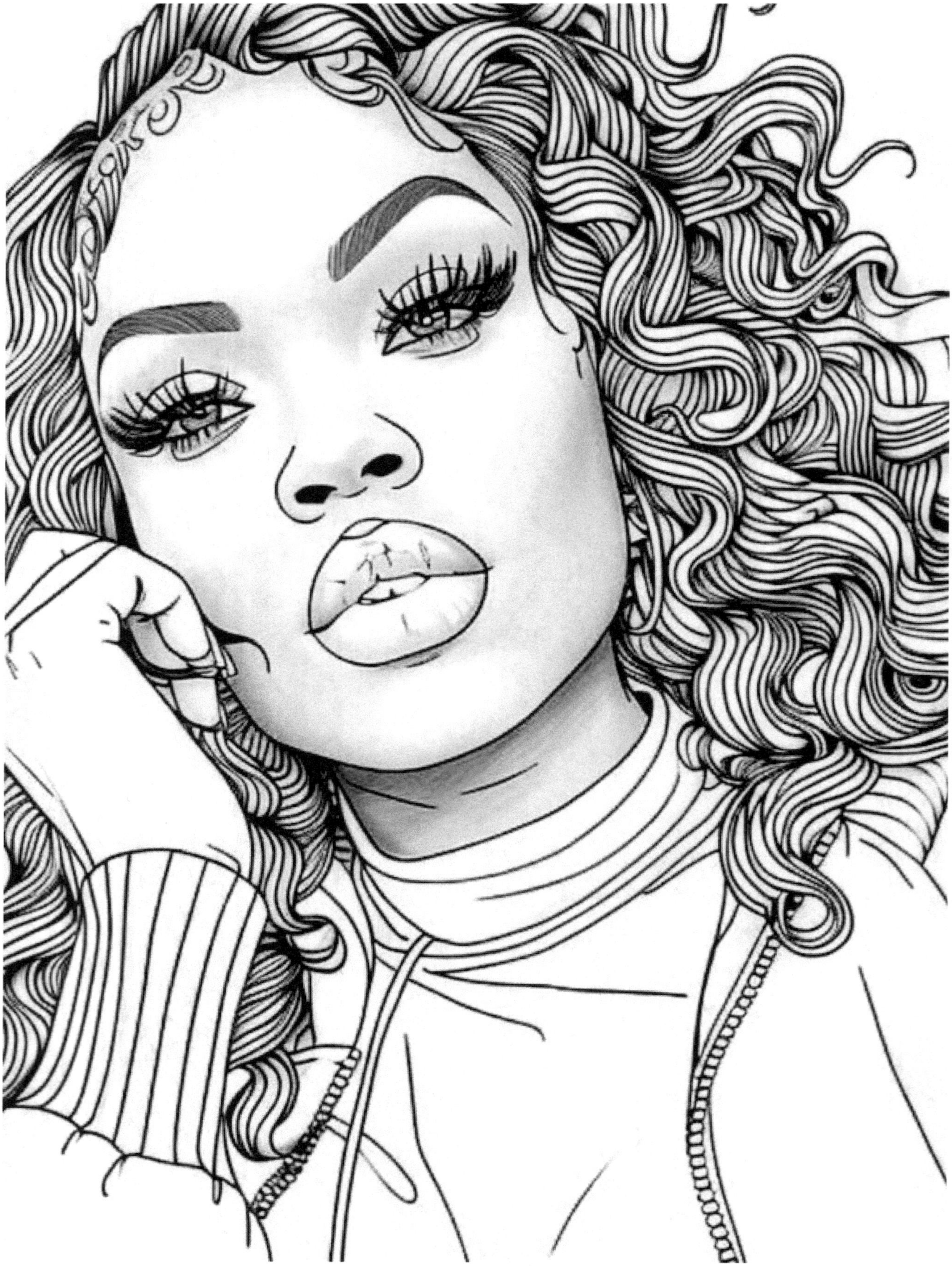

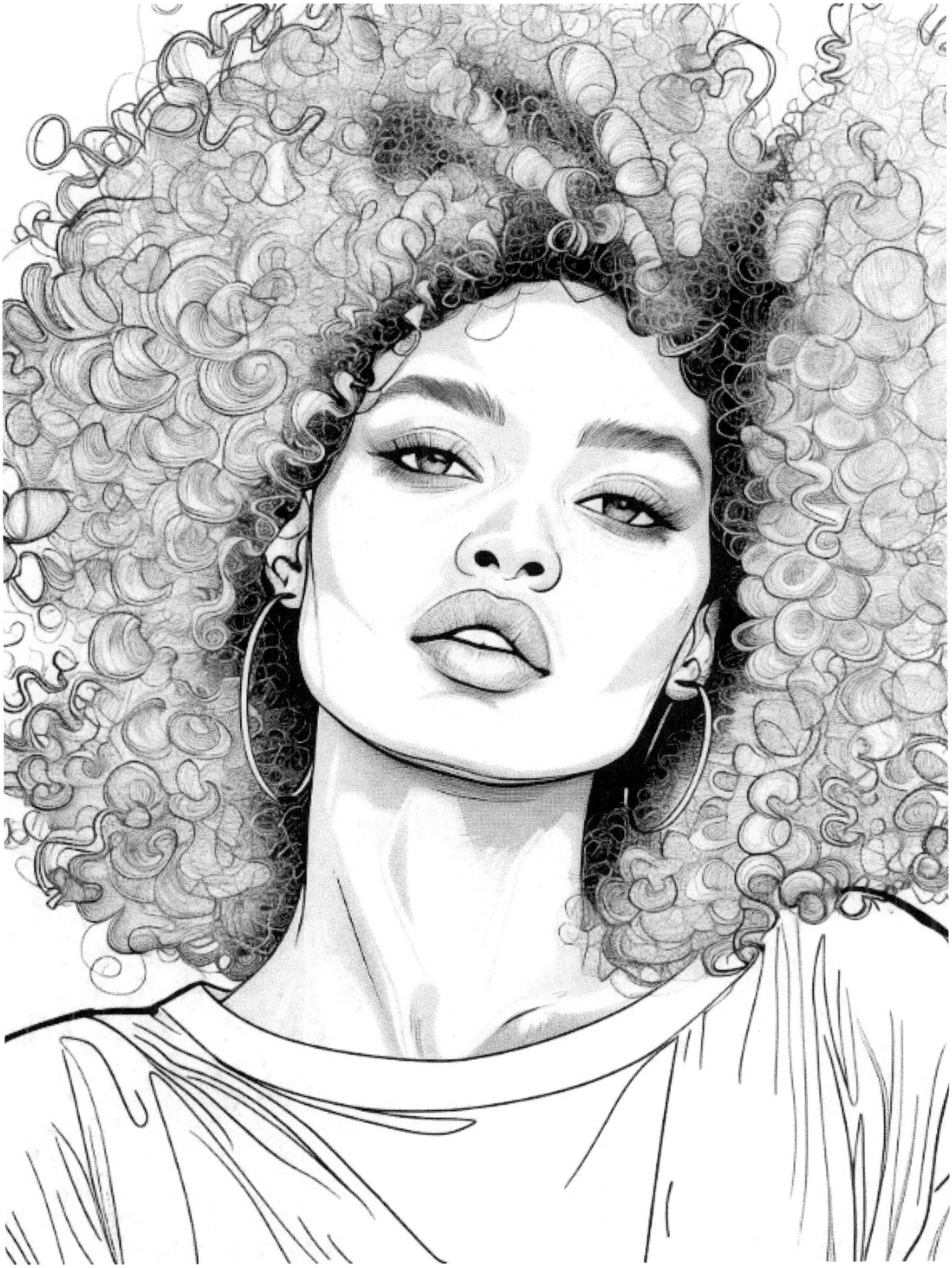

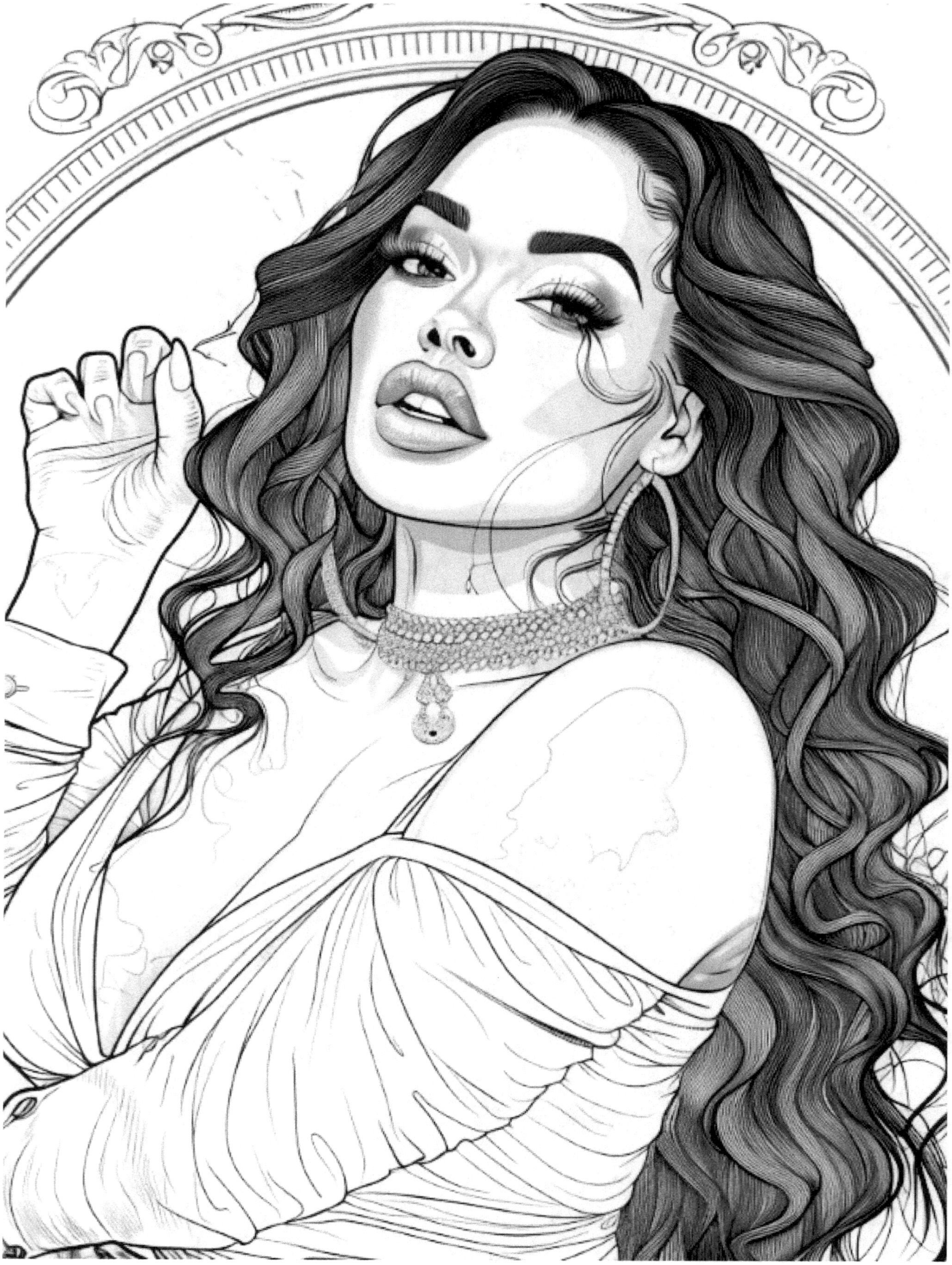

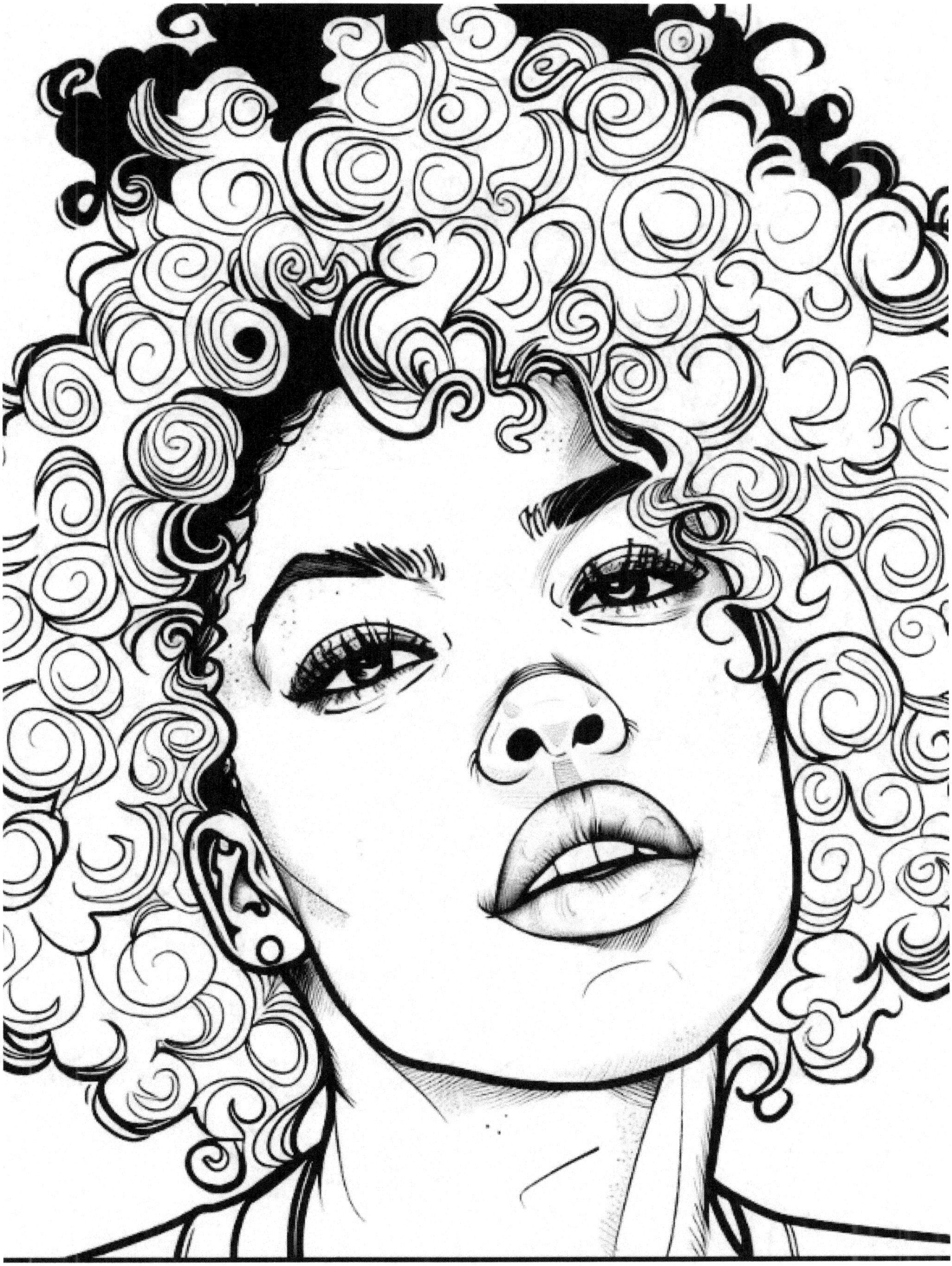

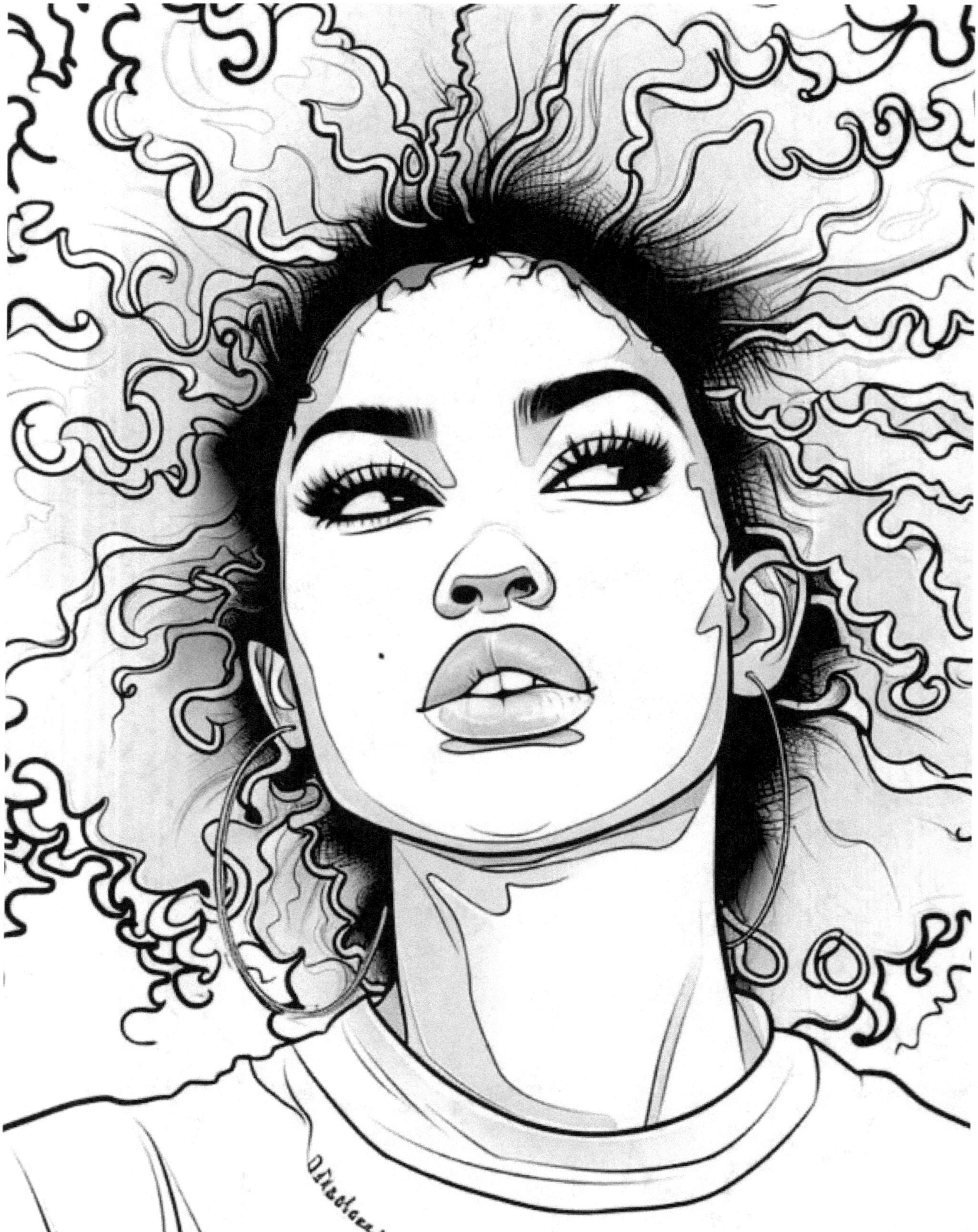

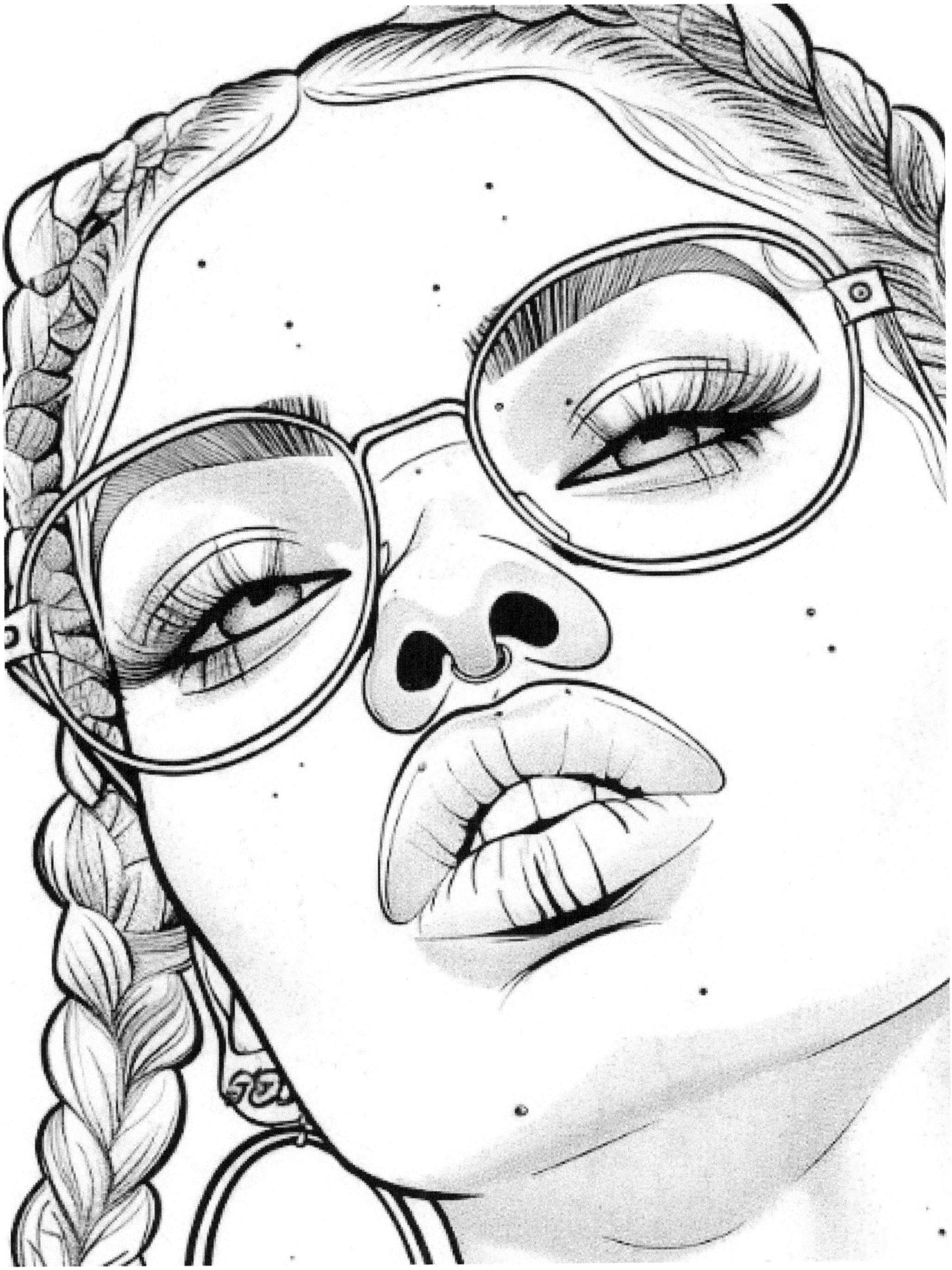

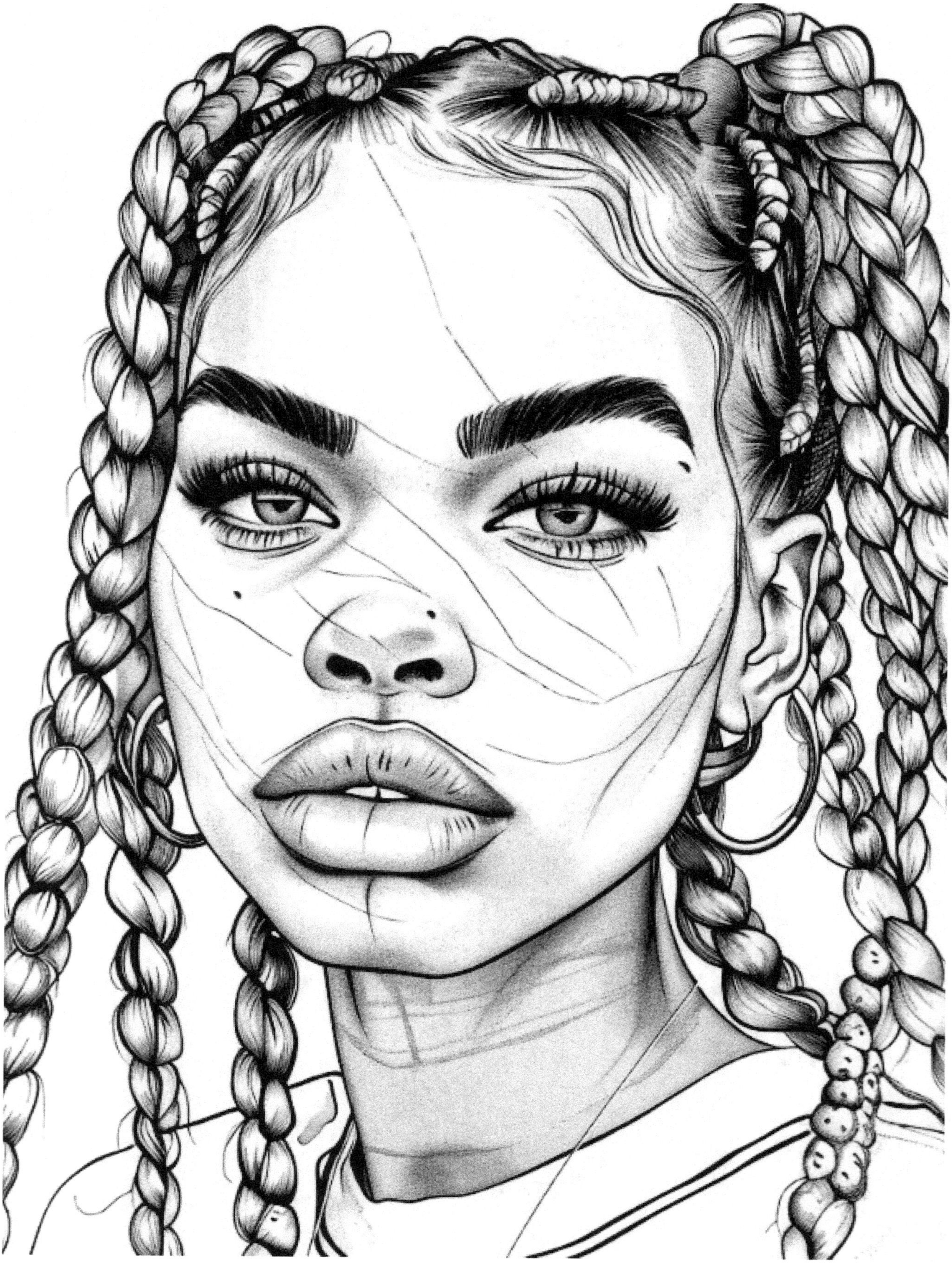

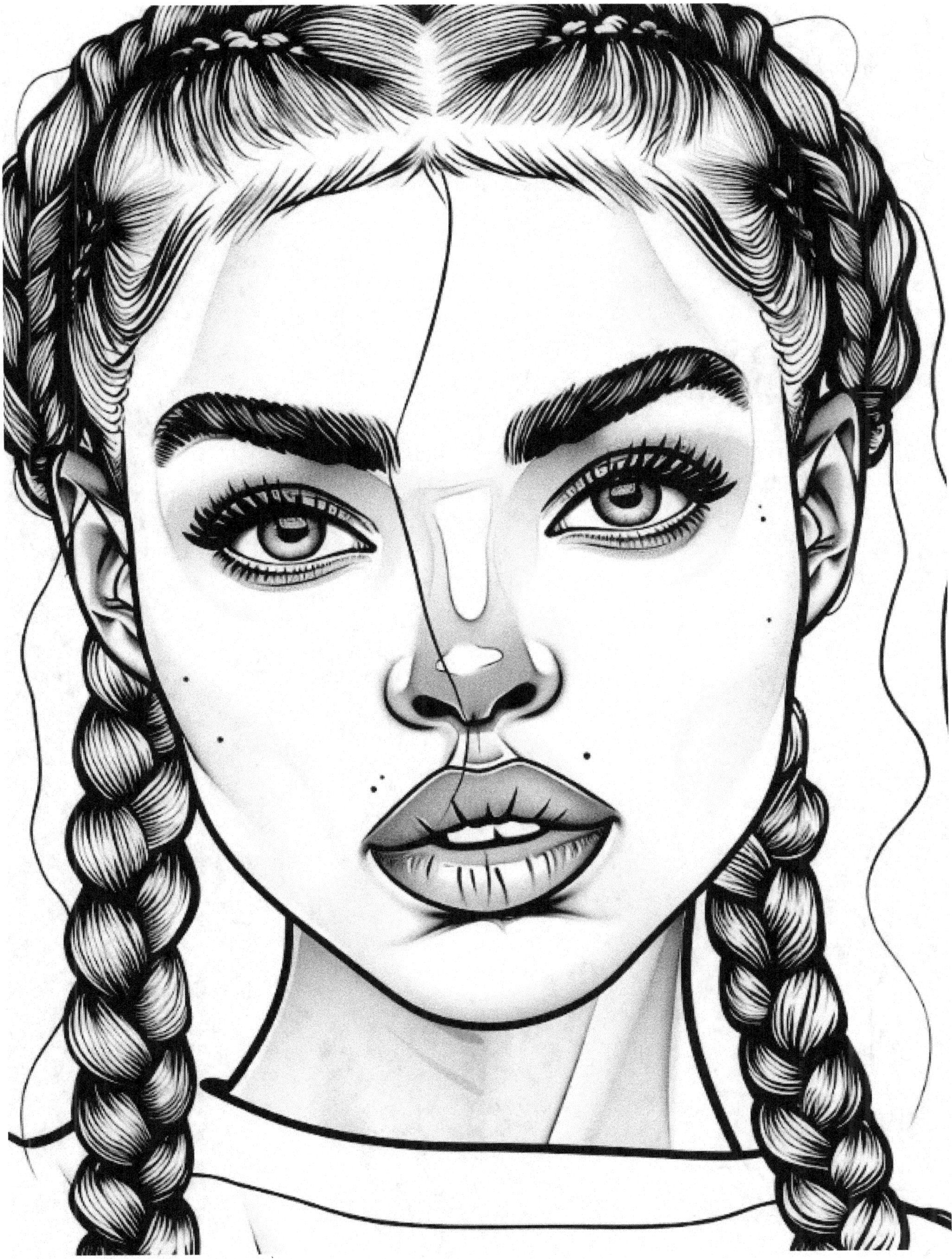

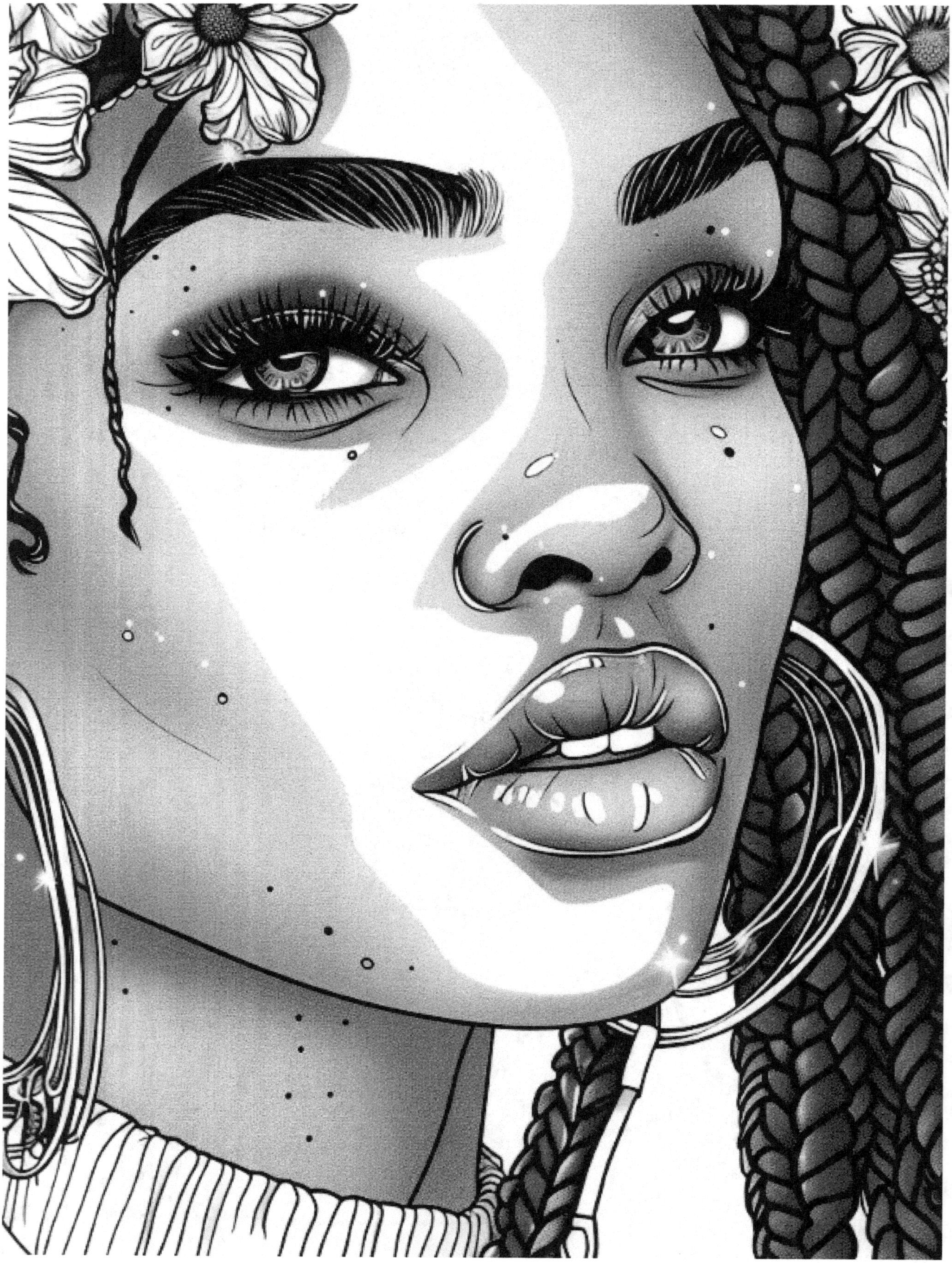

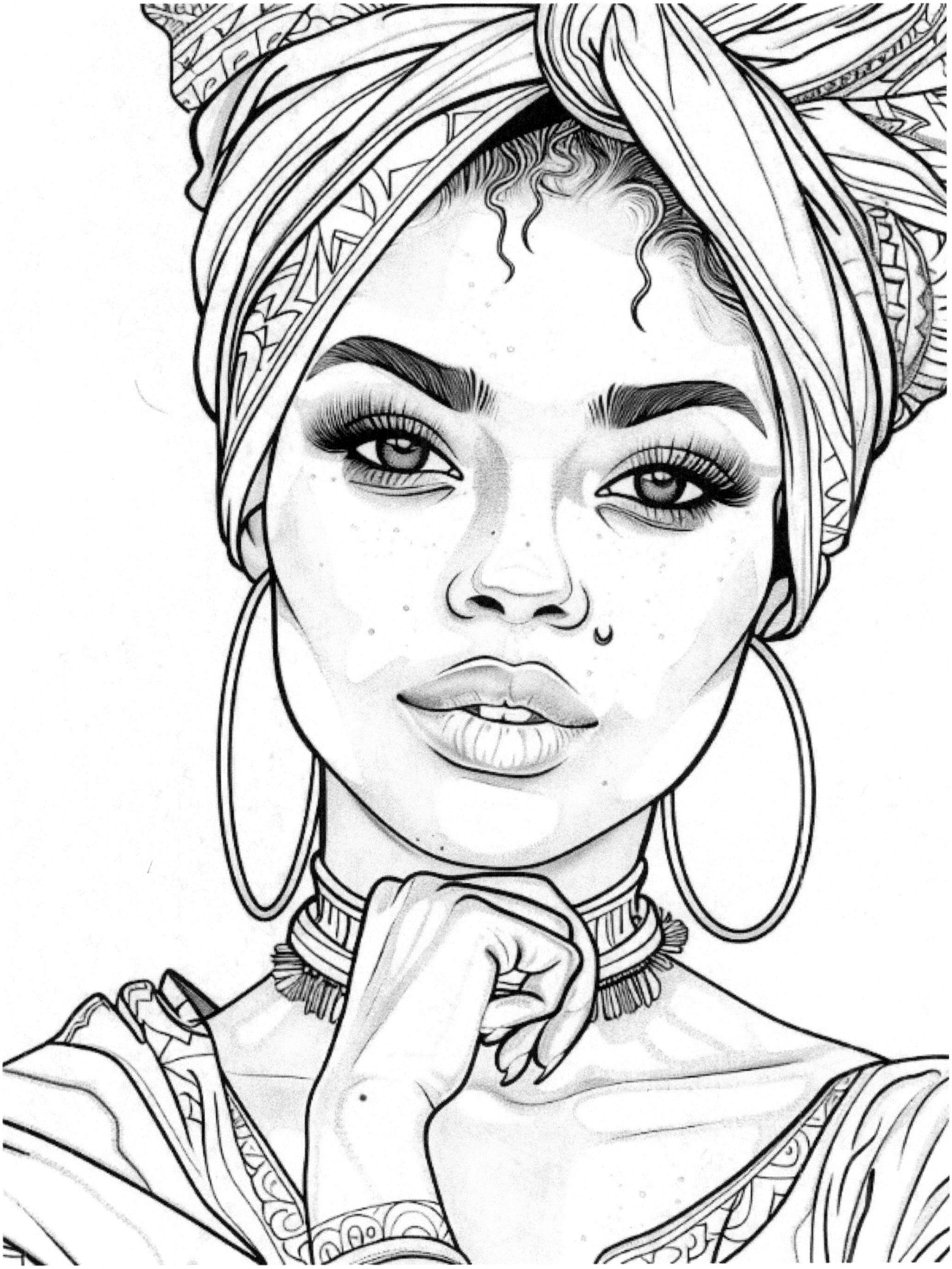

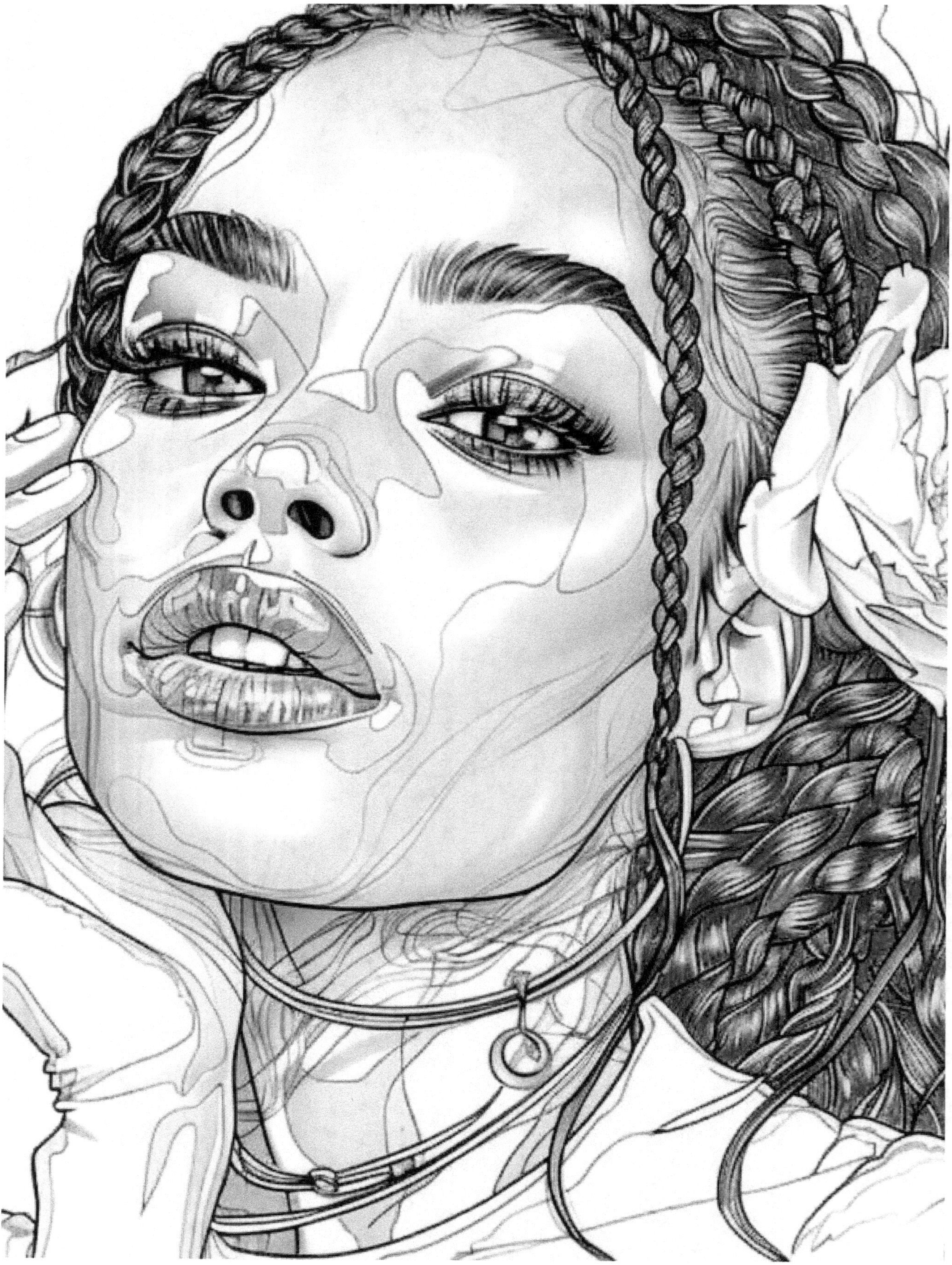

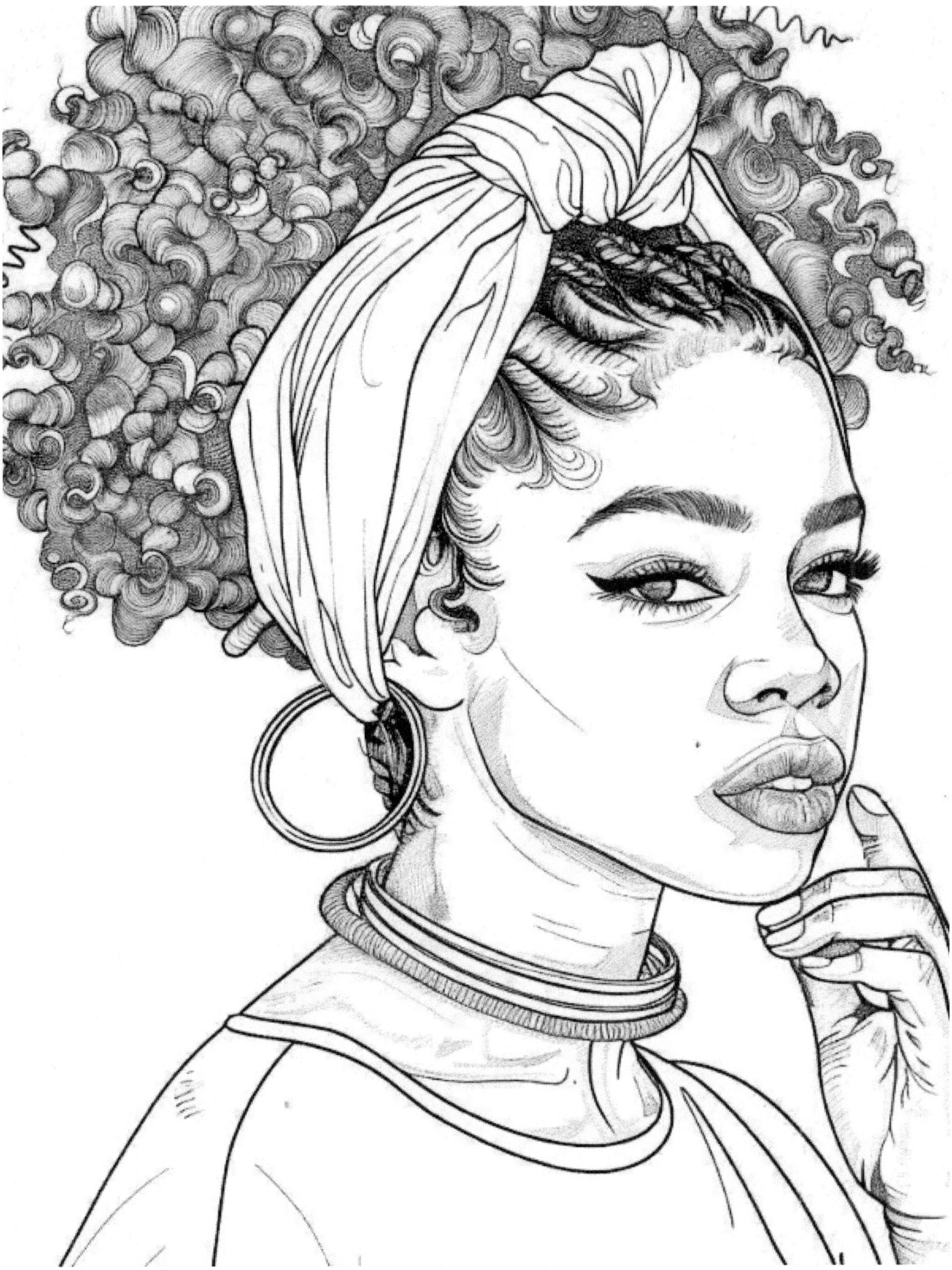

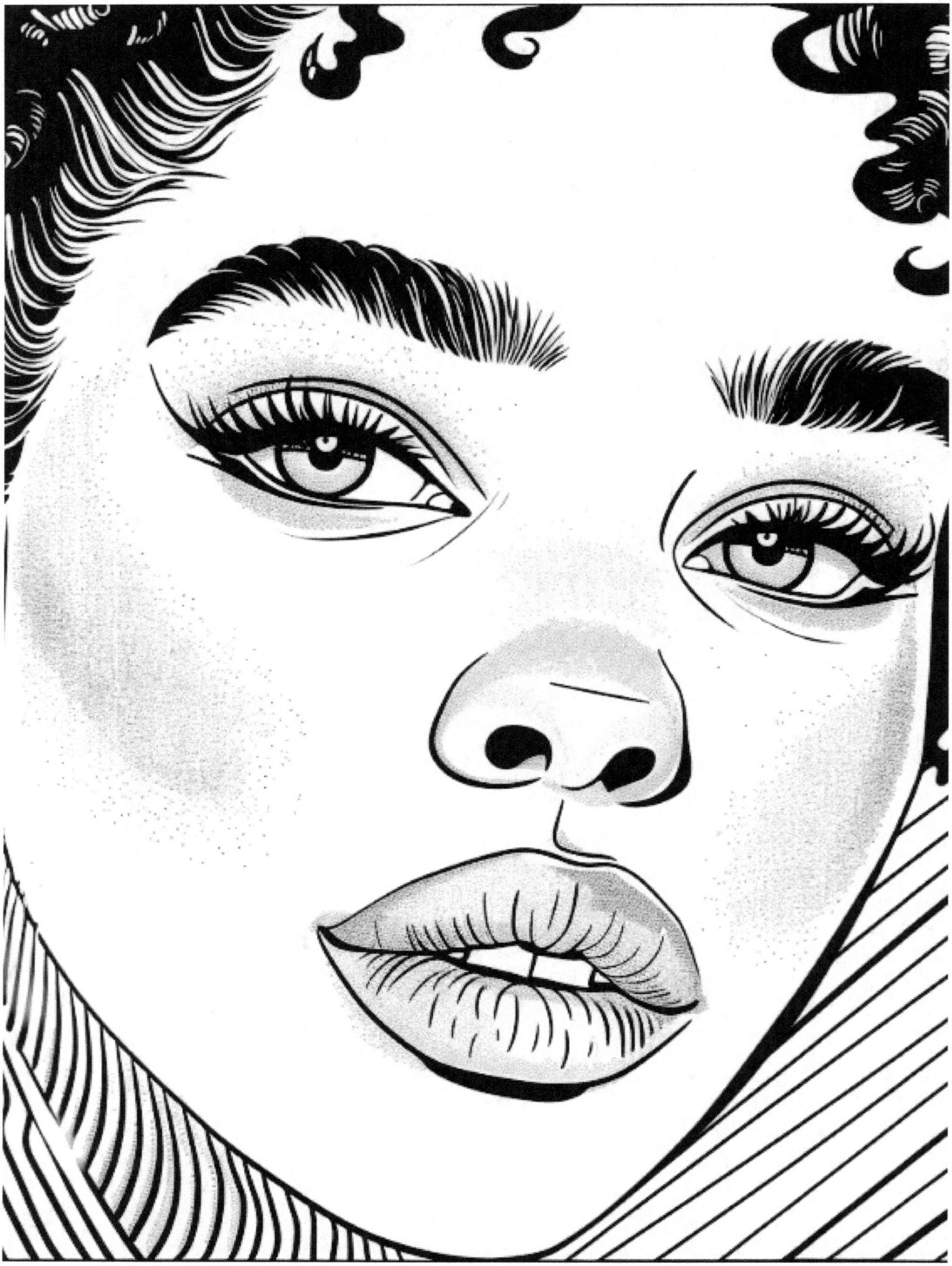

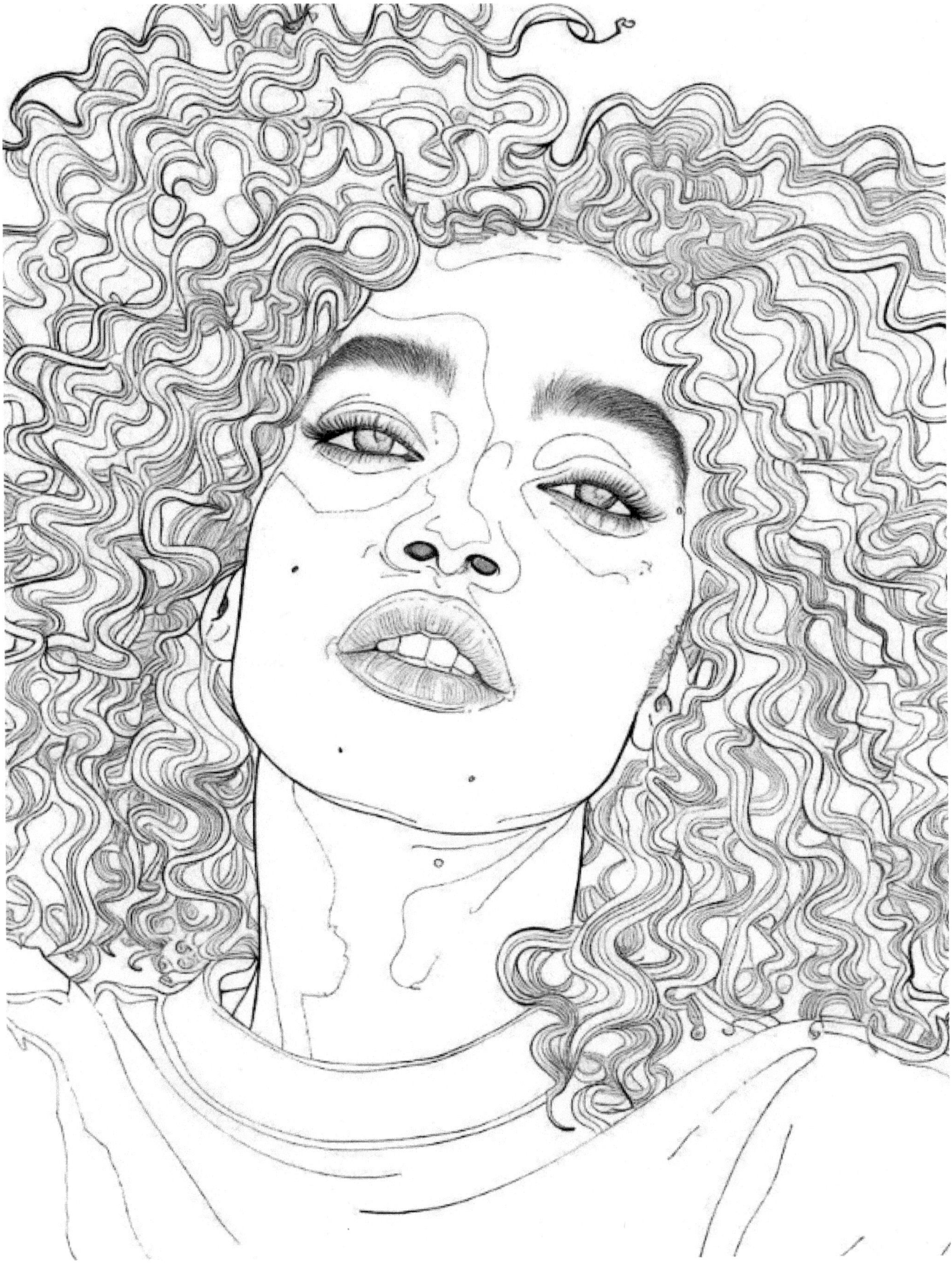

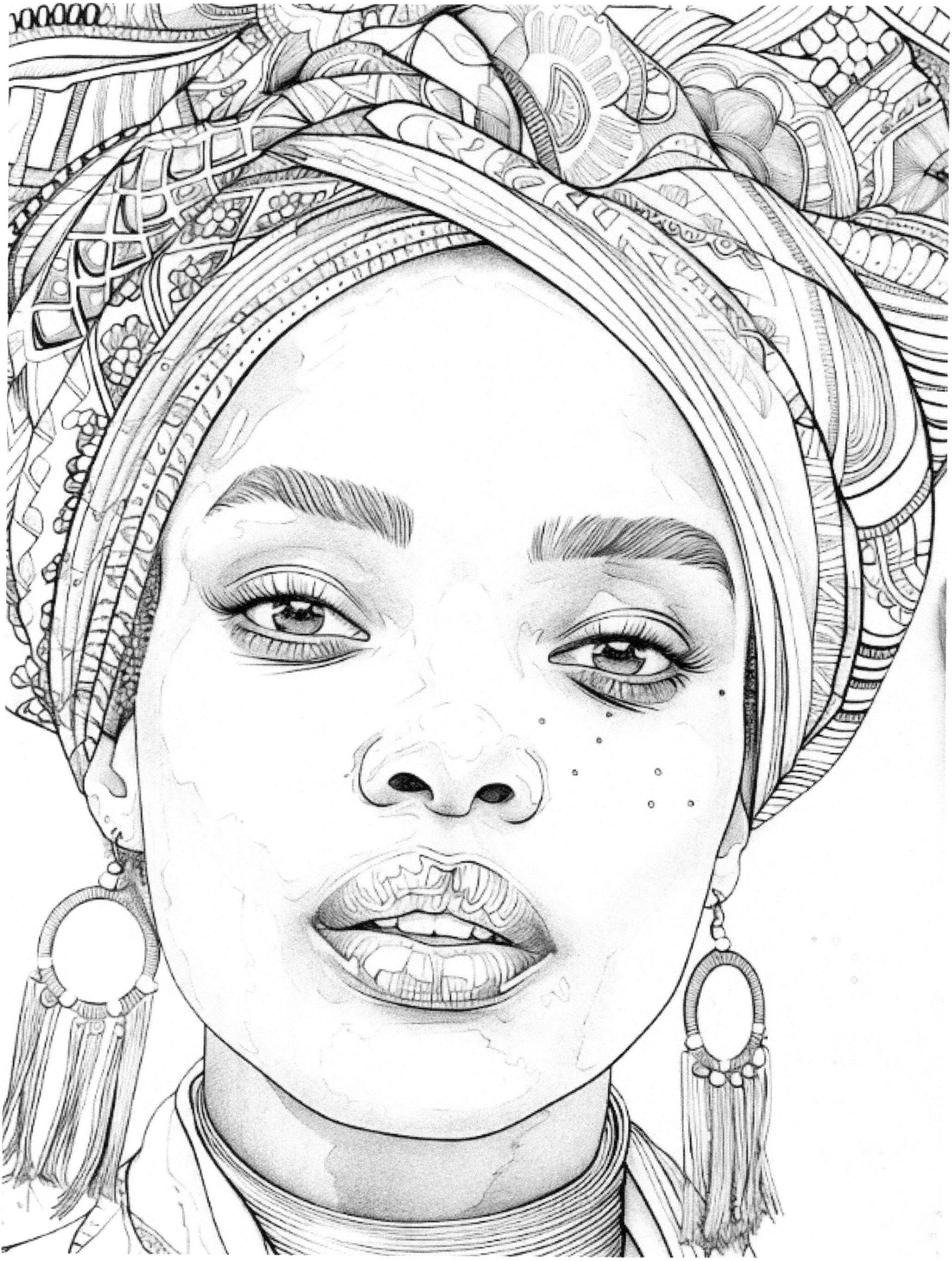

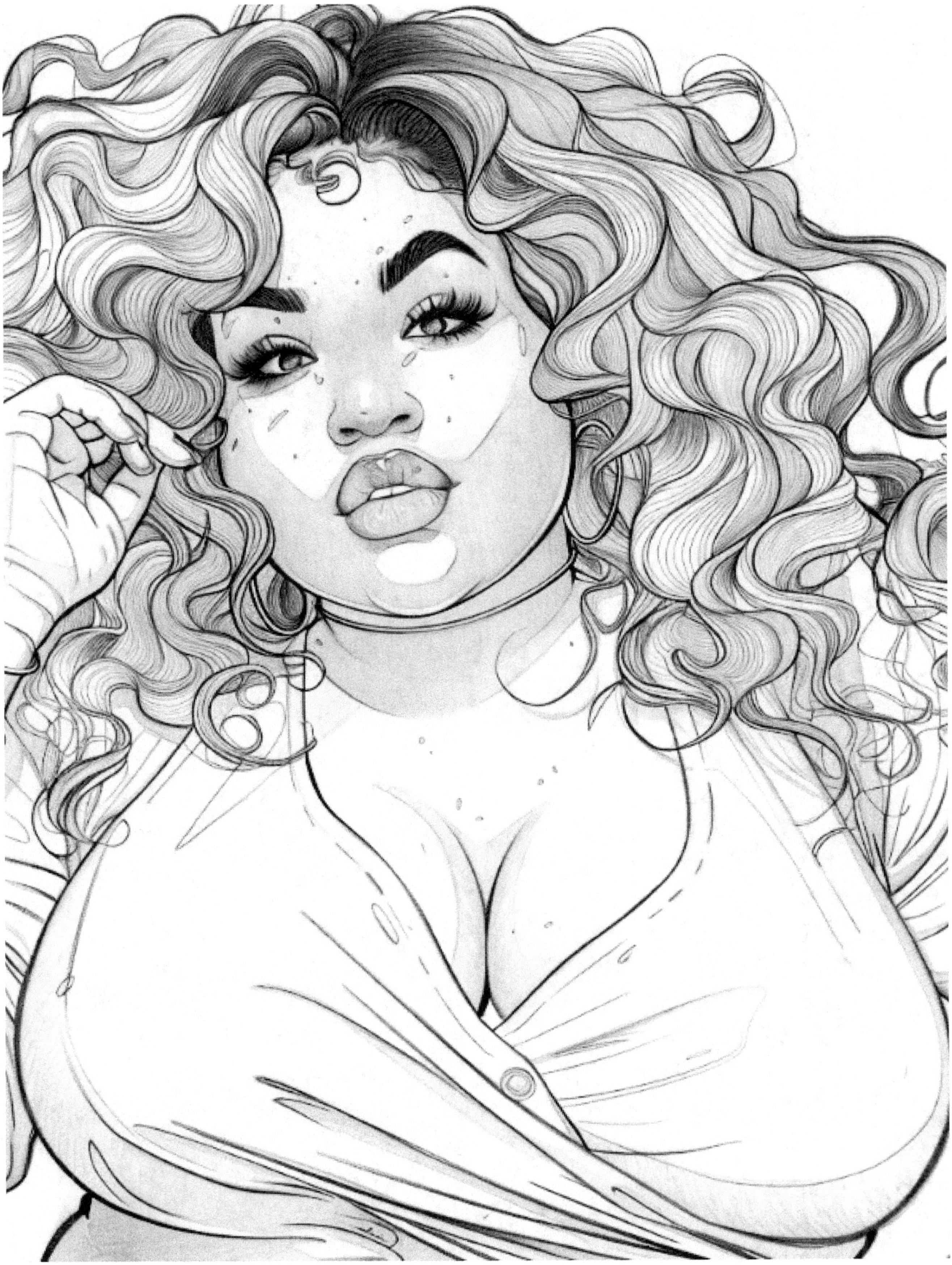

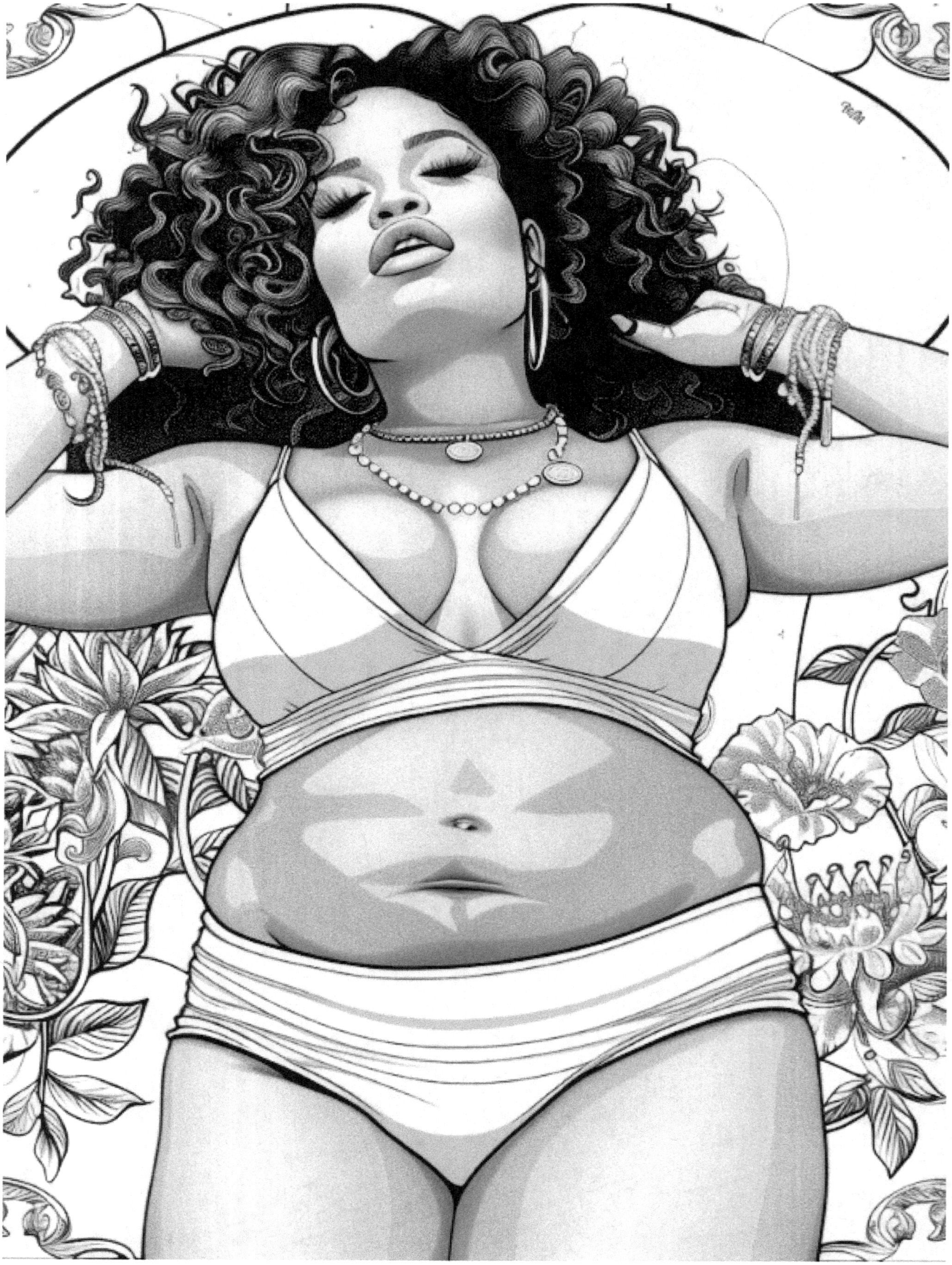

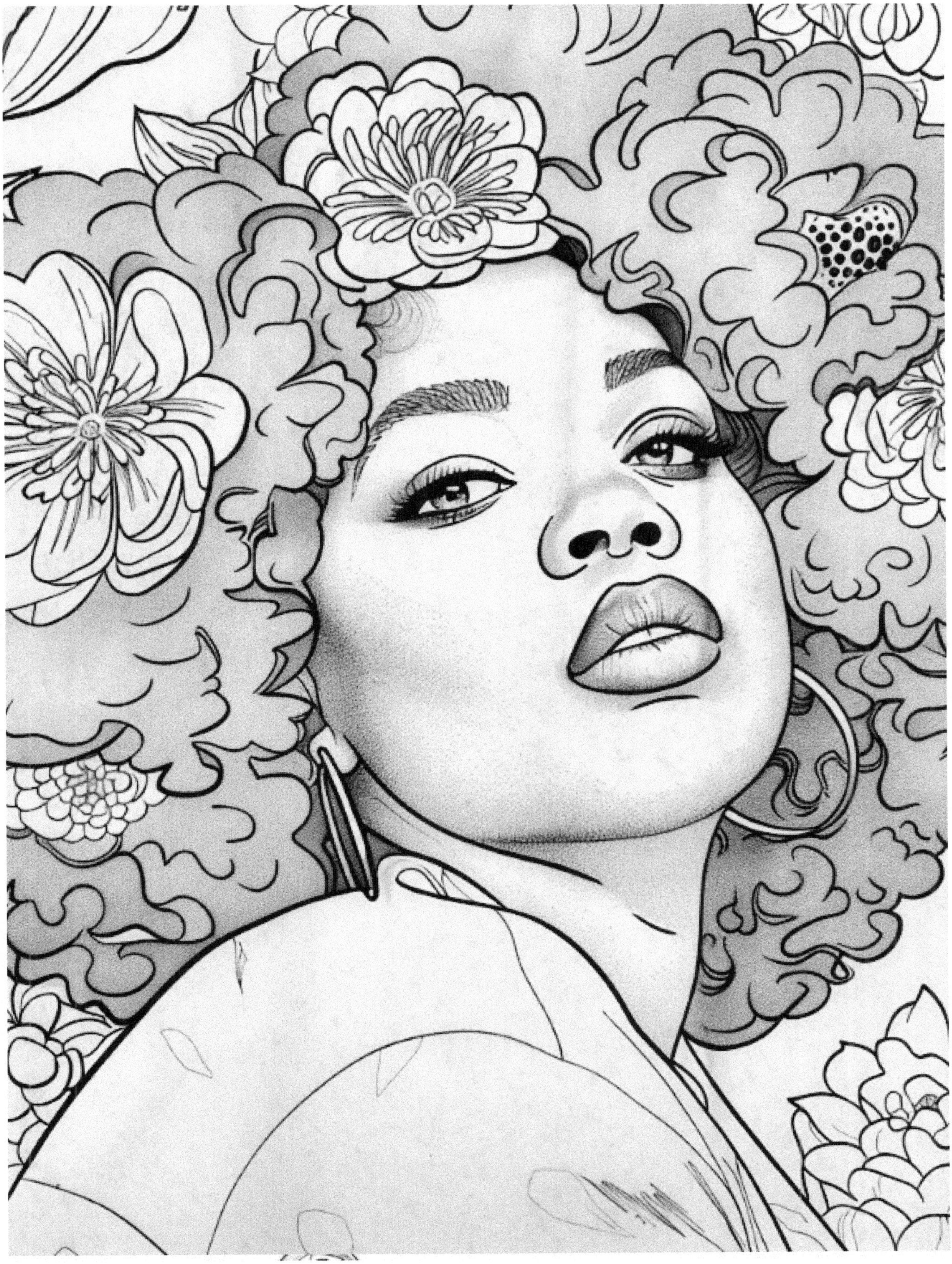

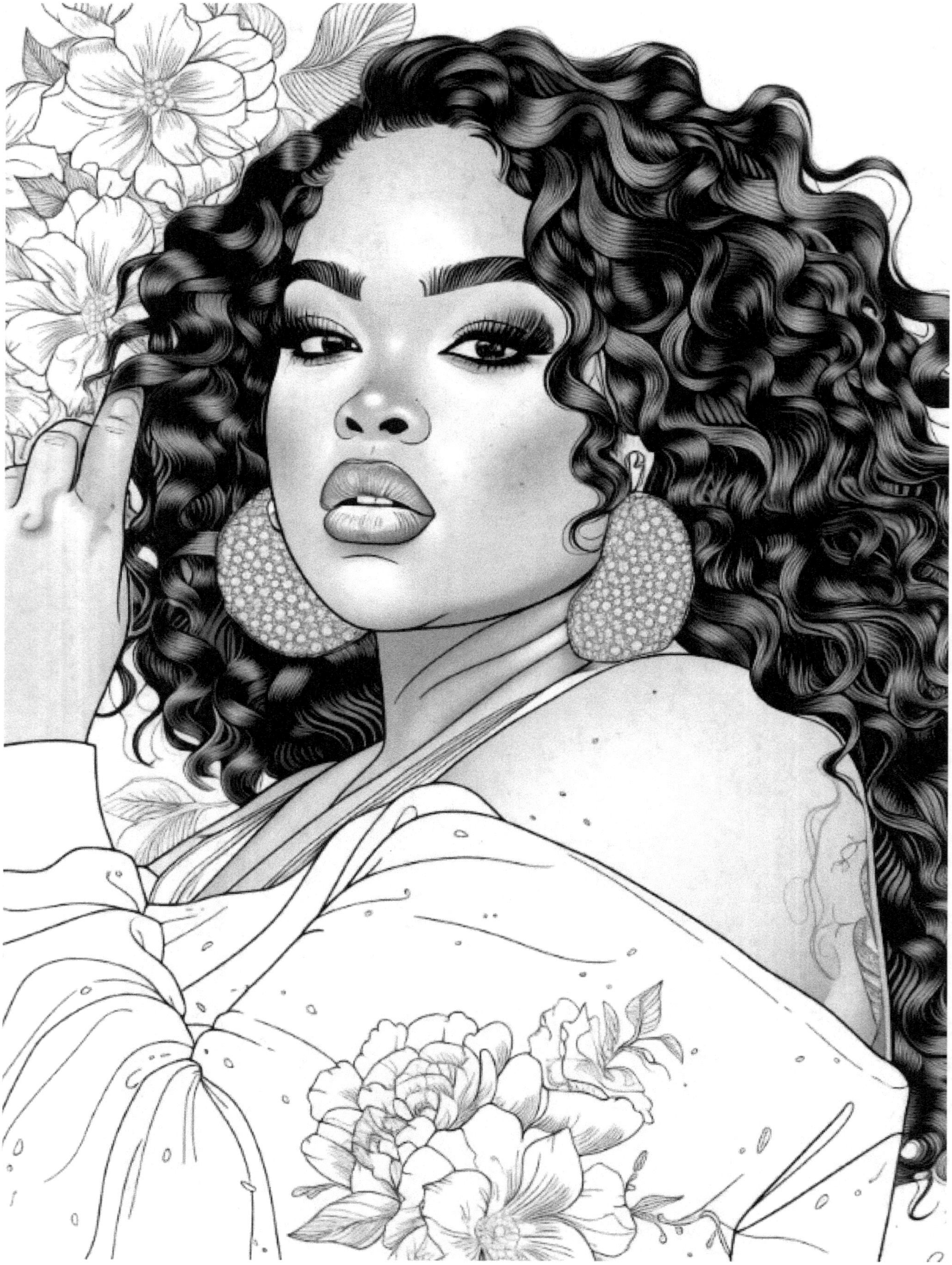

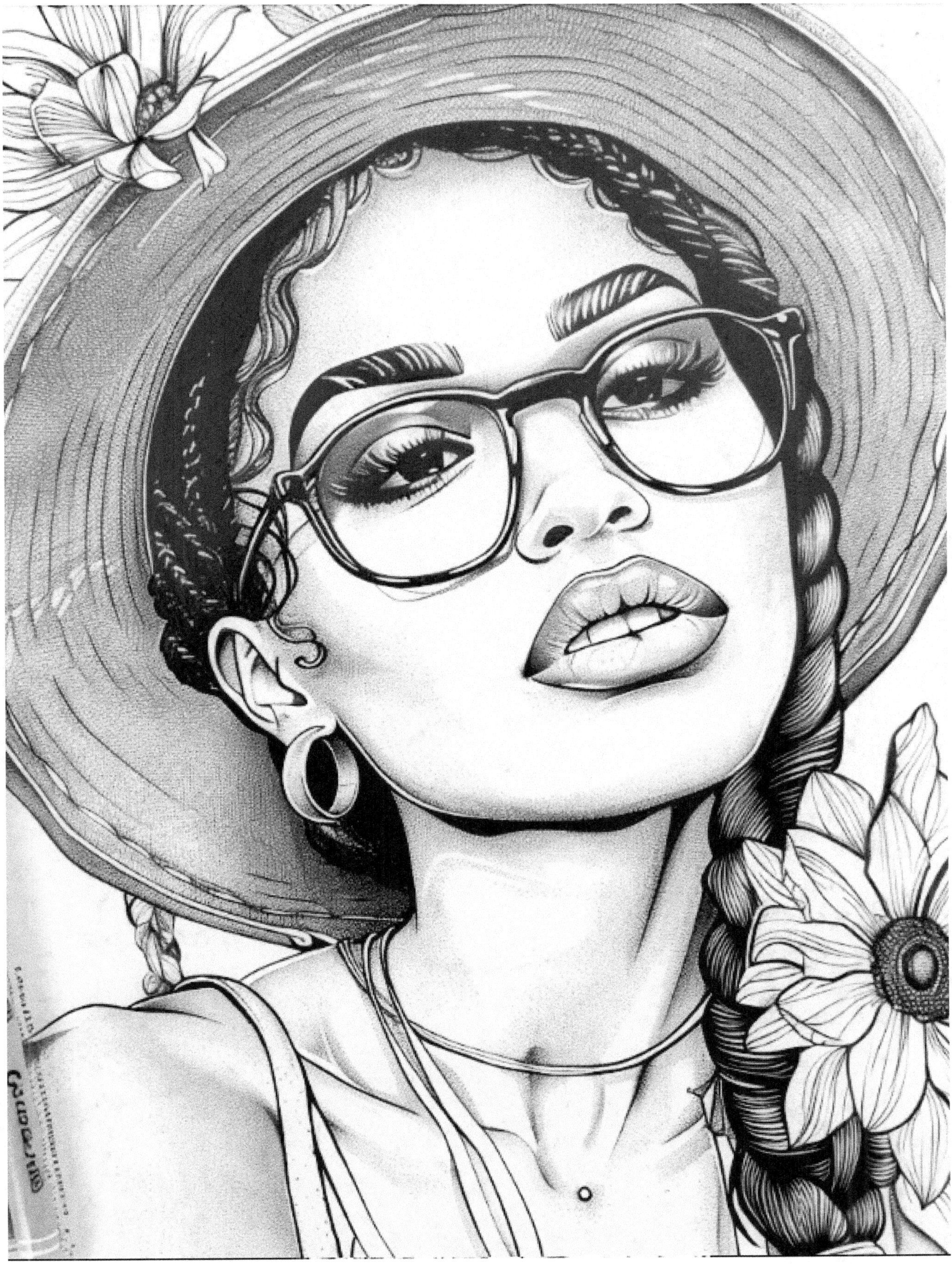

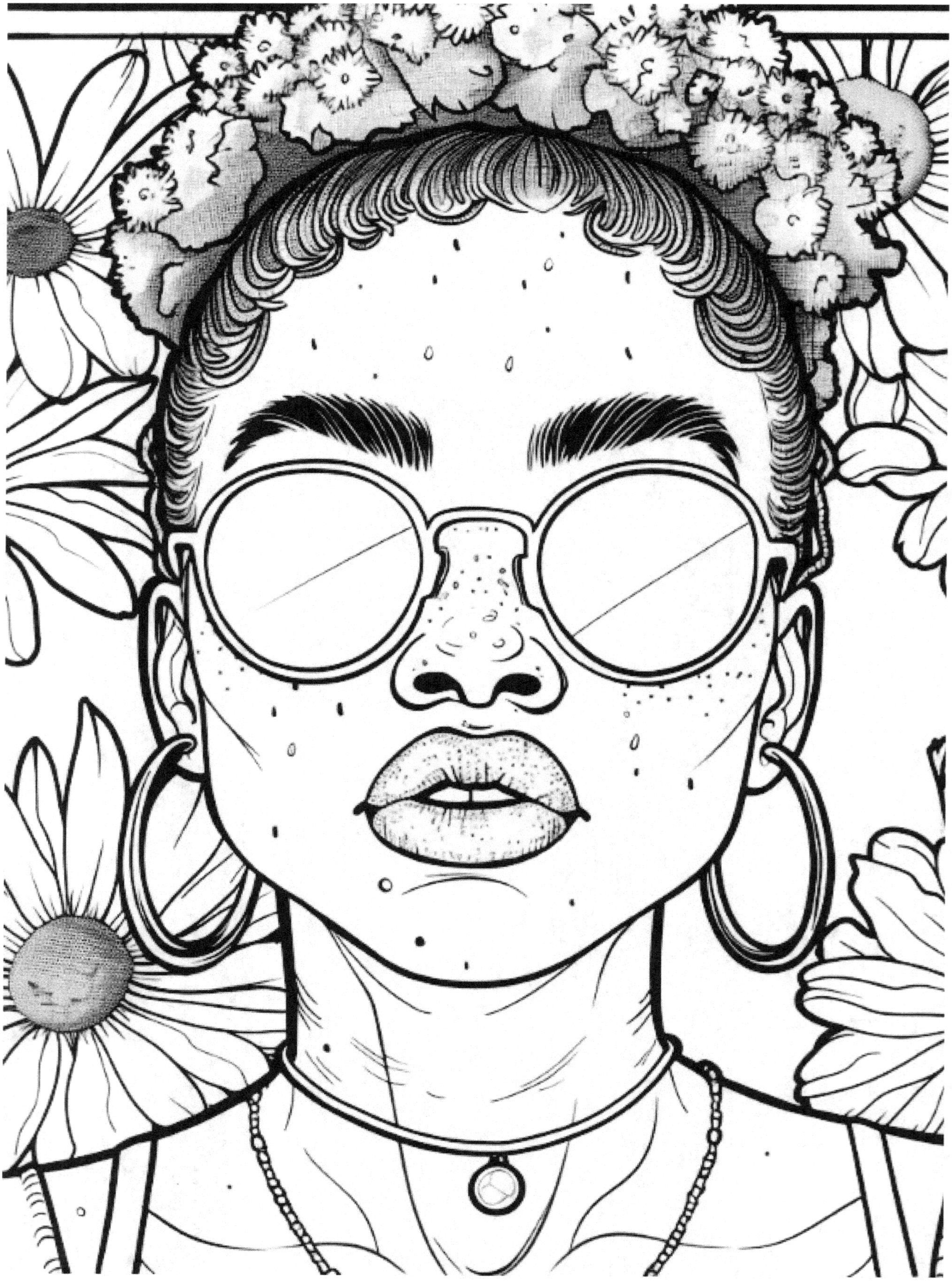

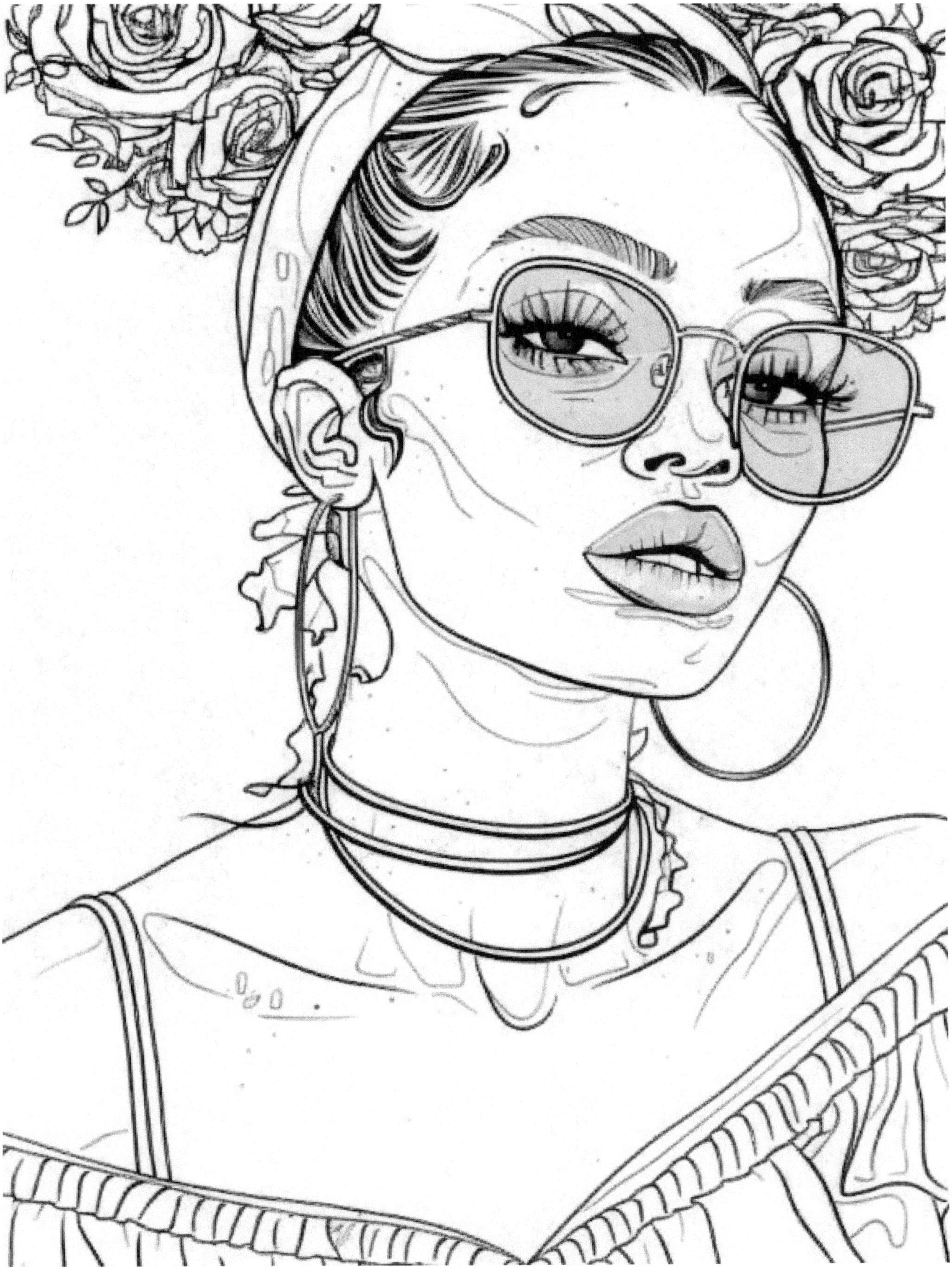

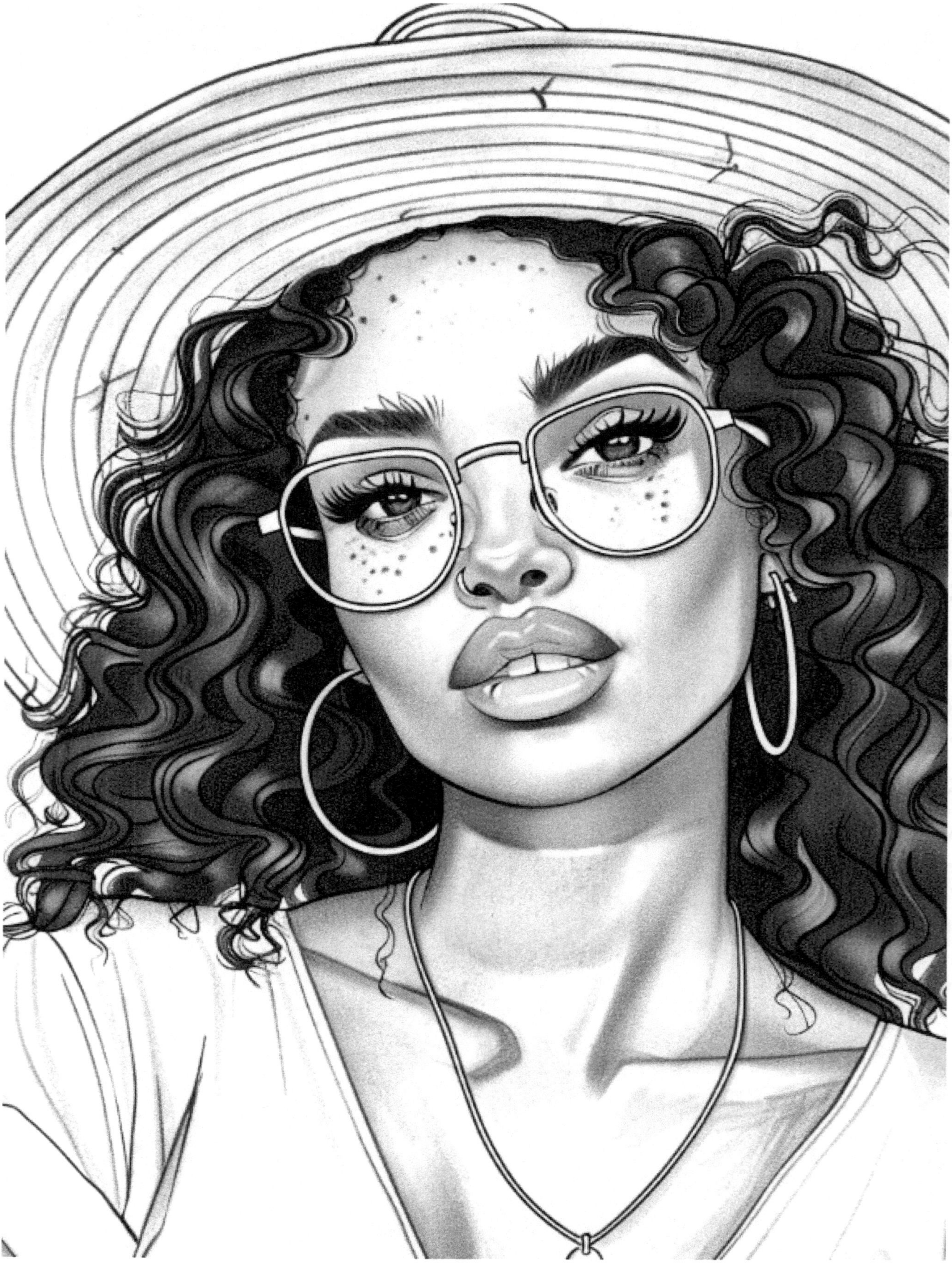

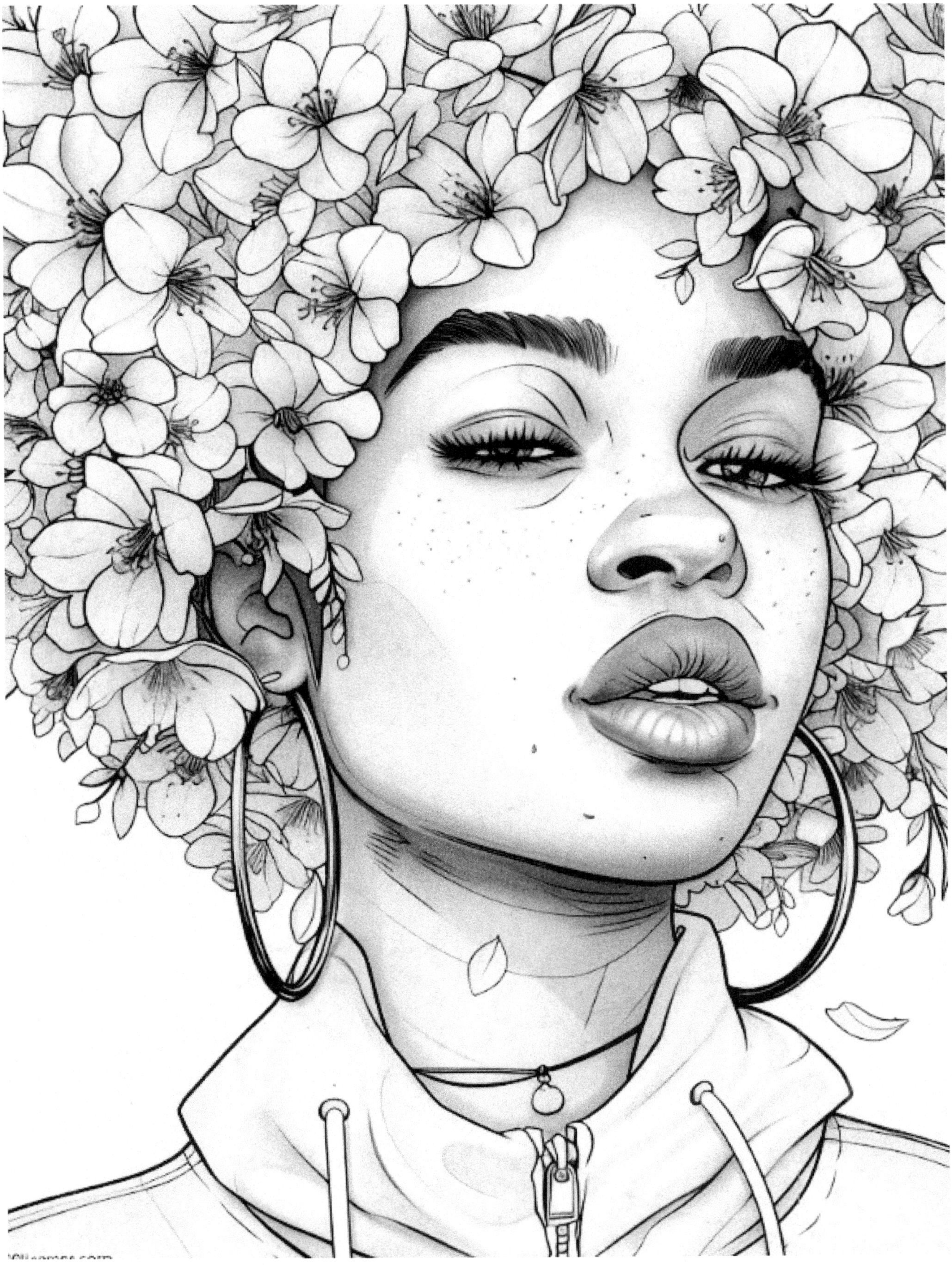

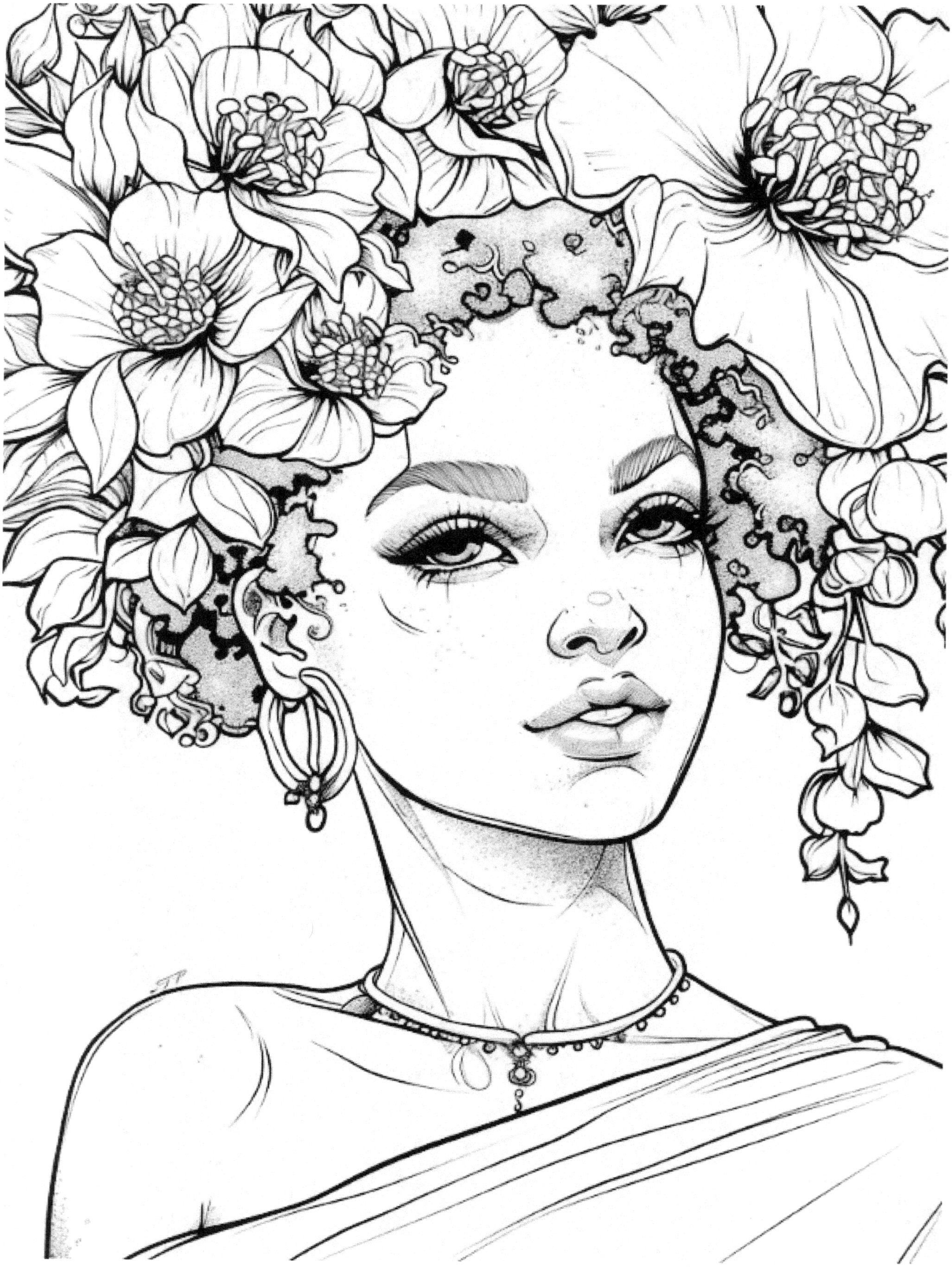

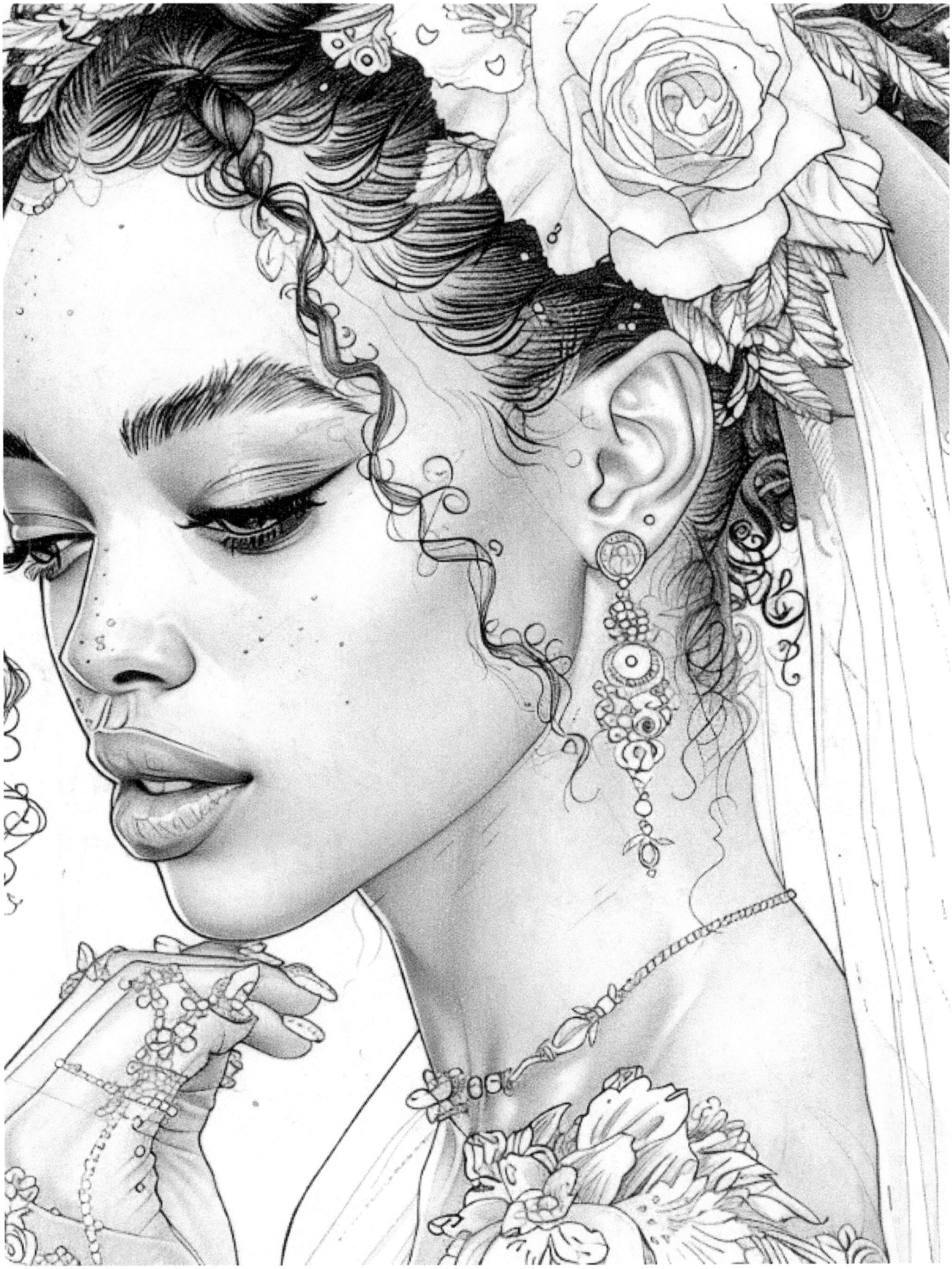

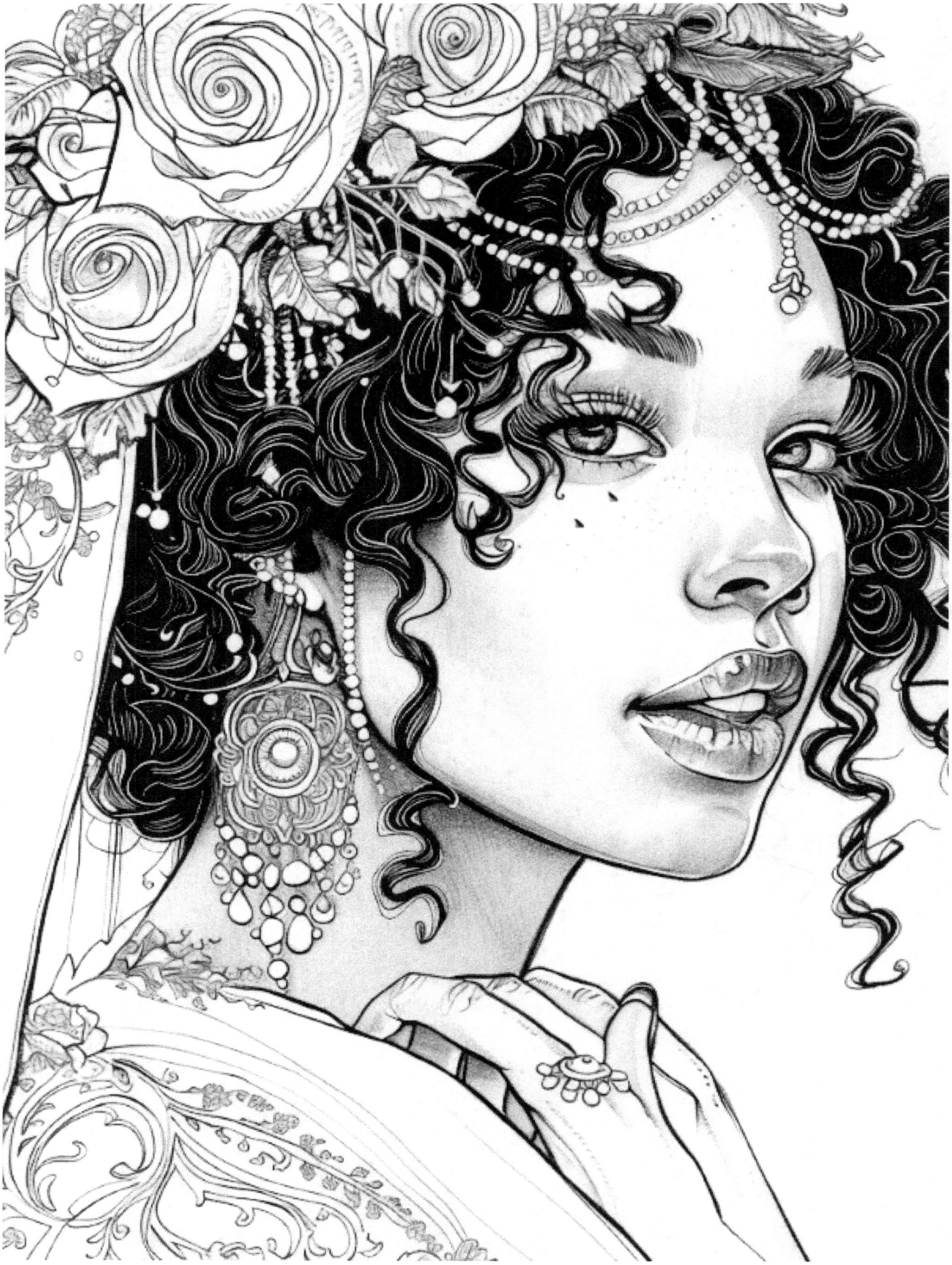

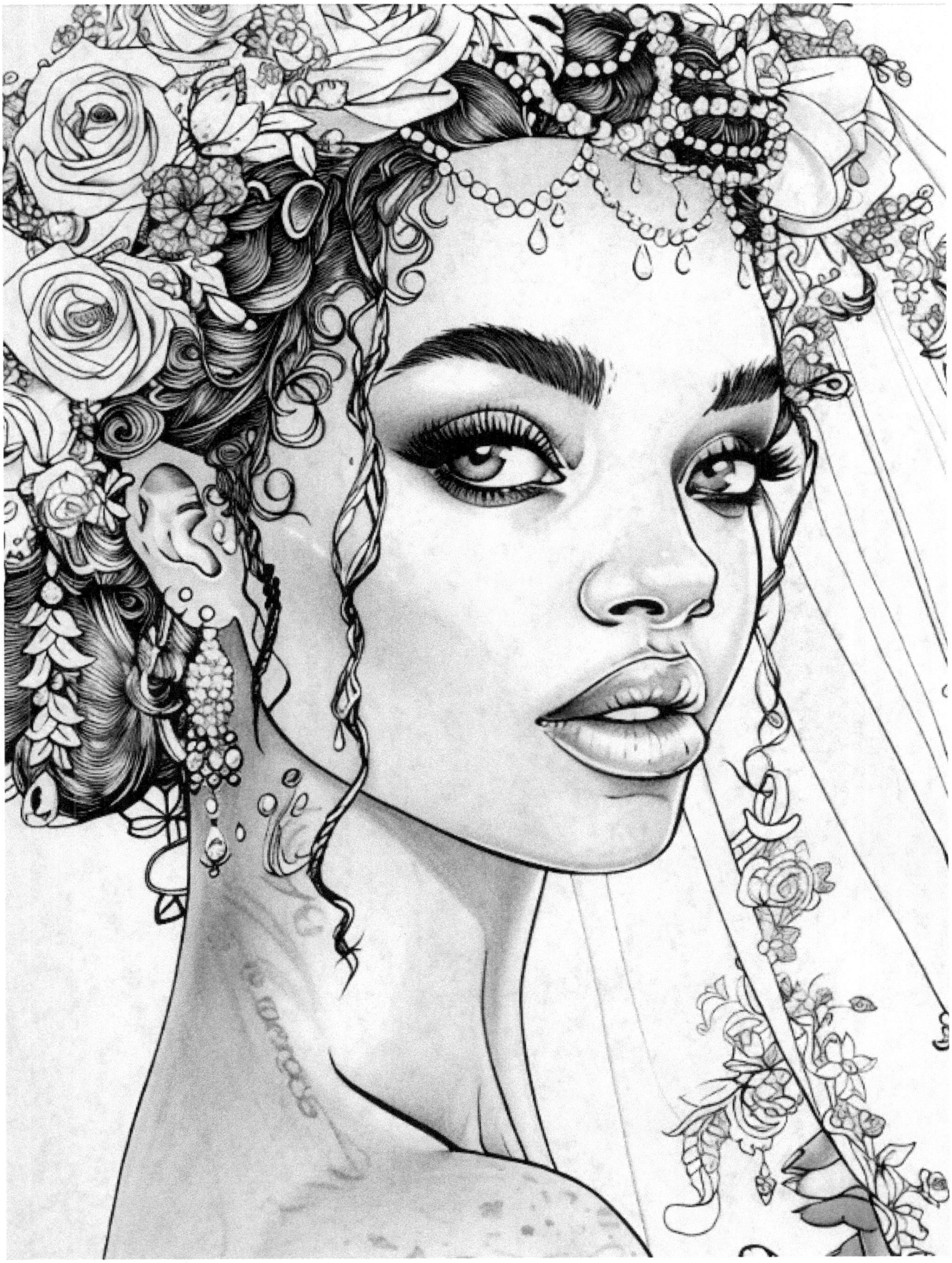

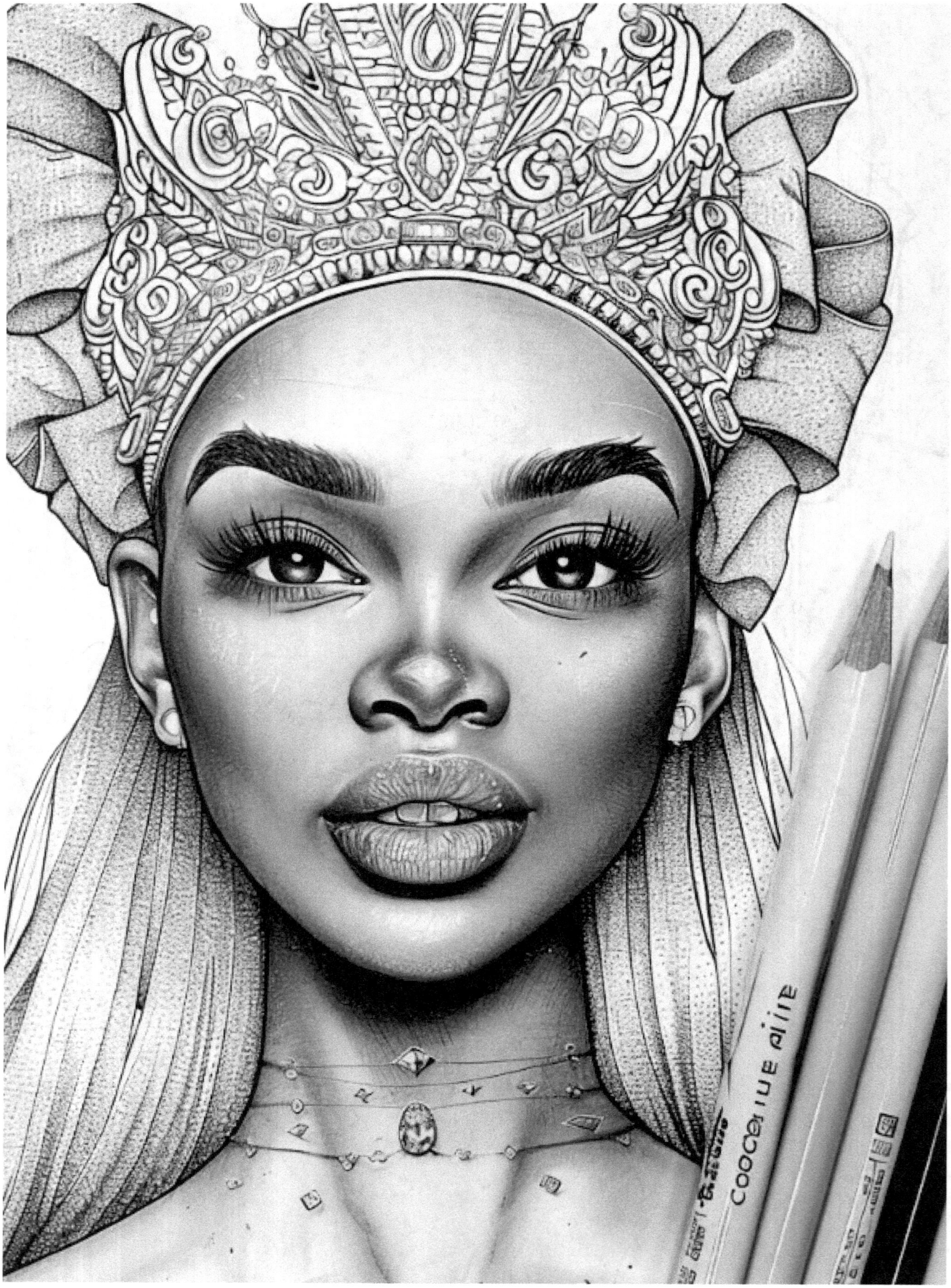

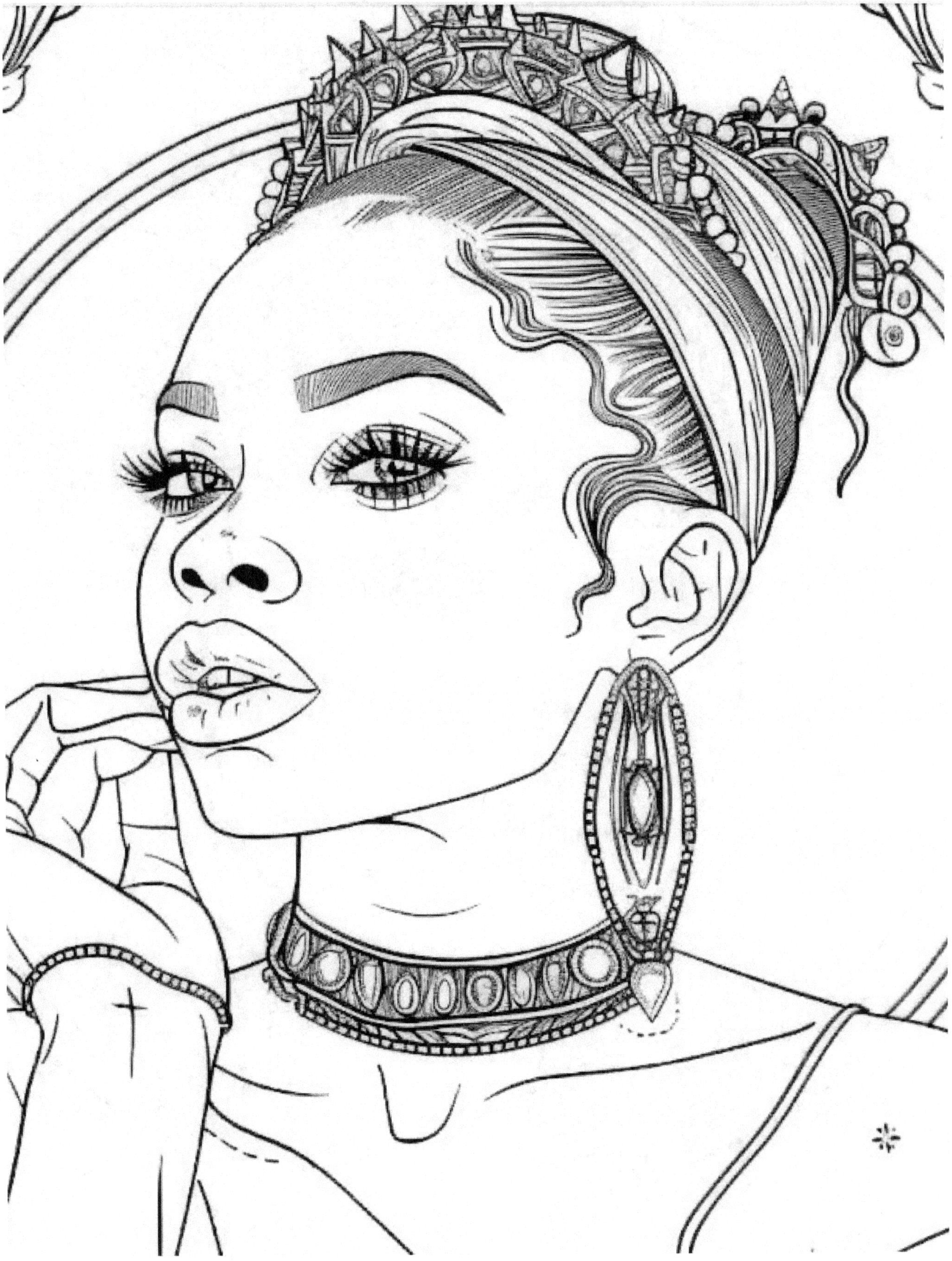

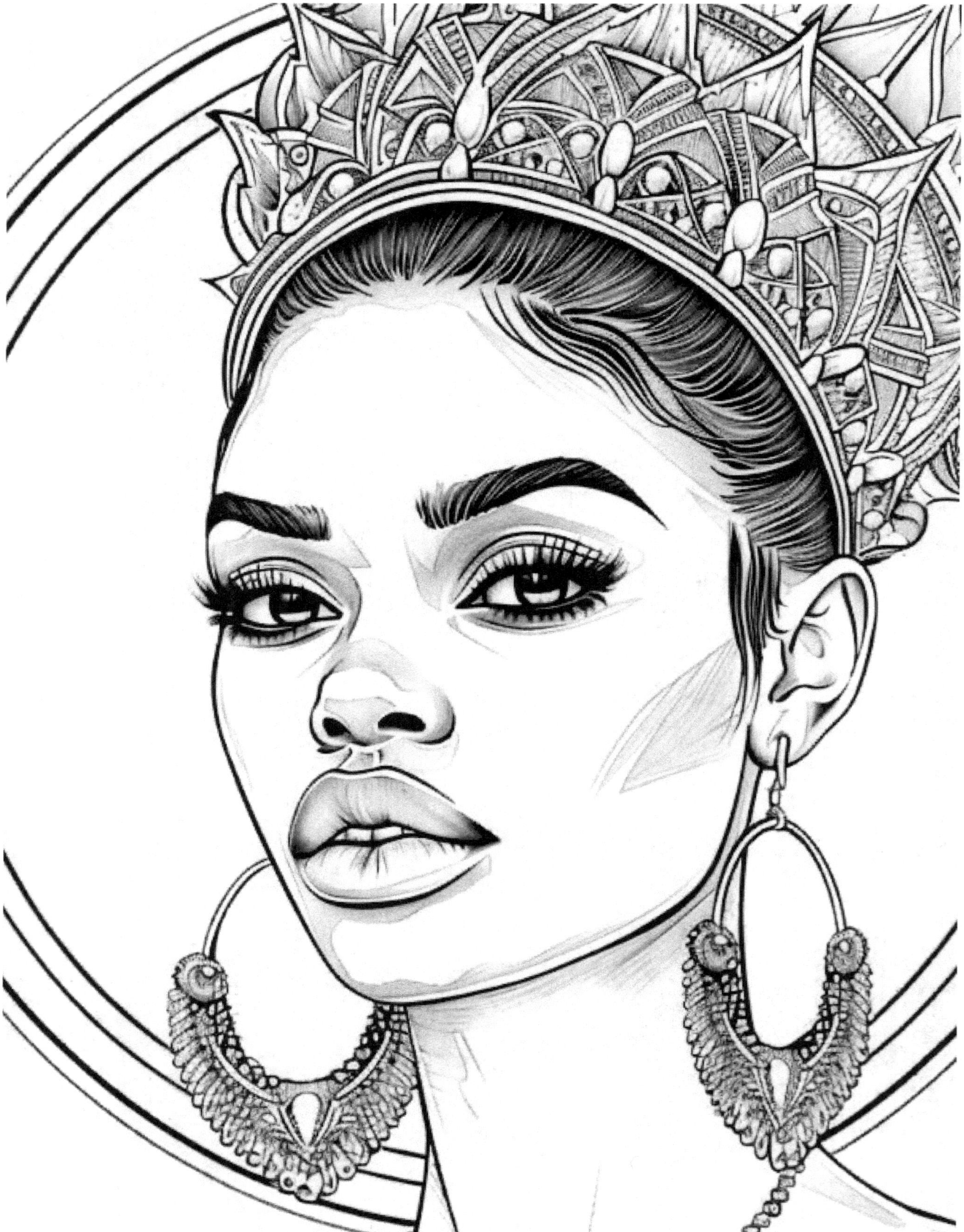

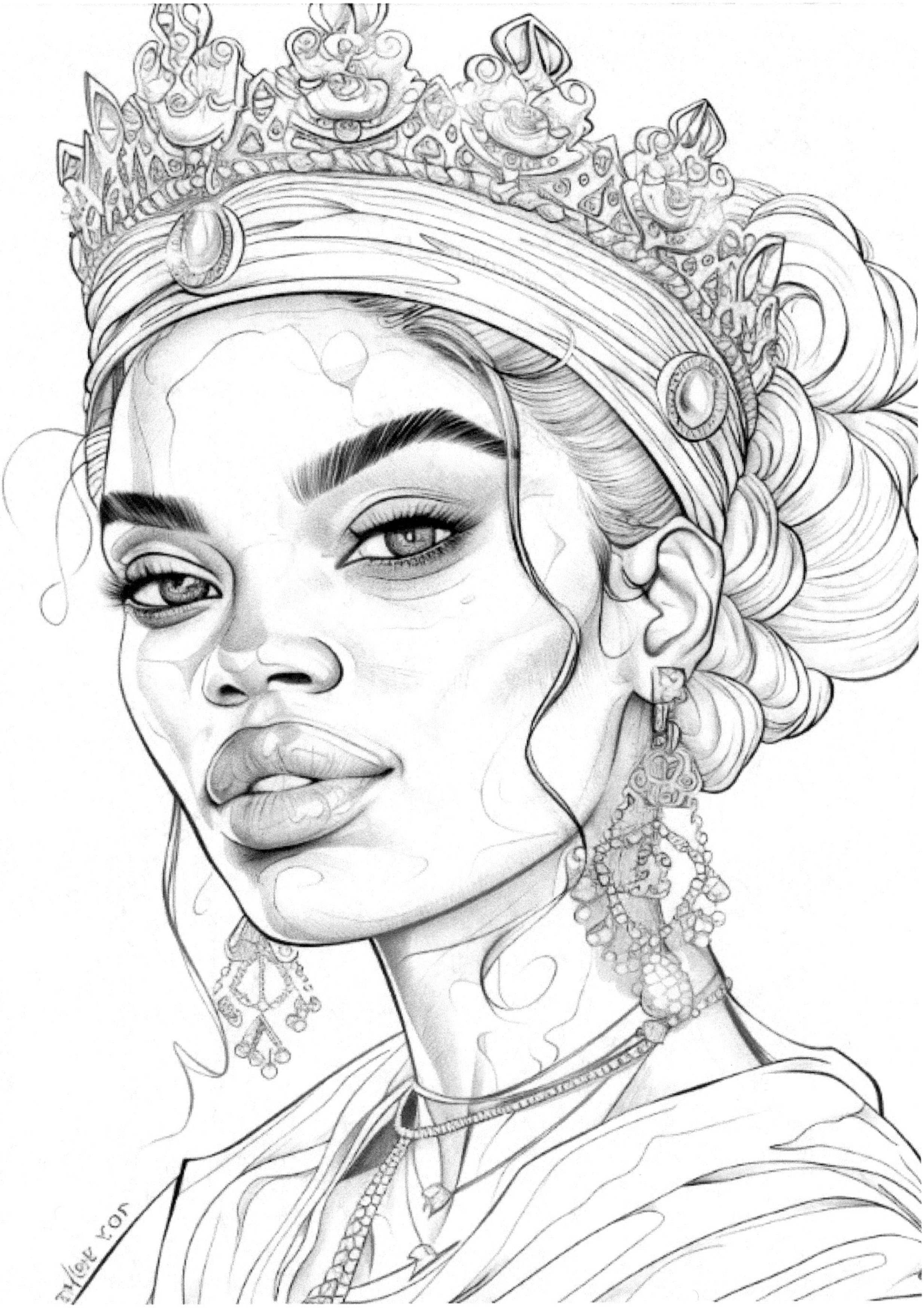

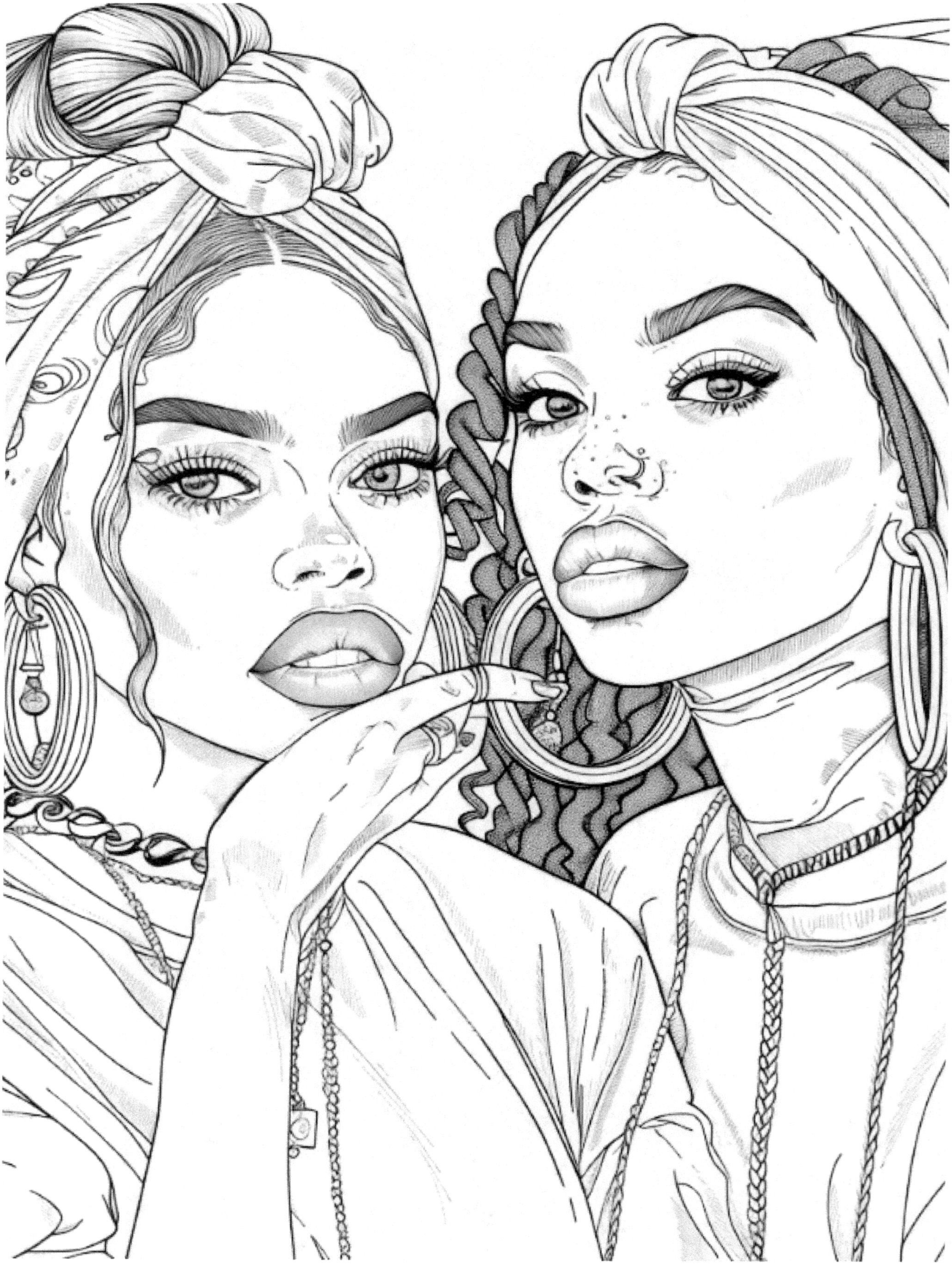

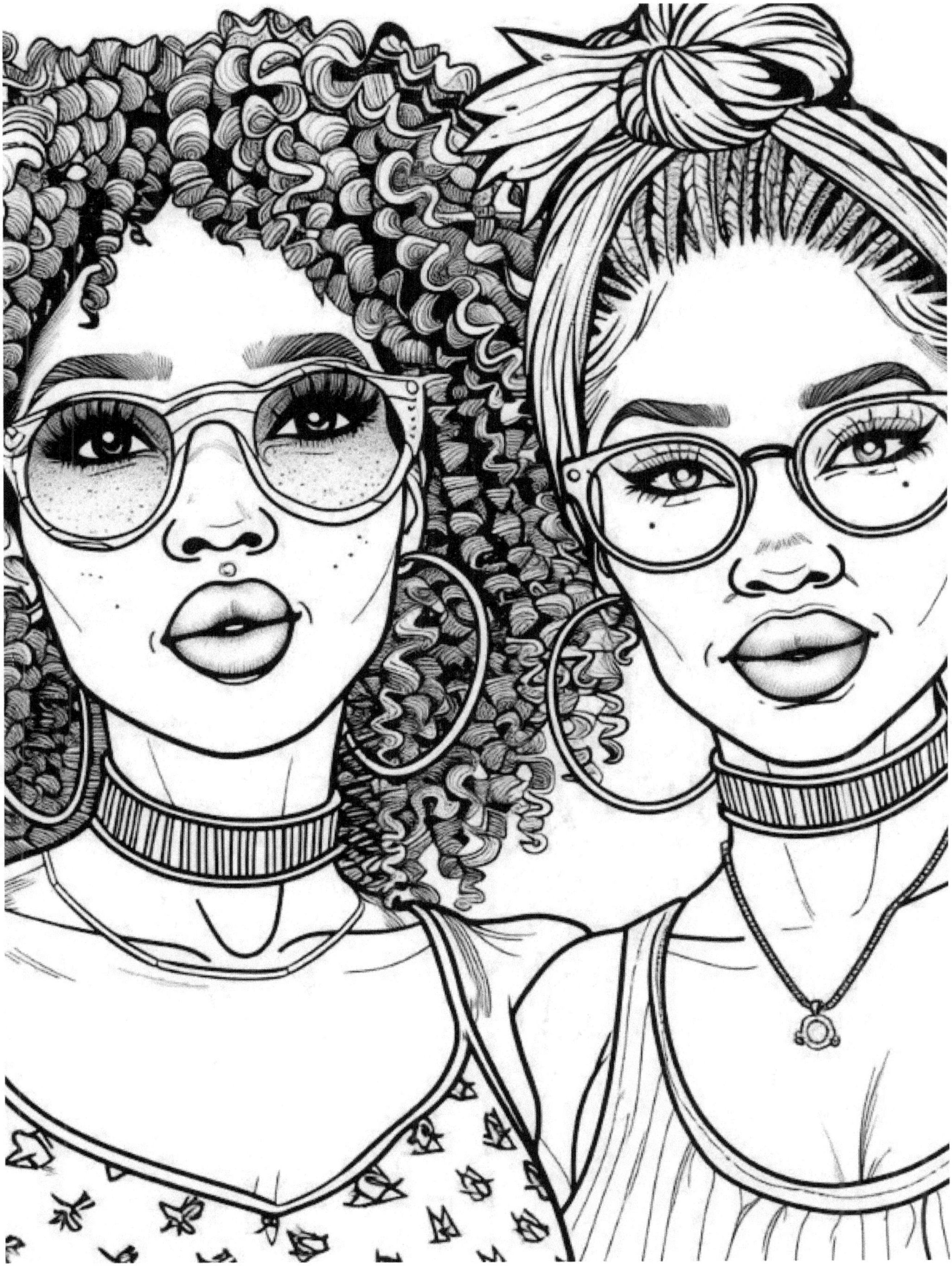

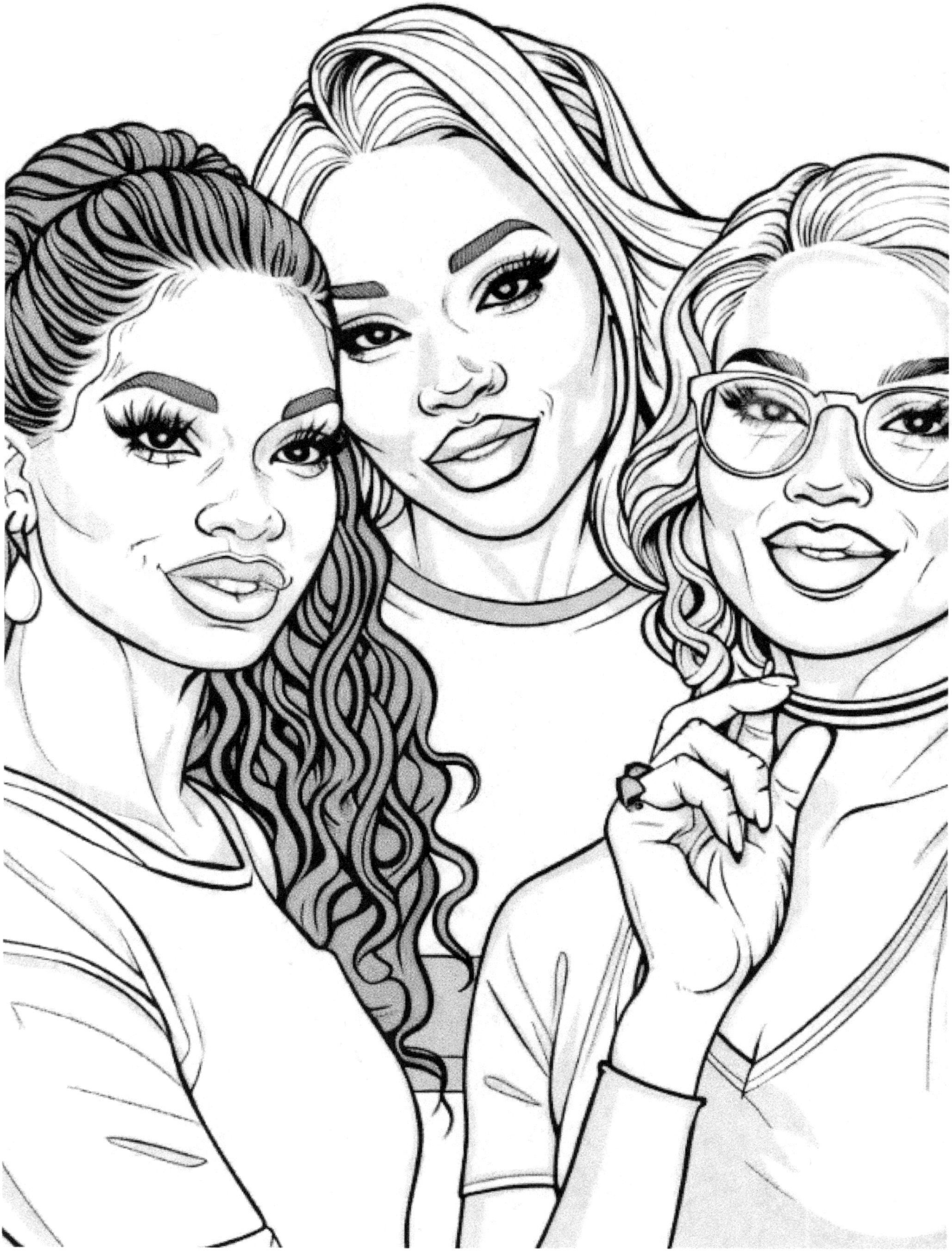

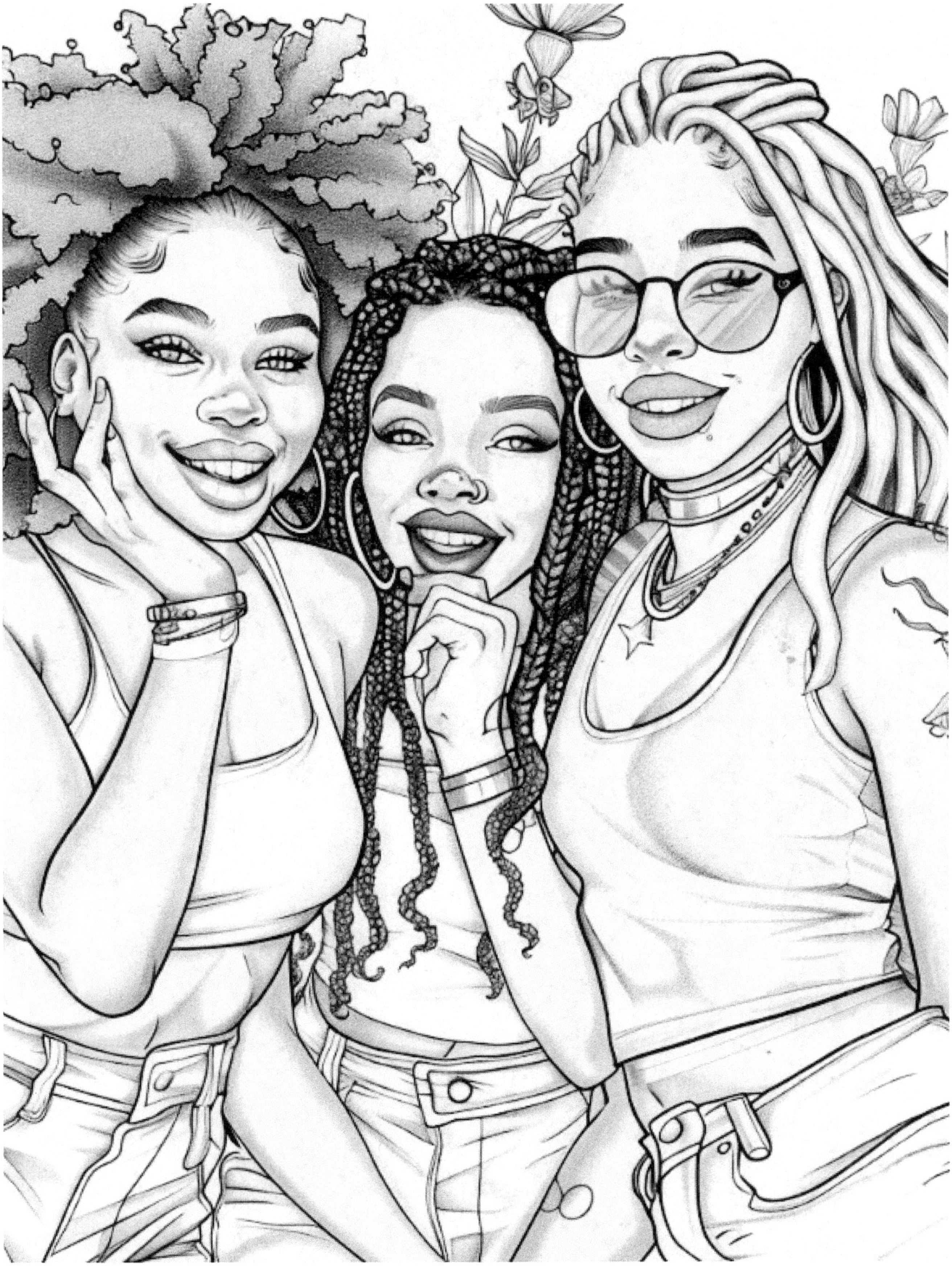

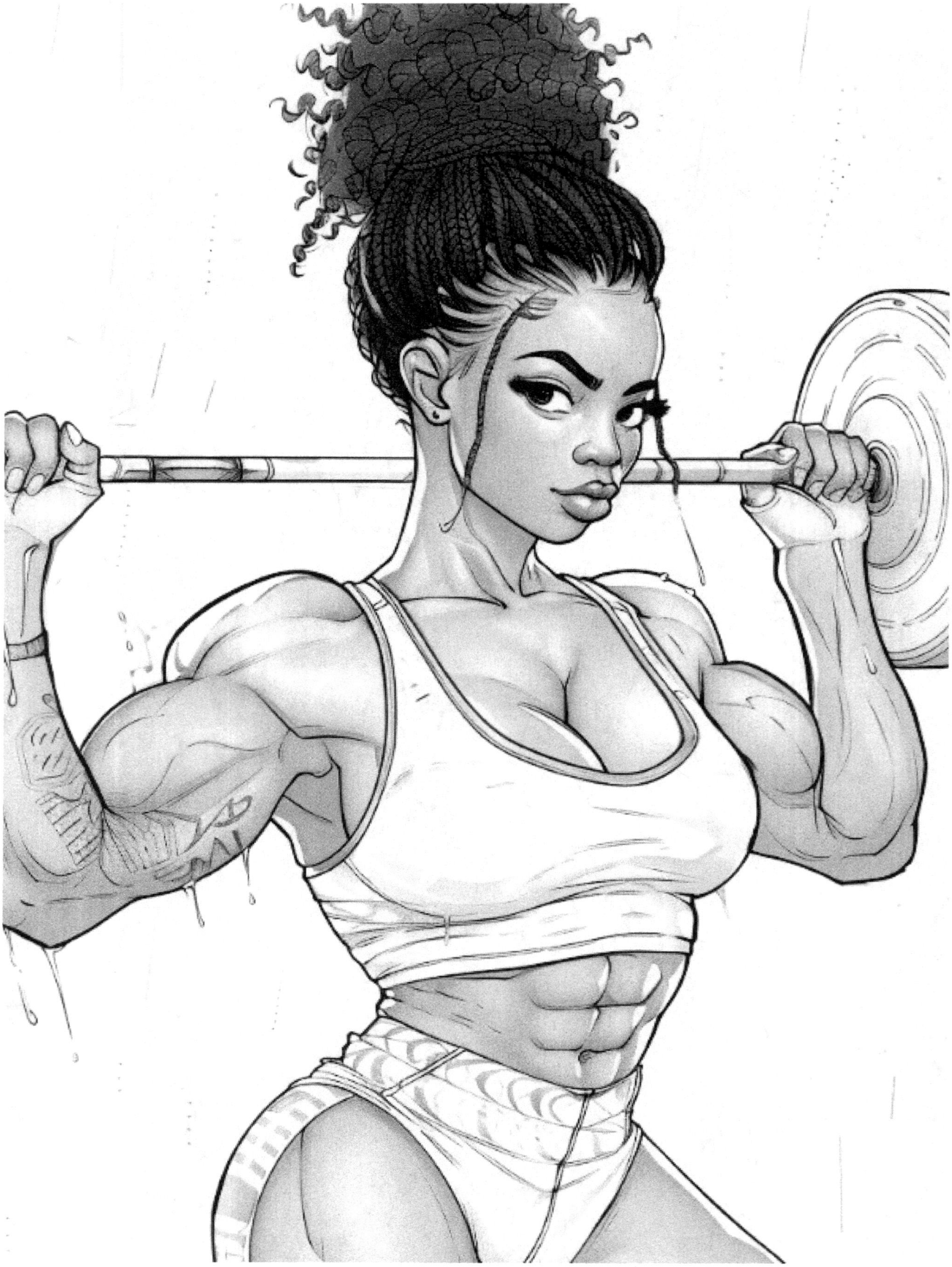

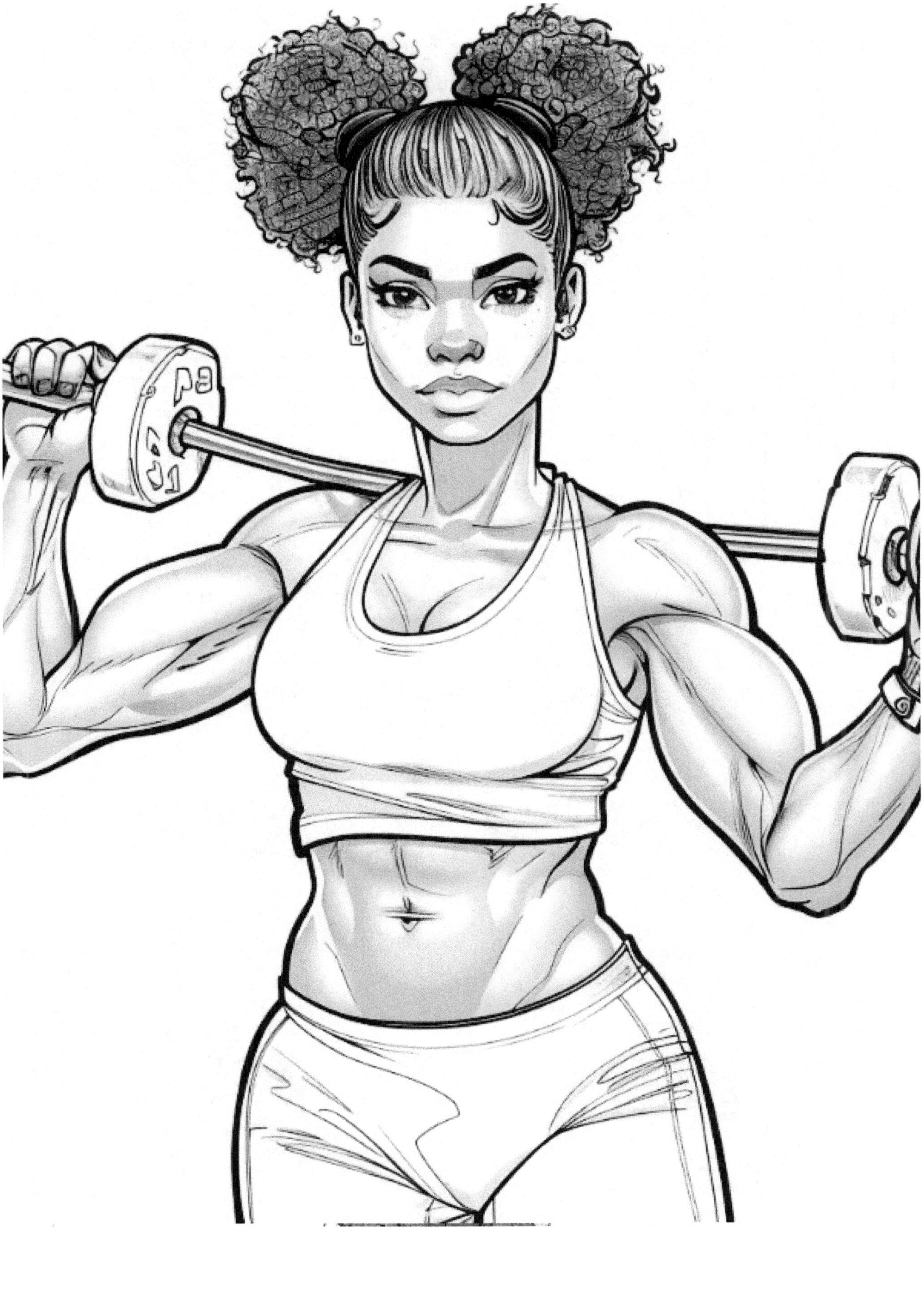

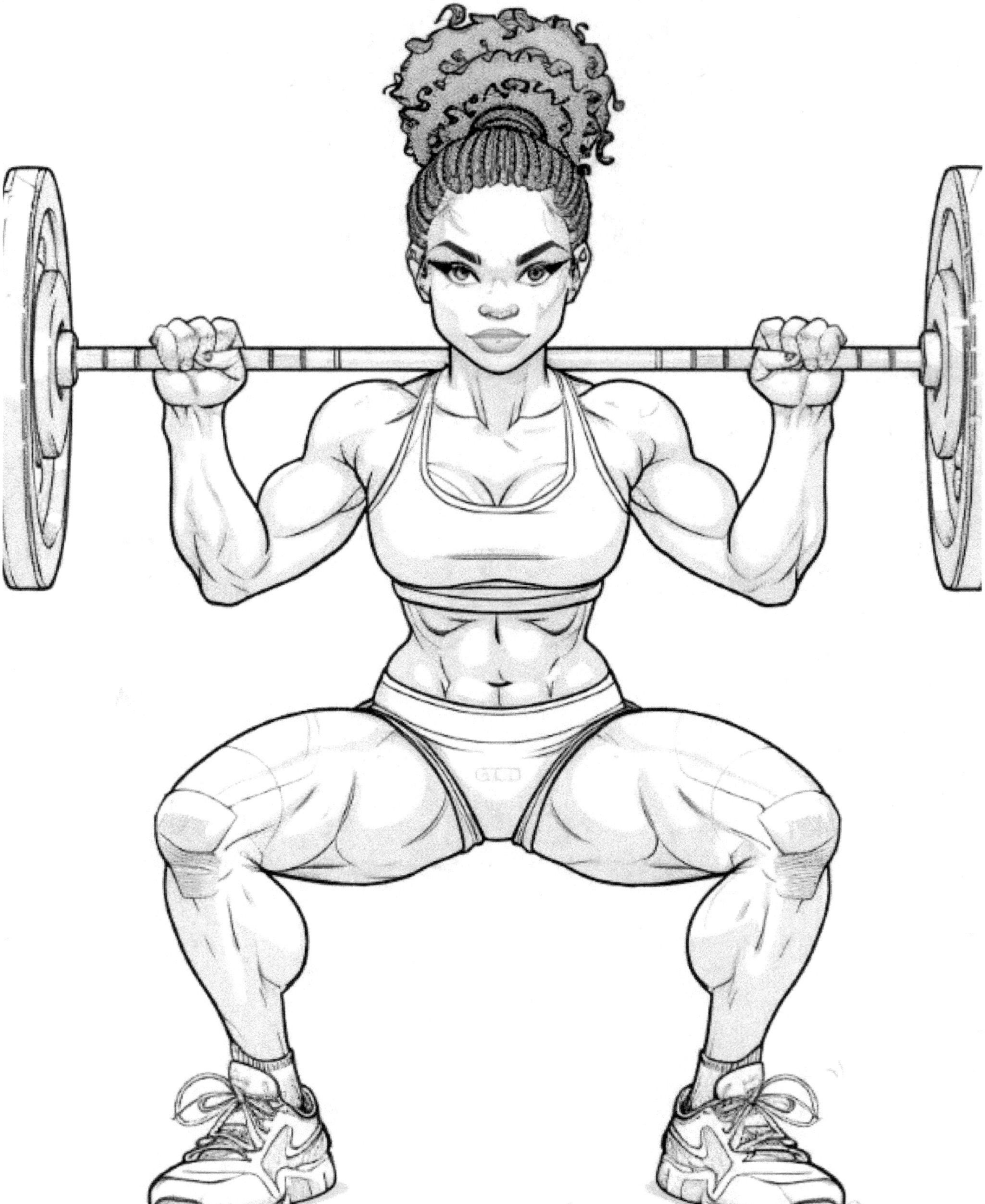

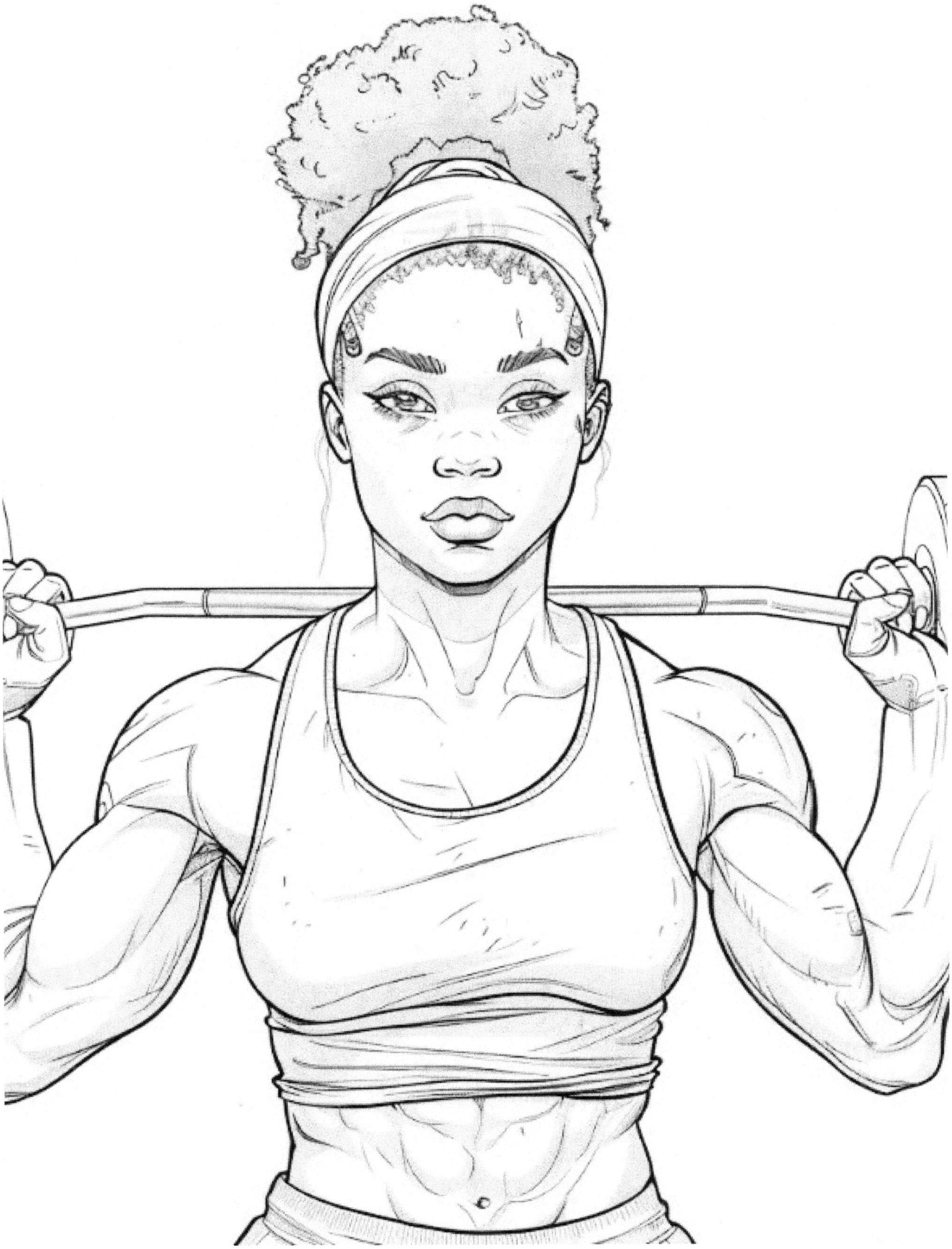

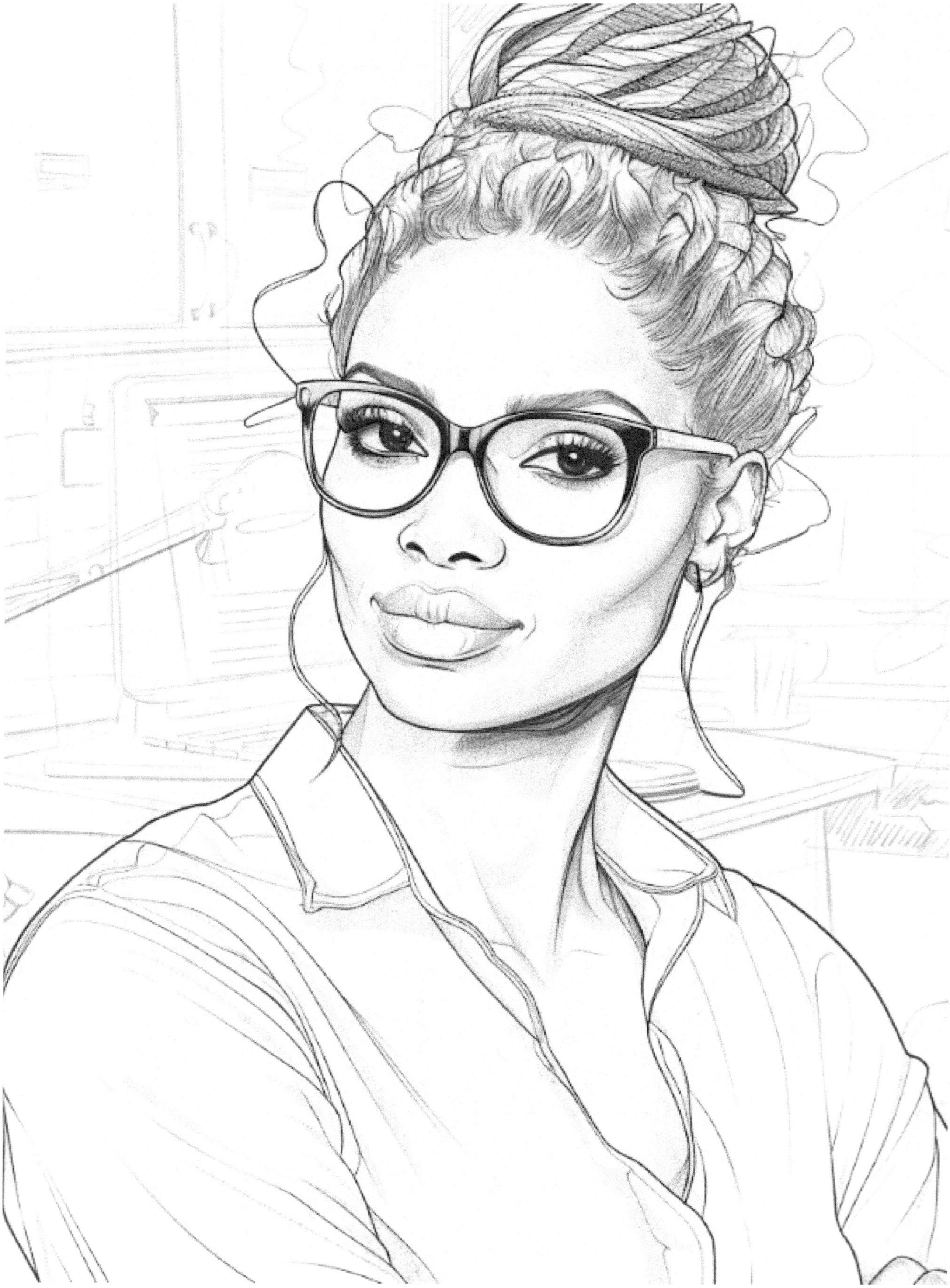

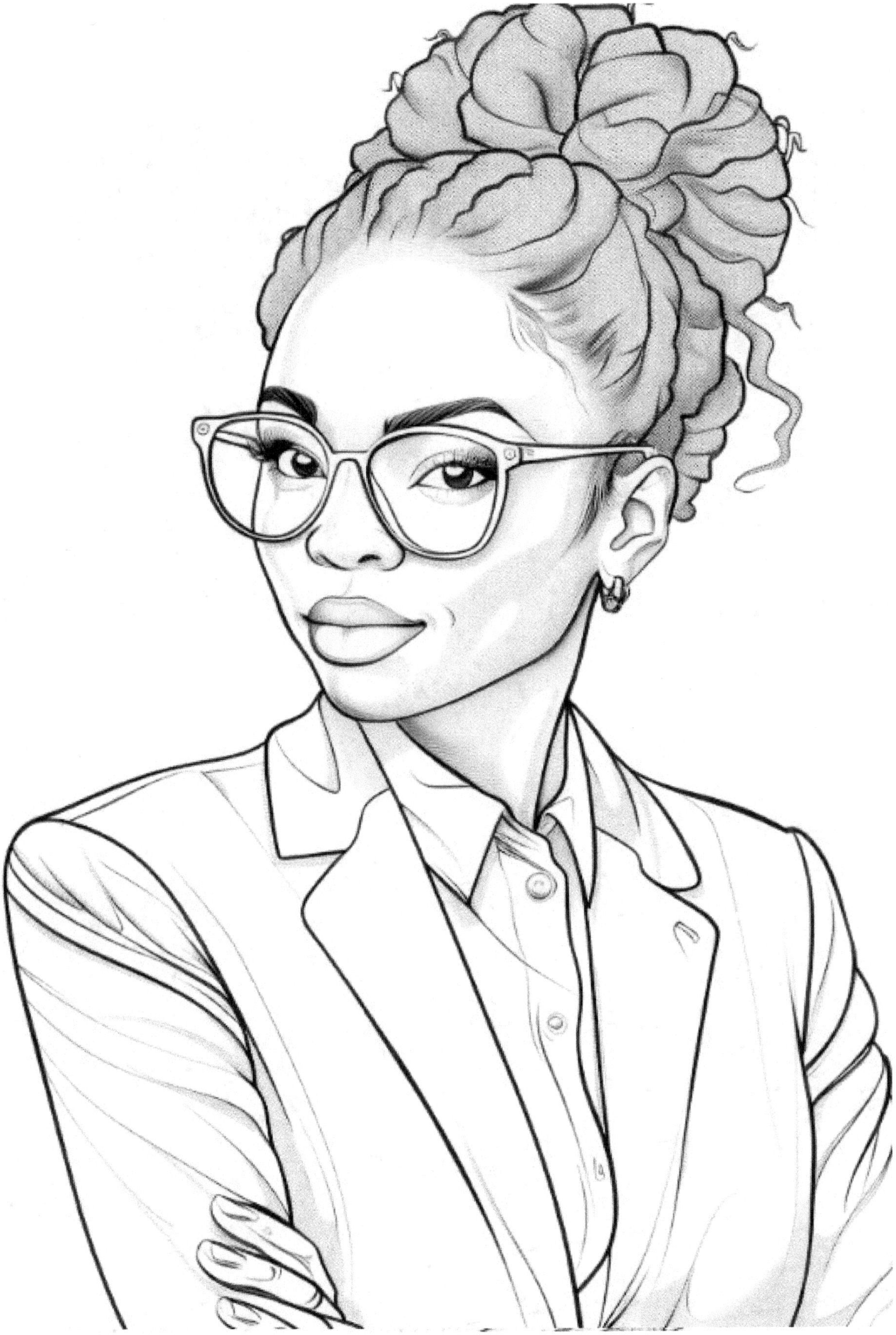

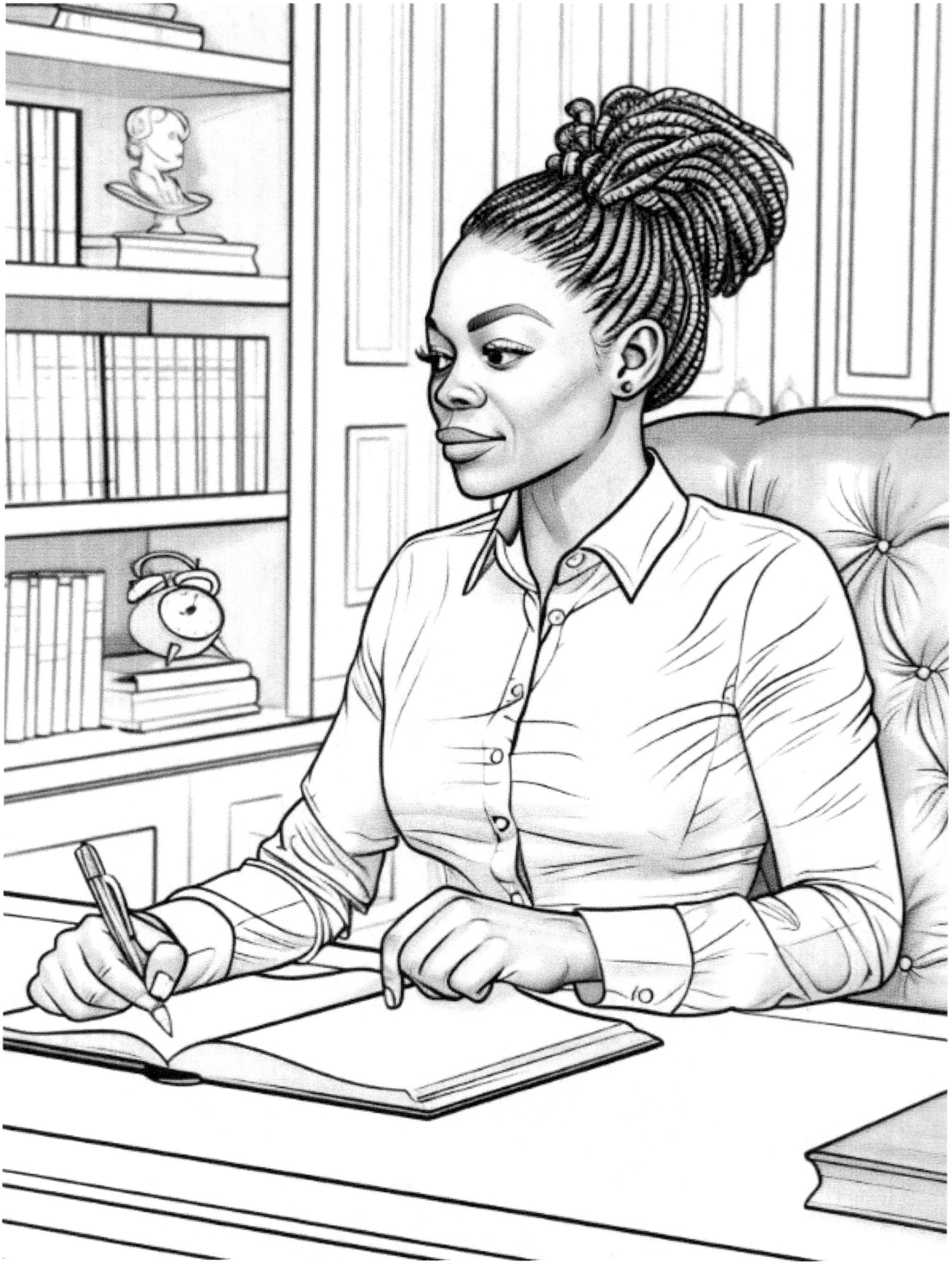

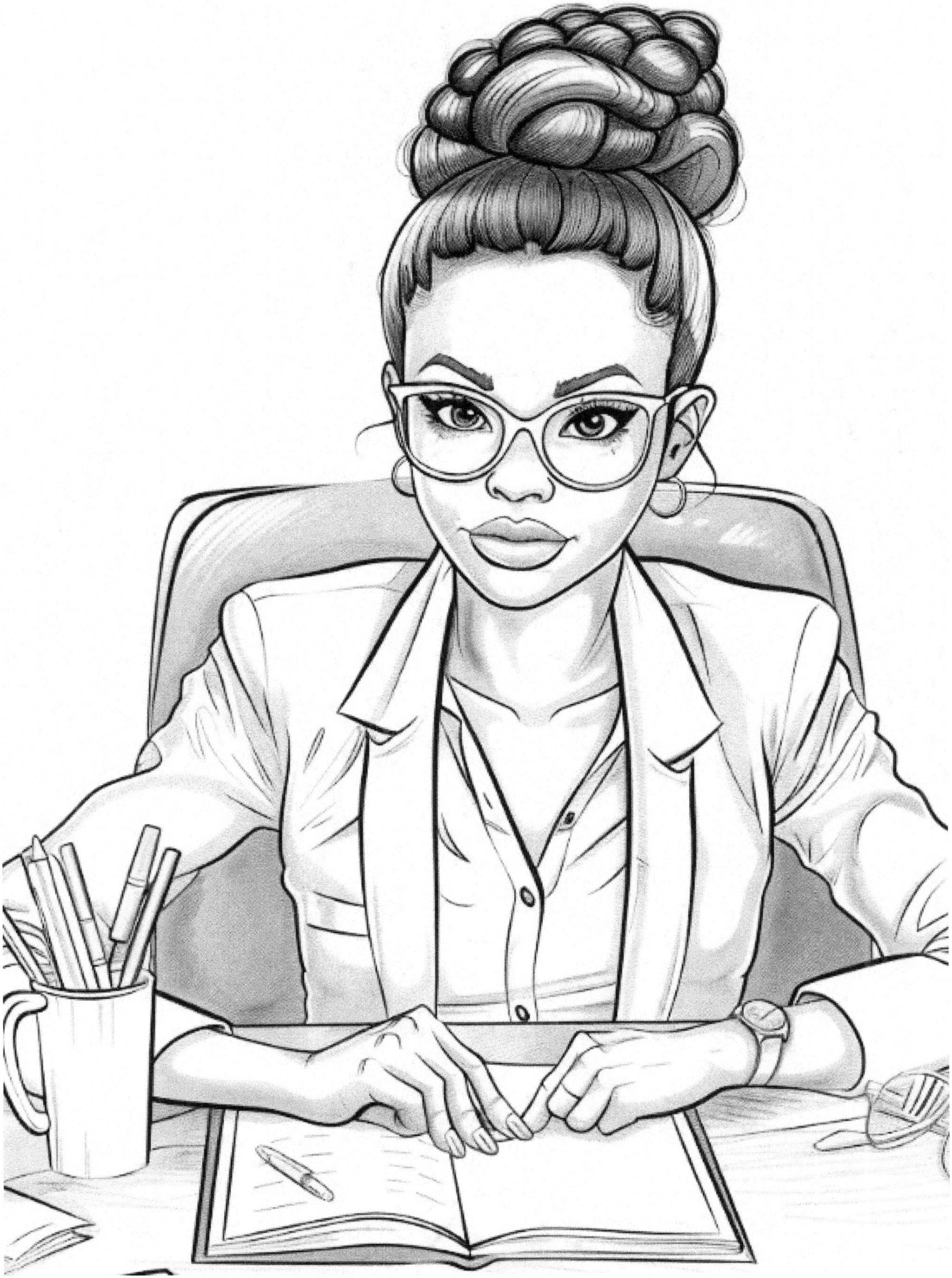

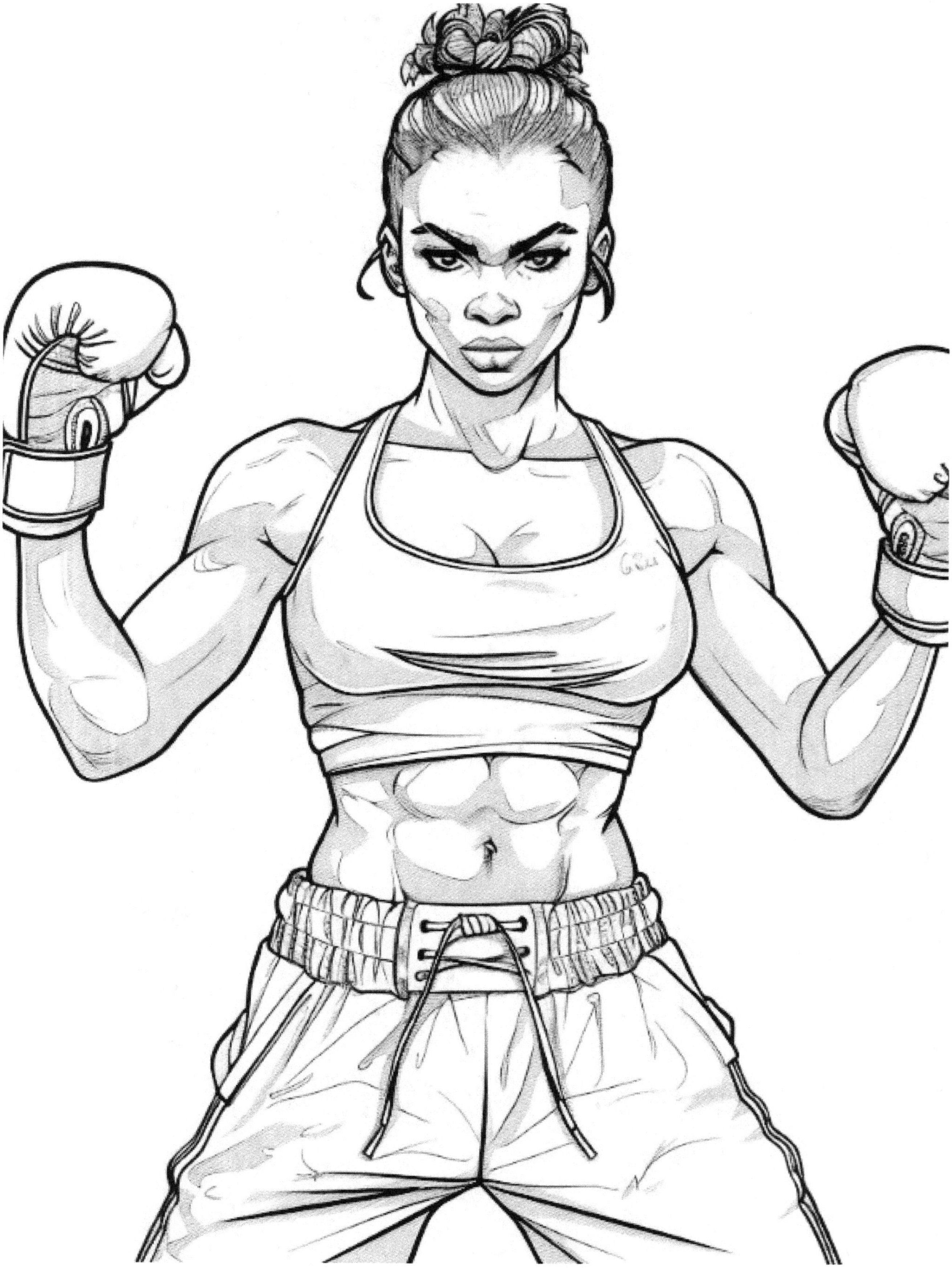

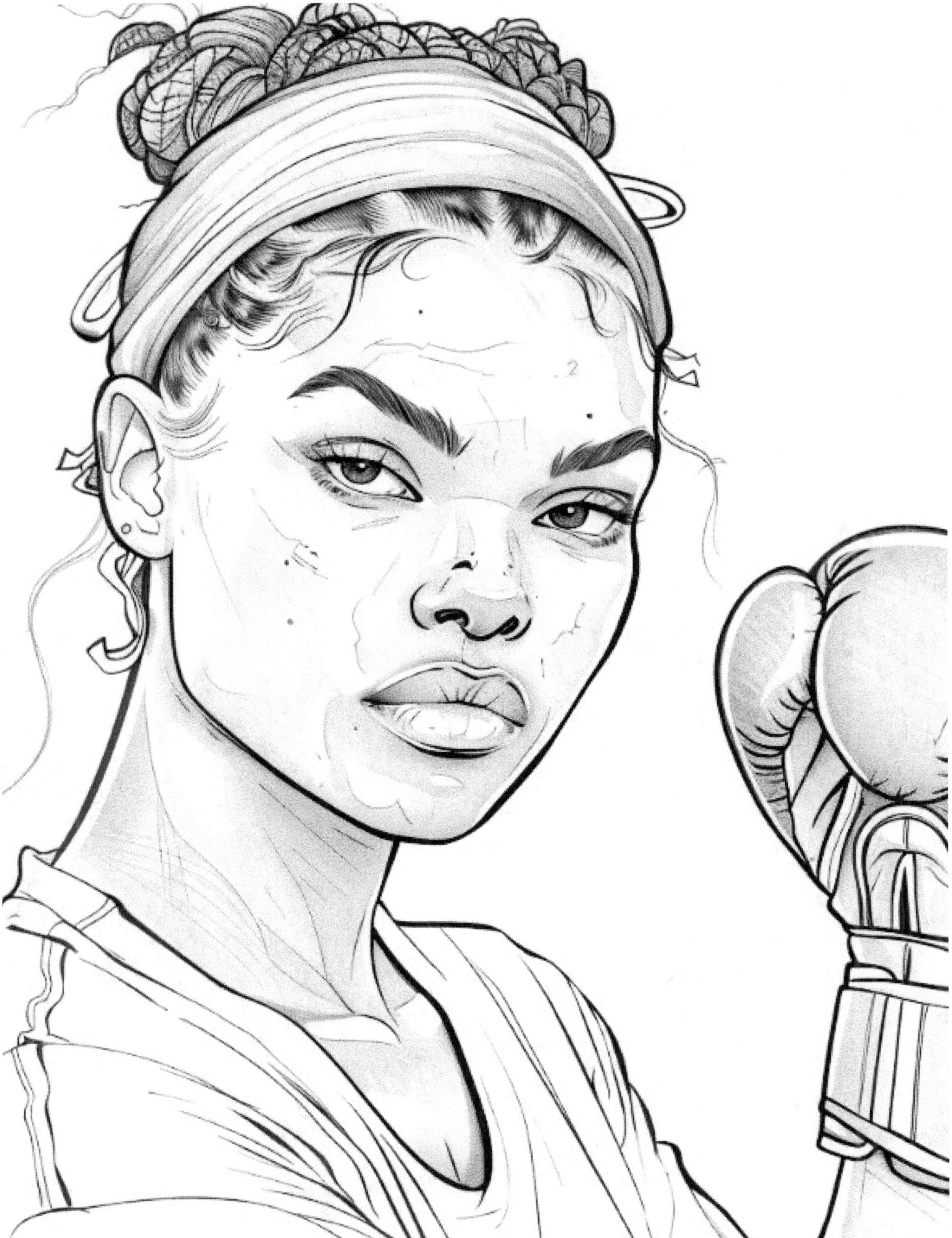

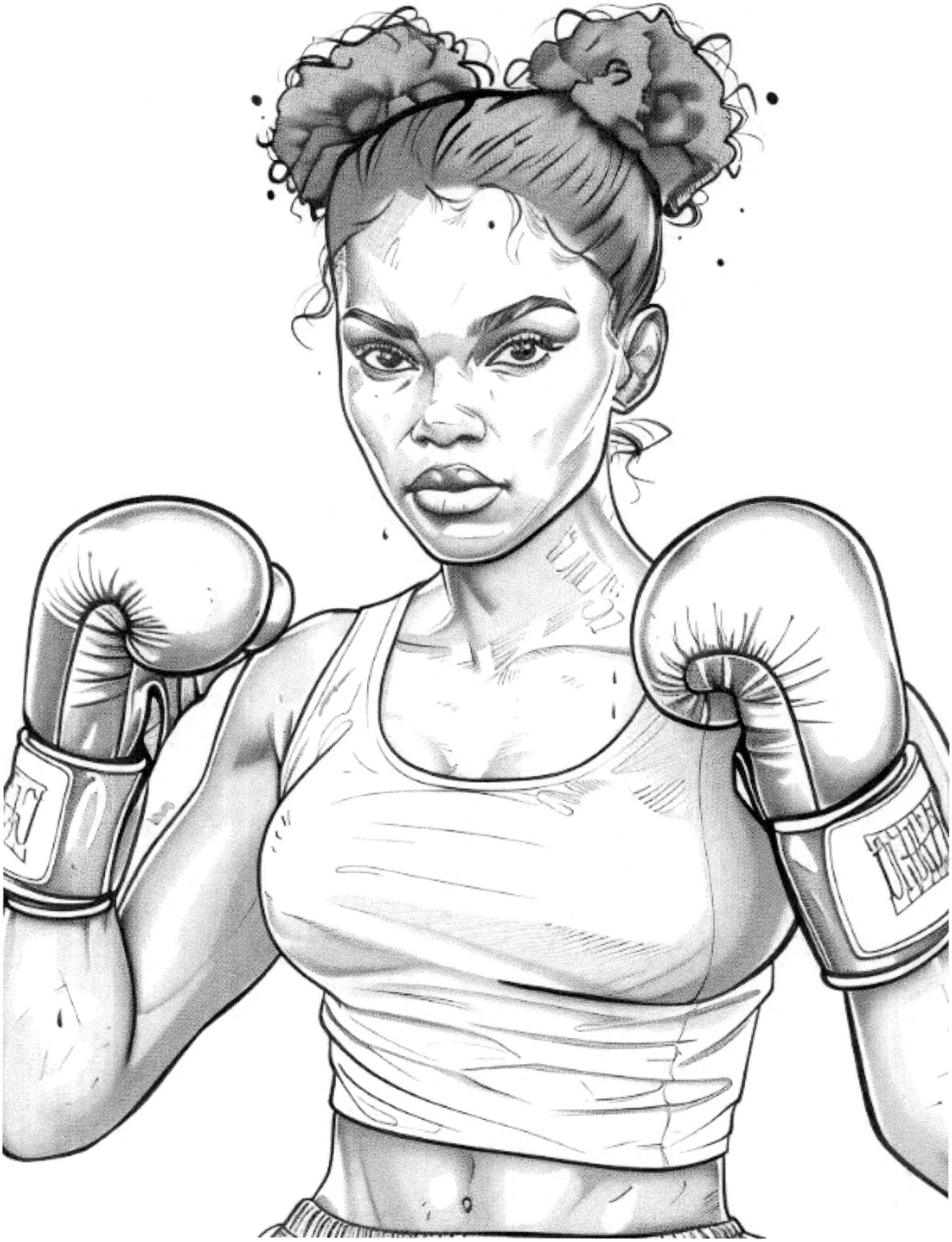

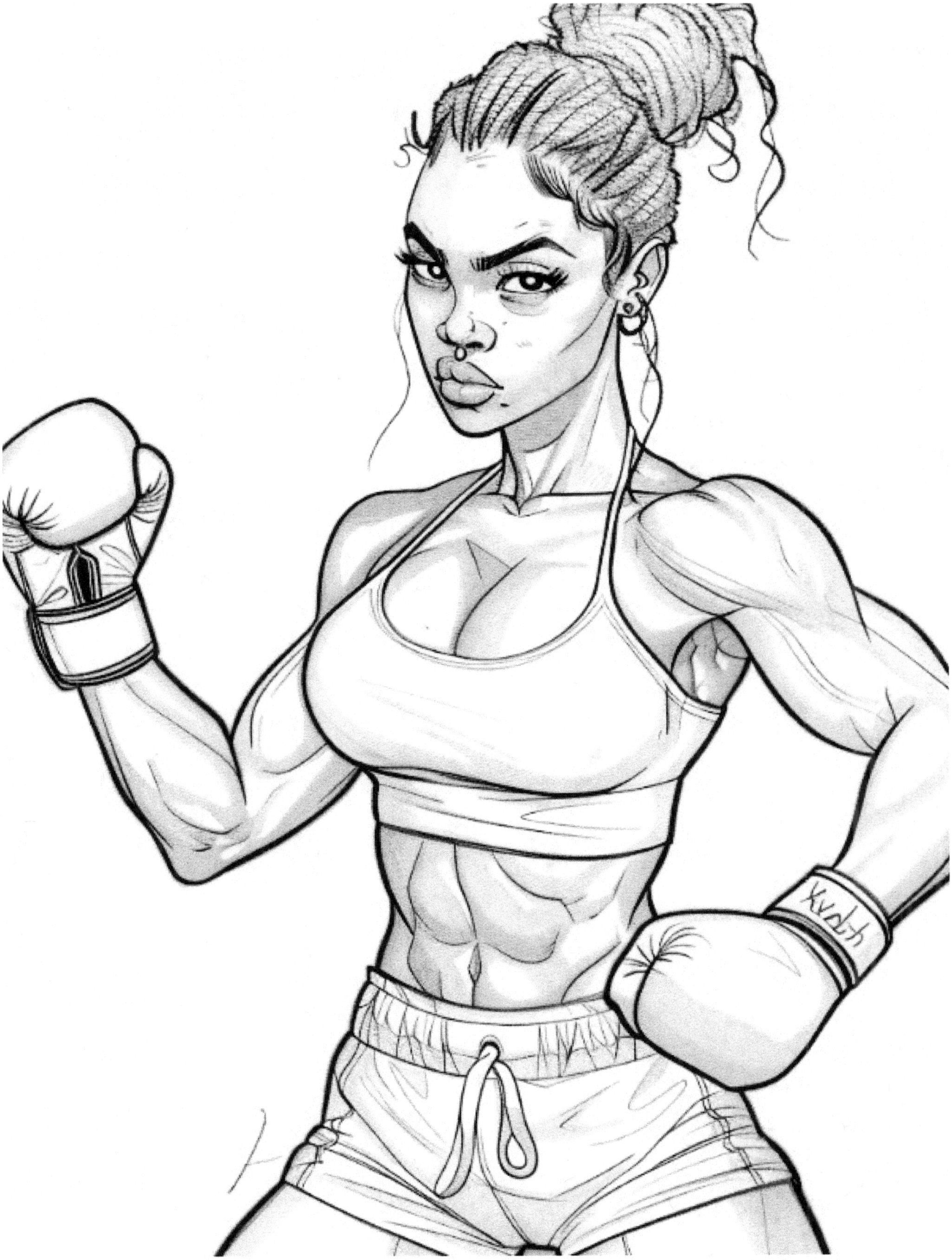

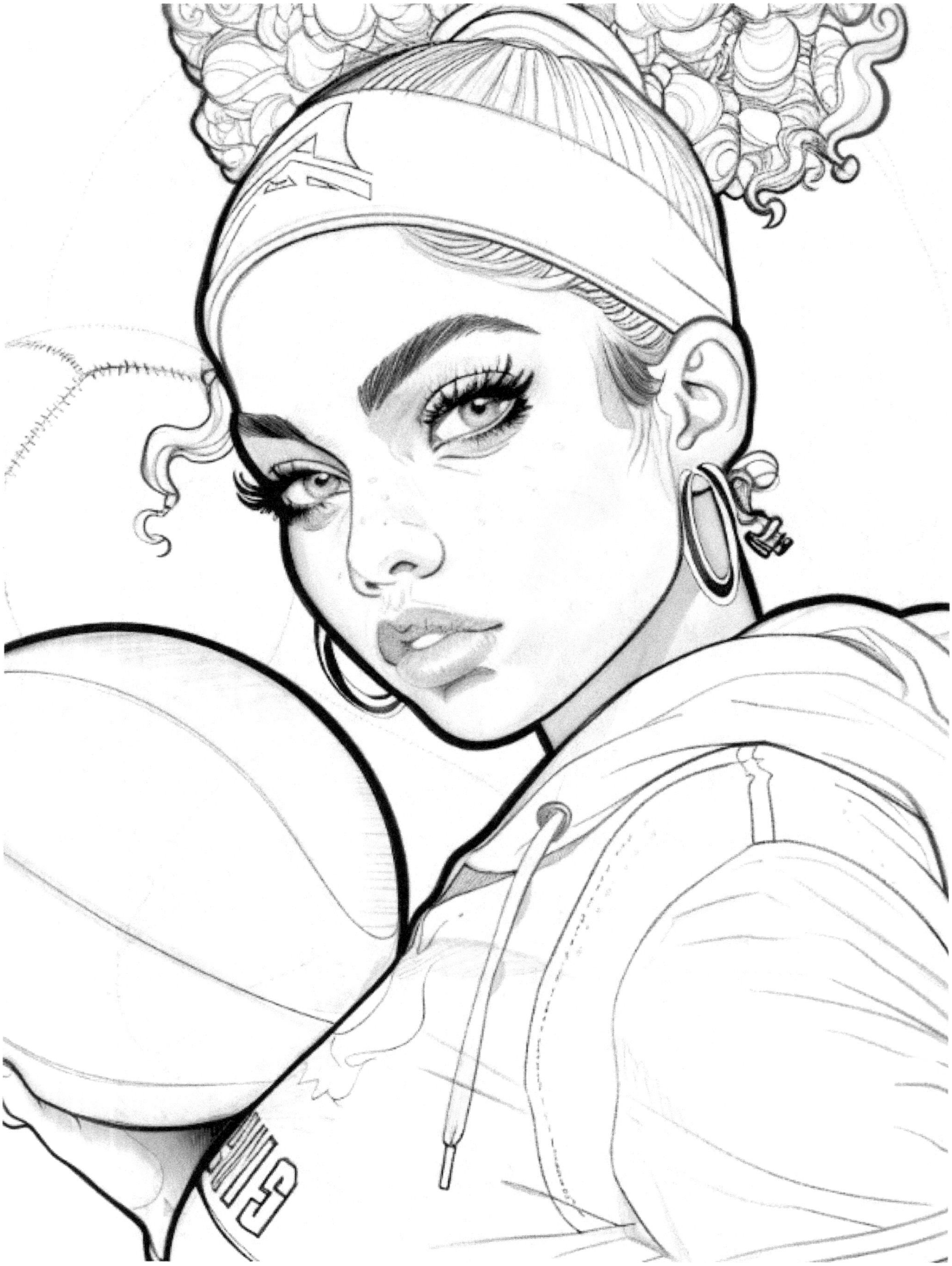

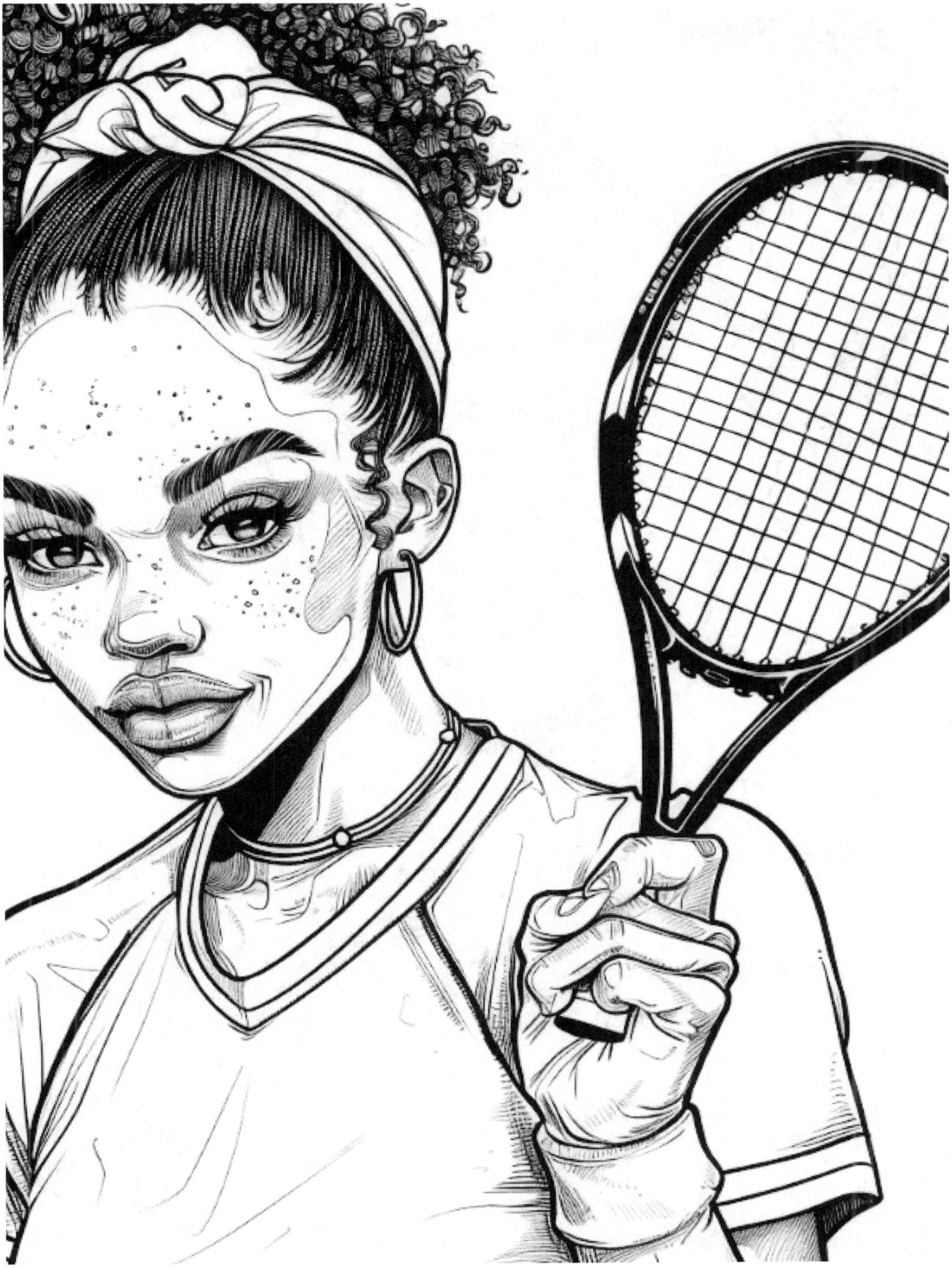

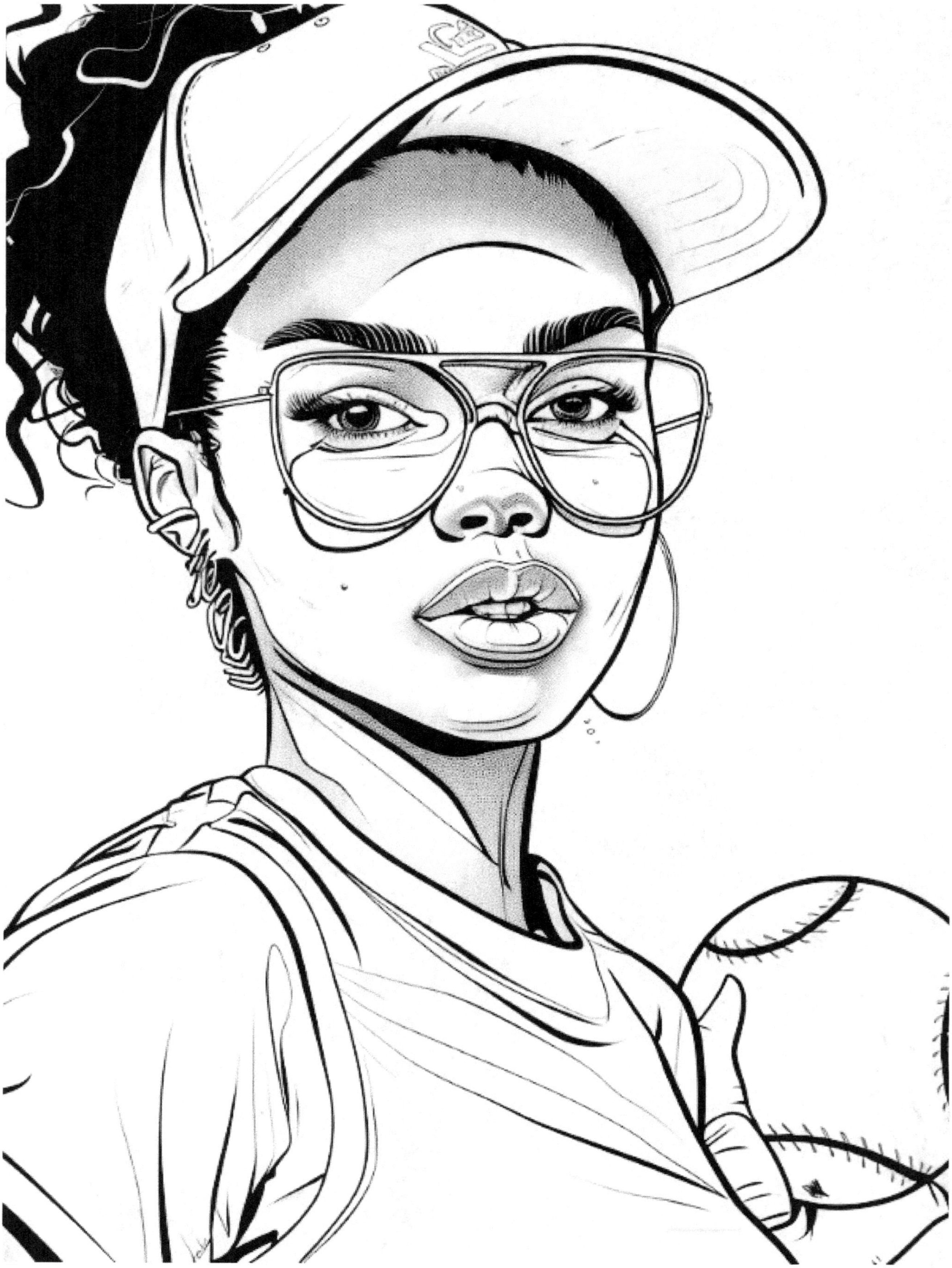

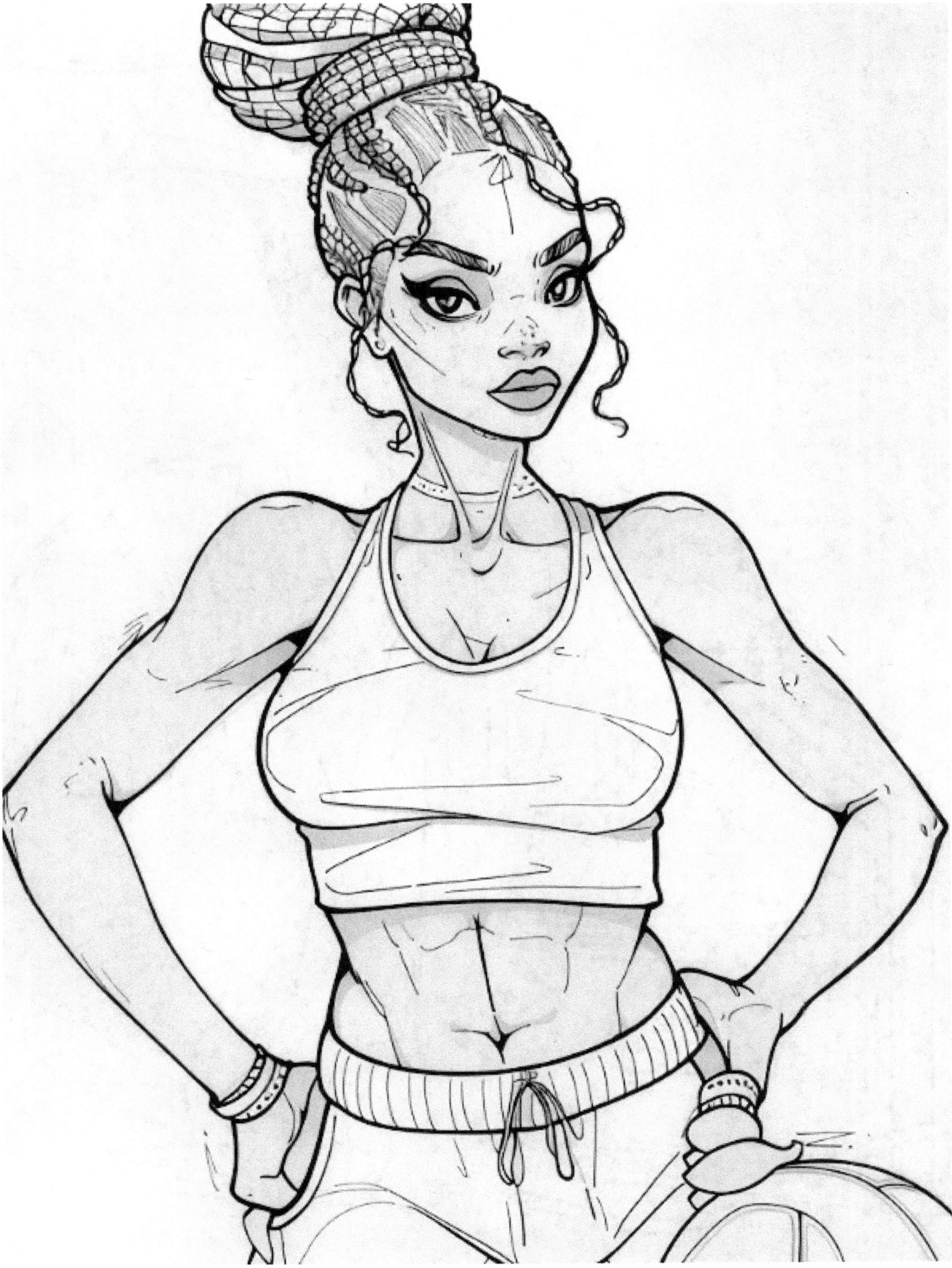

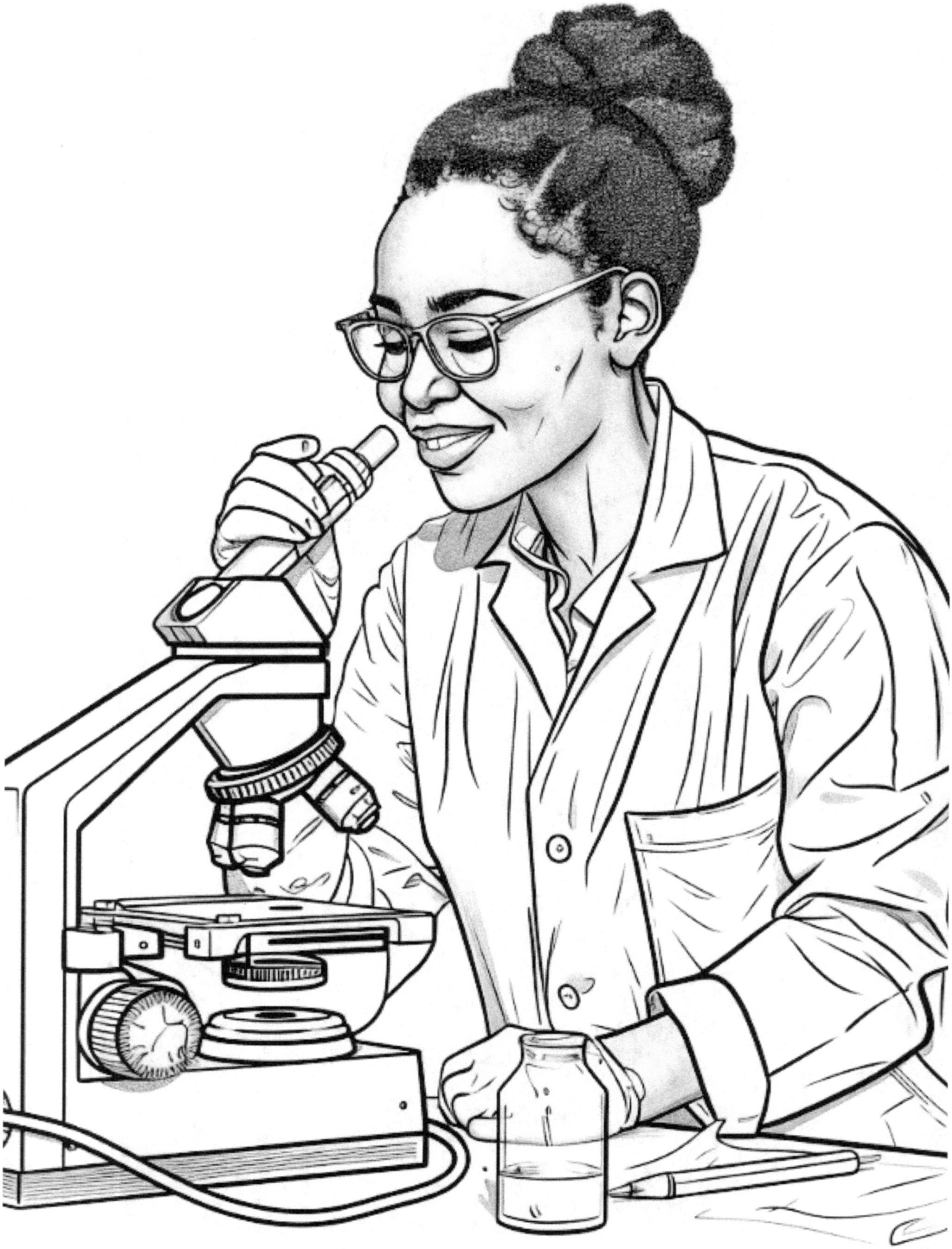

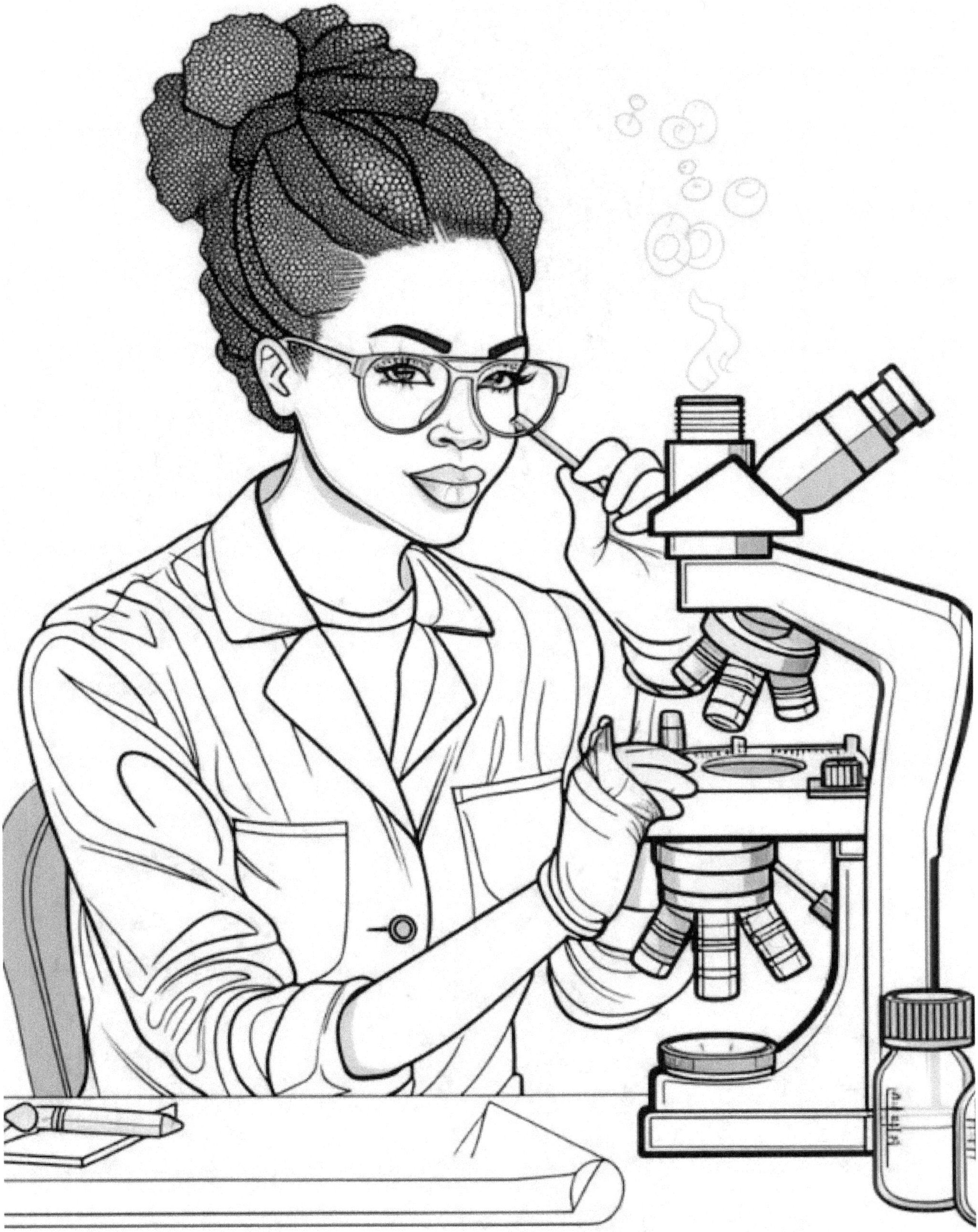

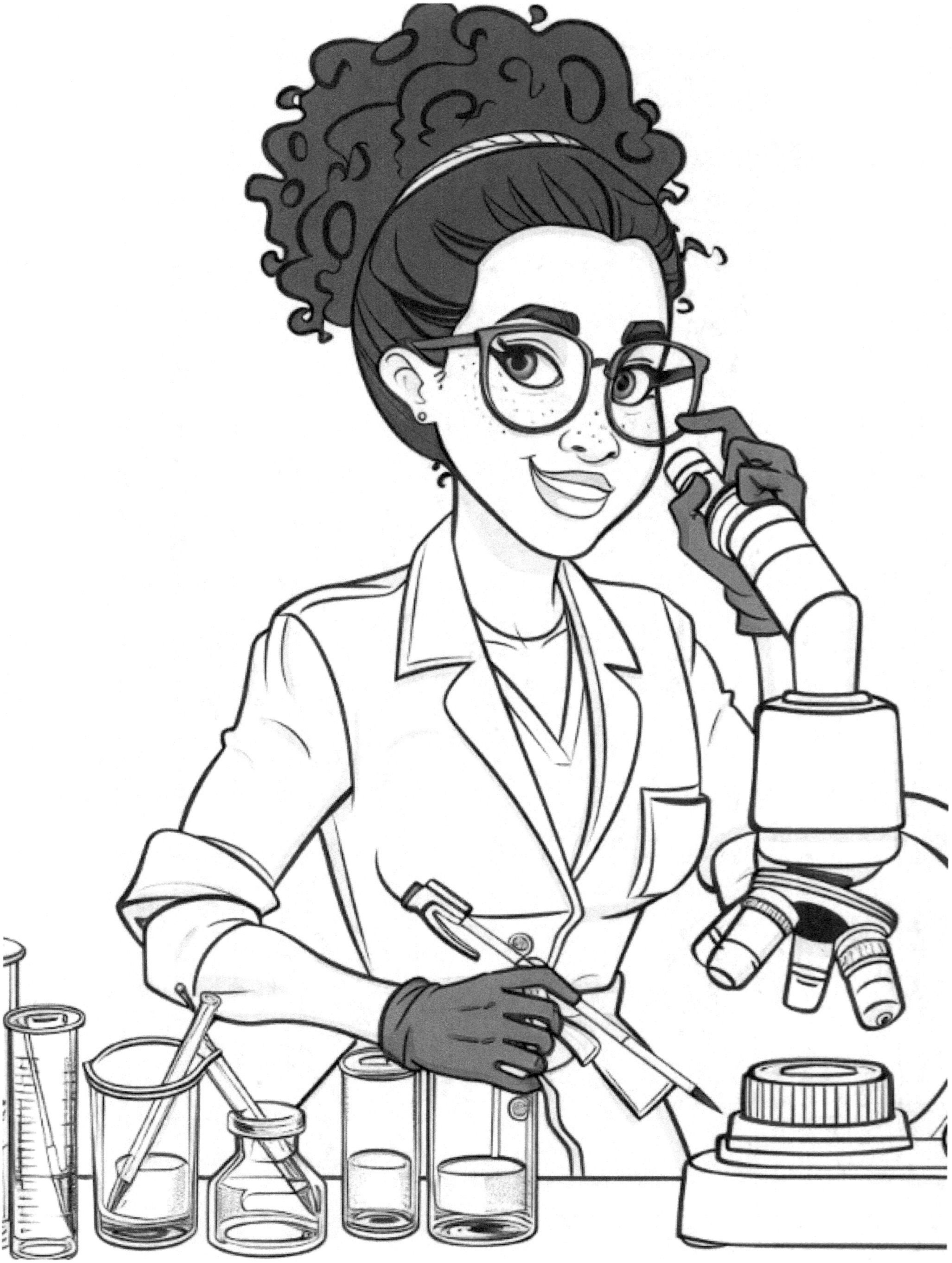

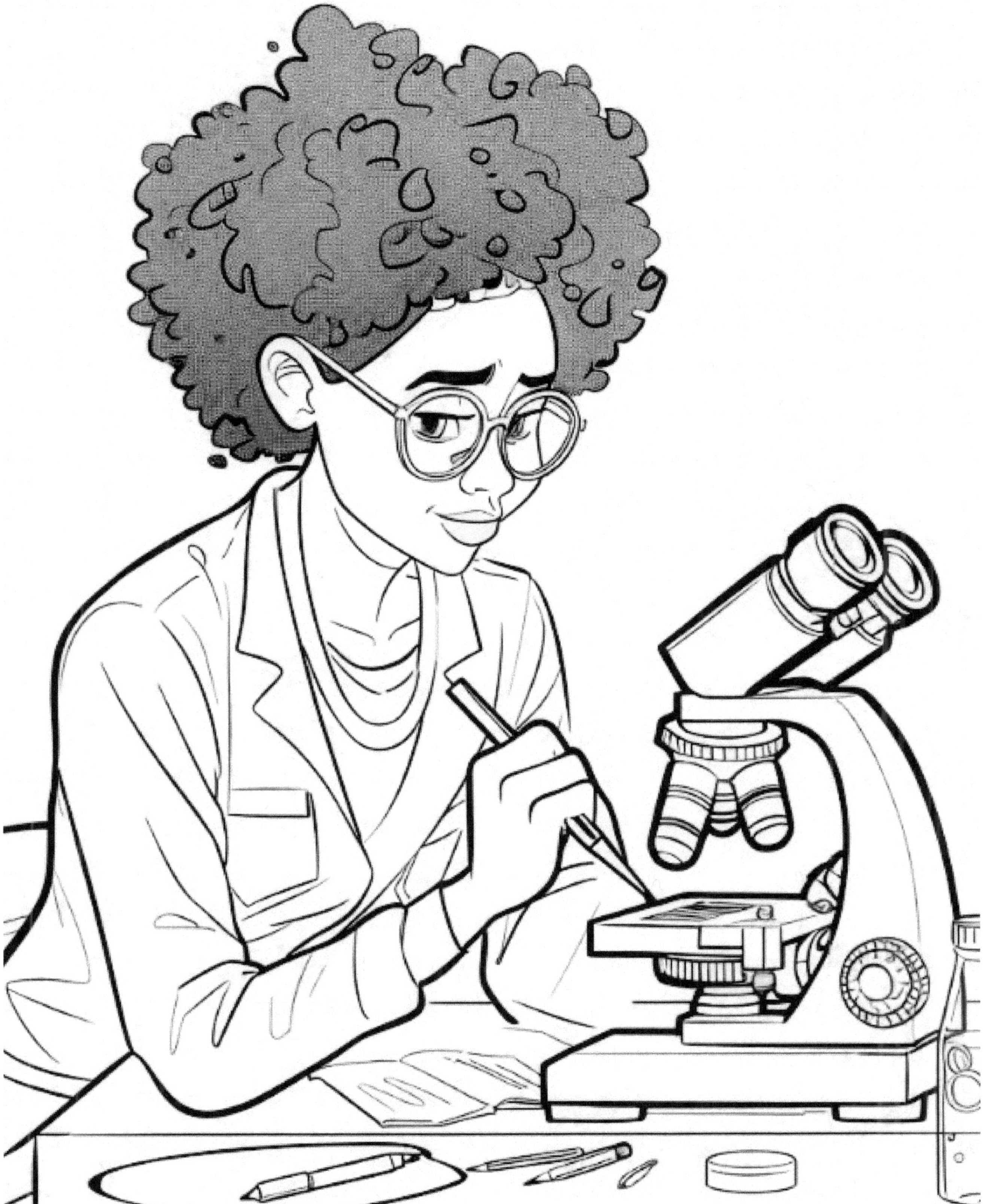

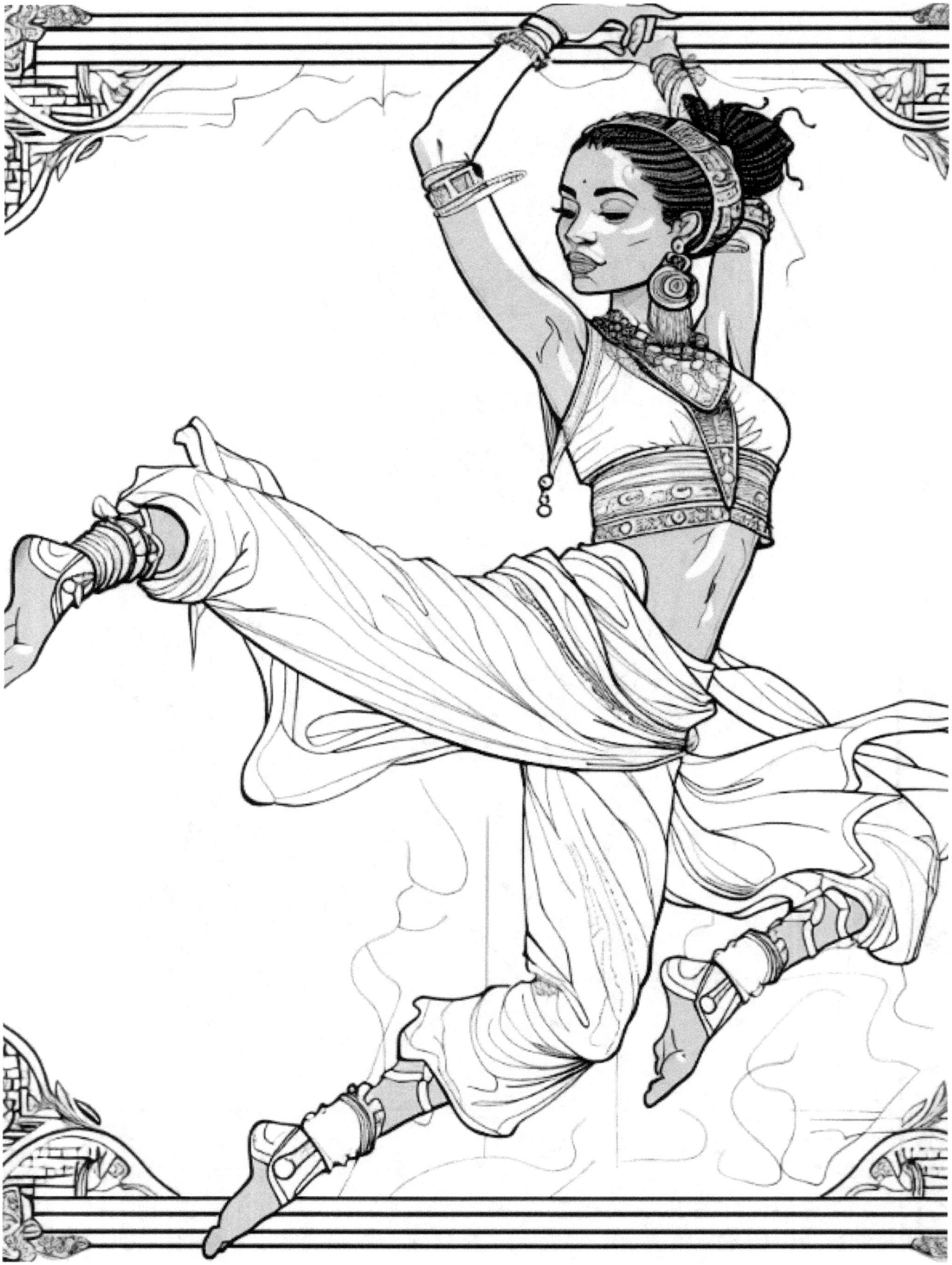

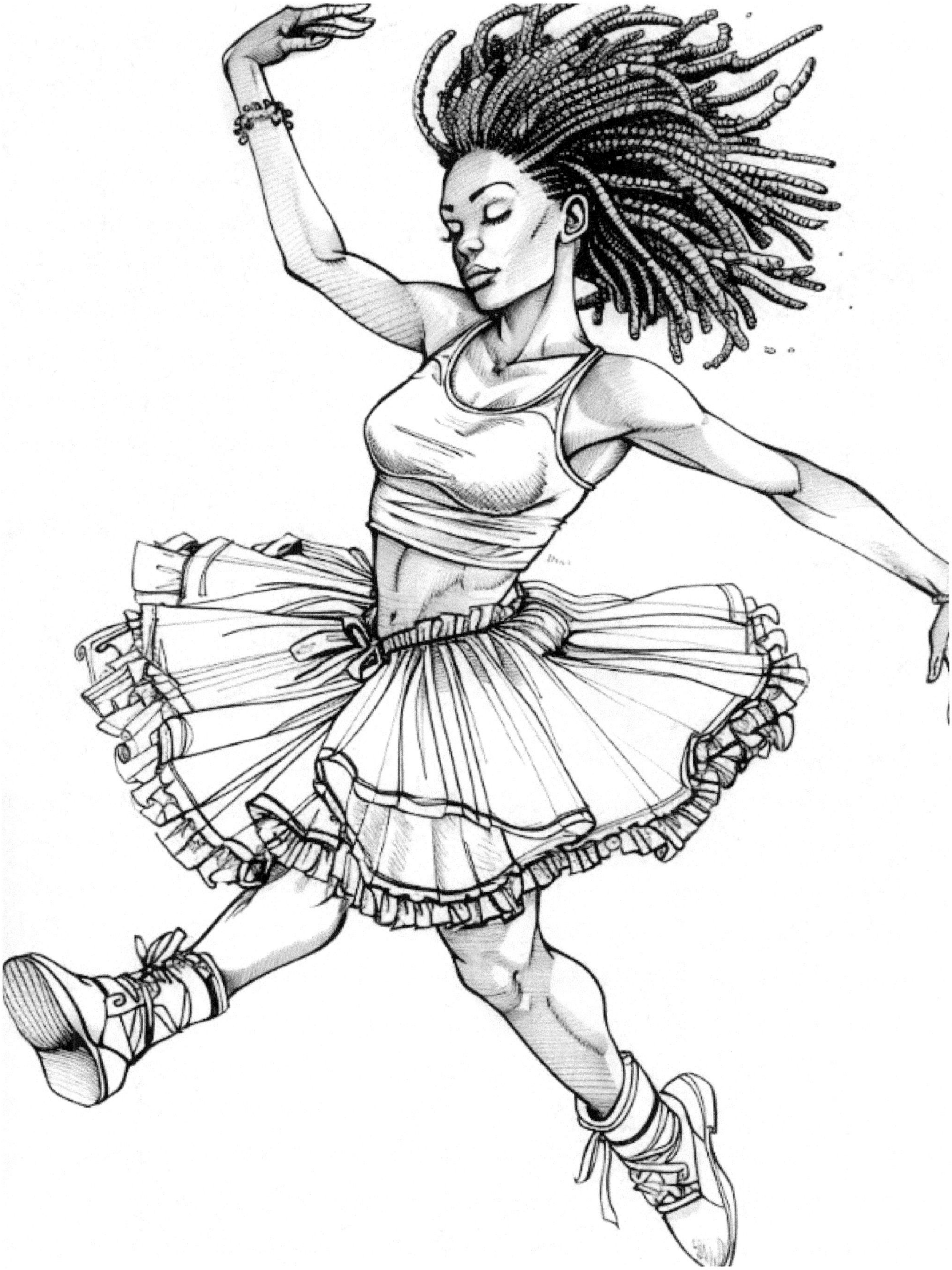

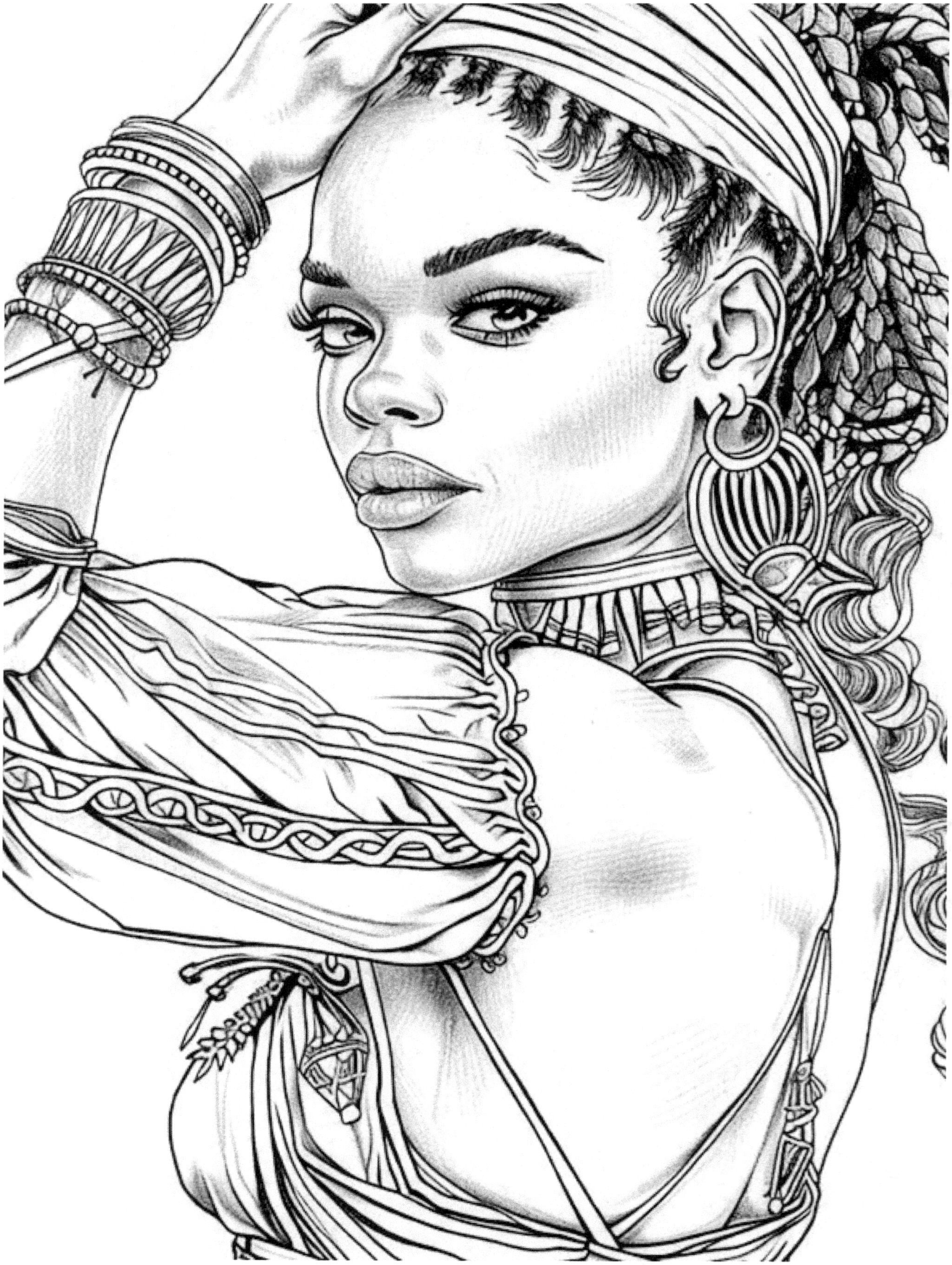

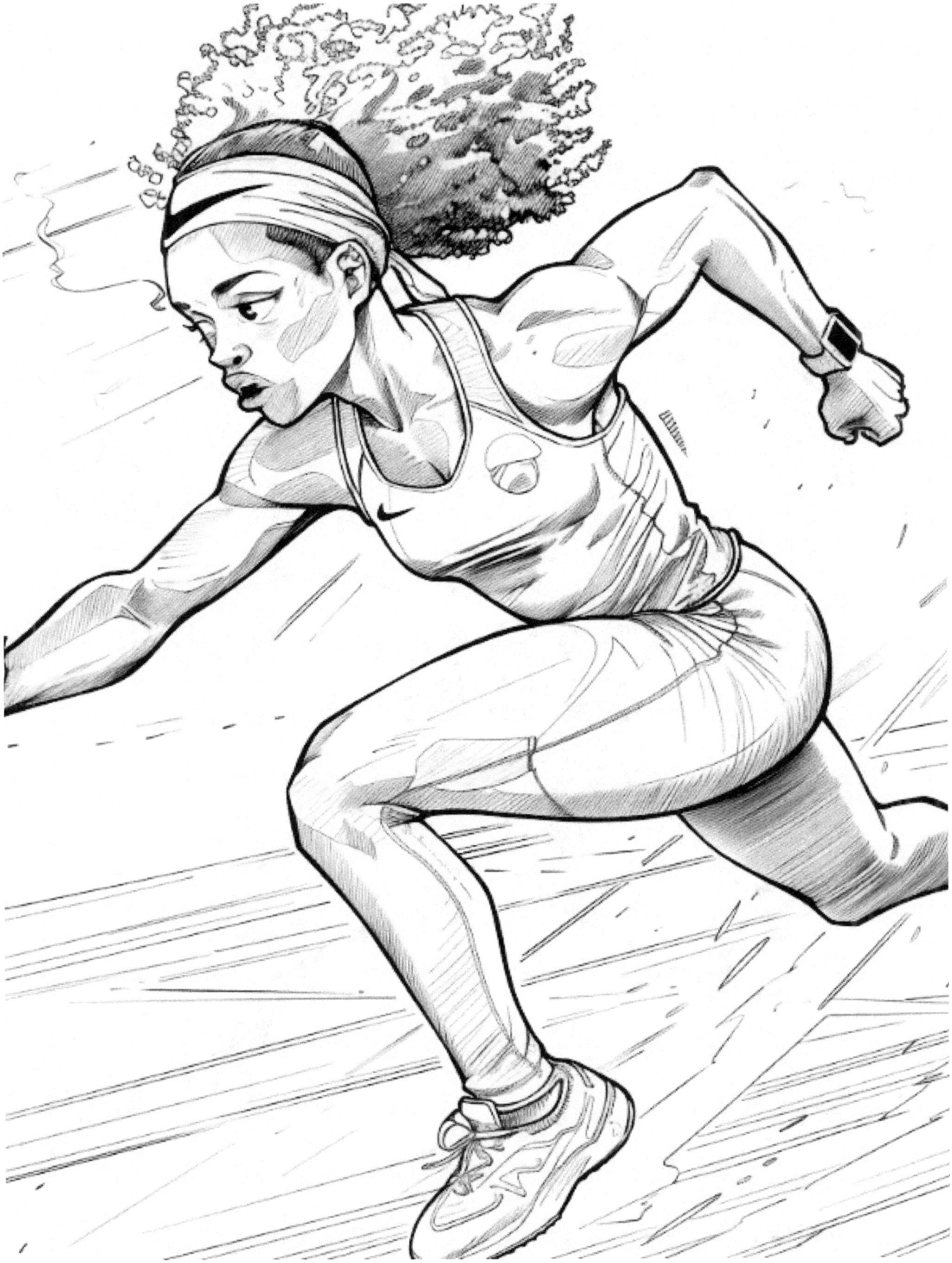

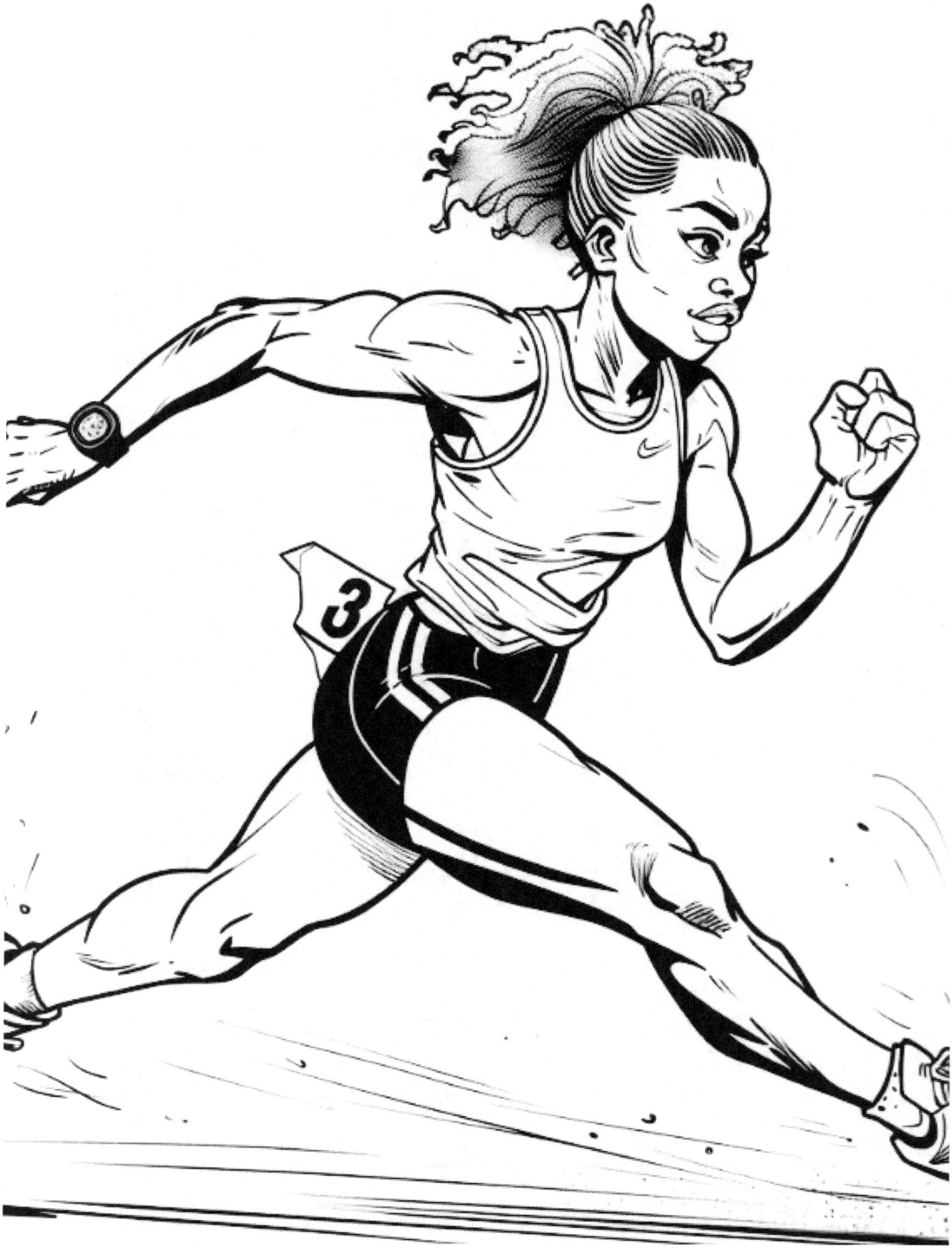
3

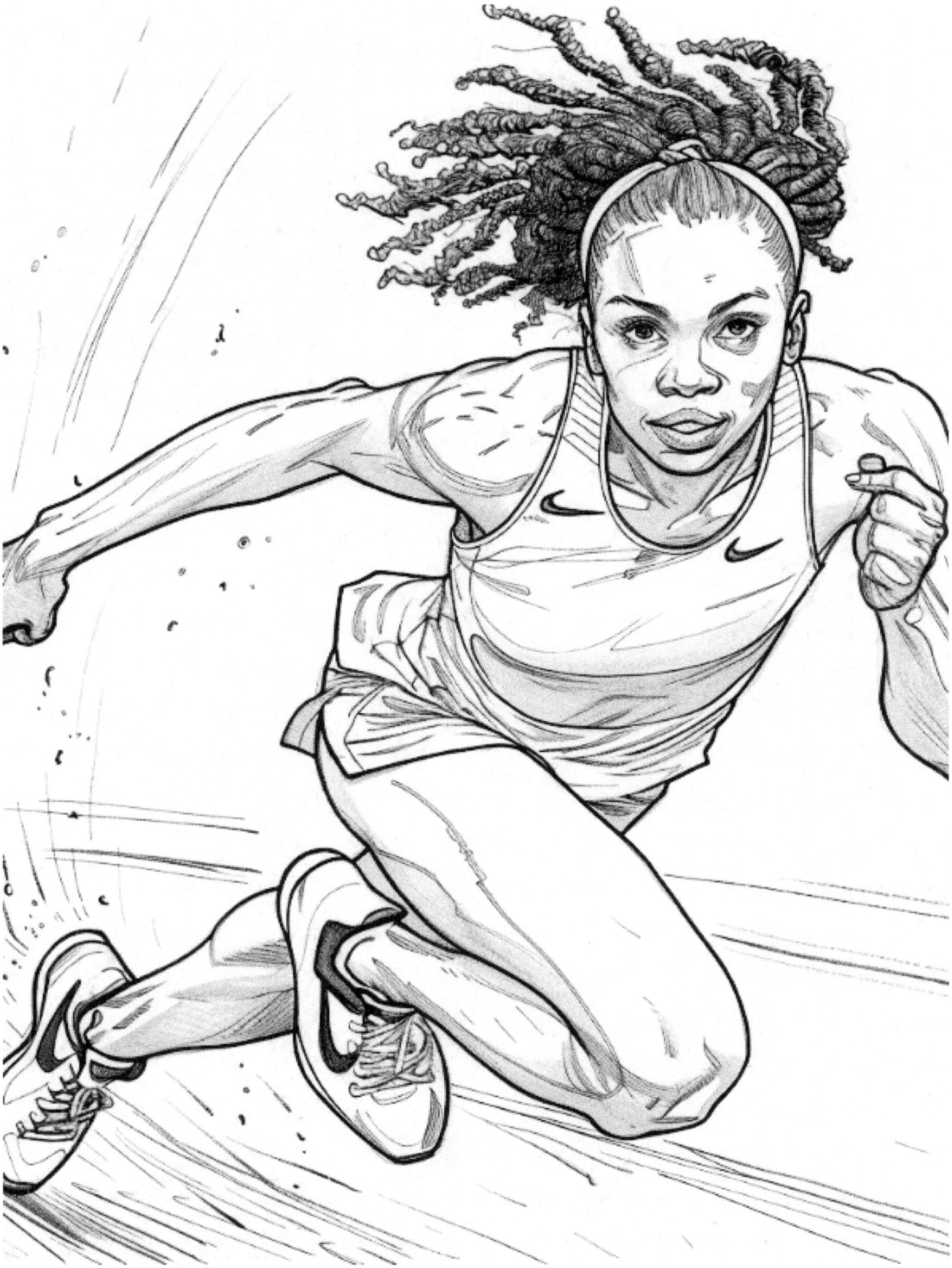

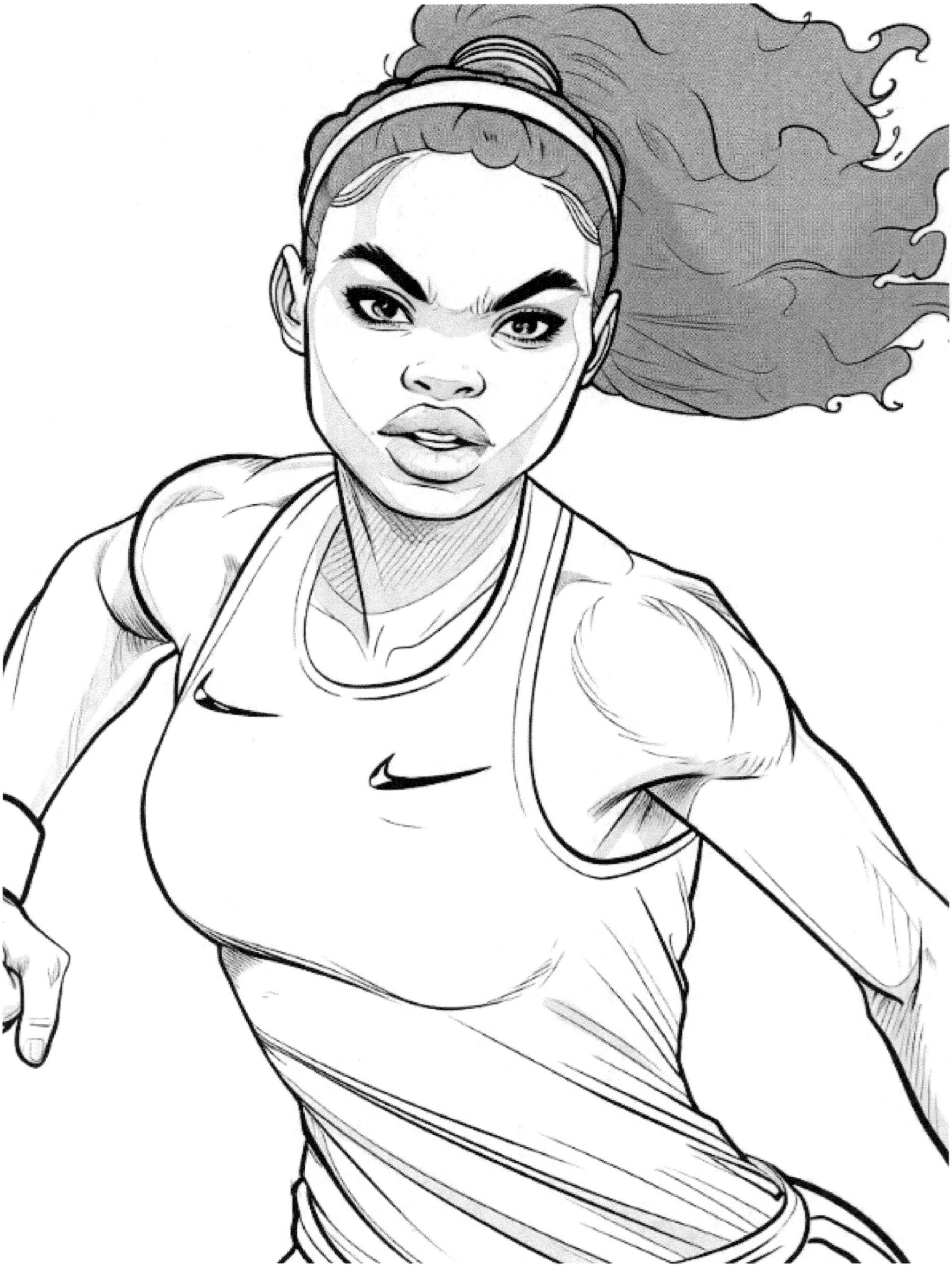

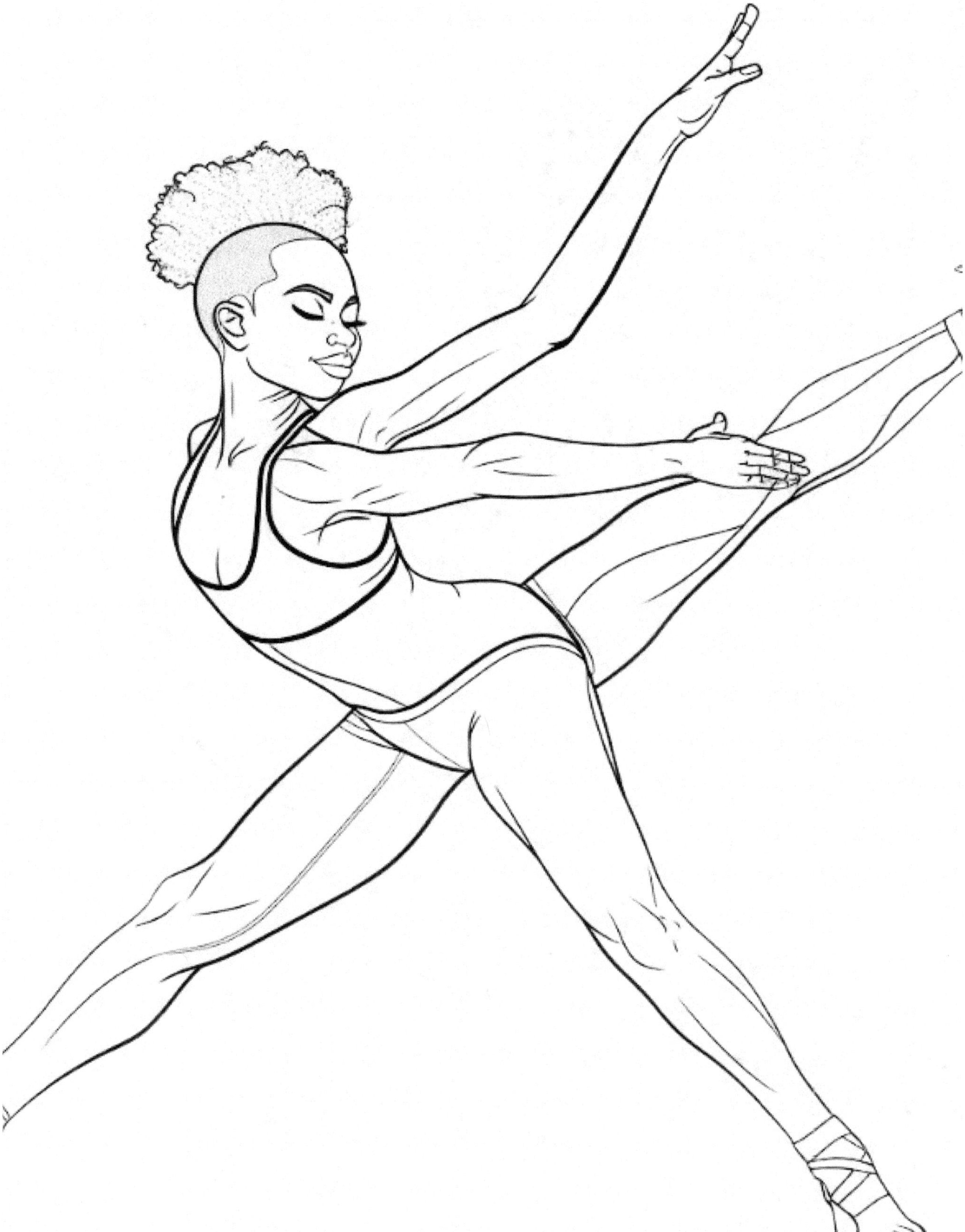

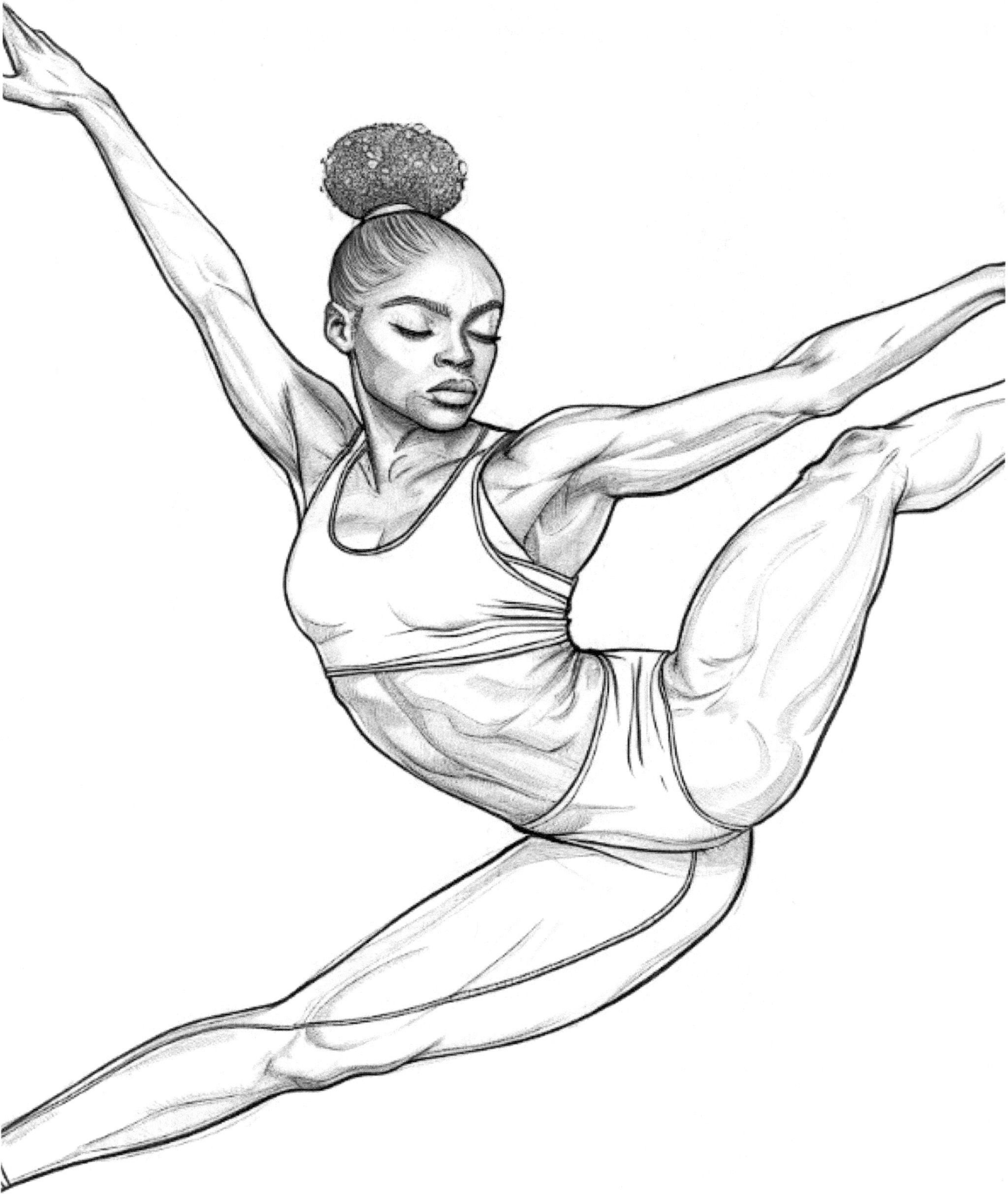

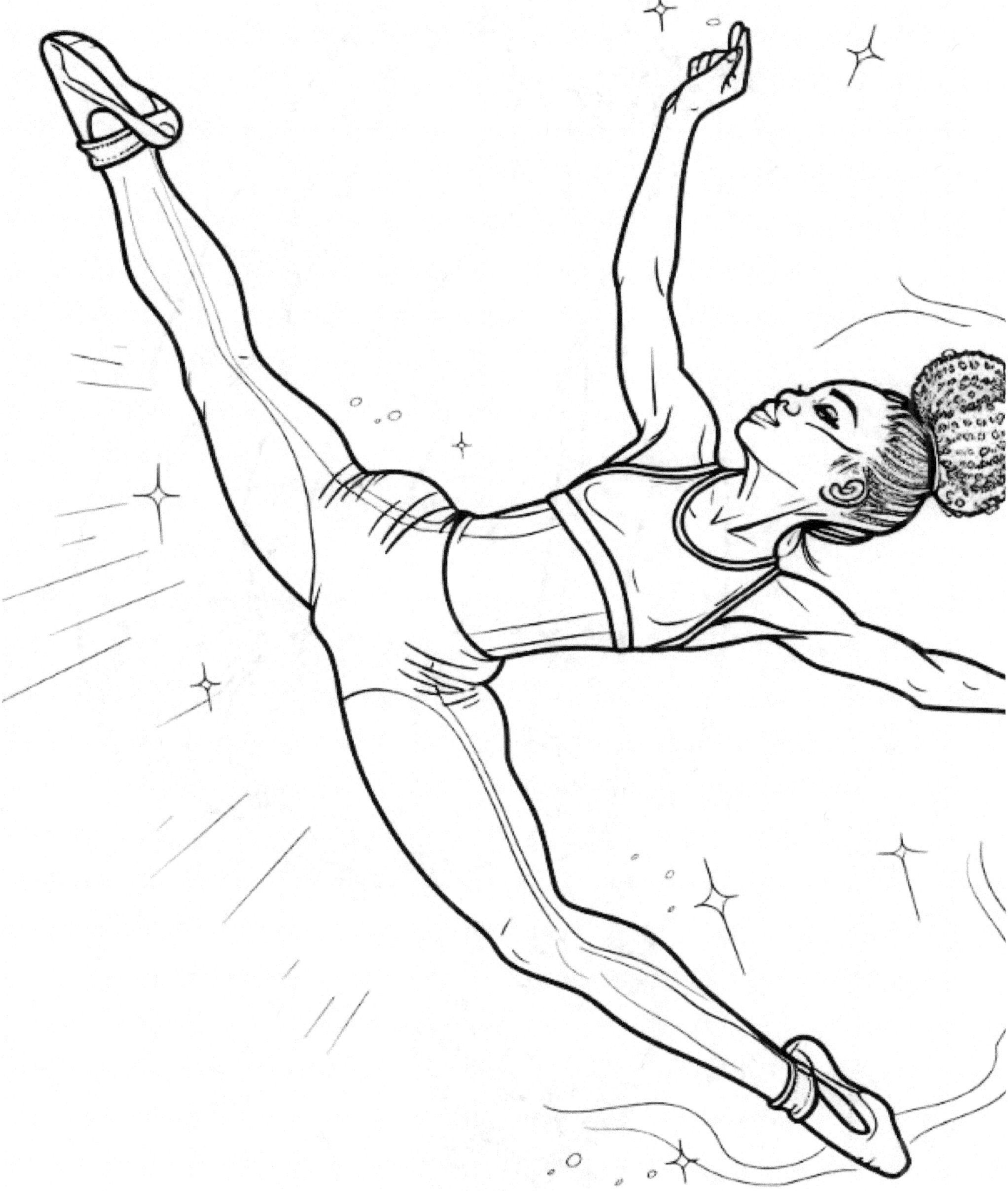

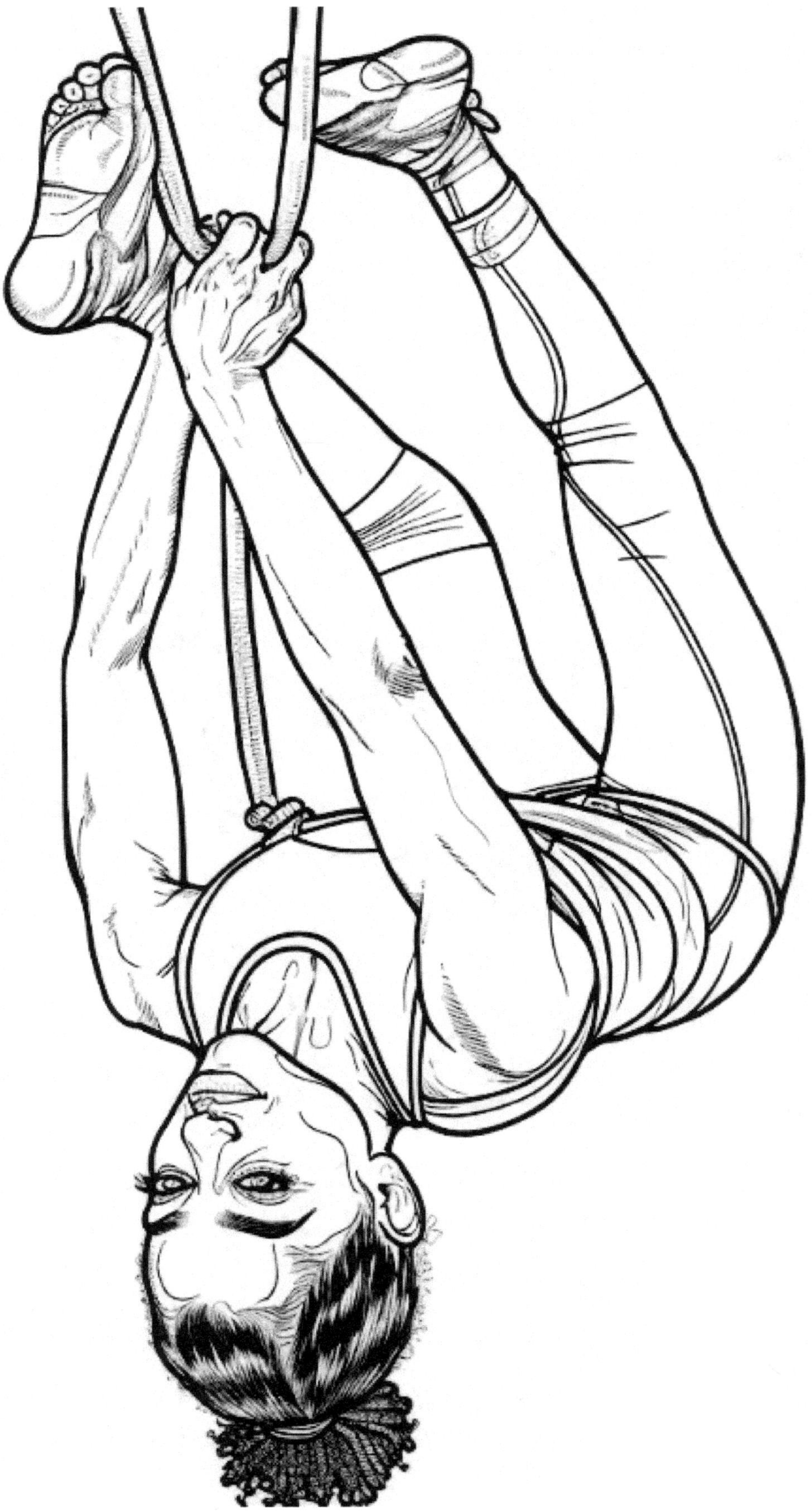

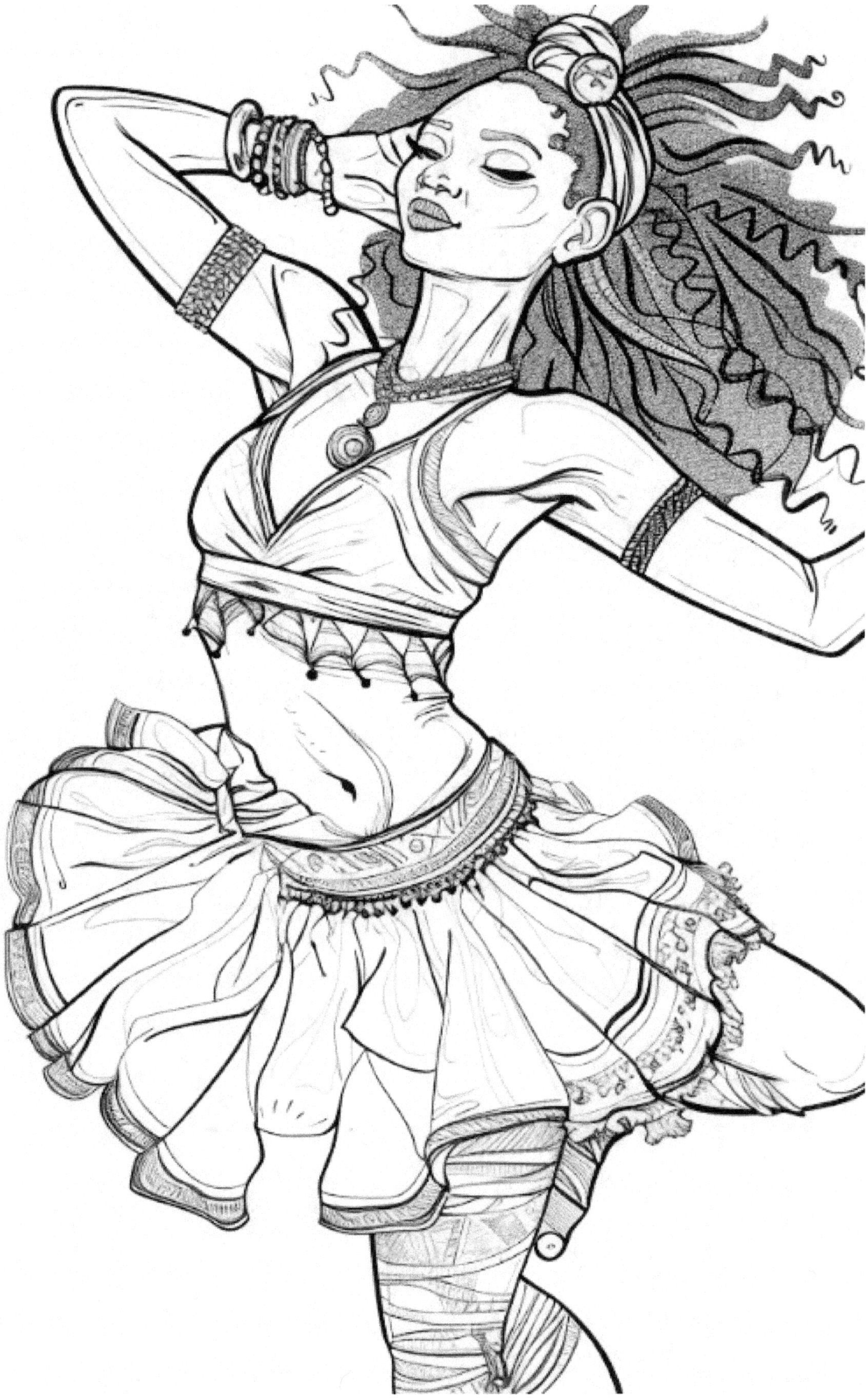

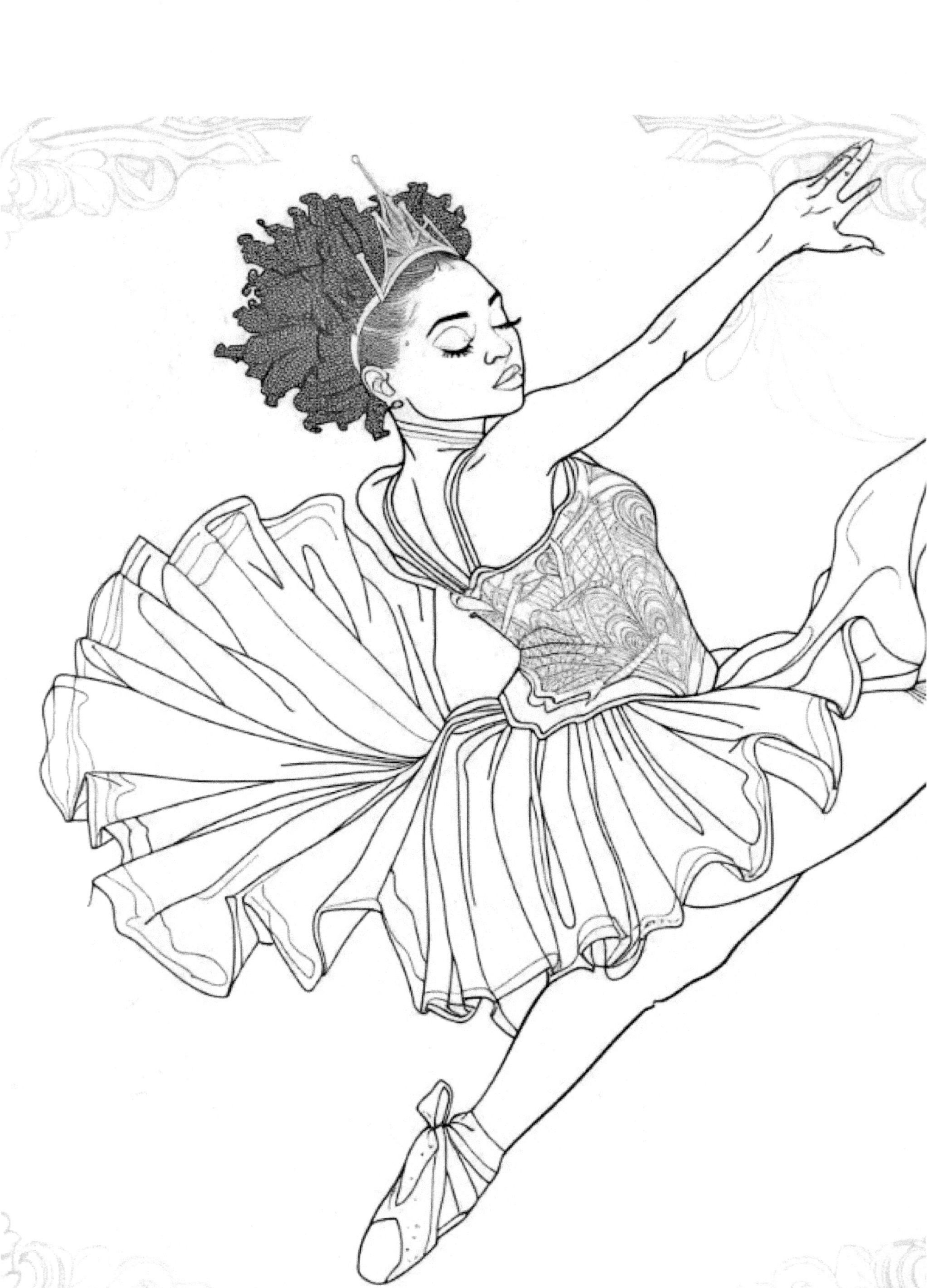

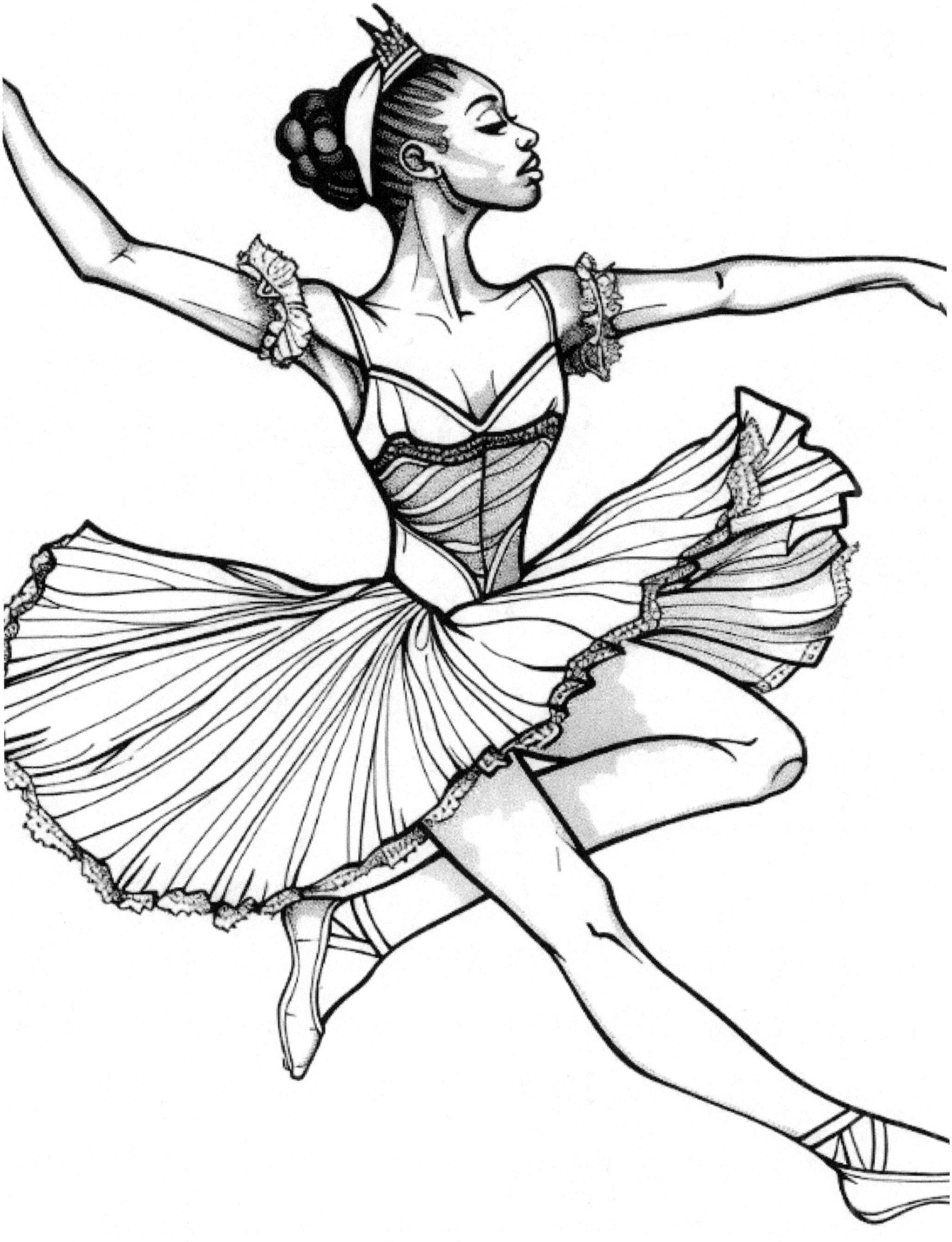

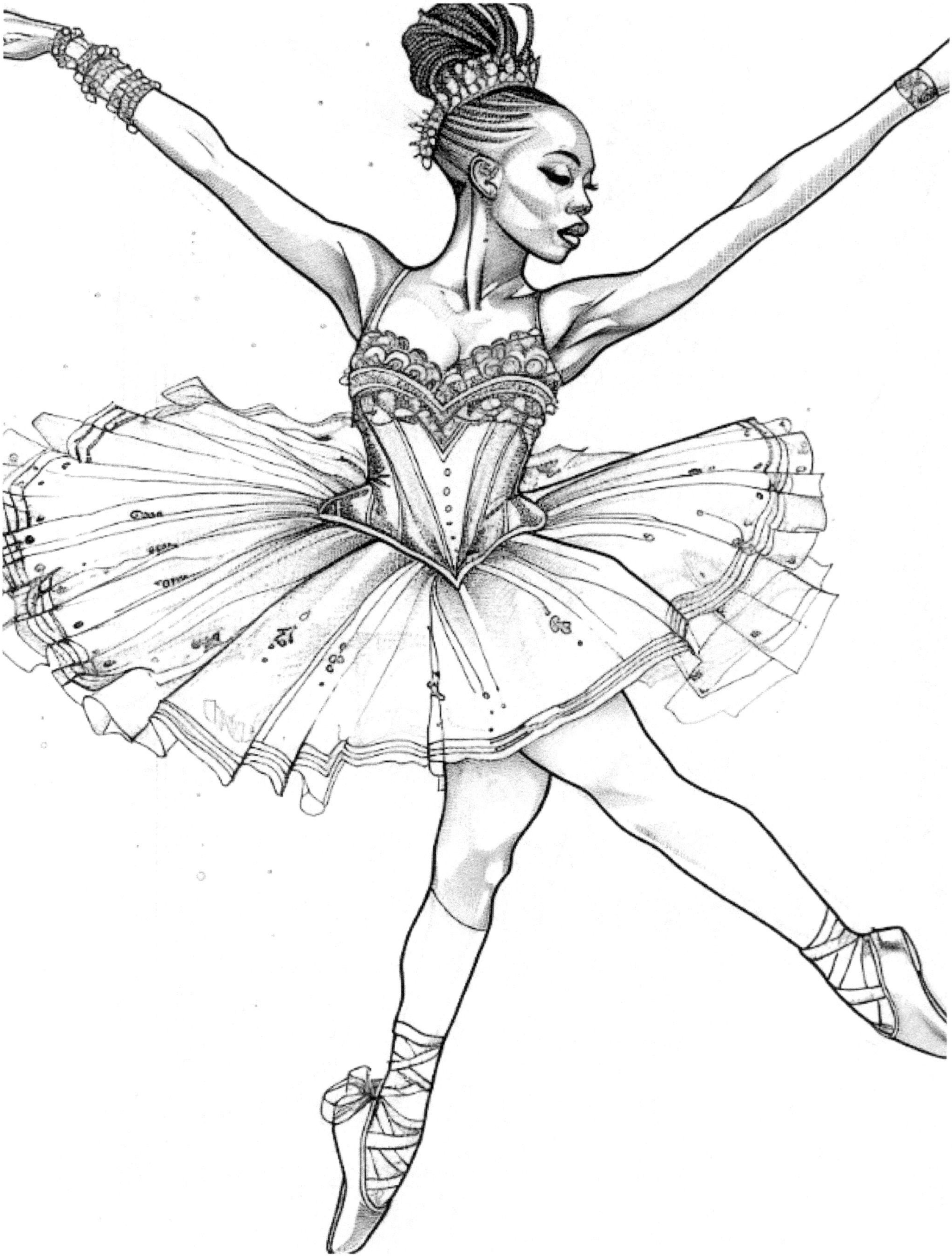

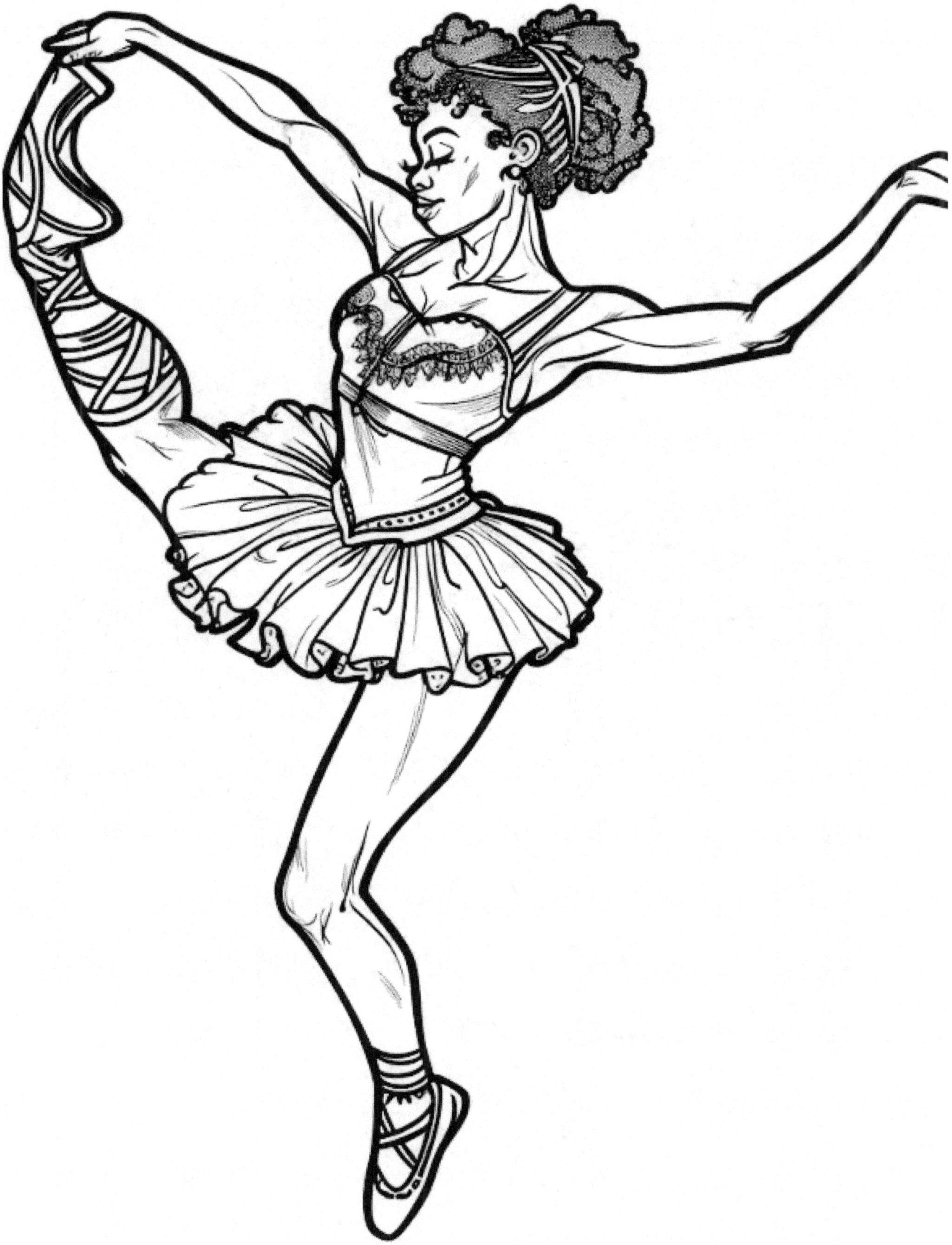

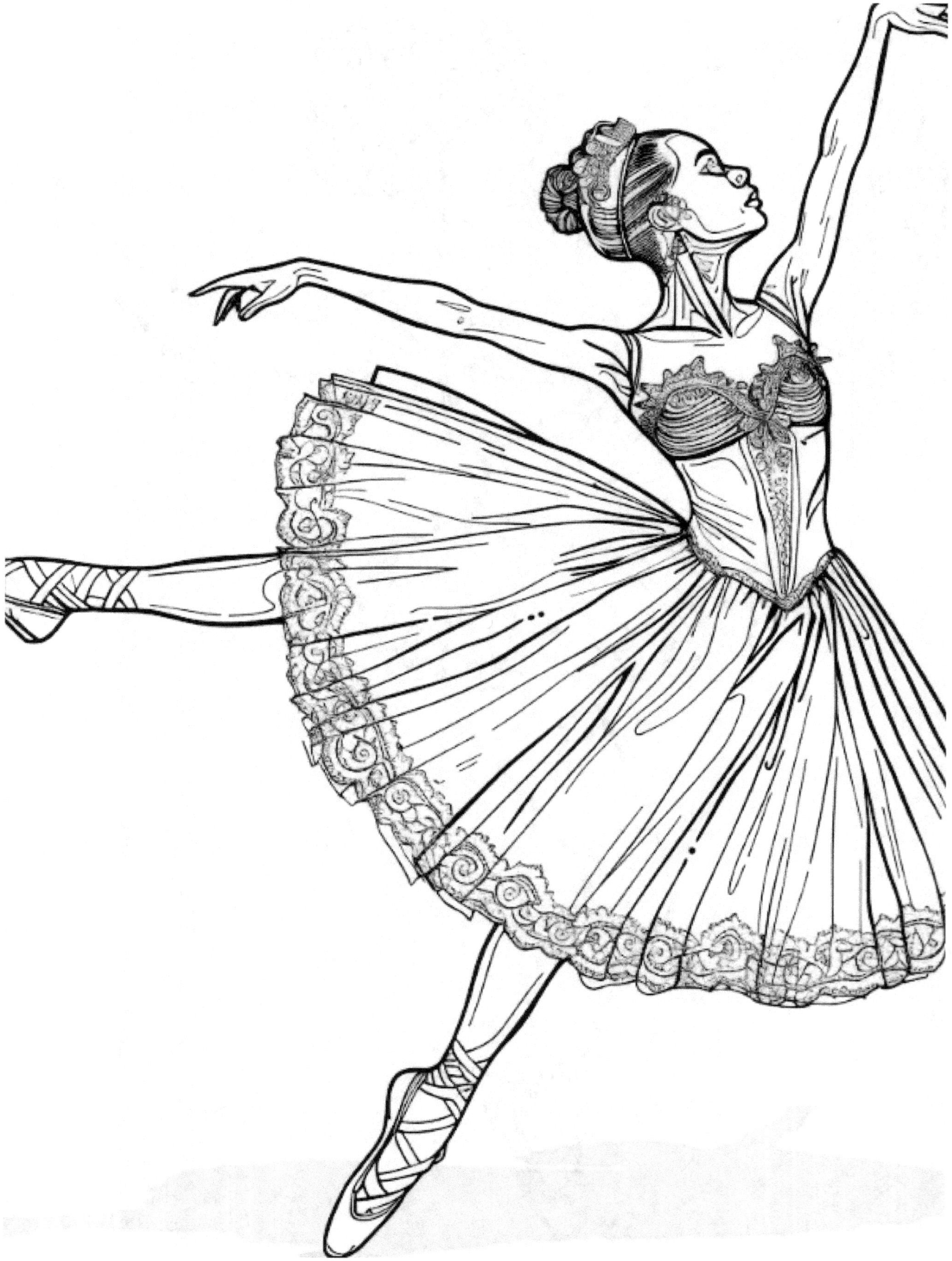

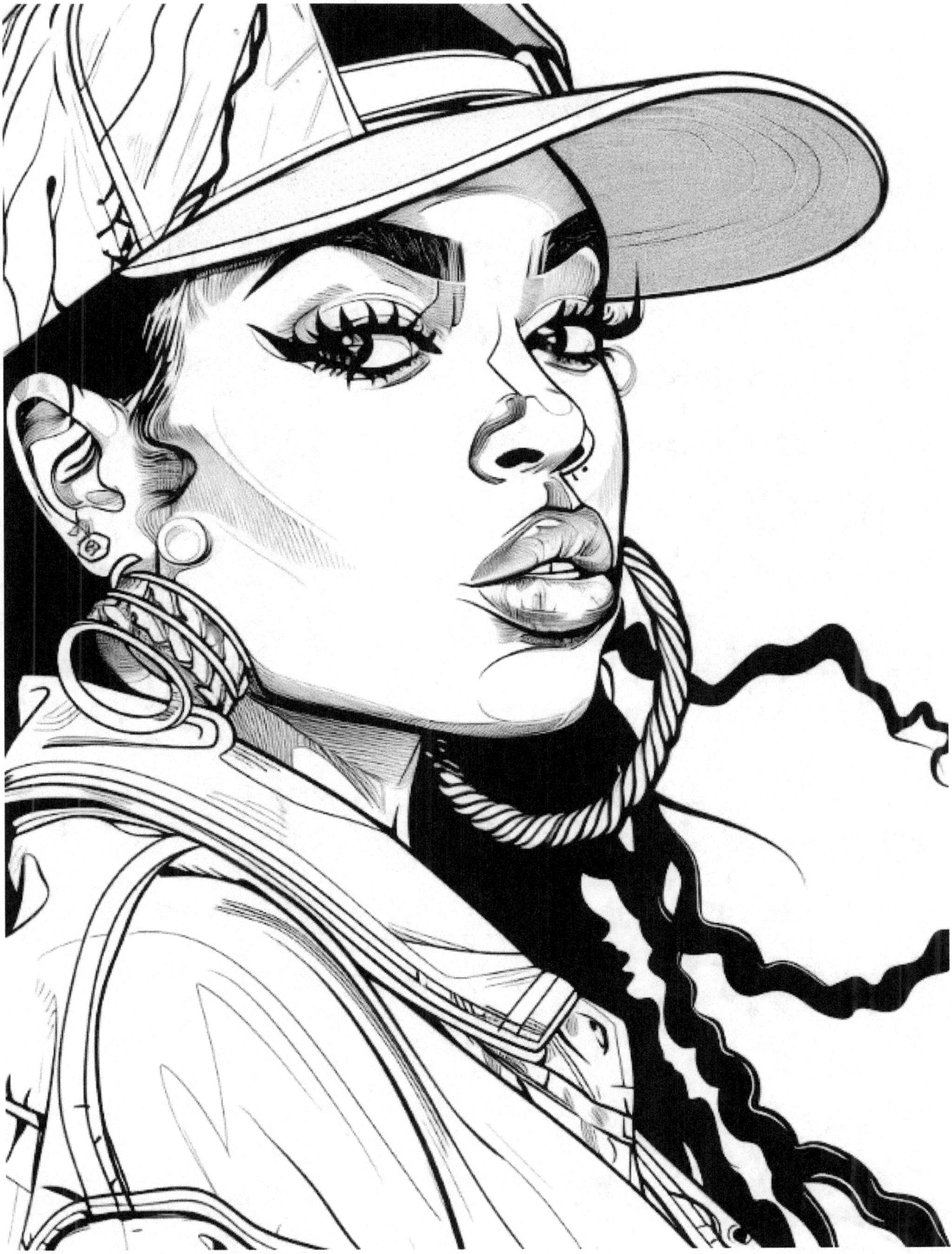

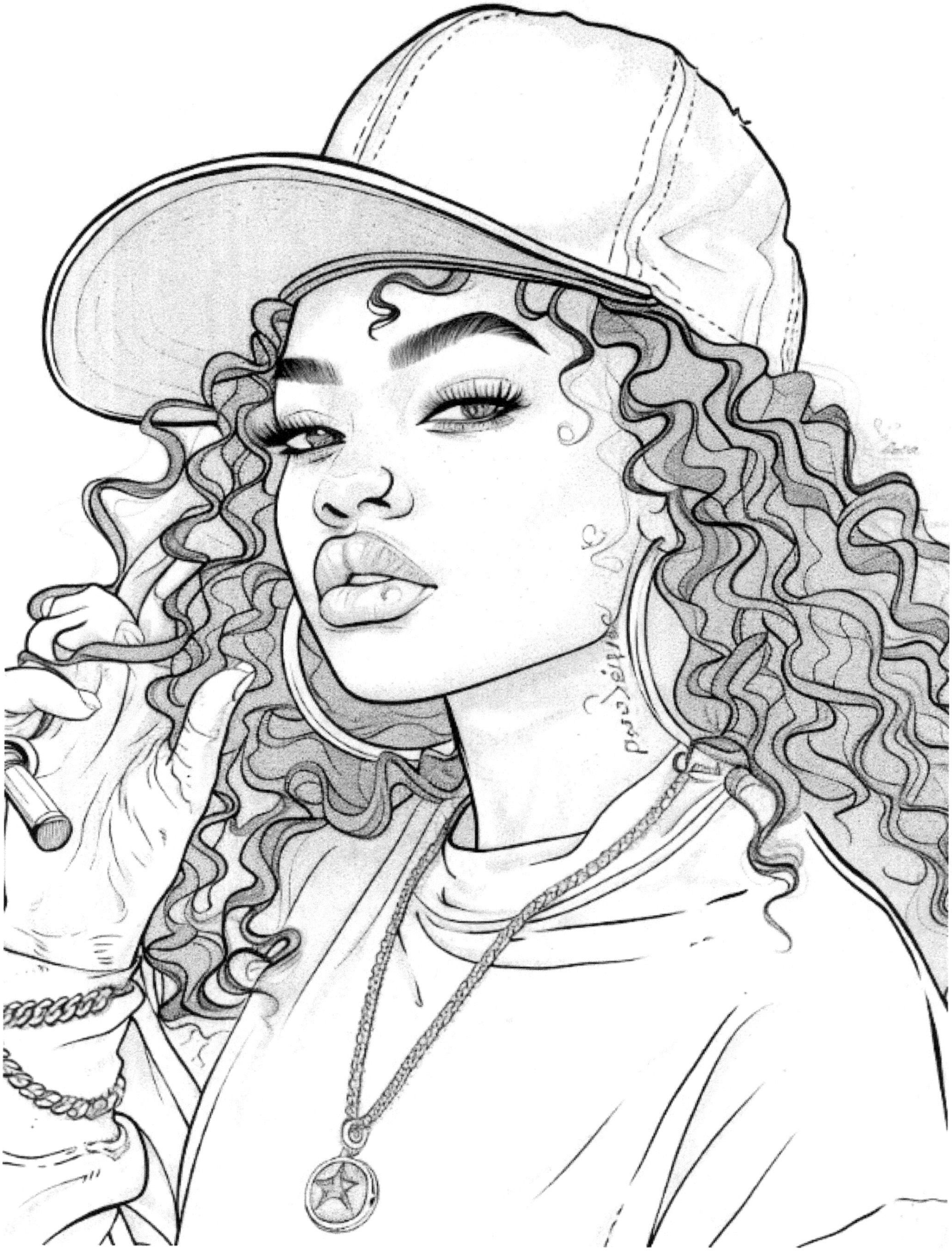

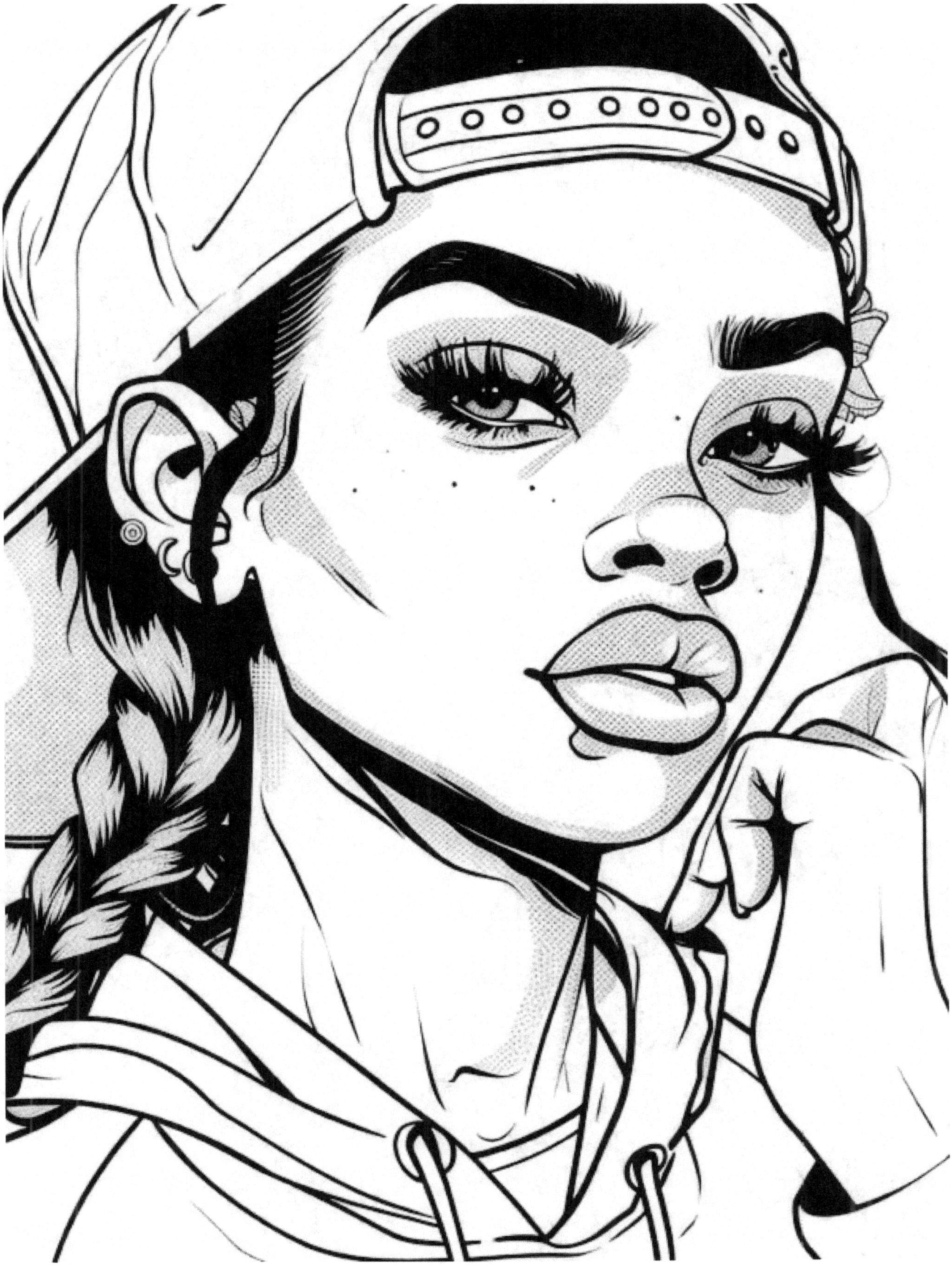

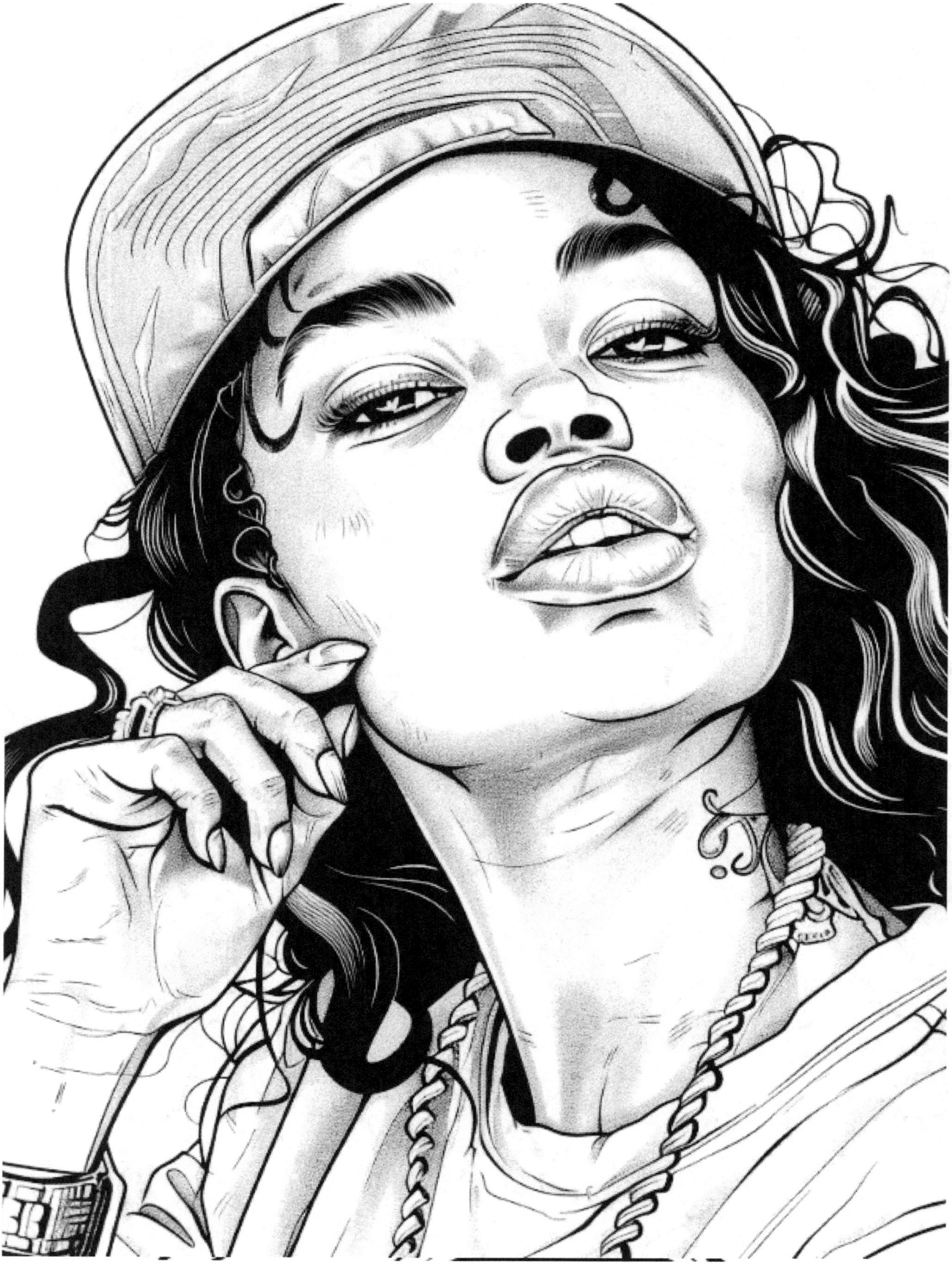

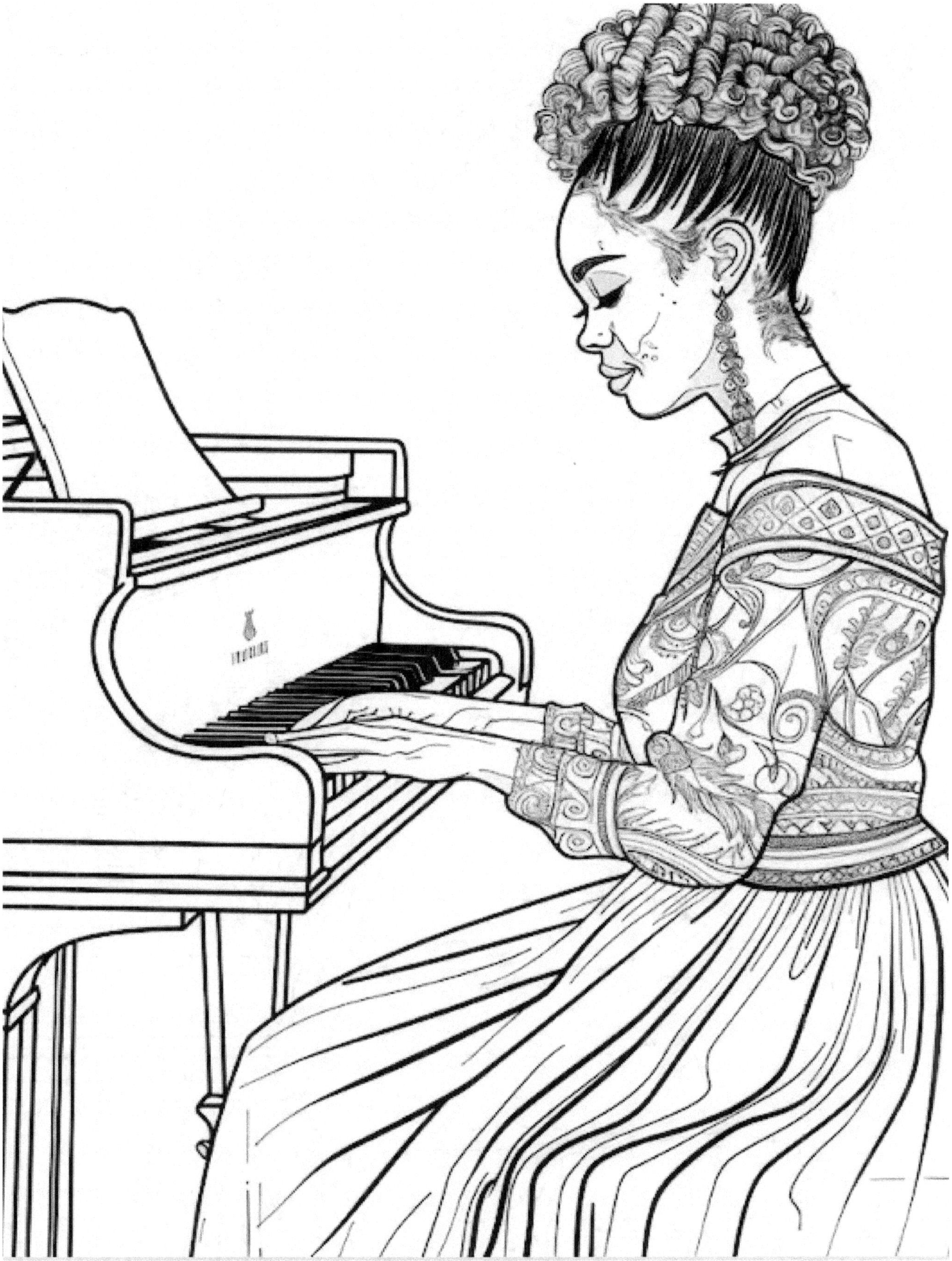

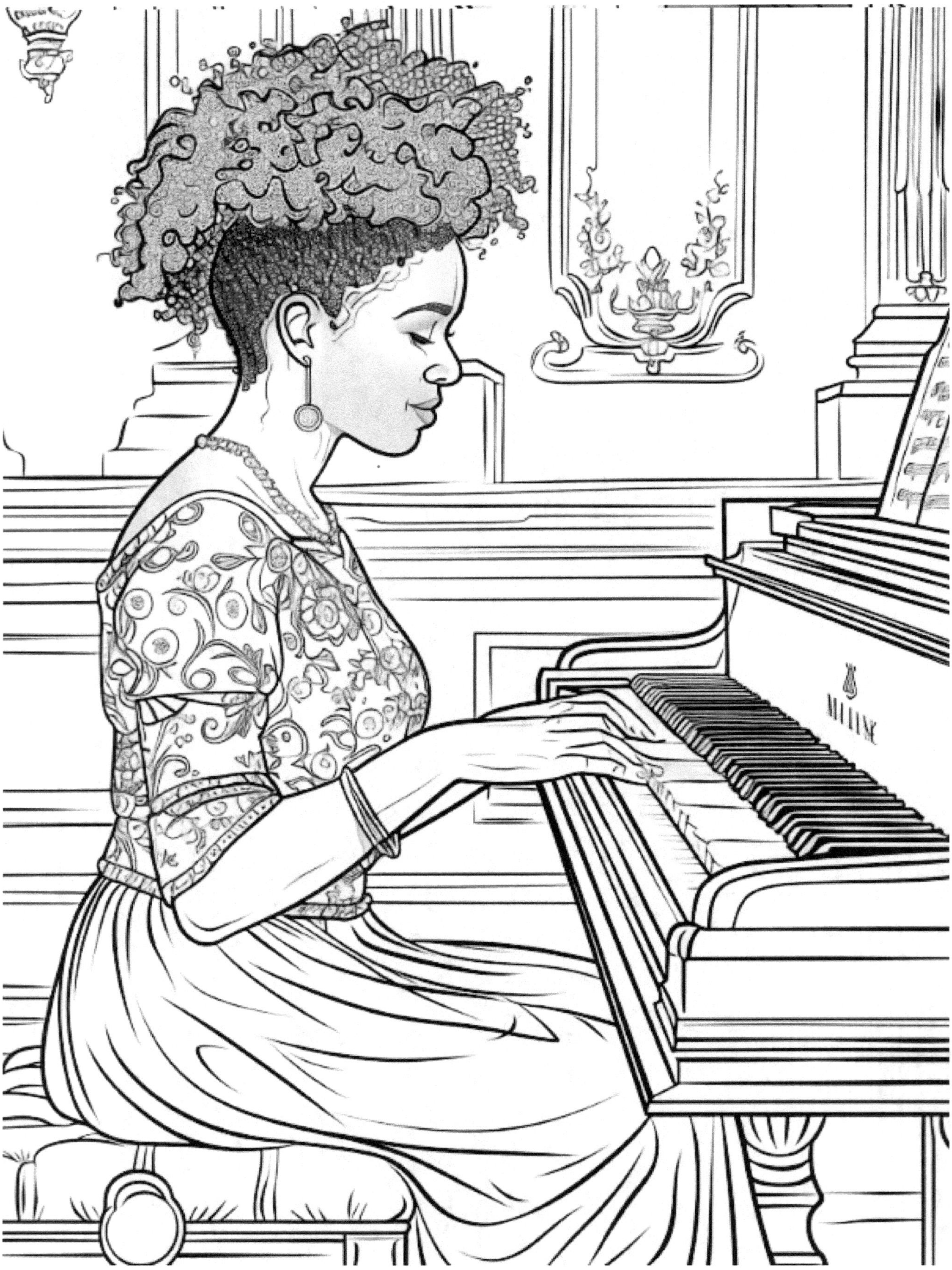

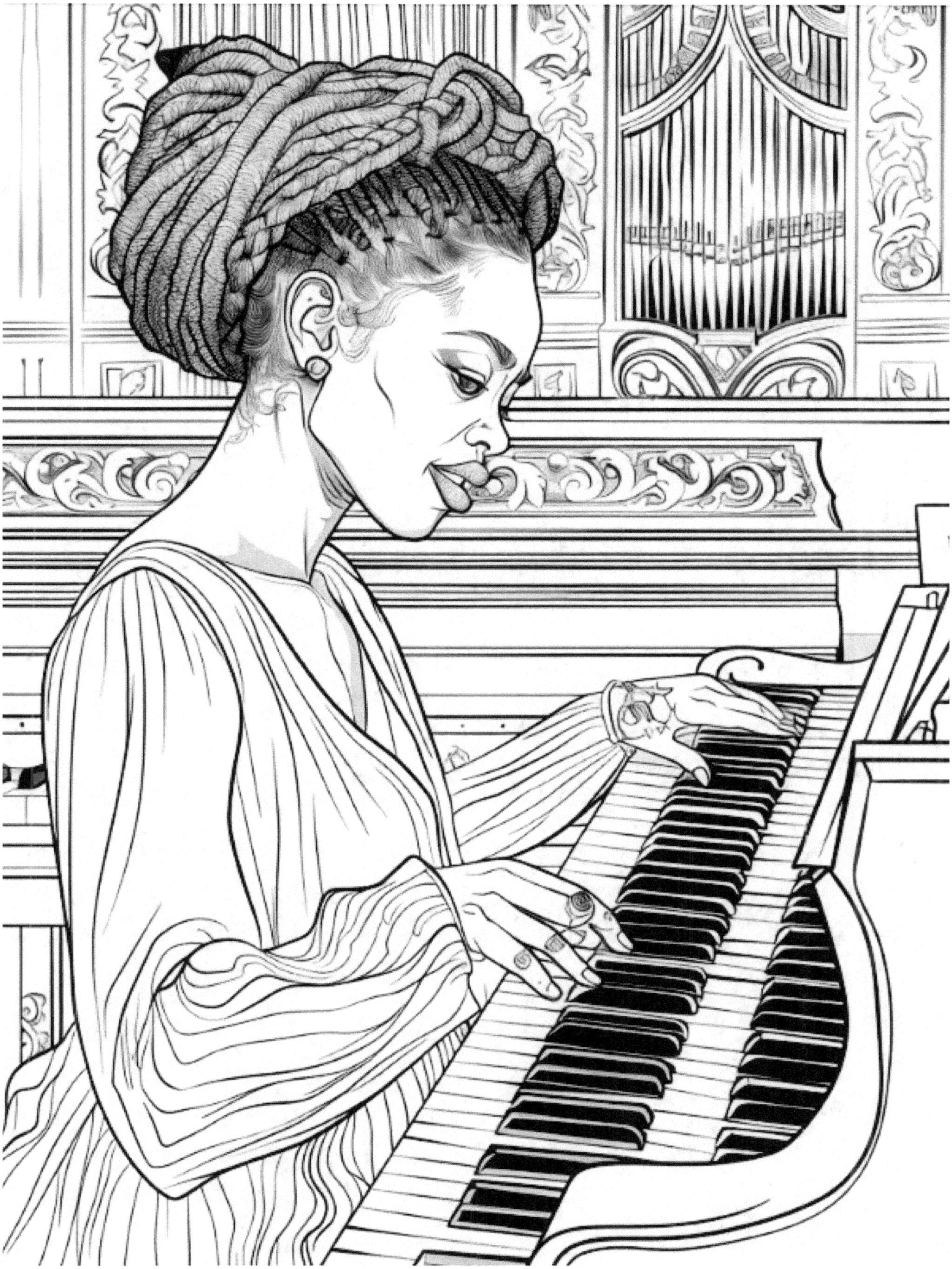

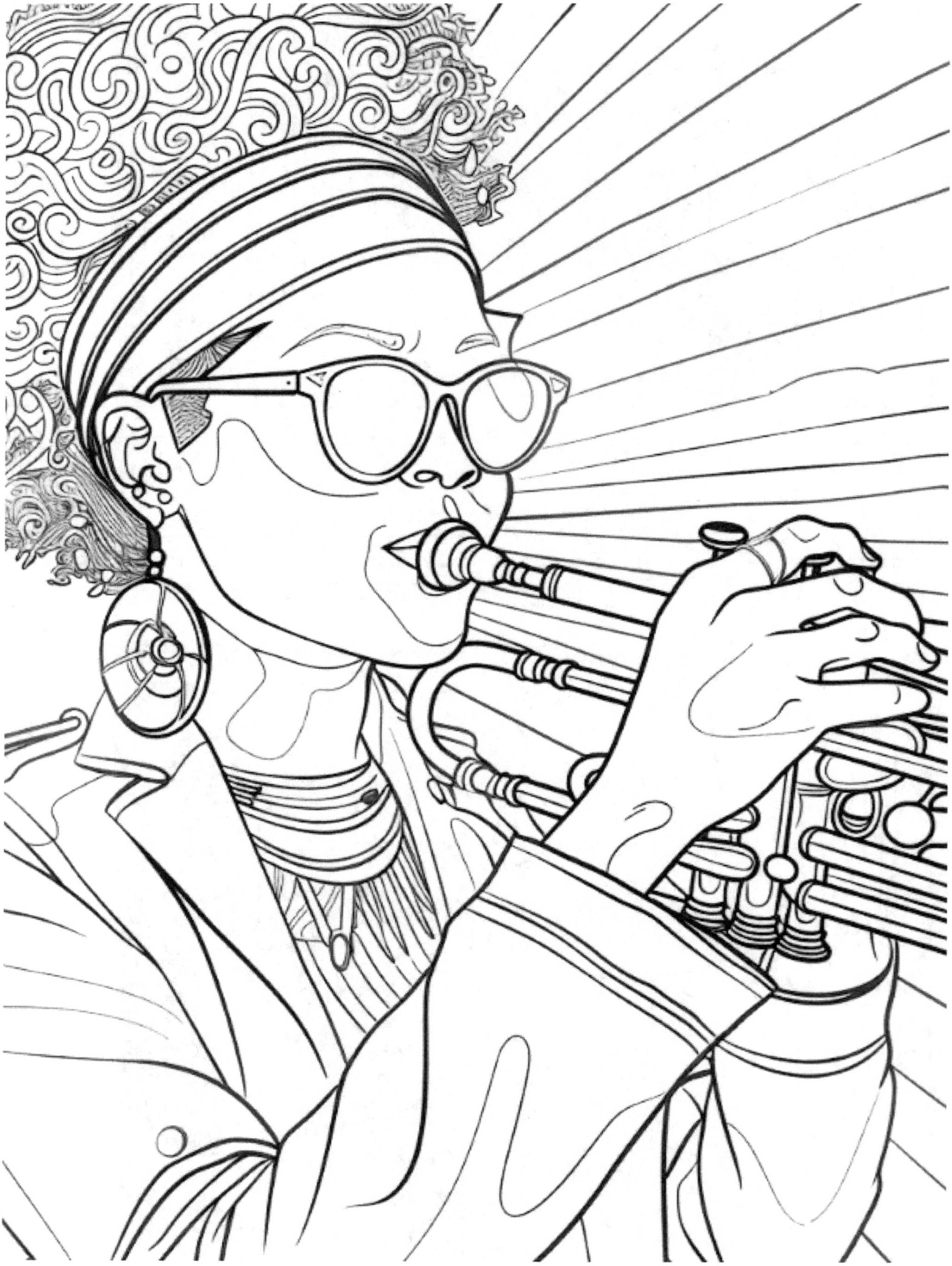

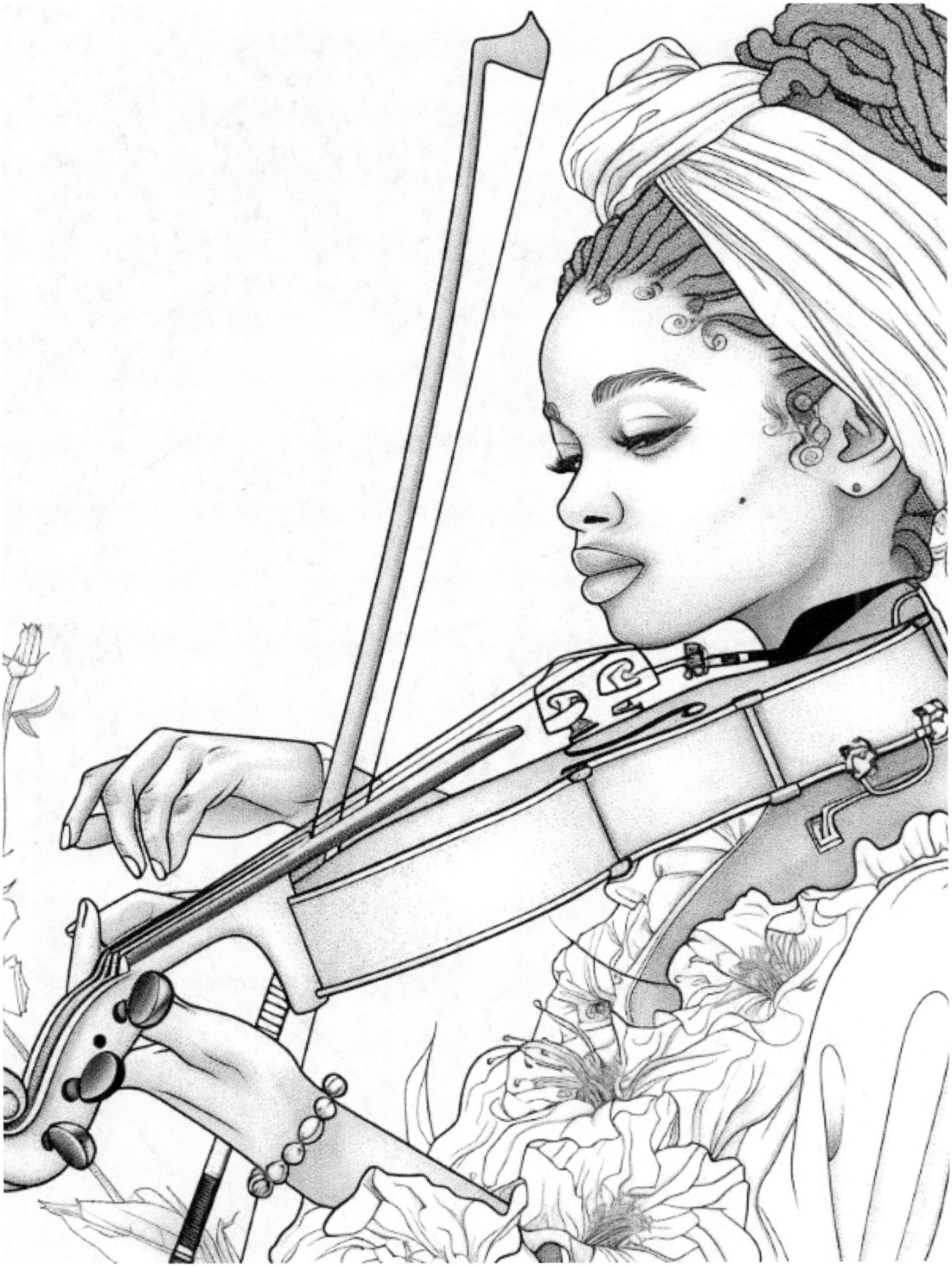

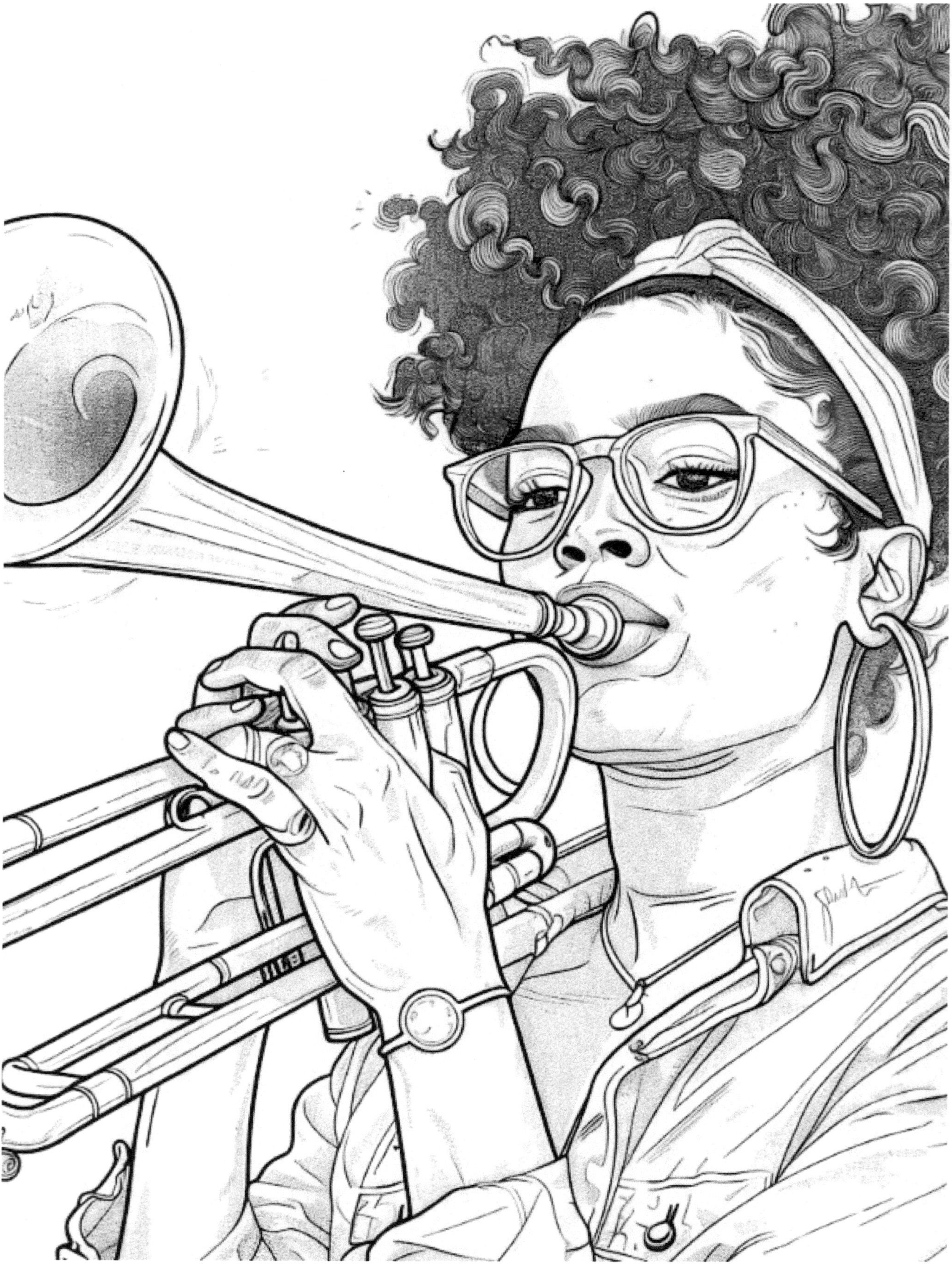

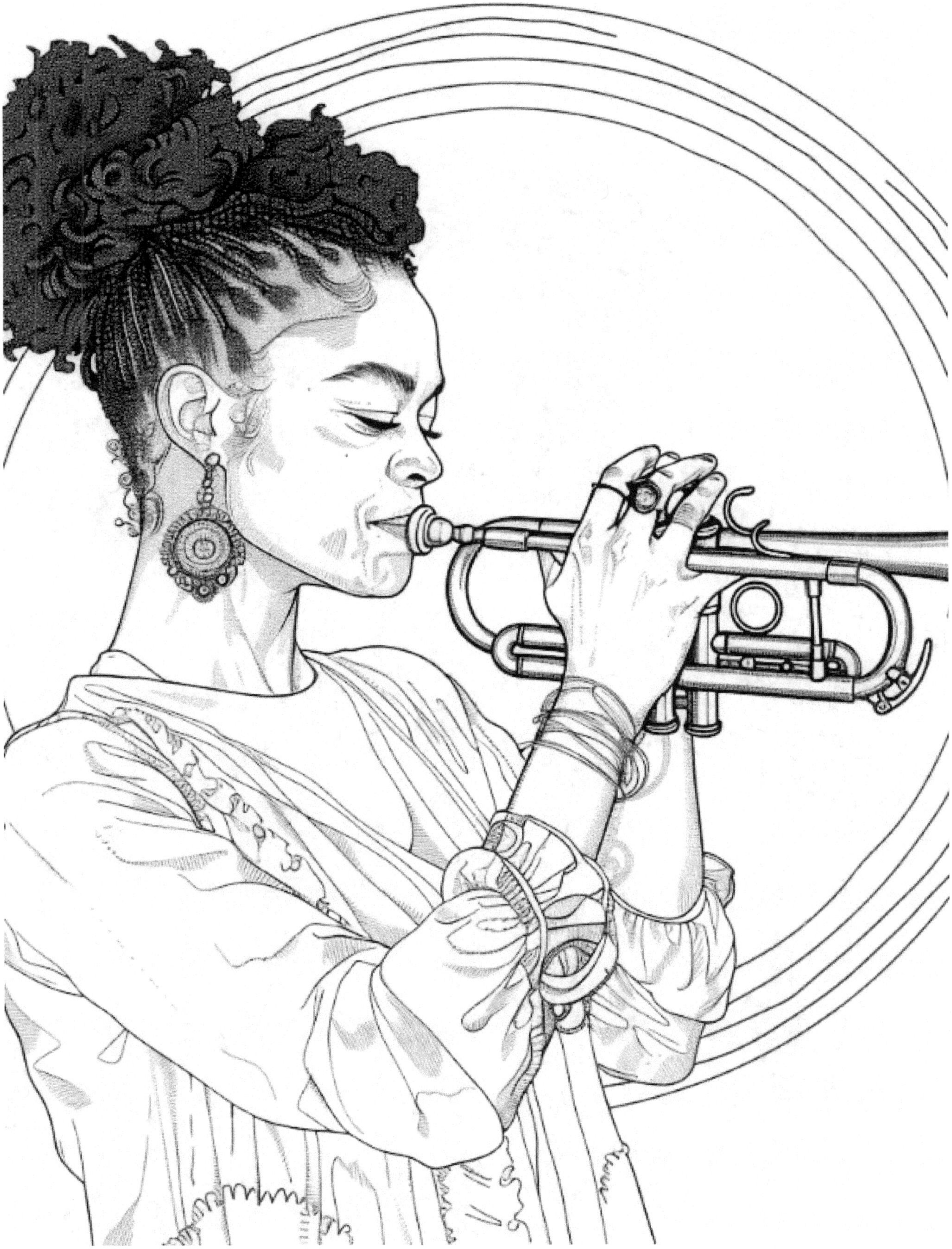

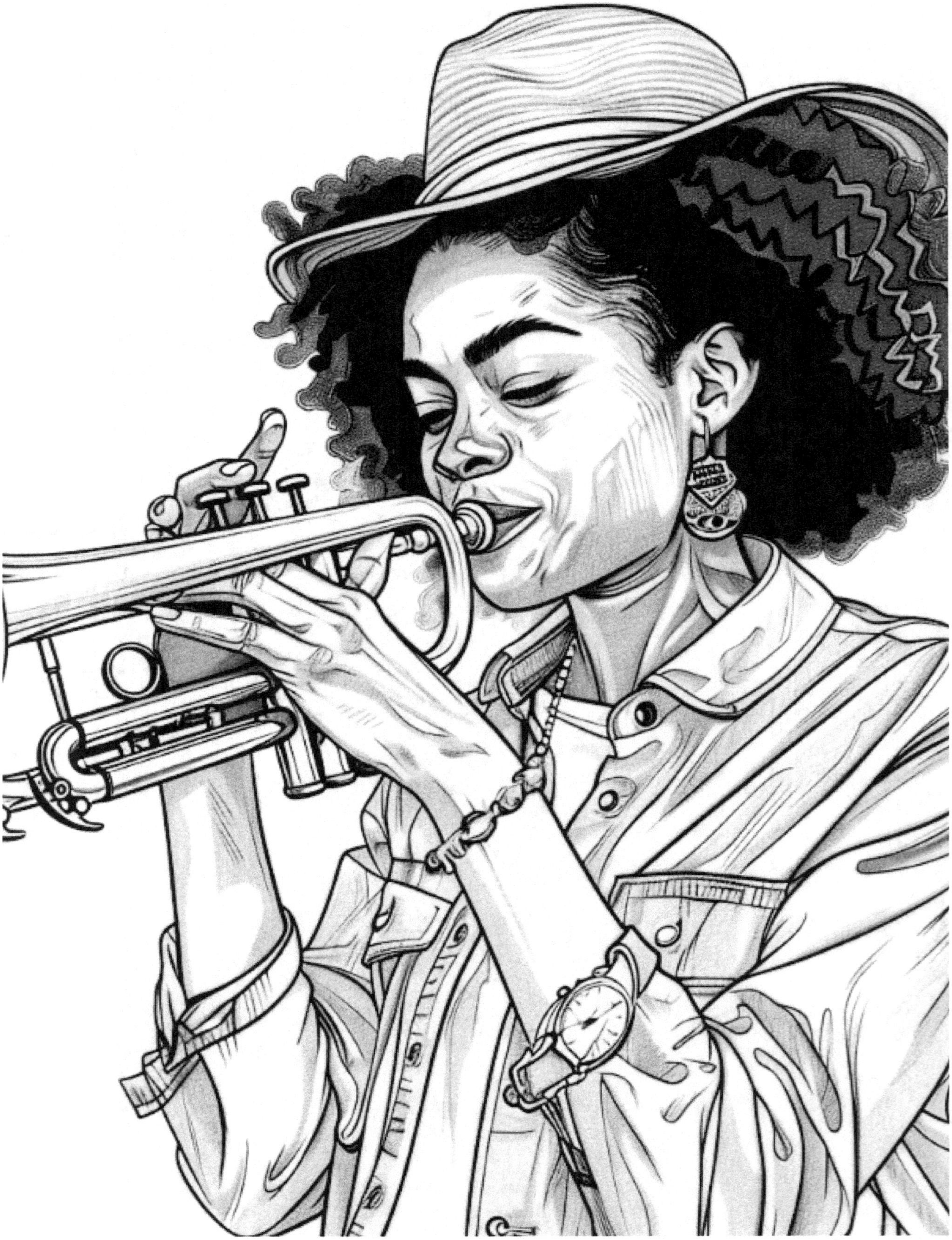

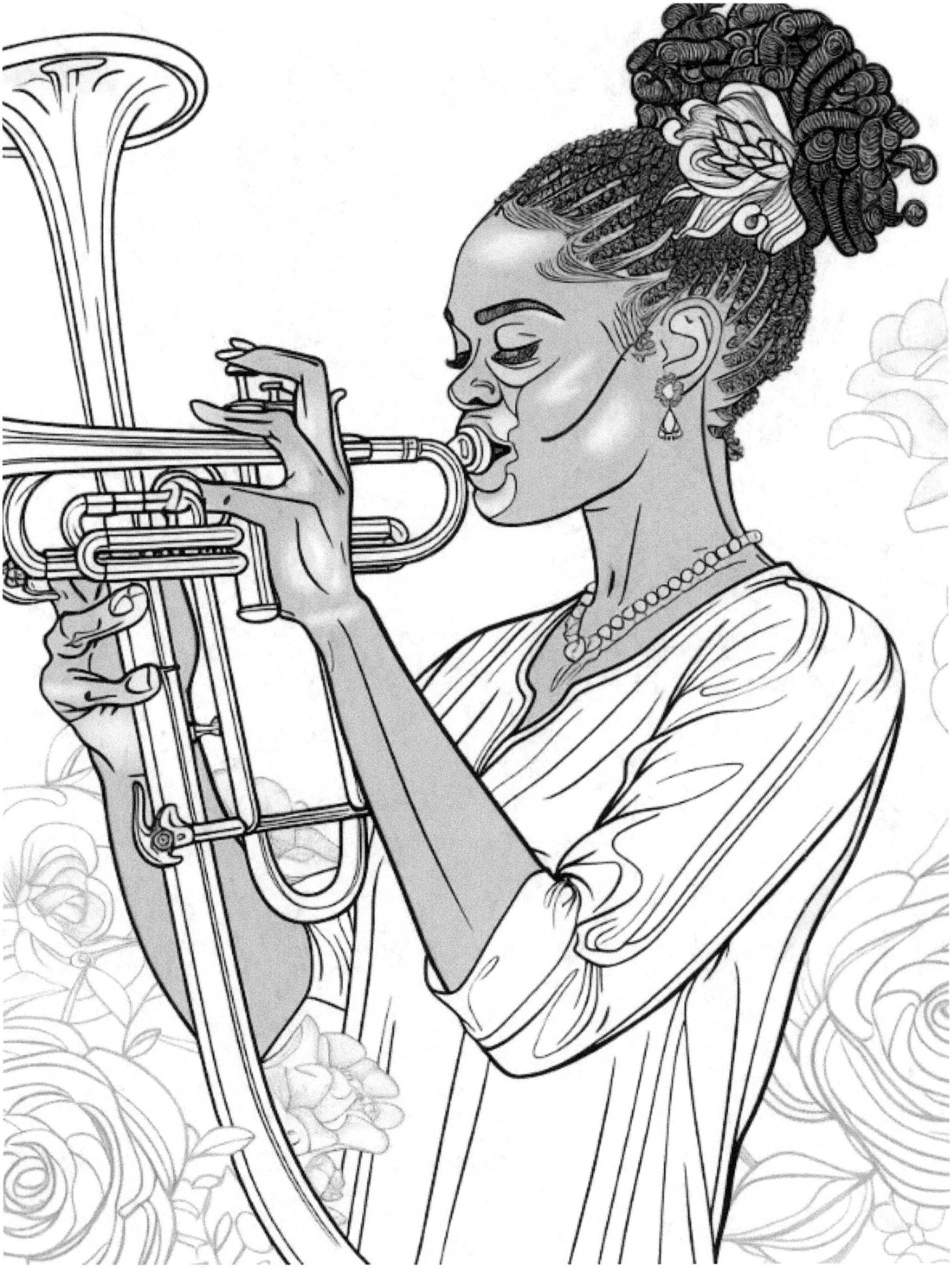

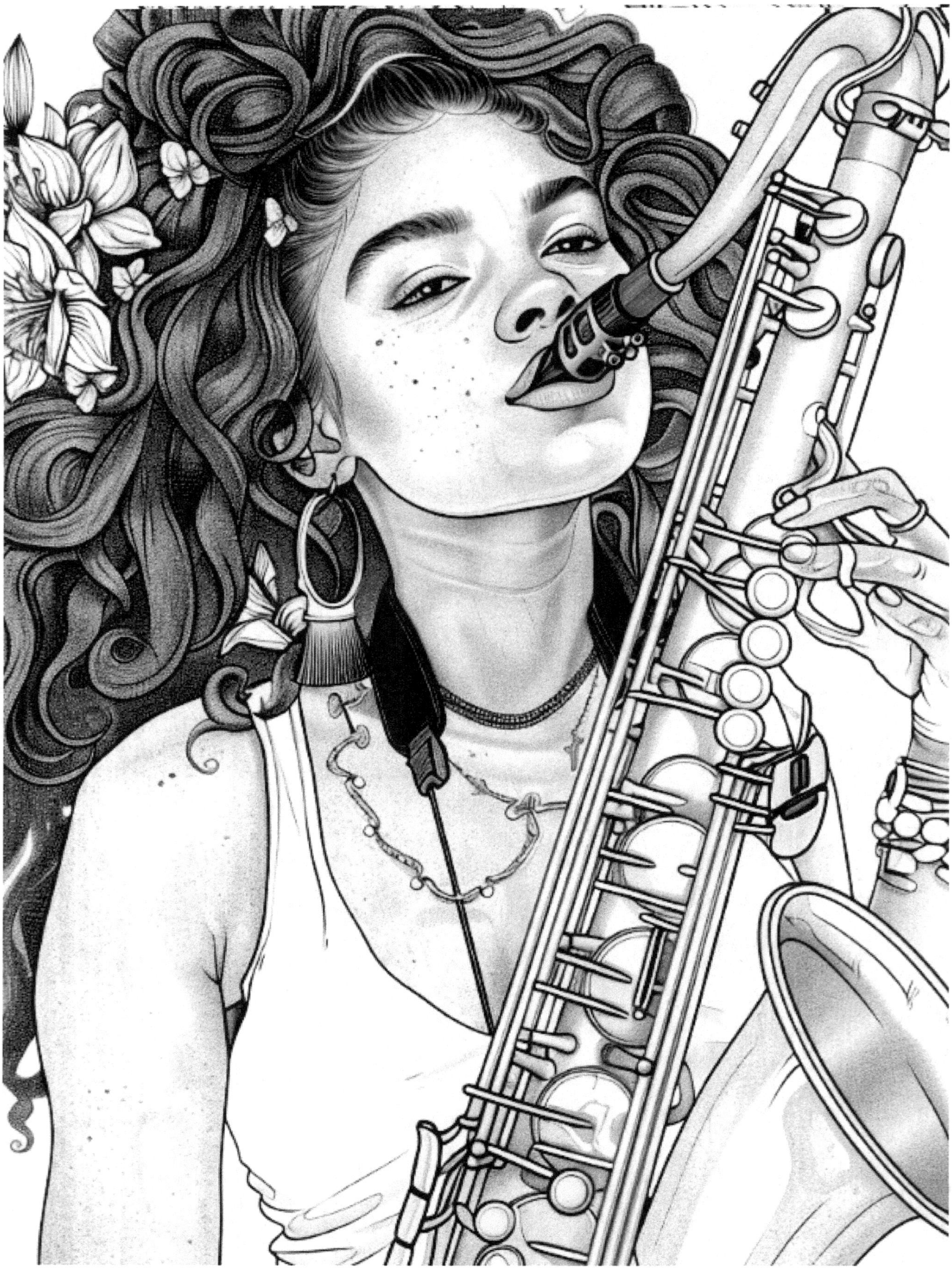

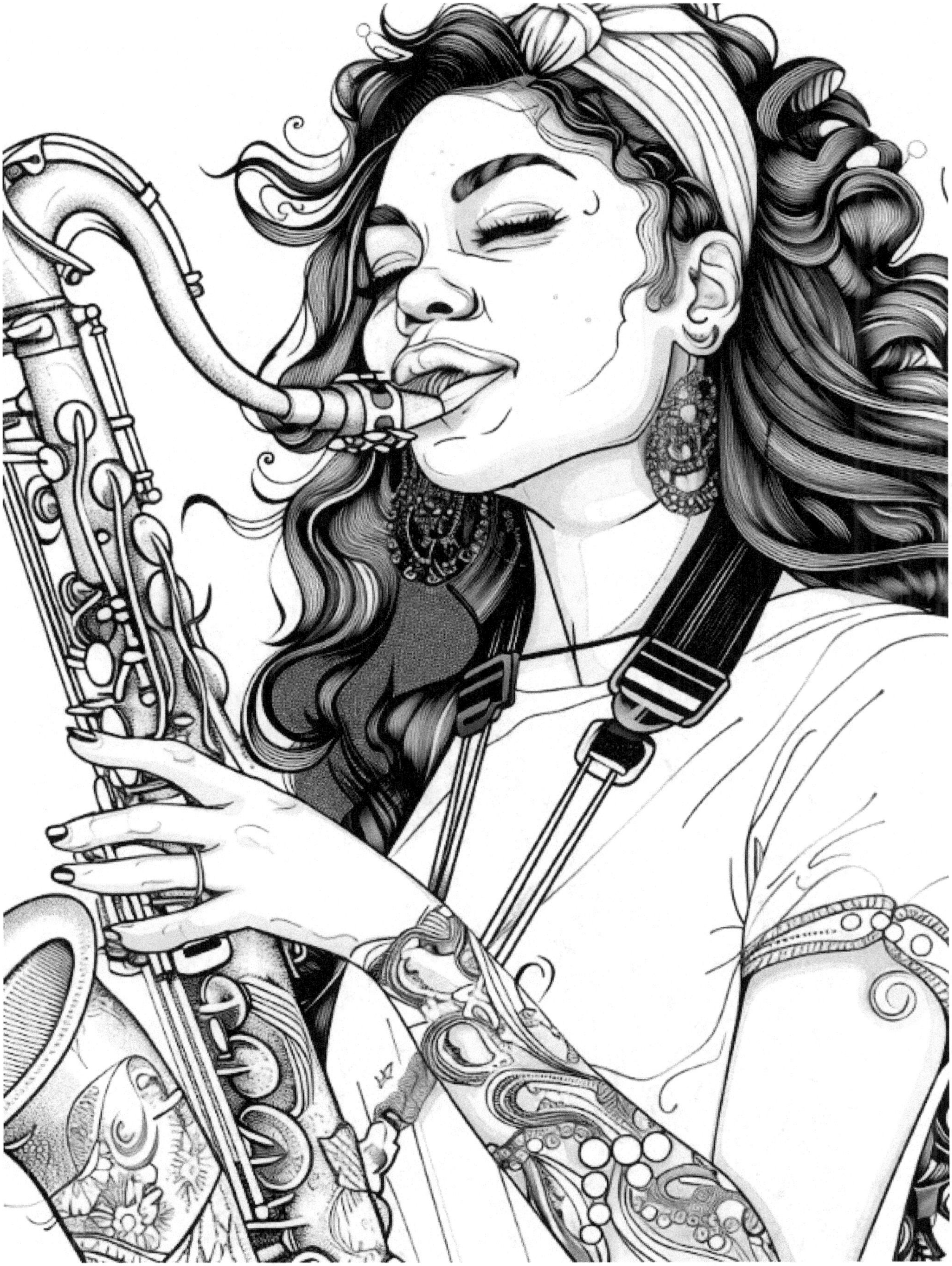

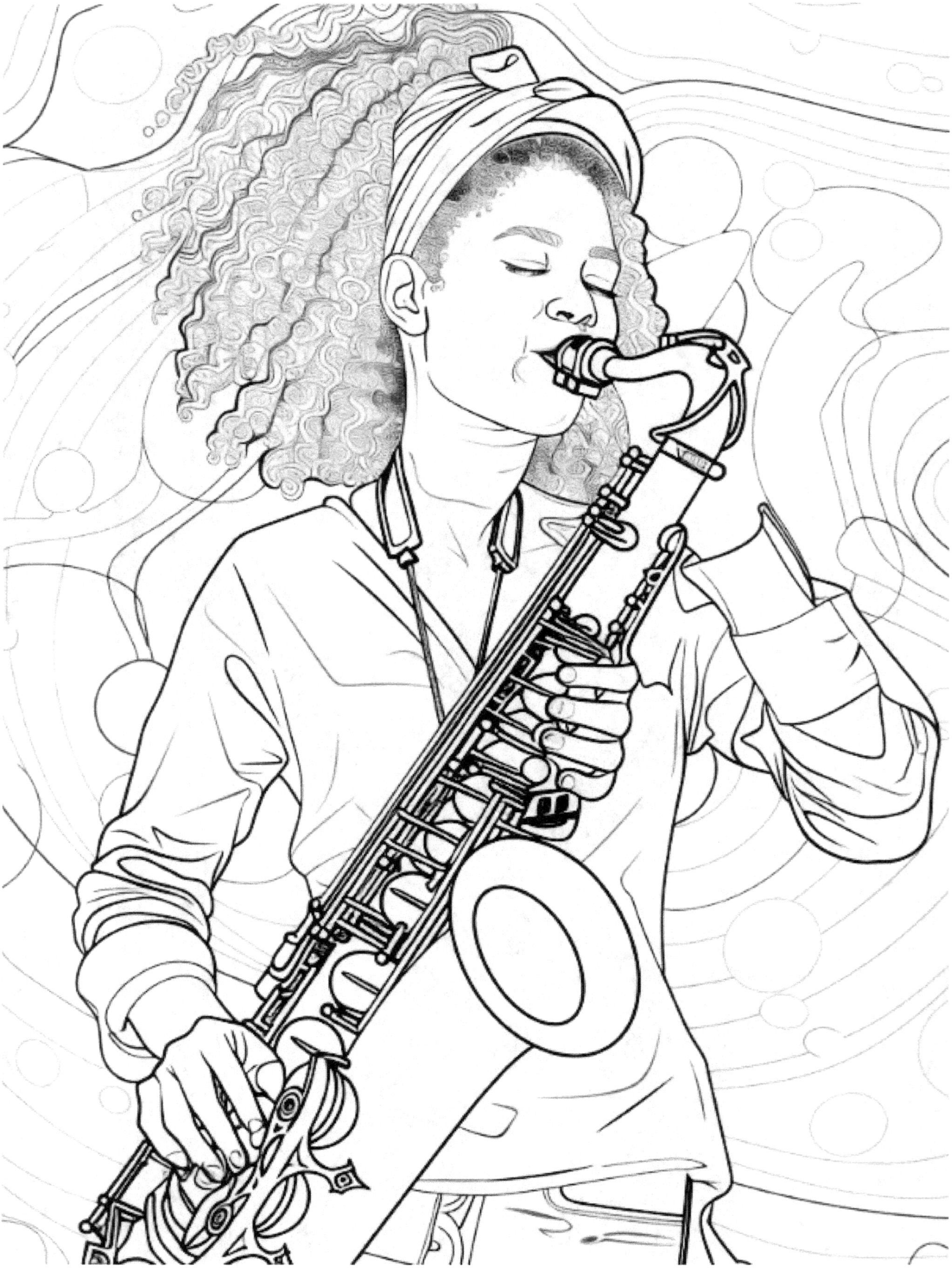

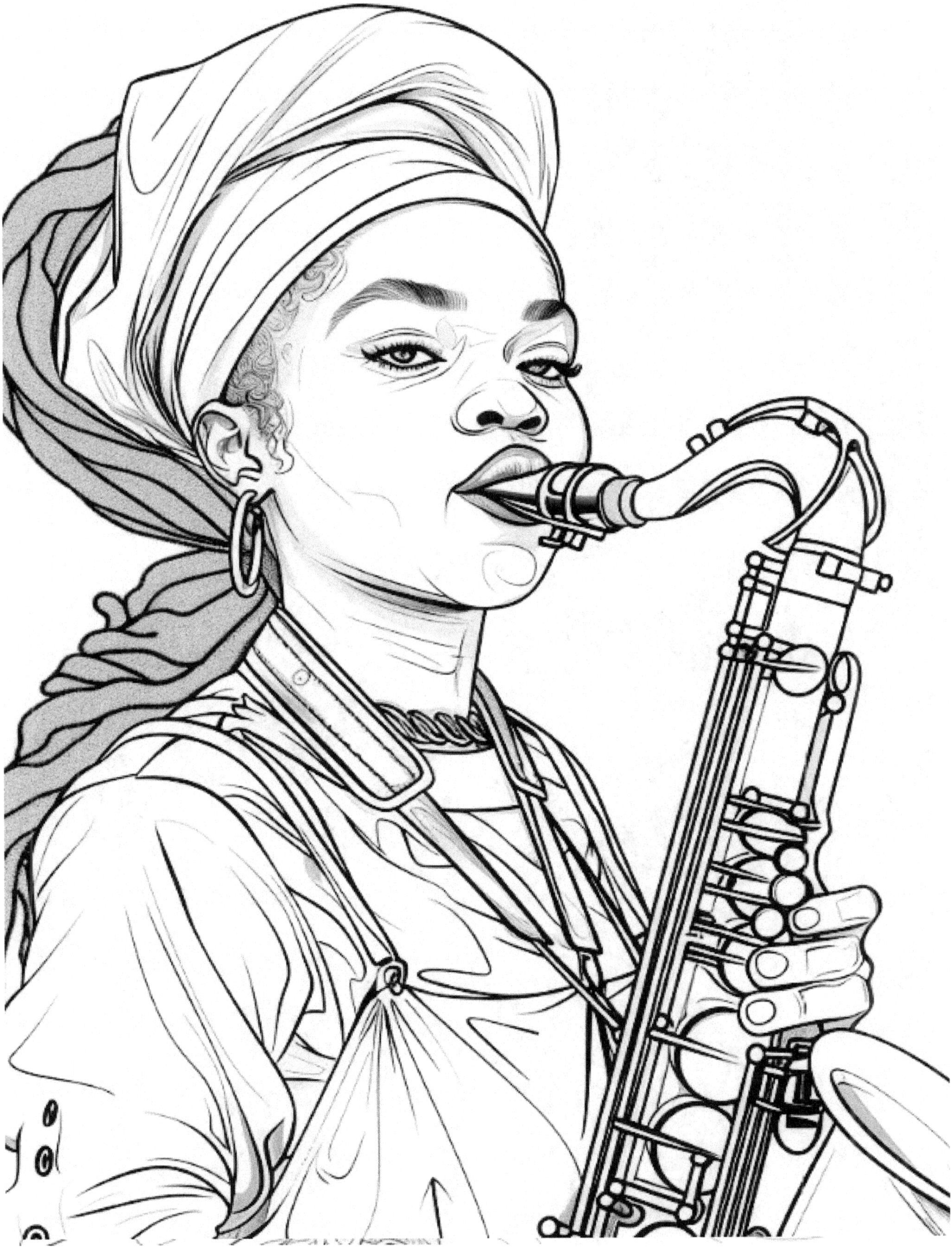

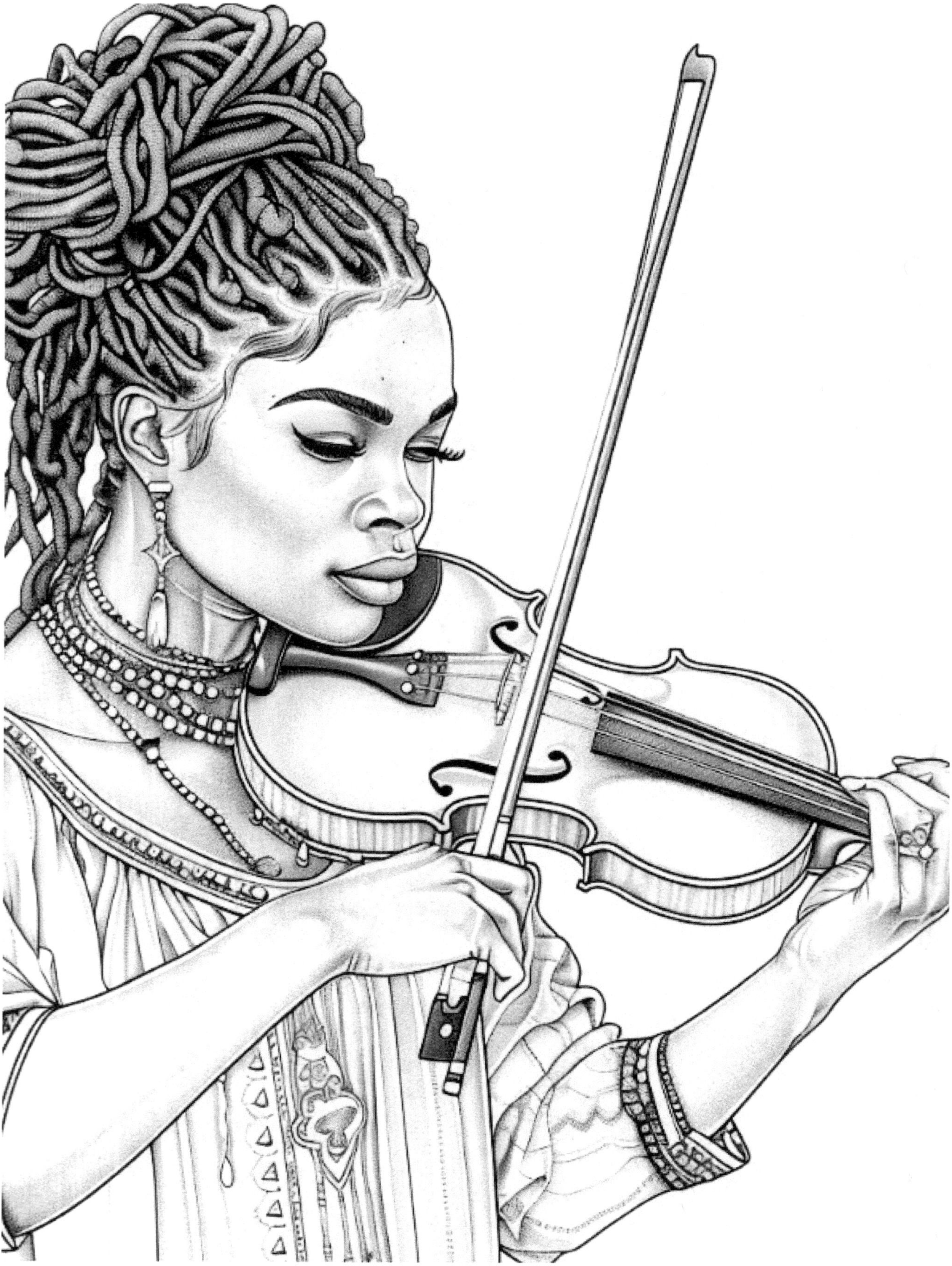

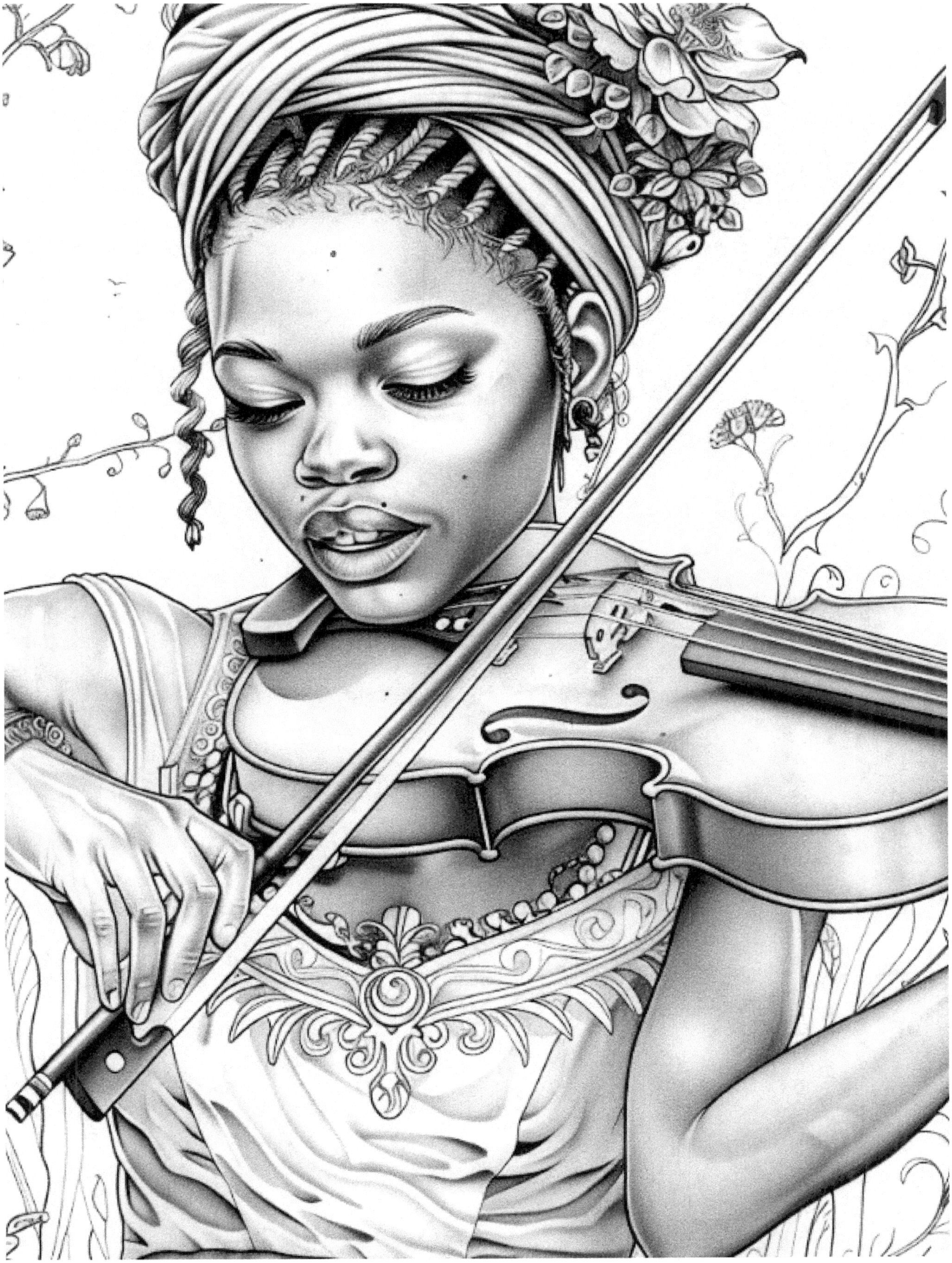

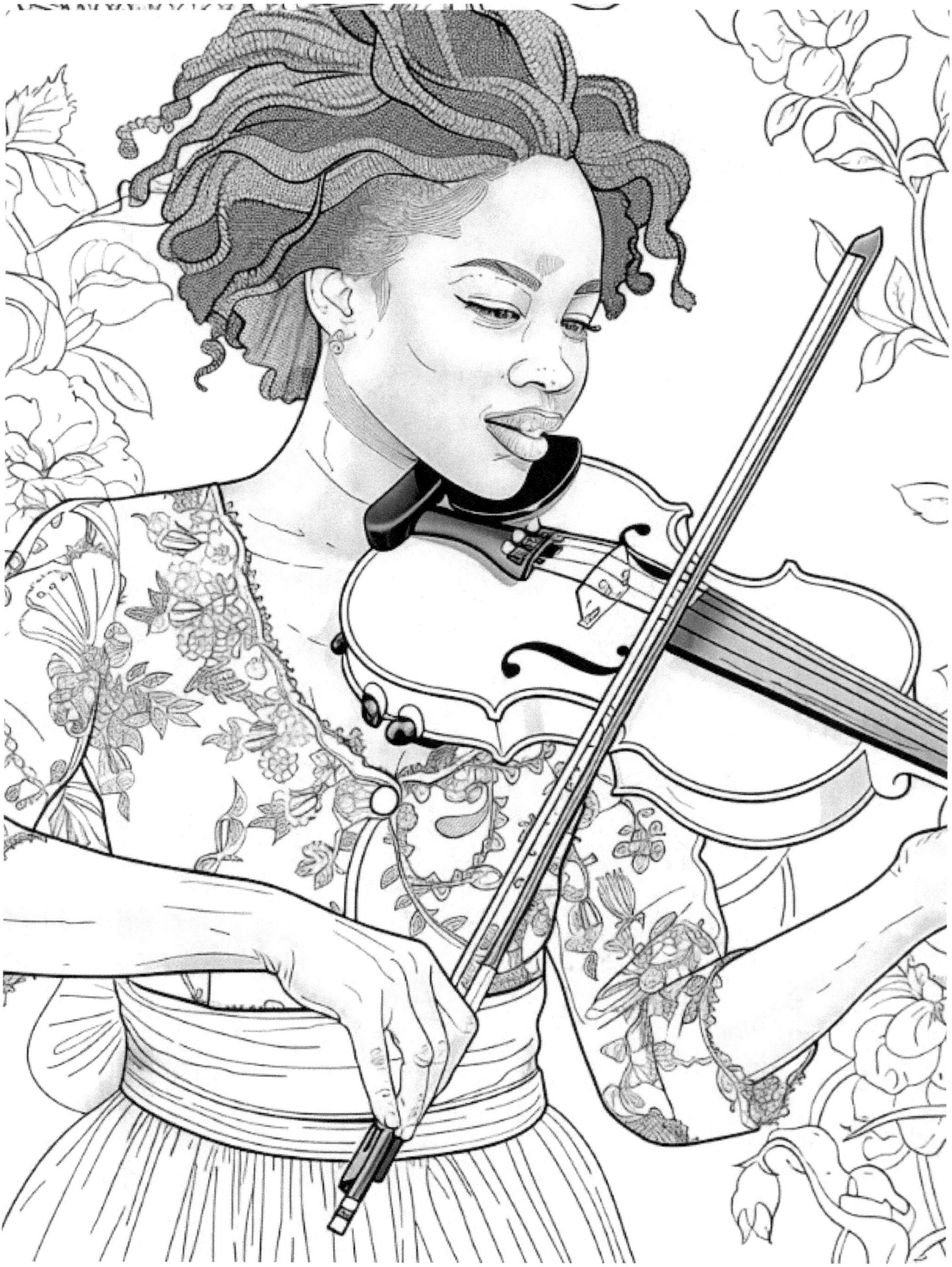

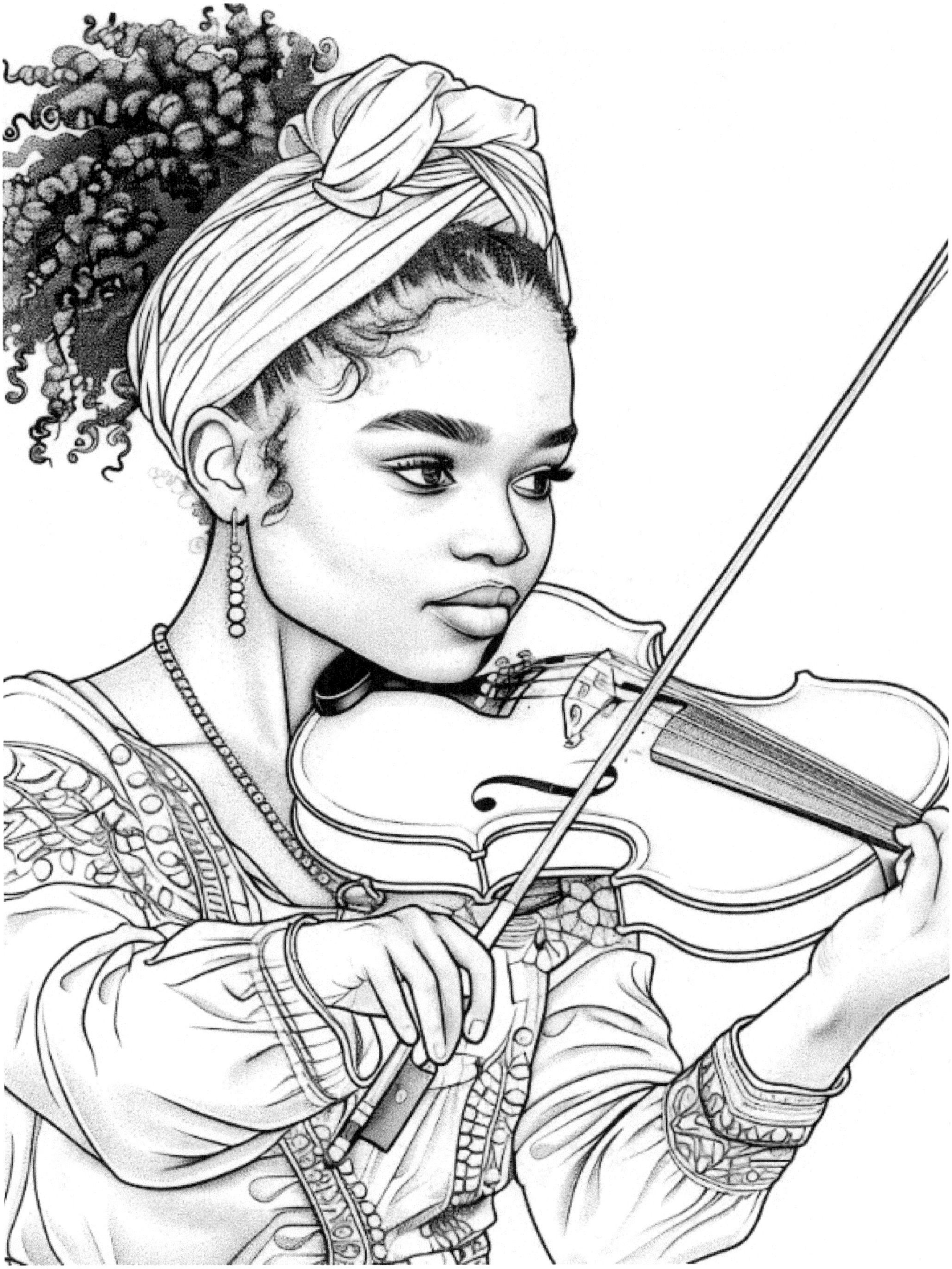

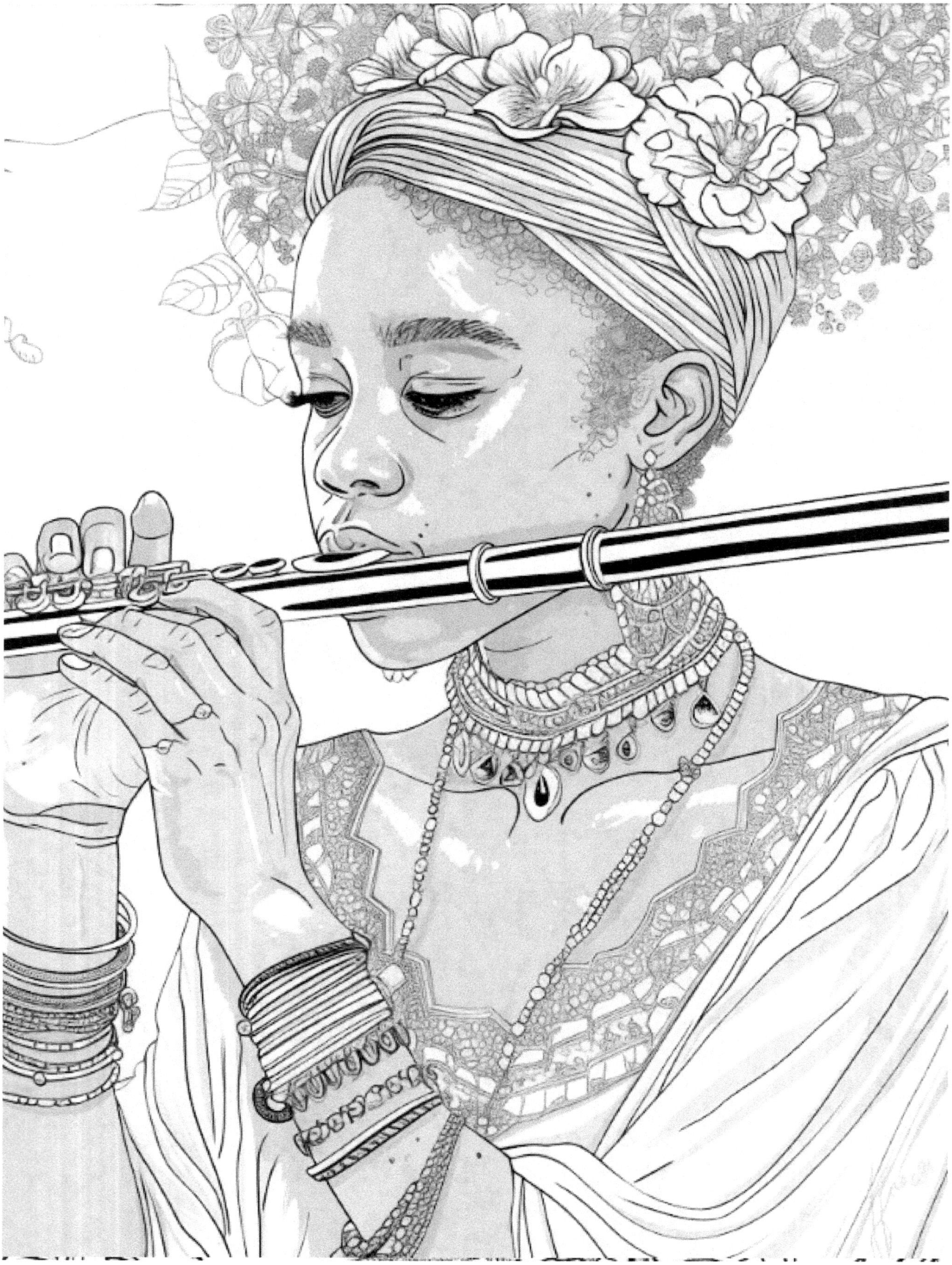

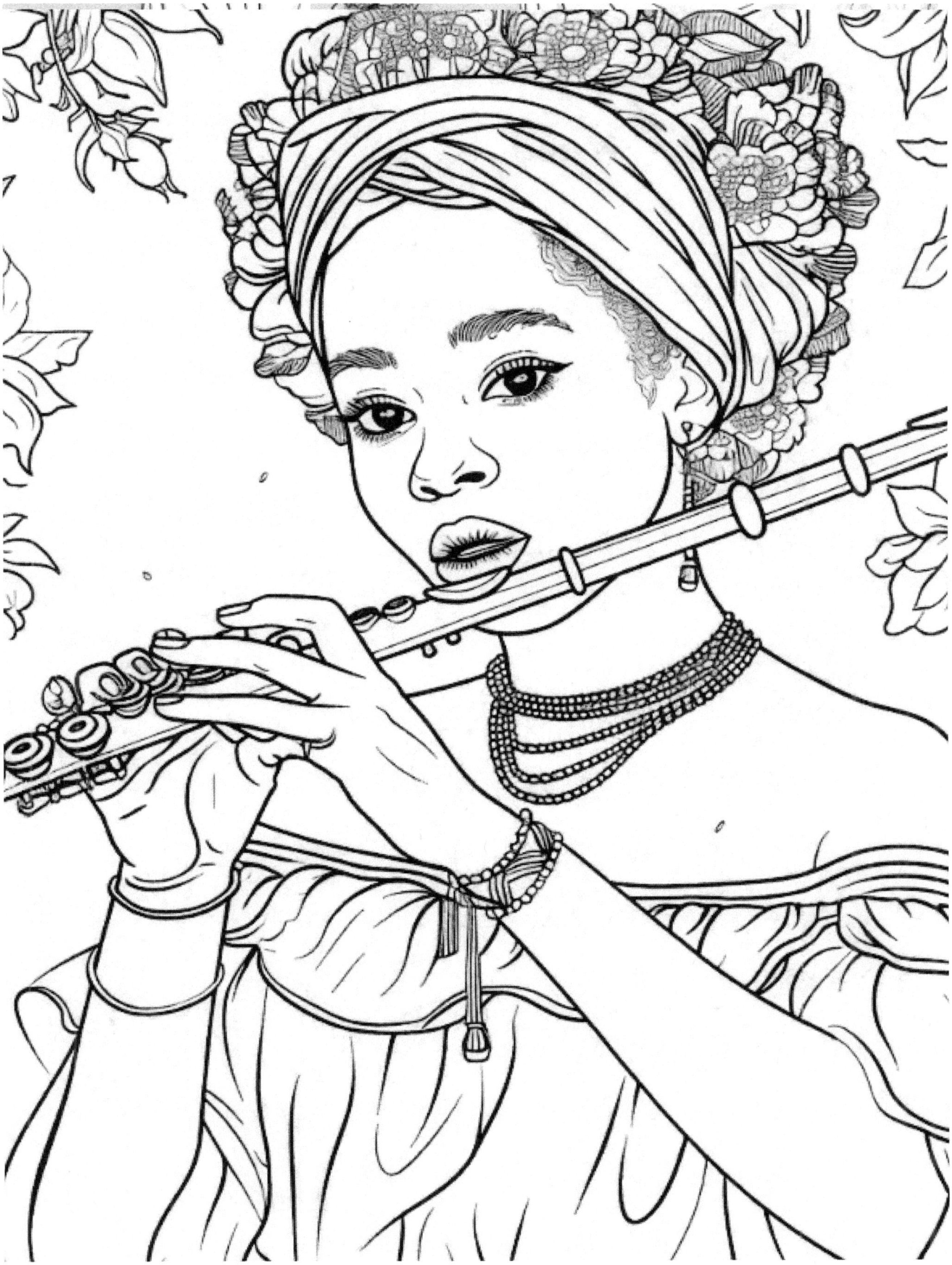

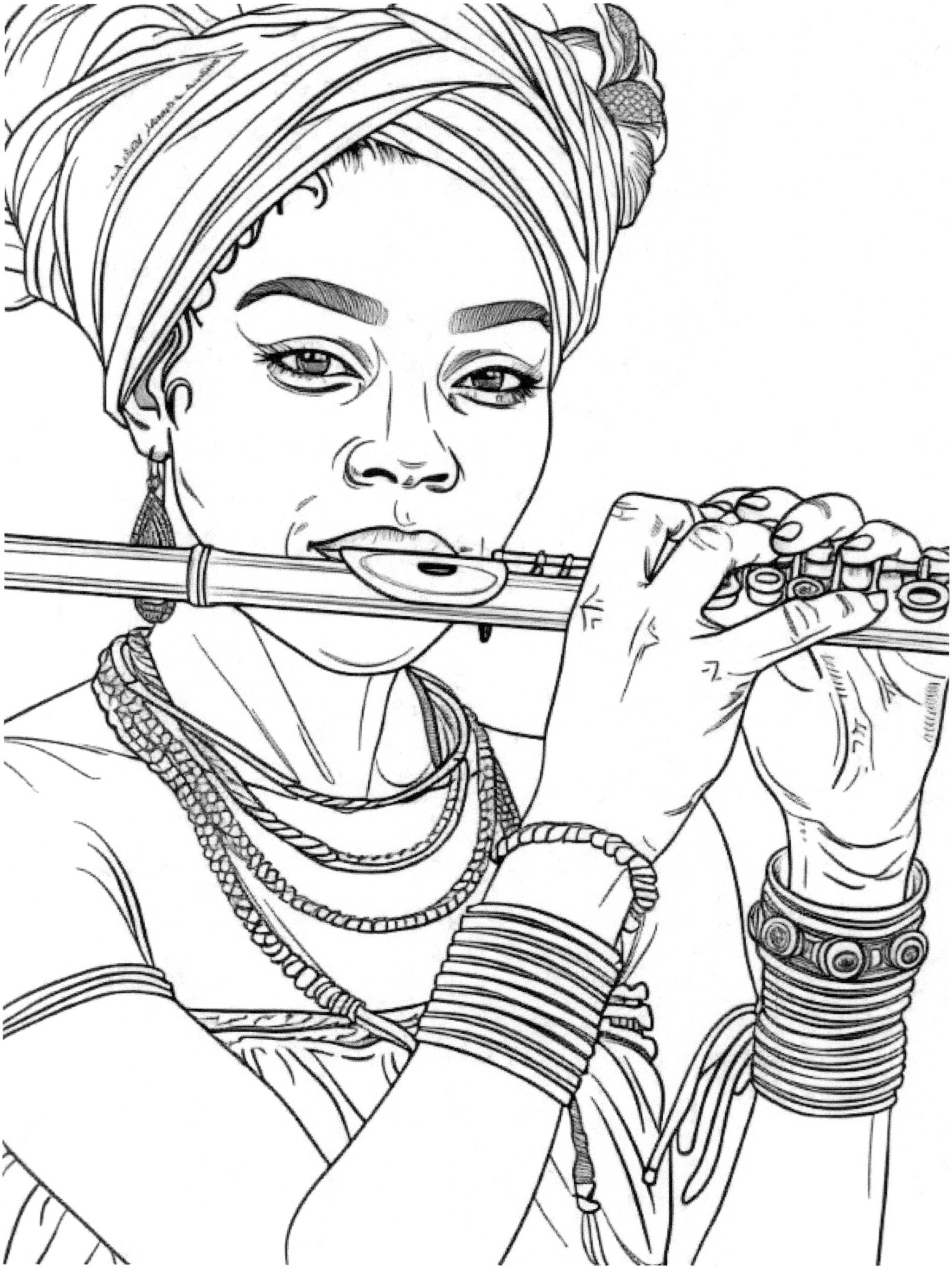

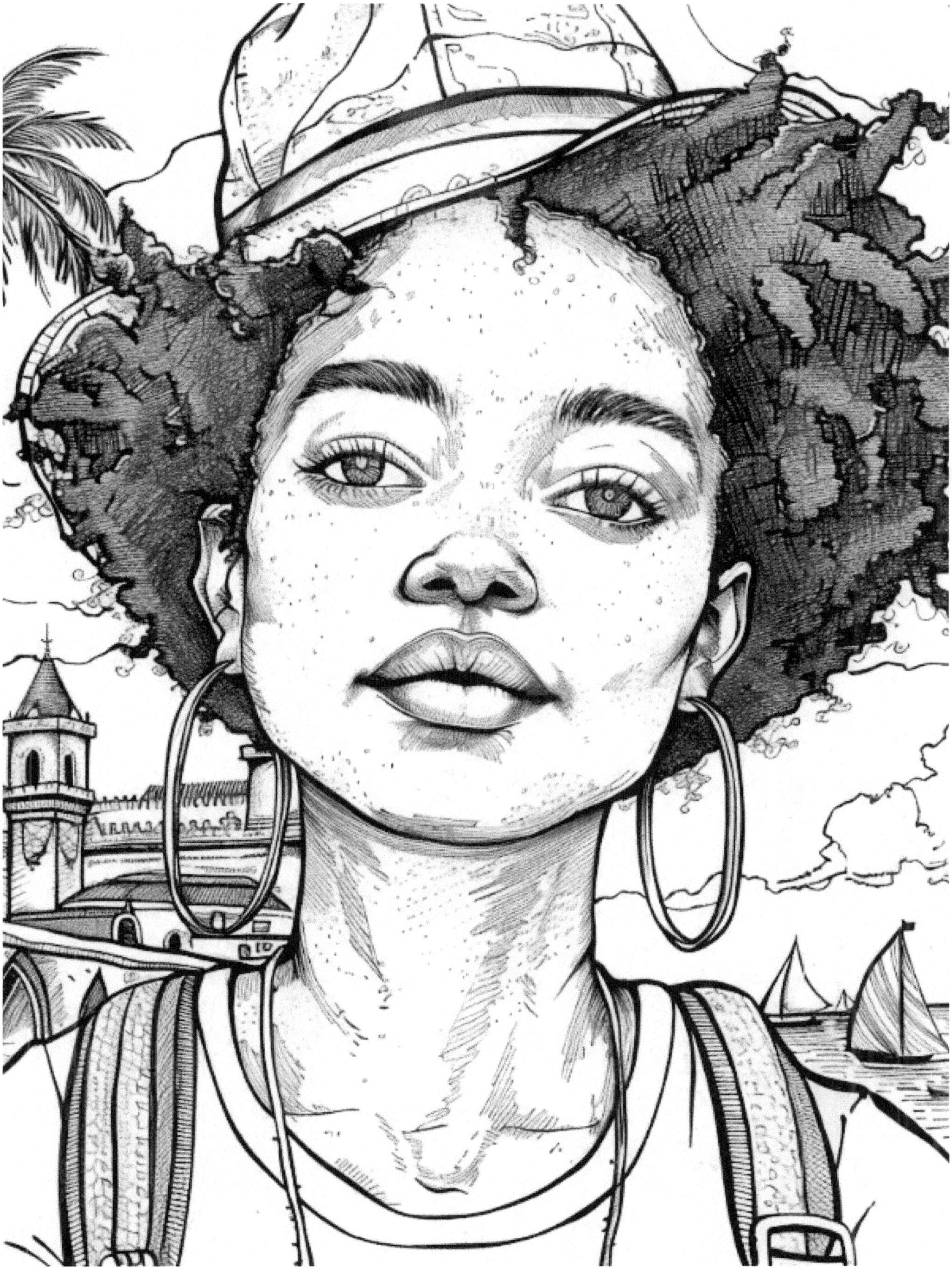

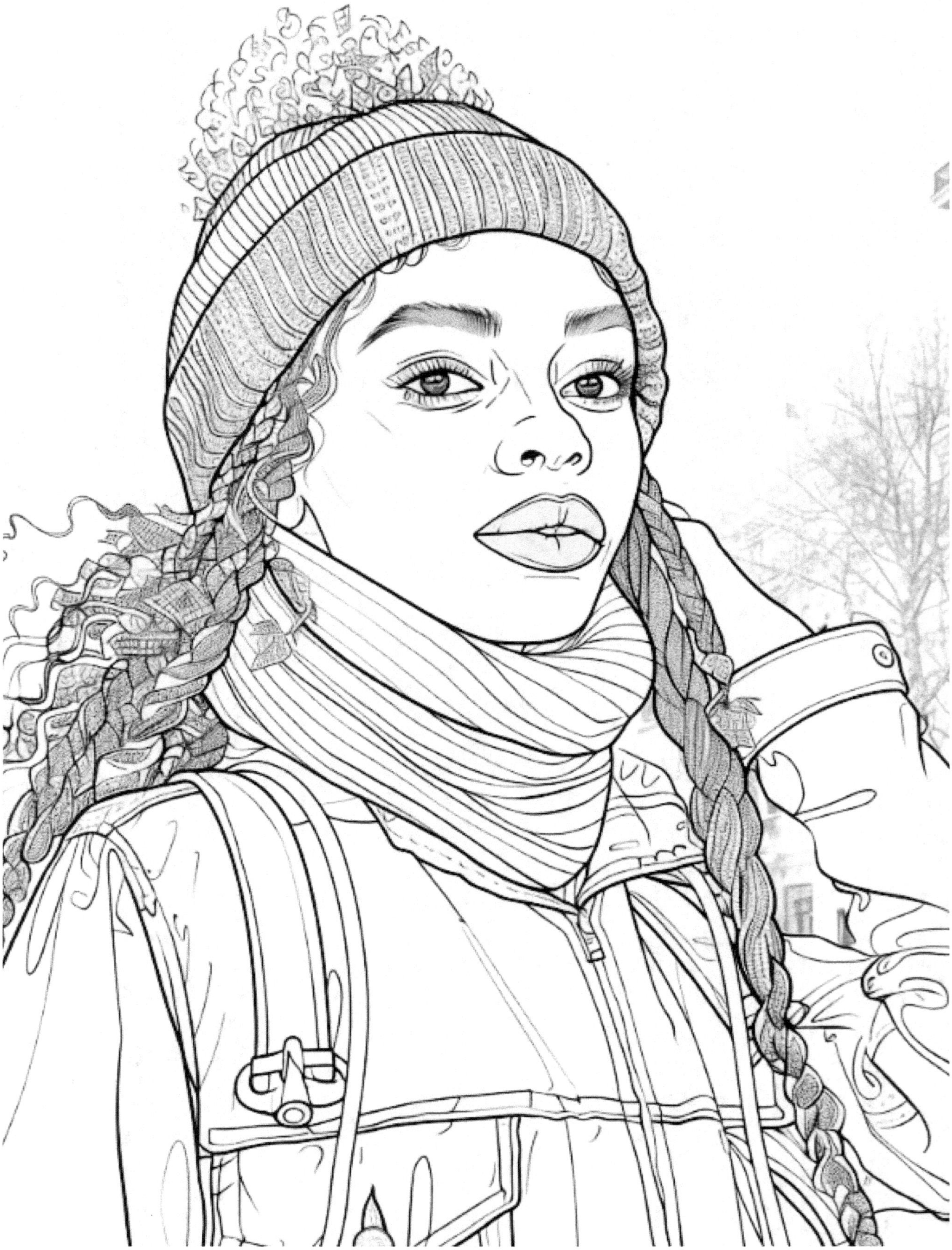

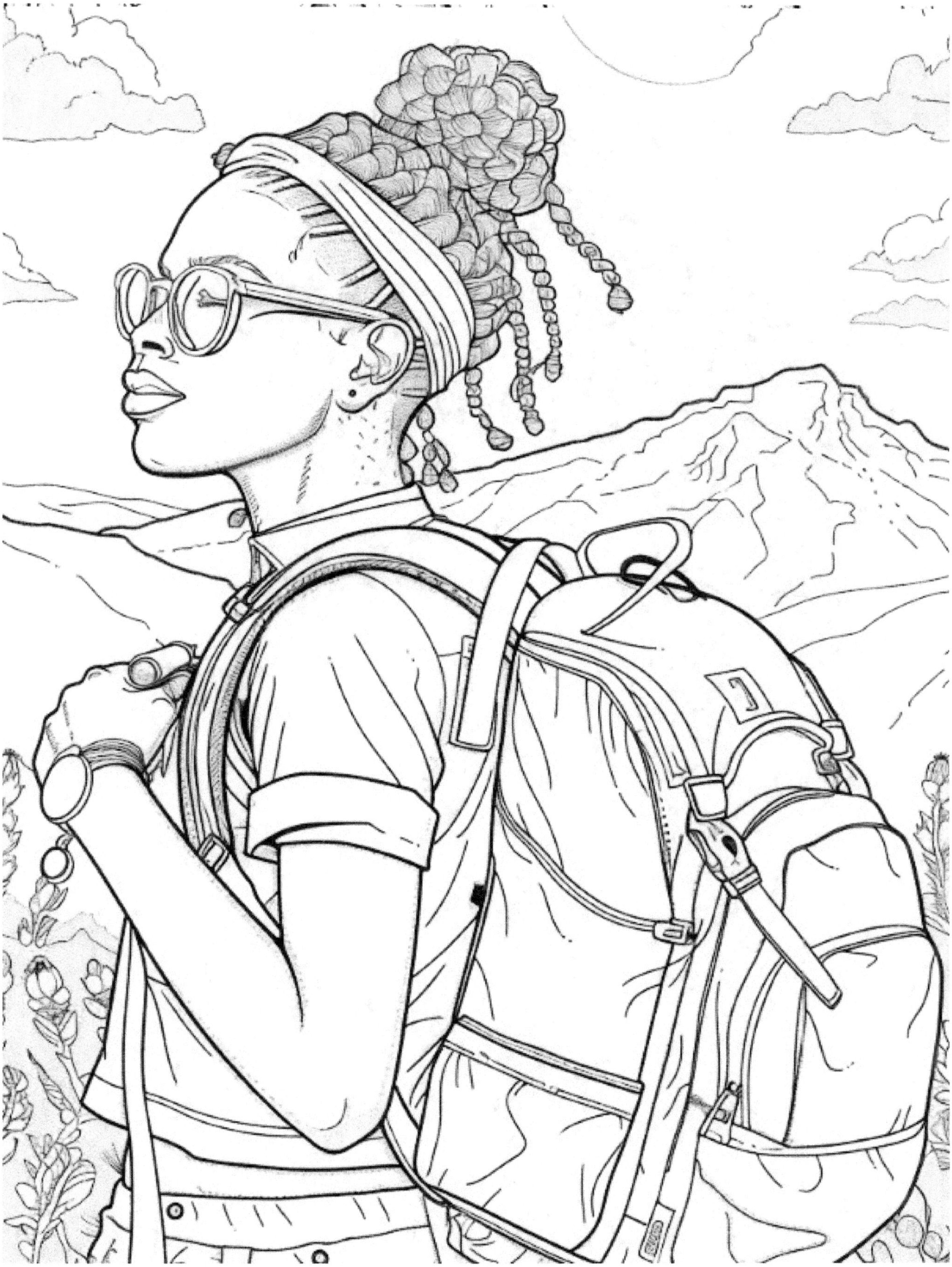

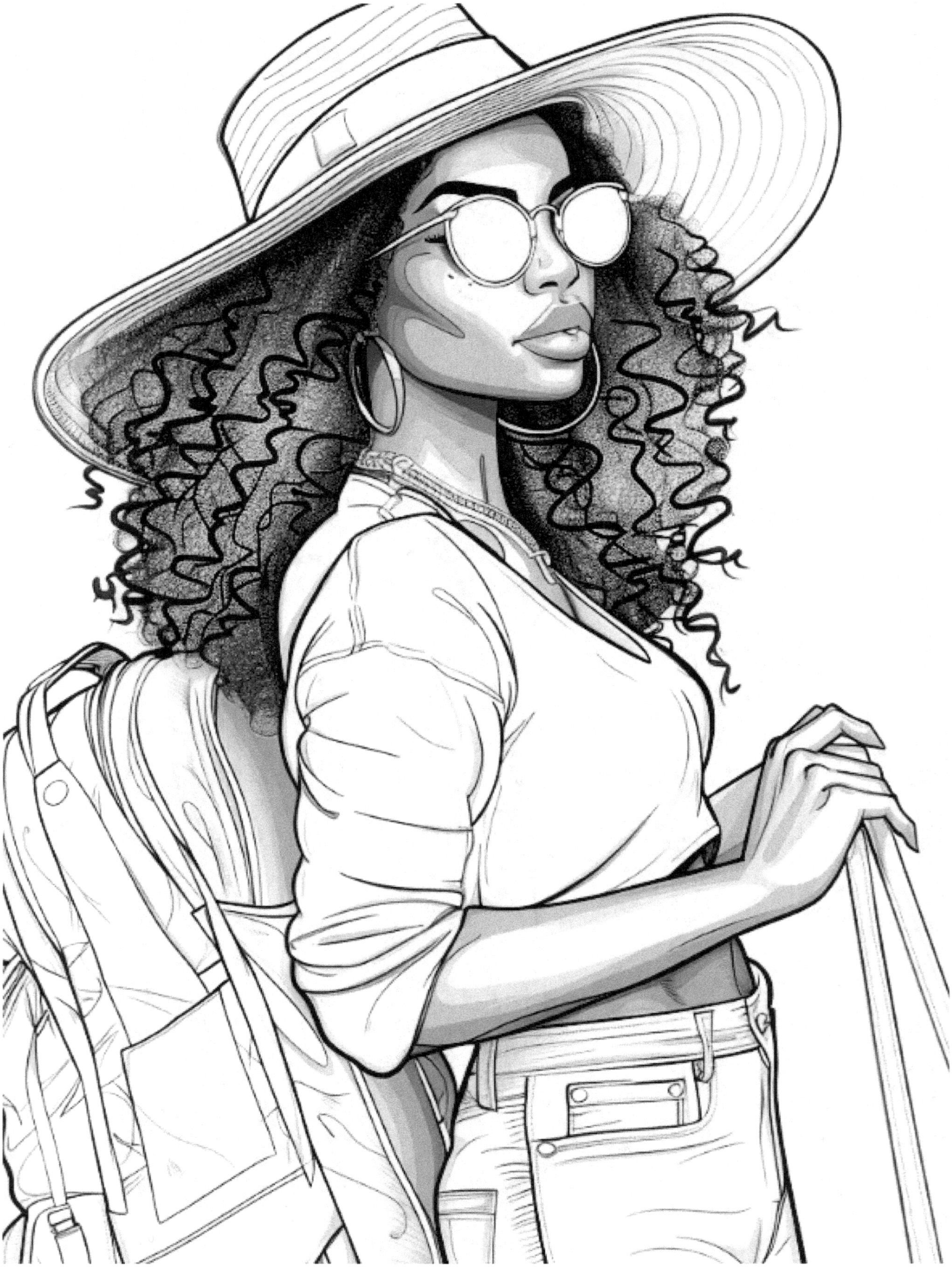

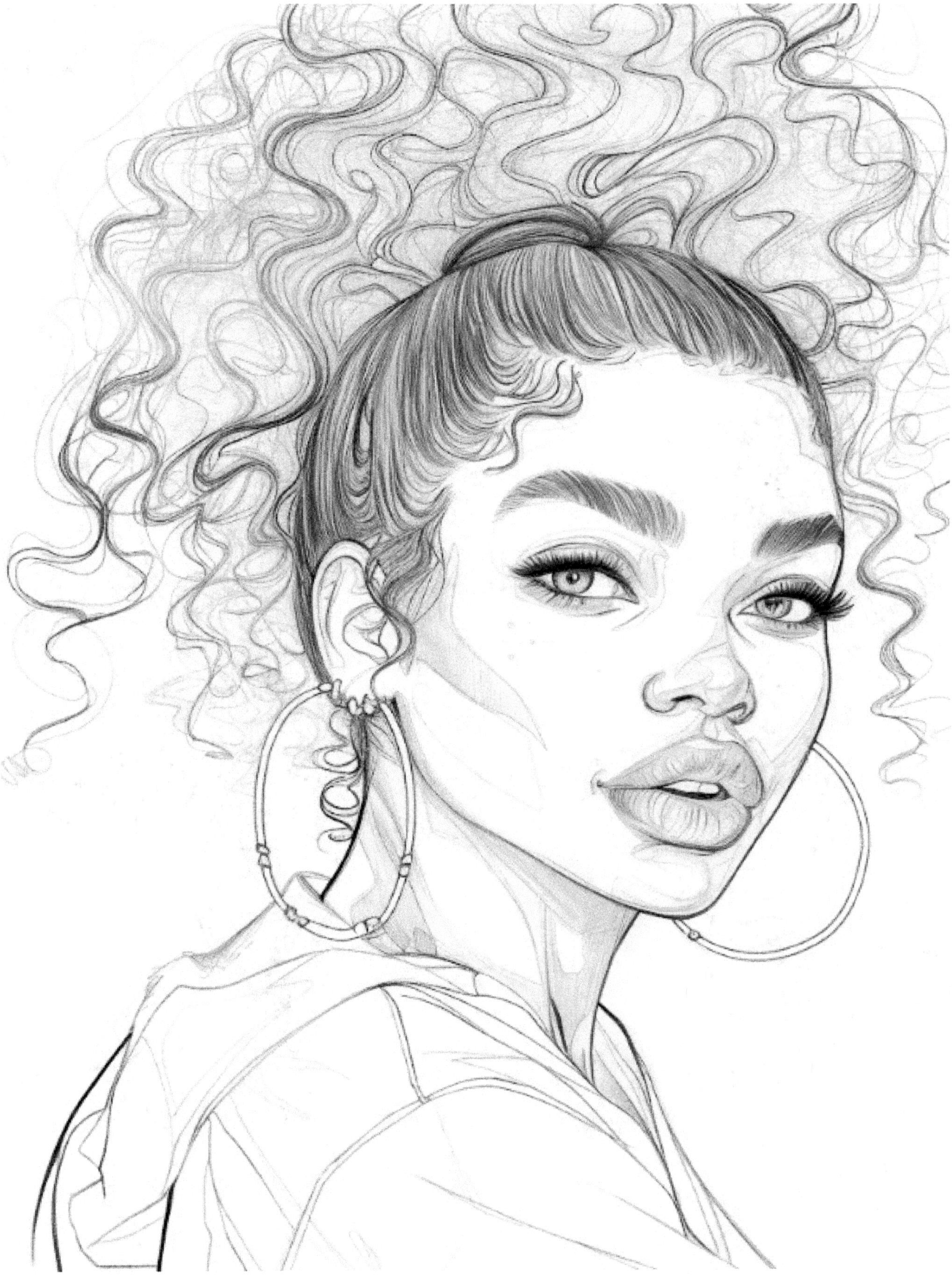

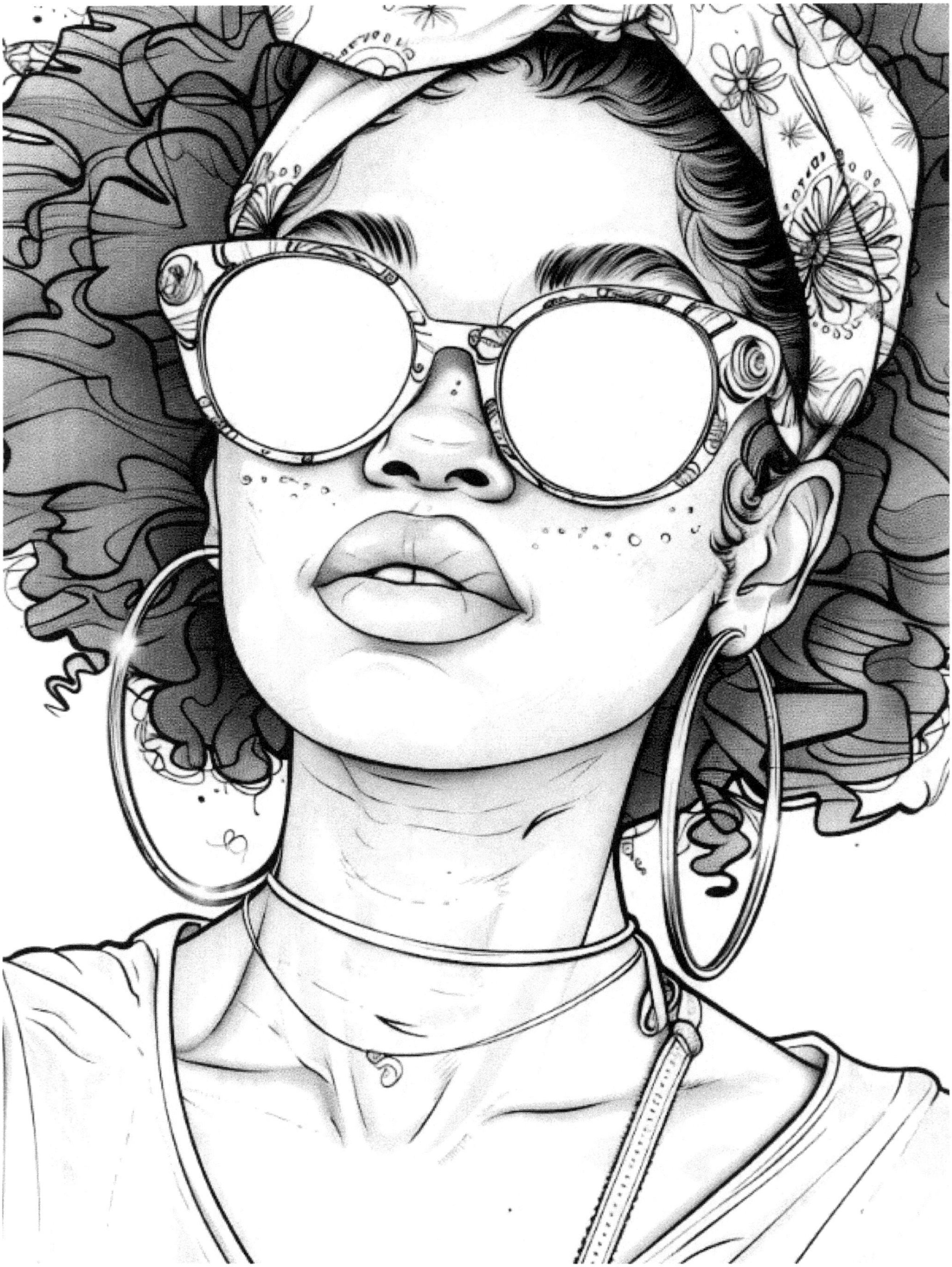

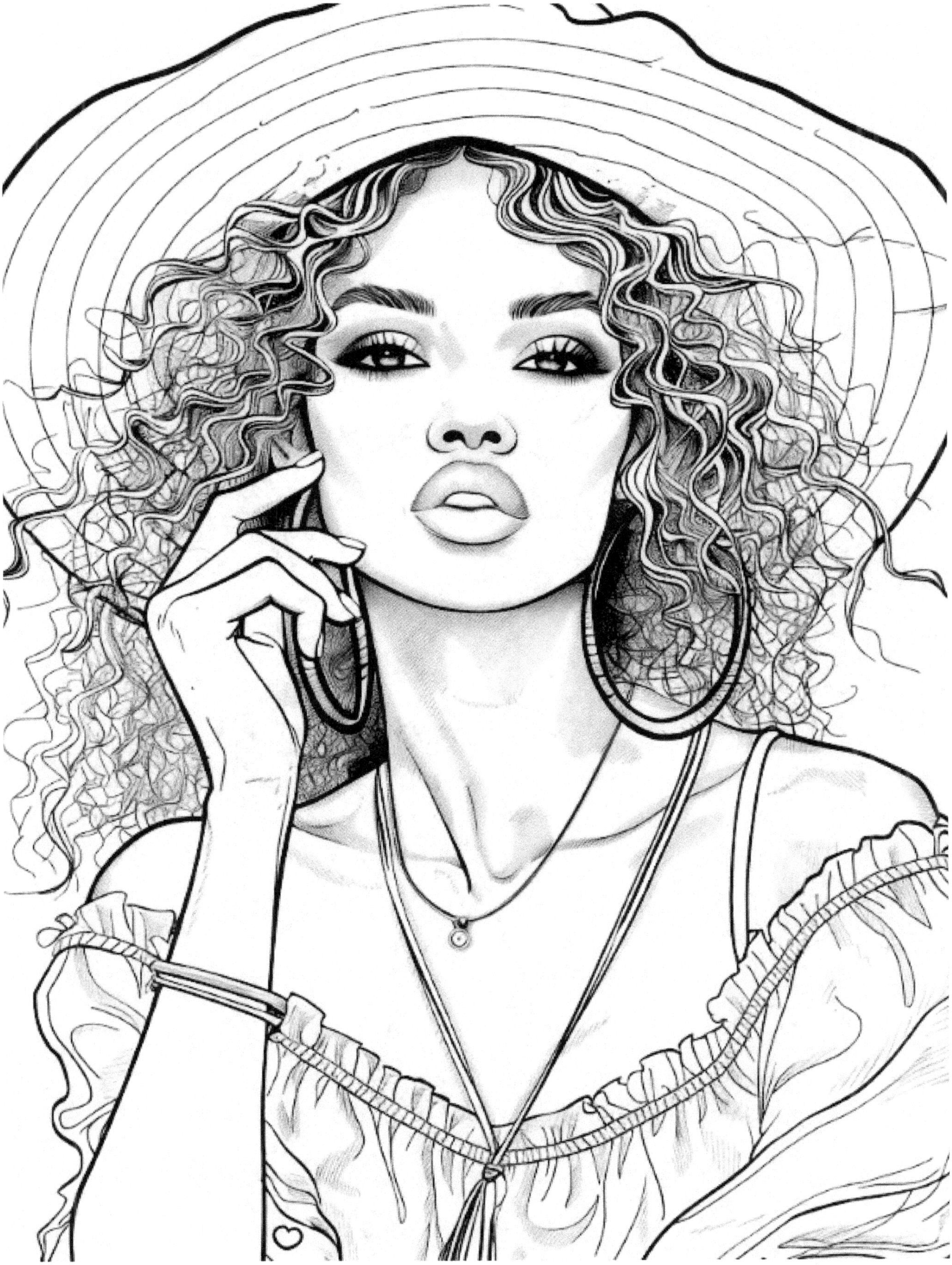

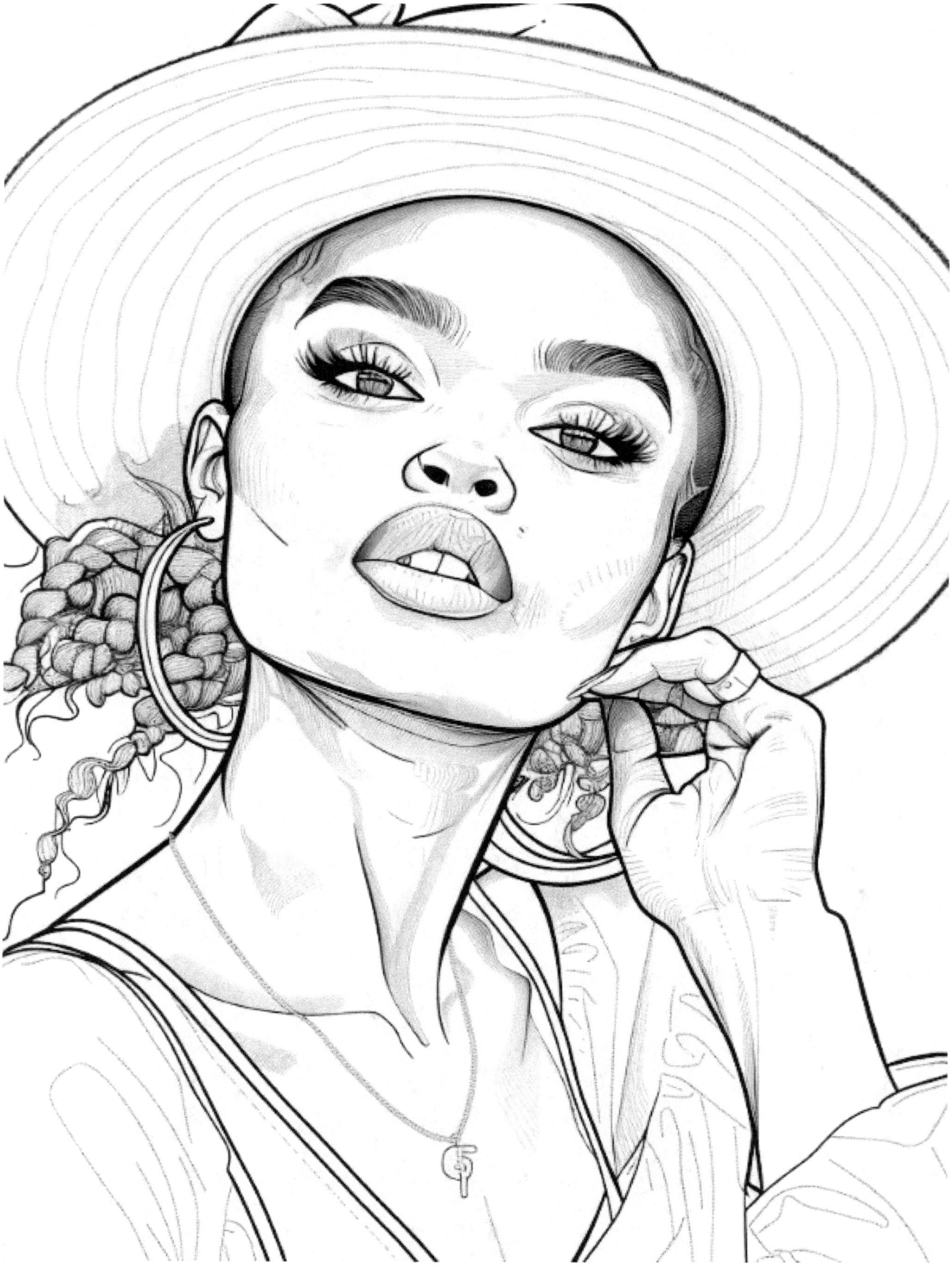

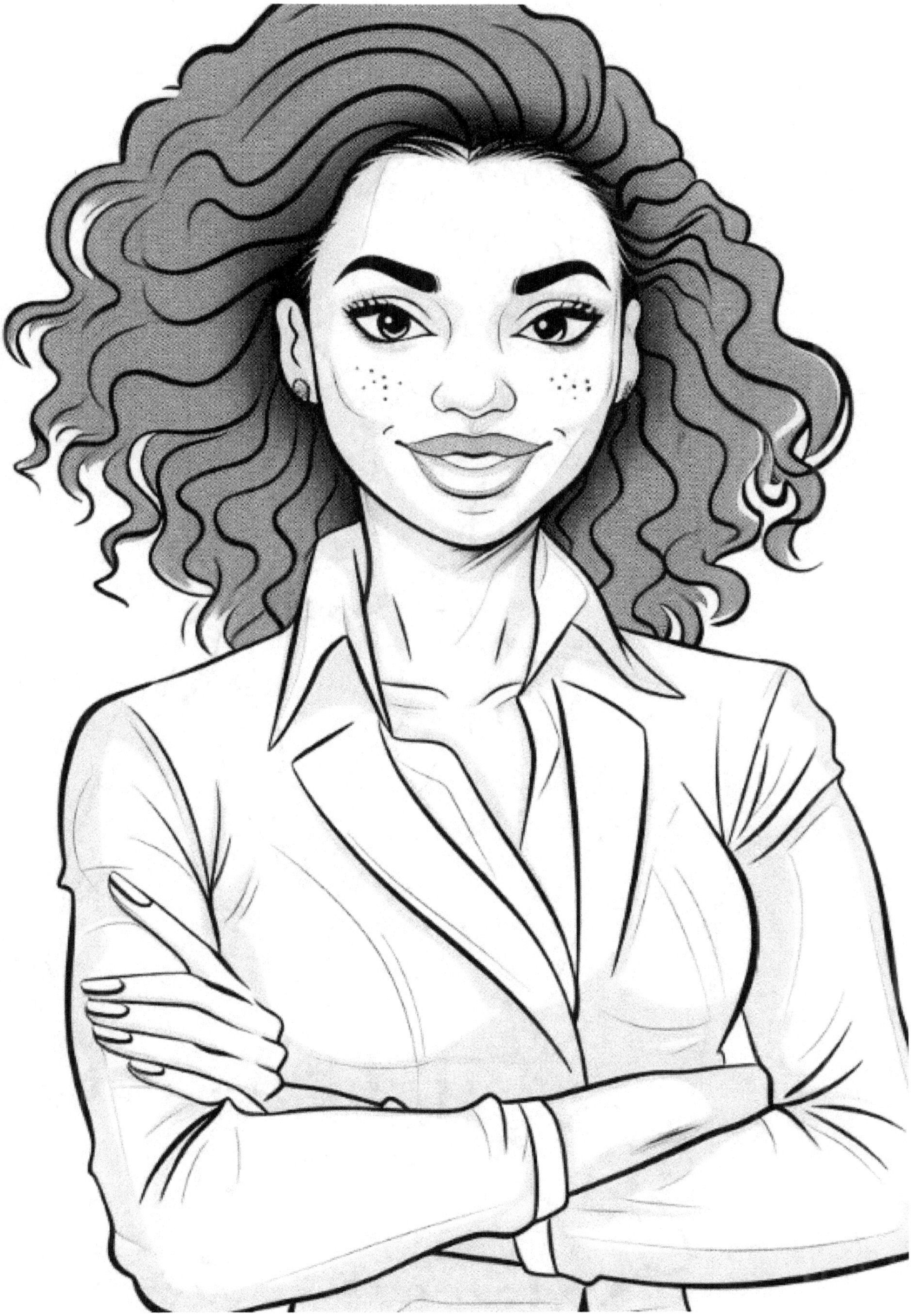

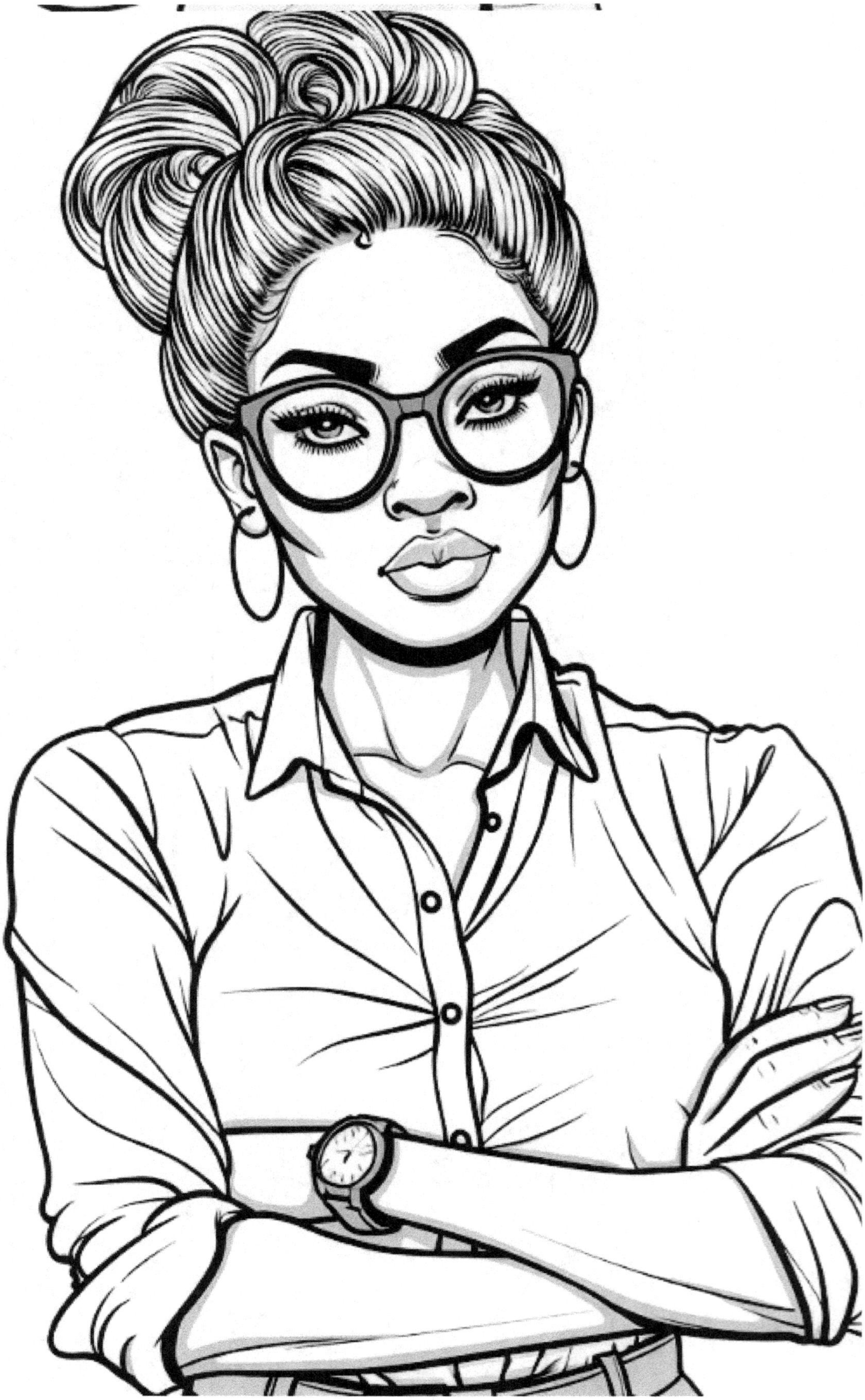

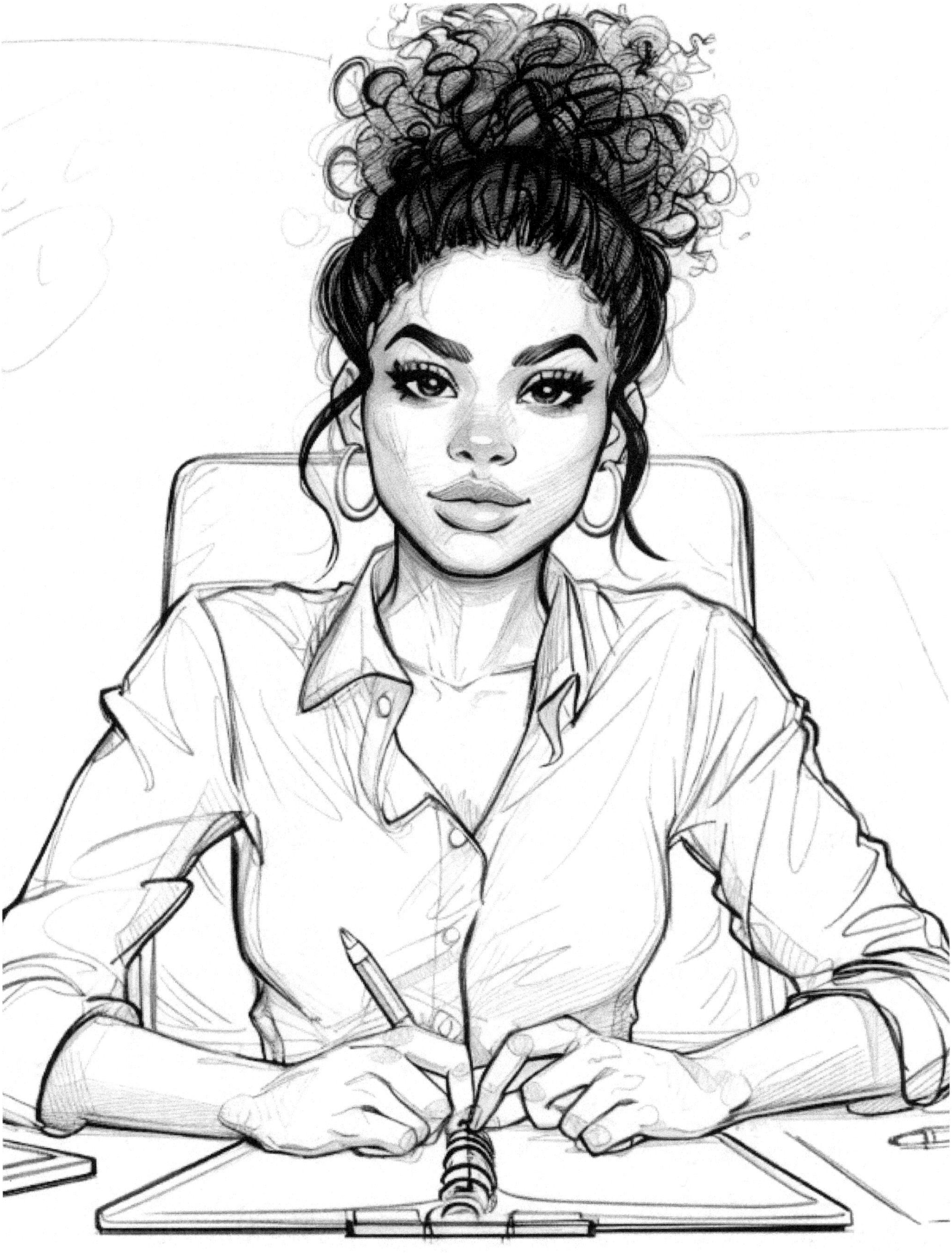

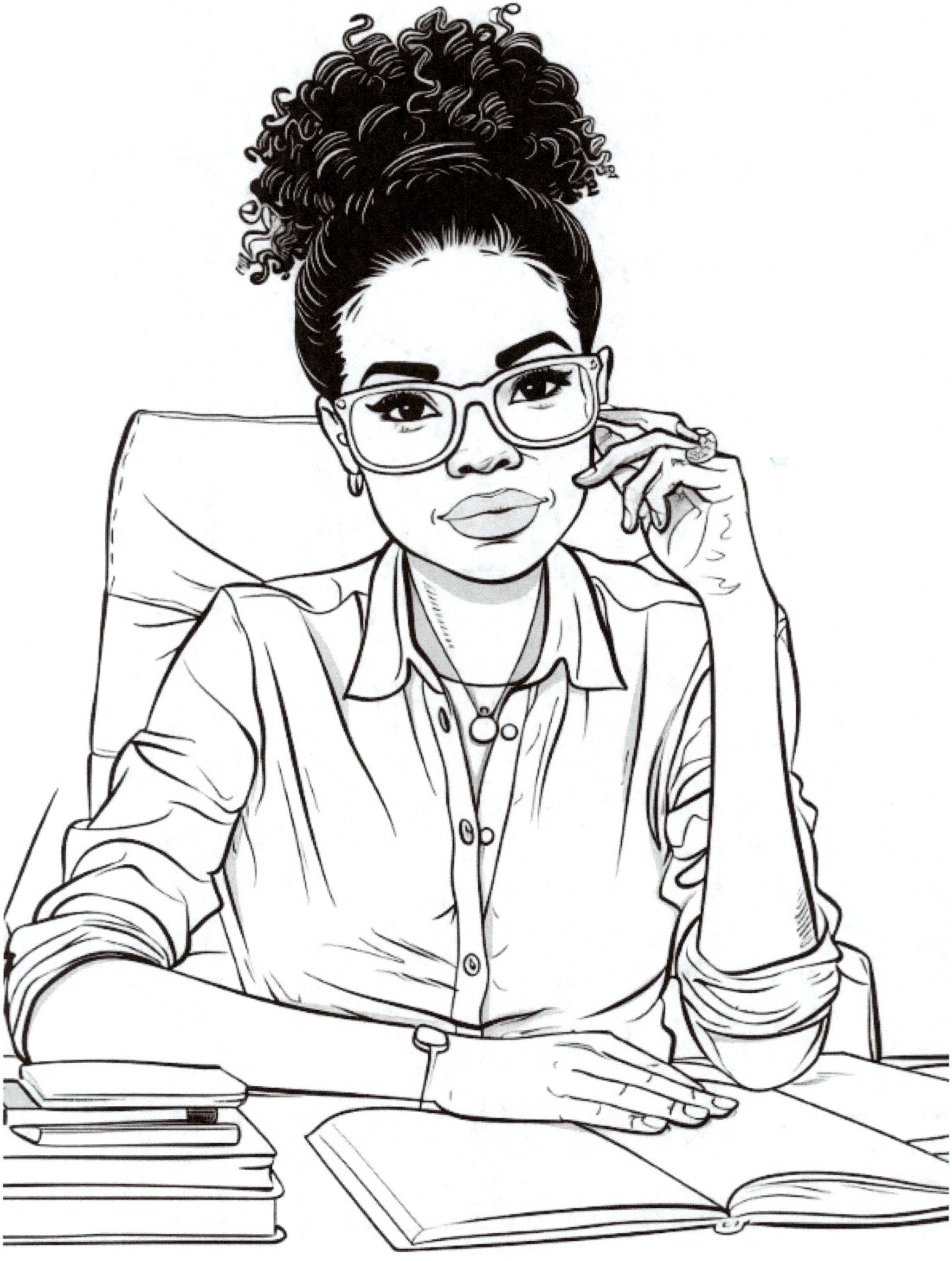

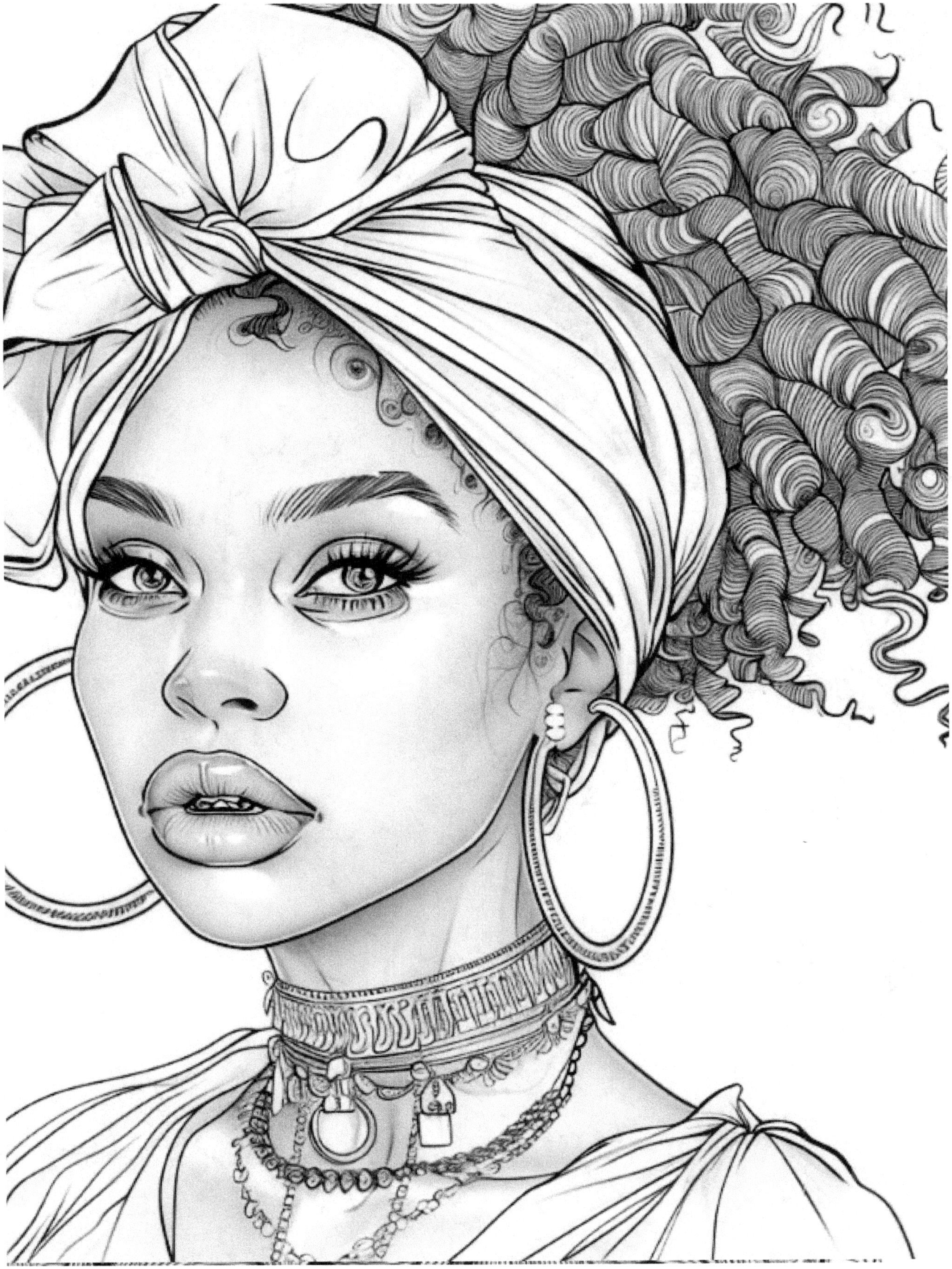

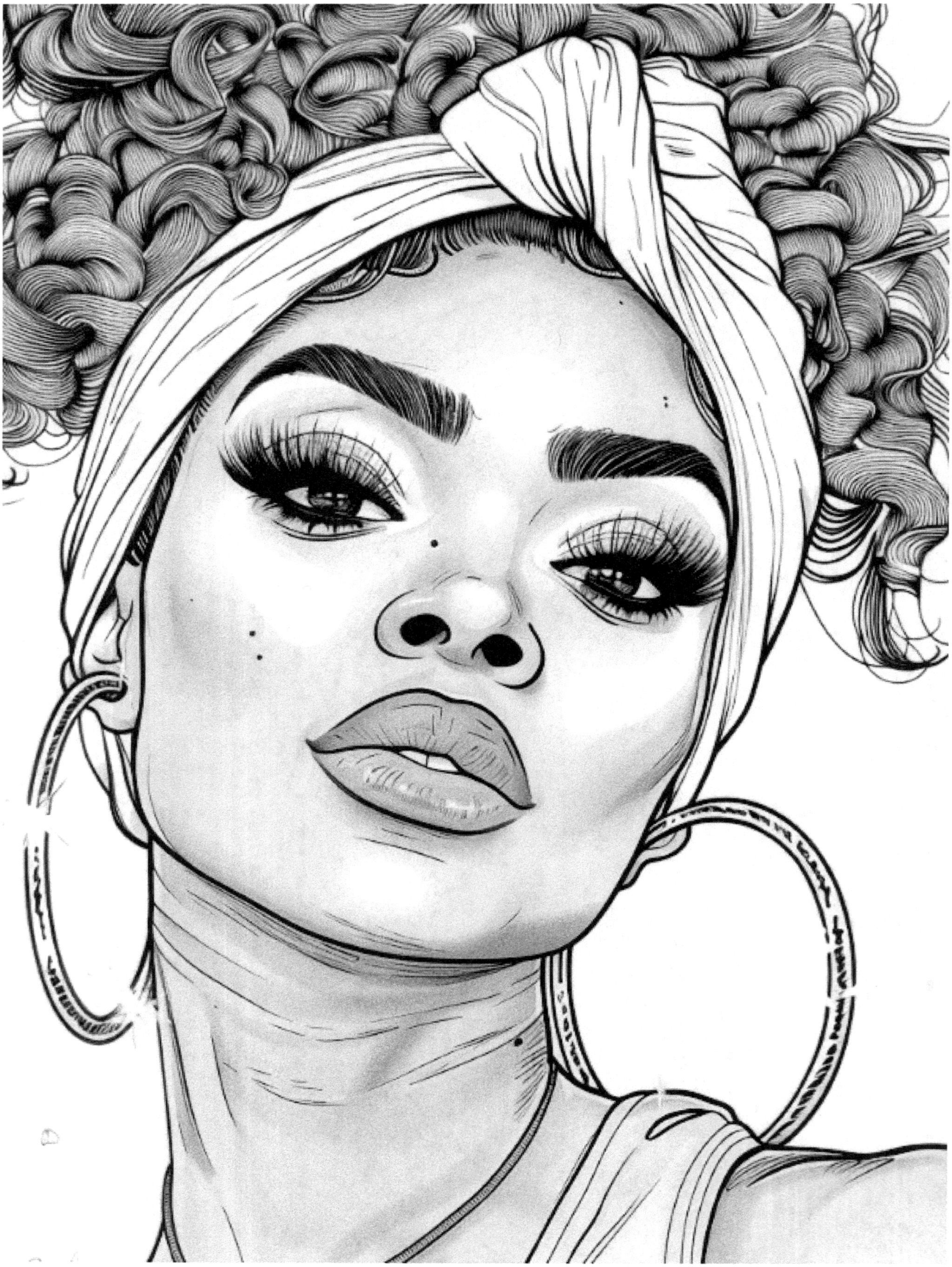

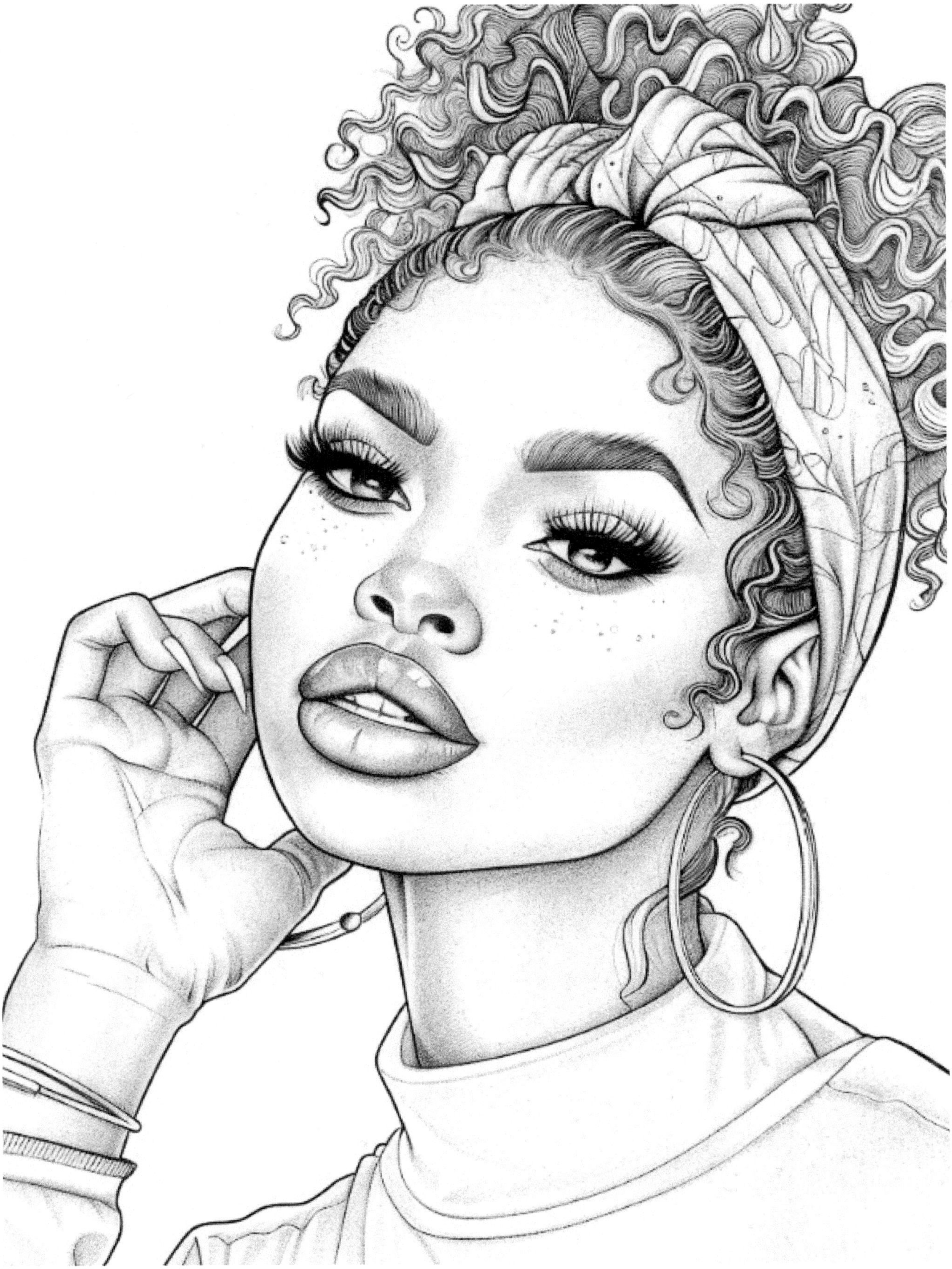

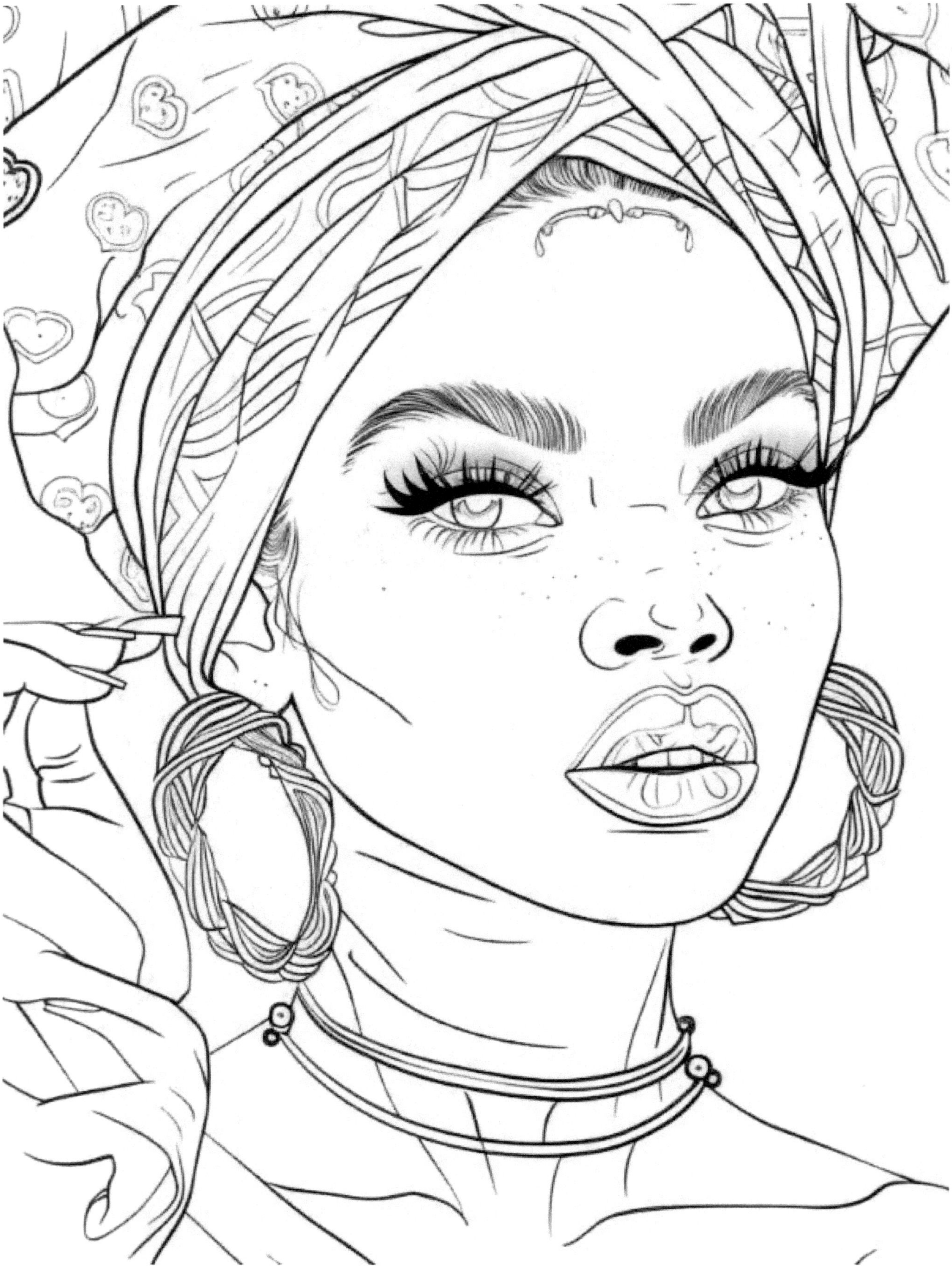

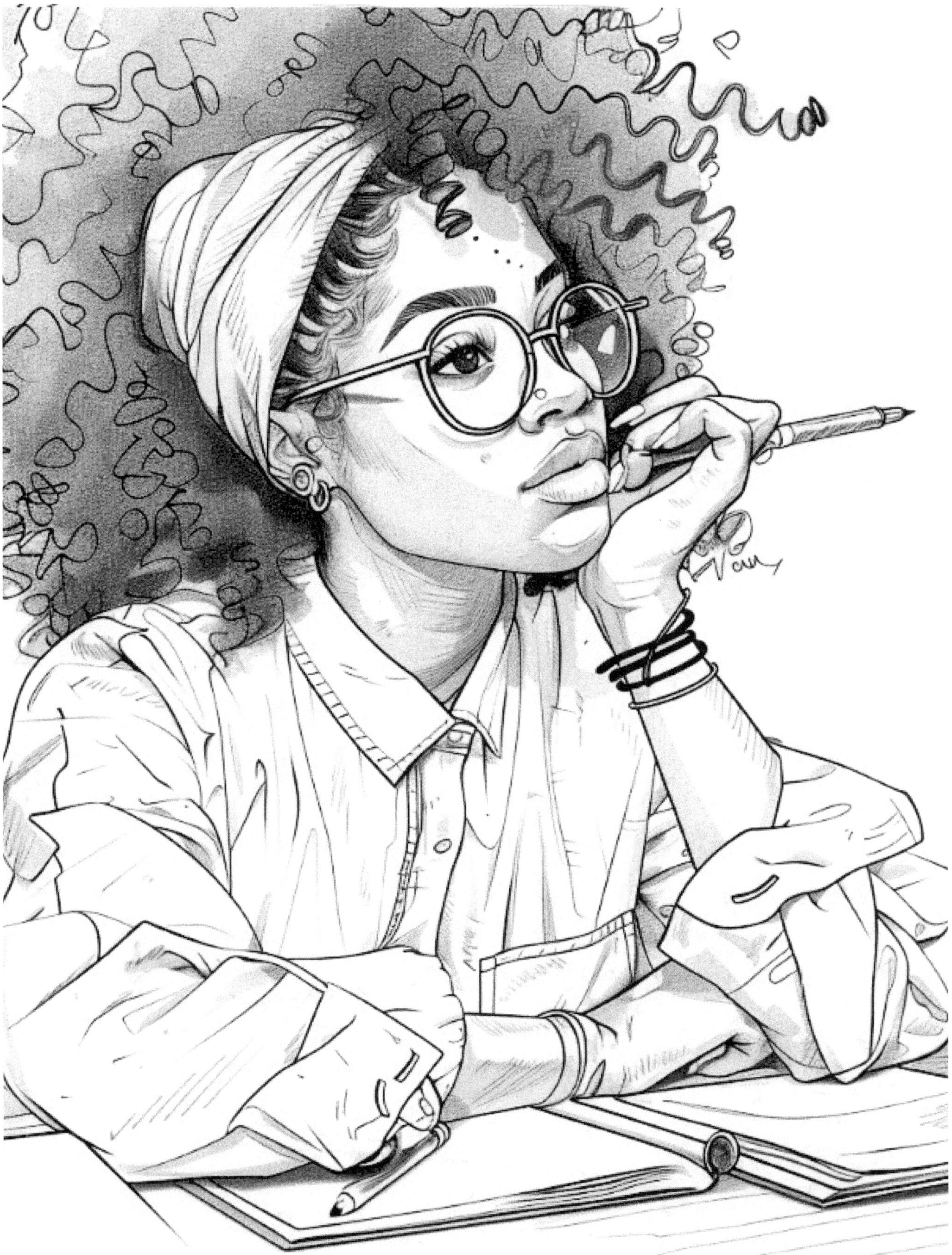

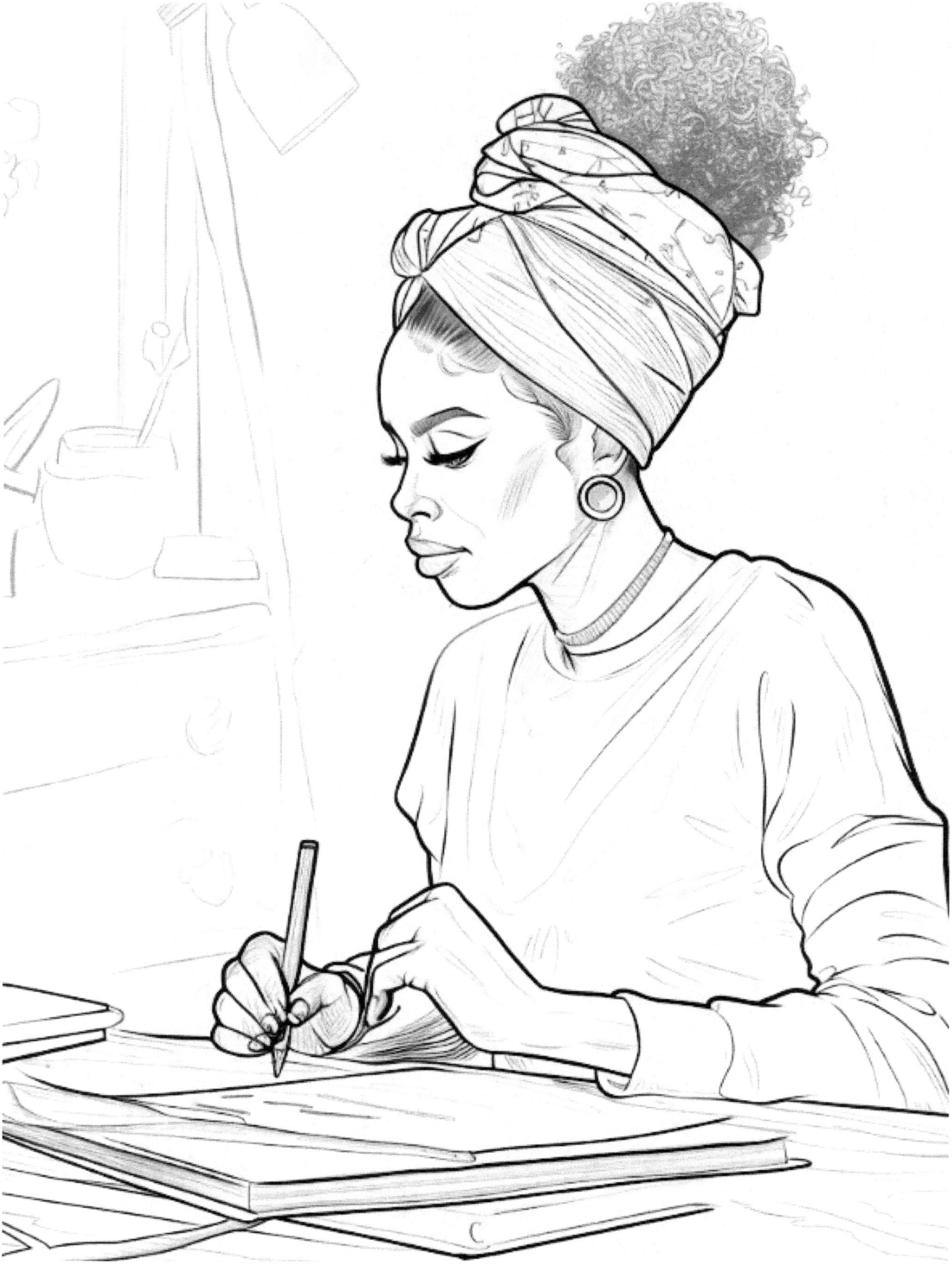

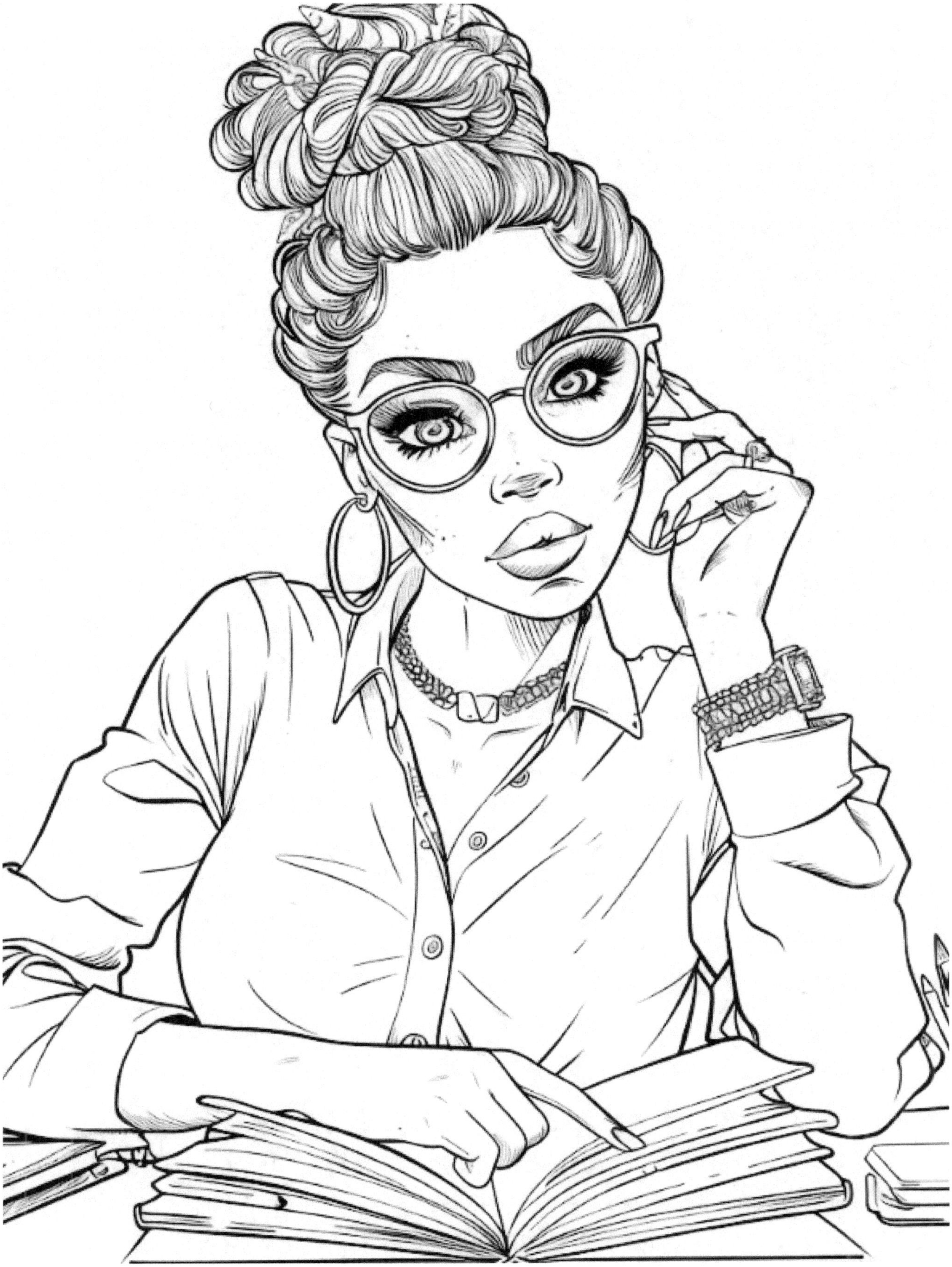

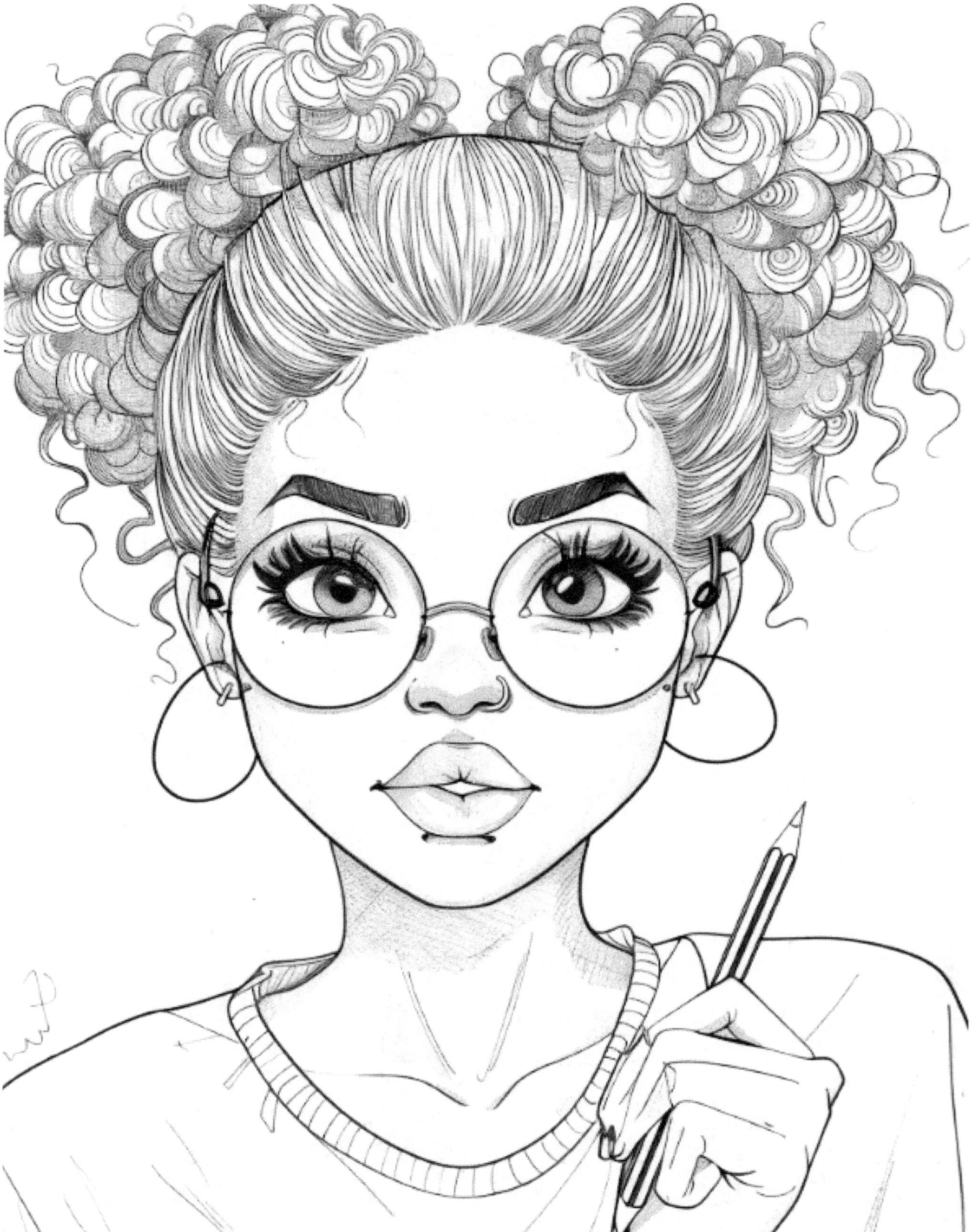

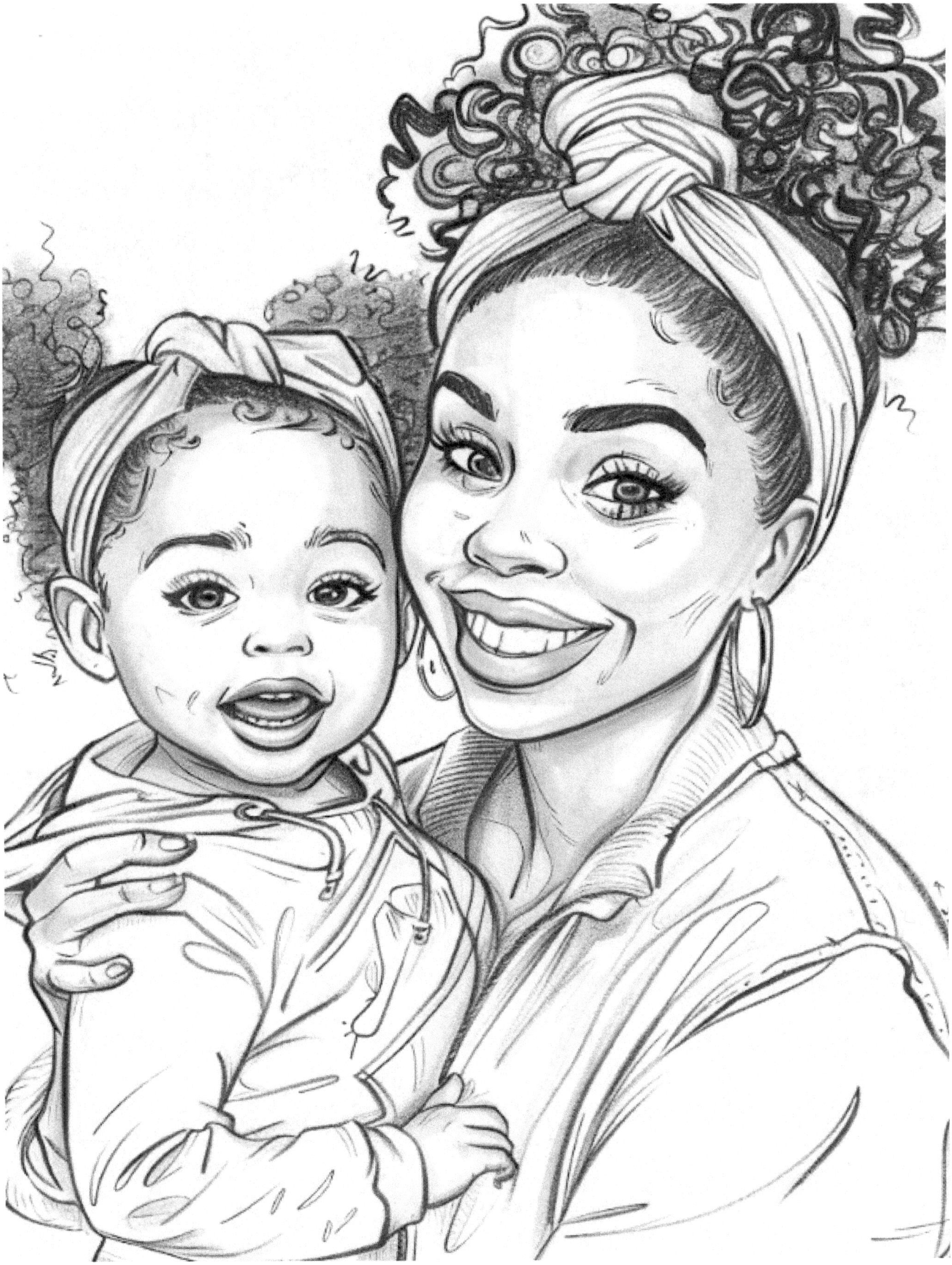

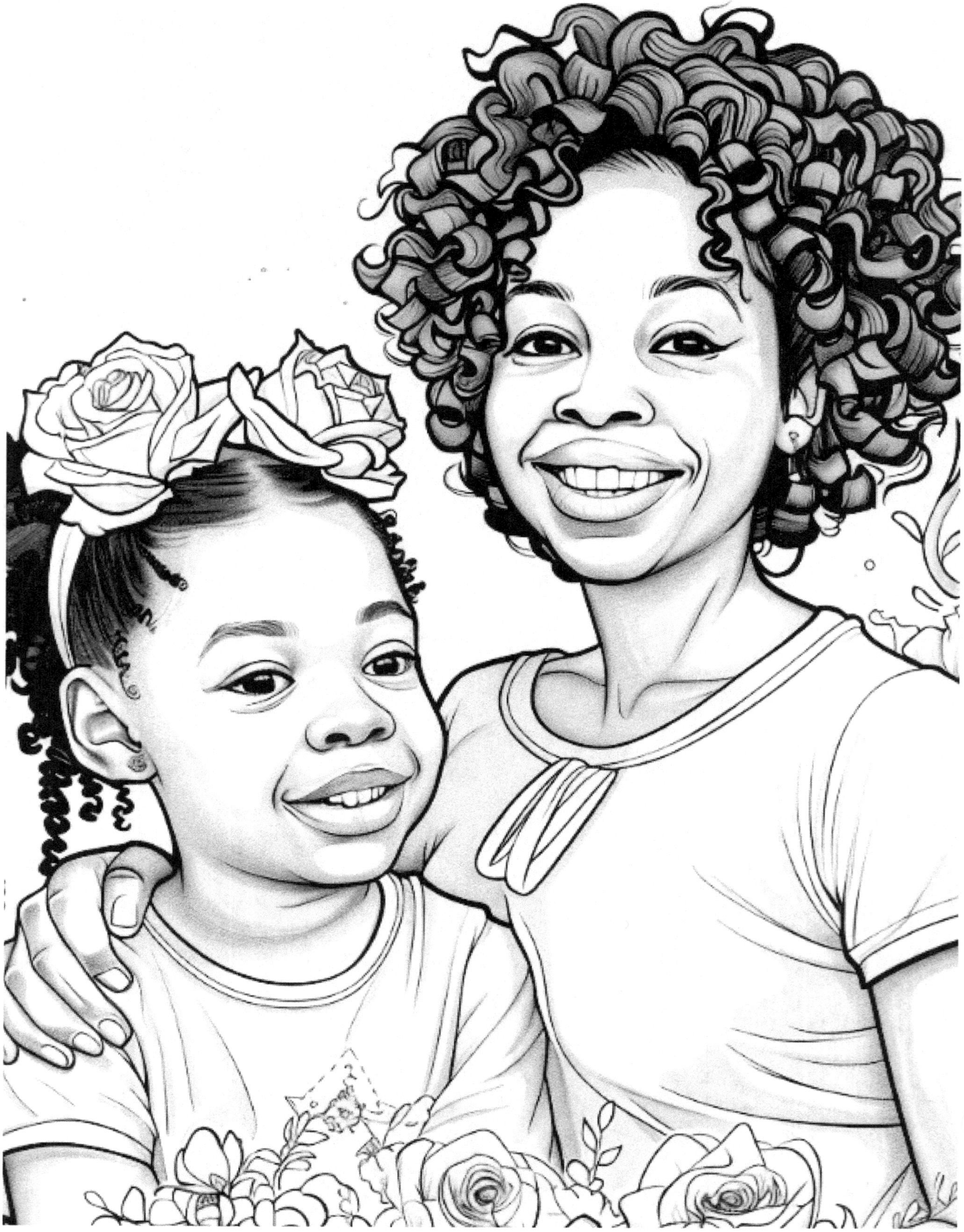

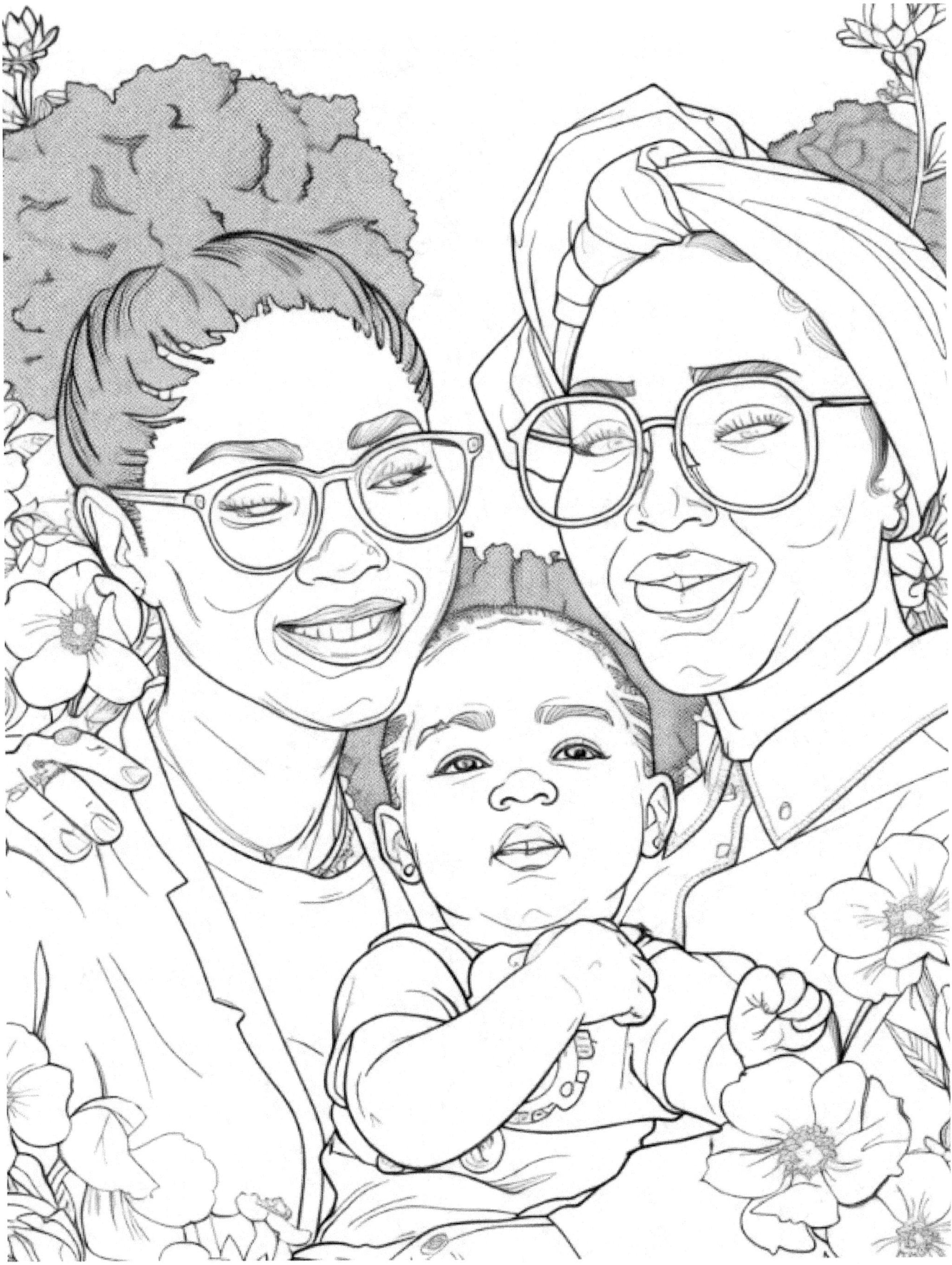

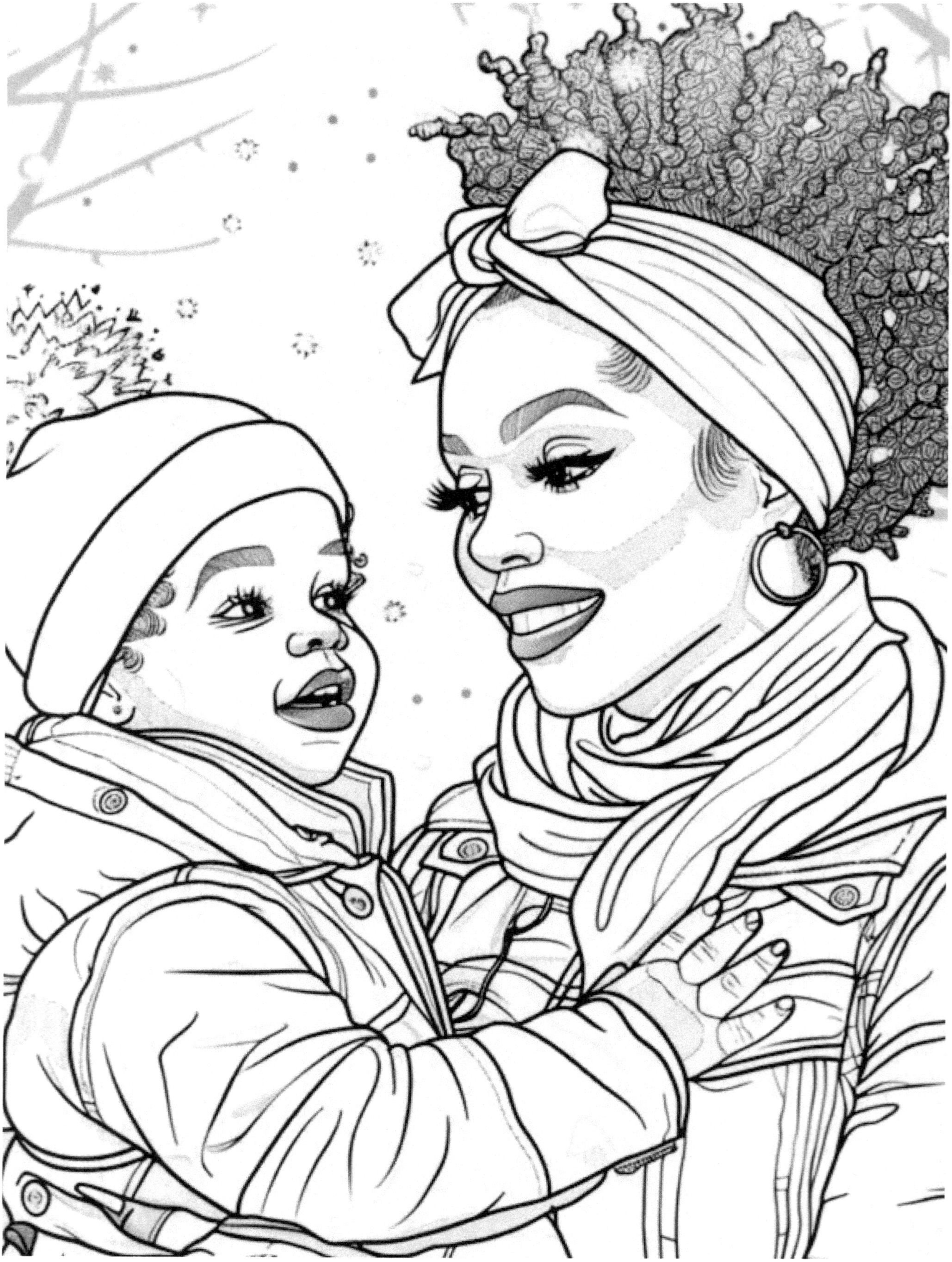

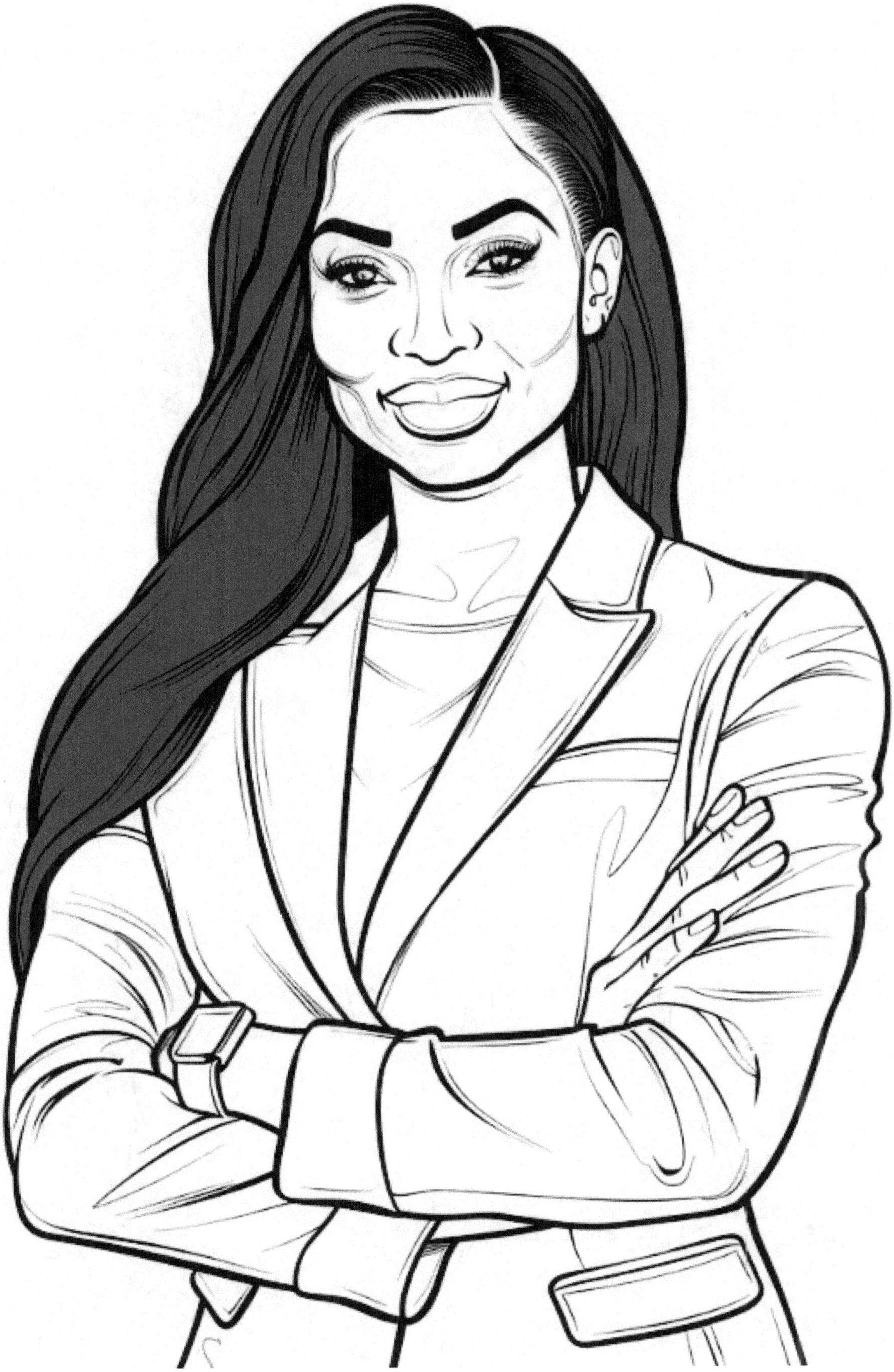

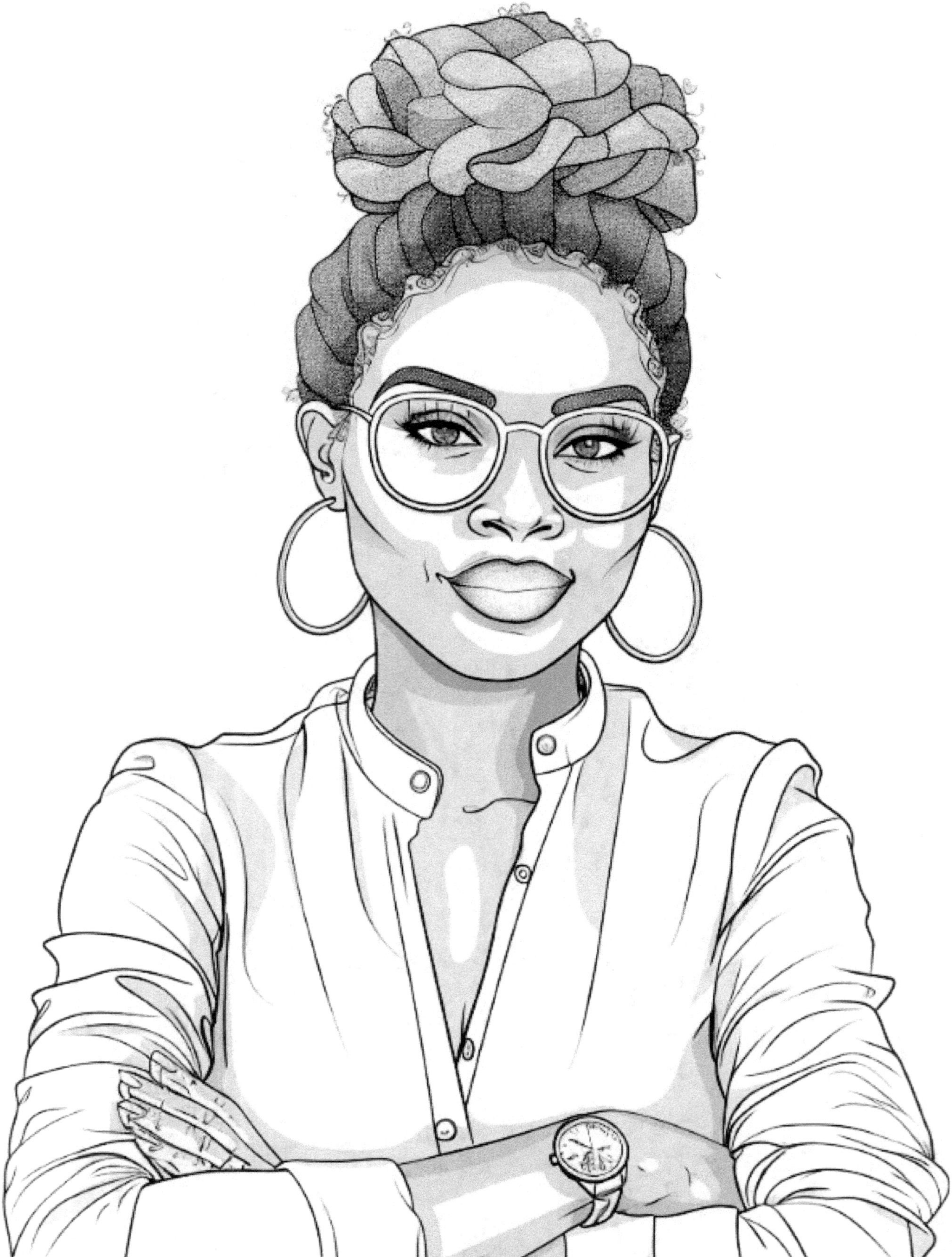

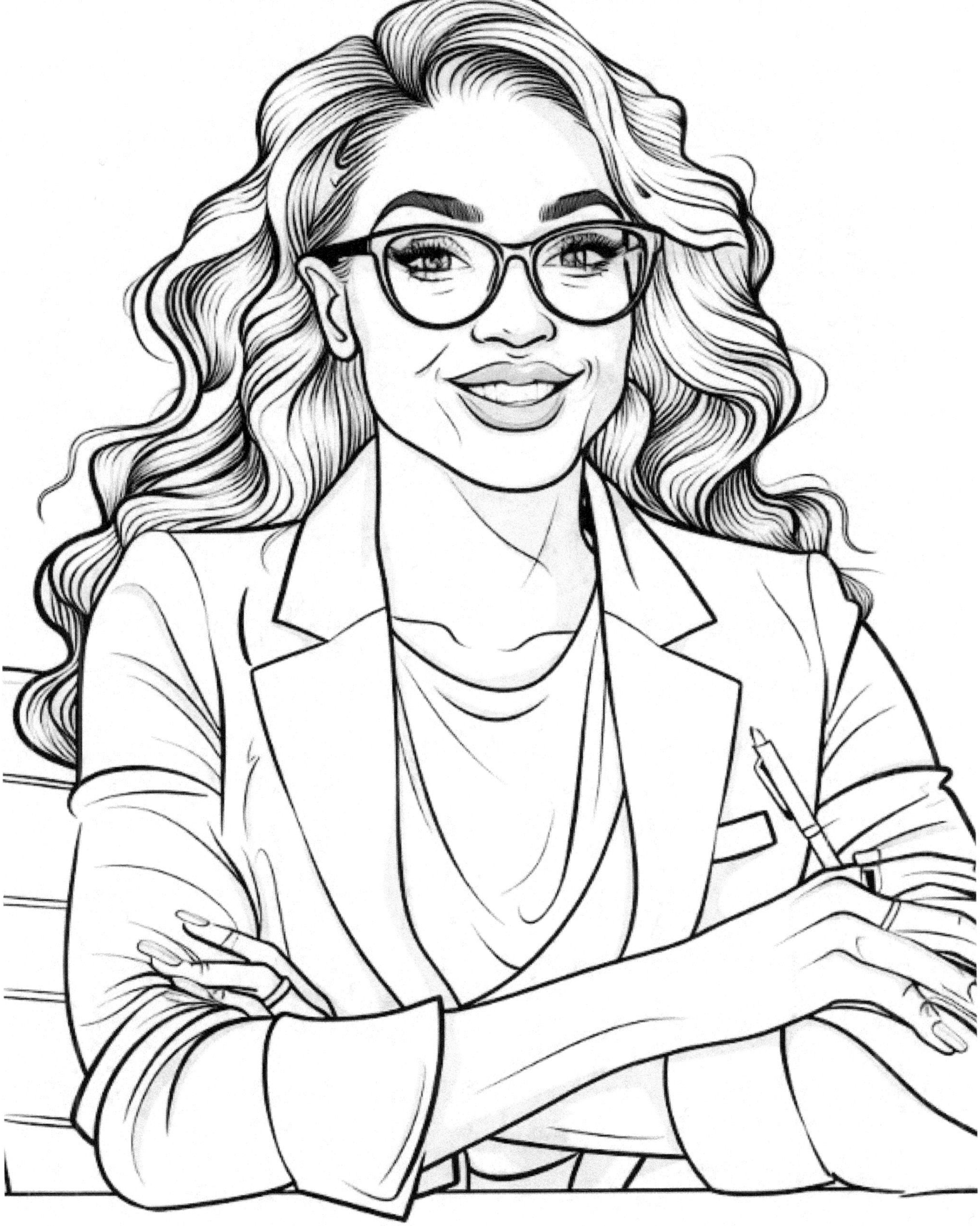

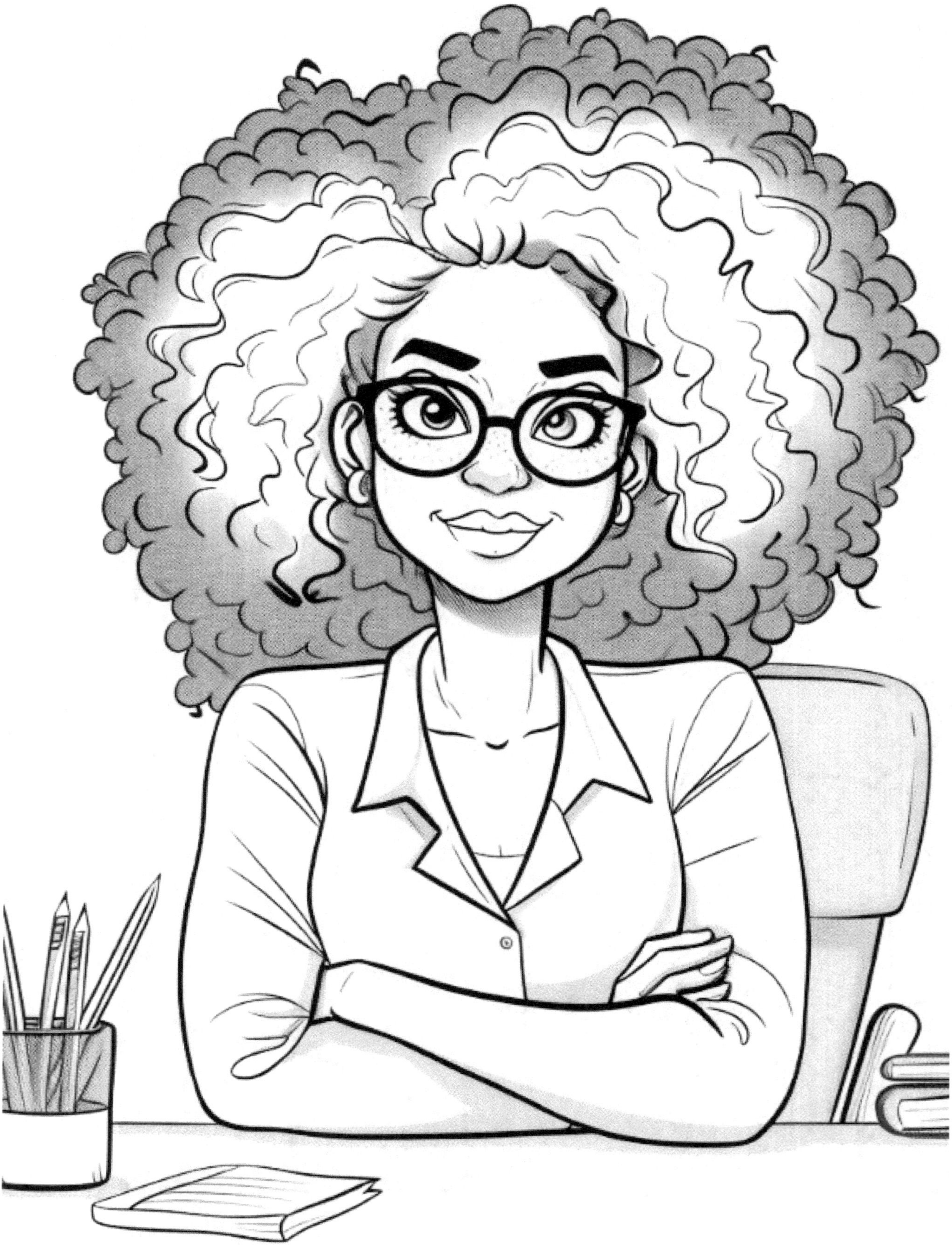

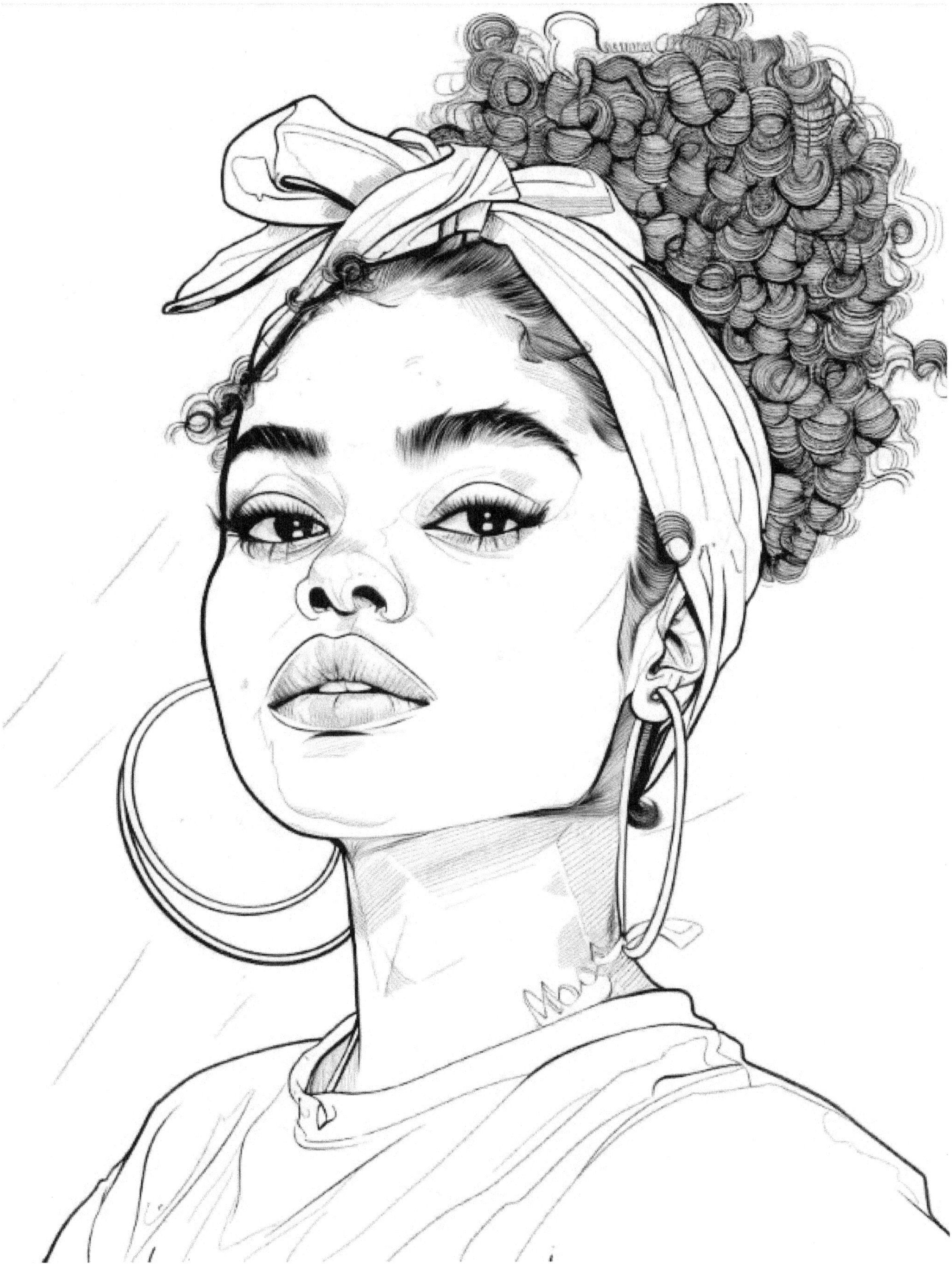

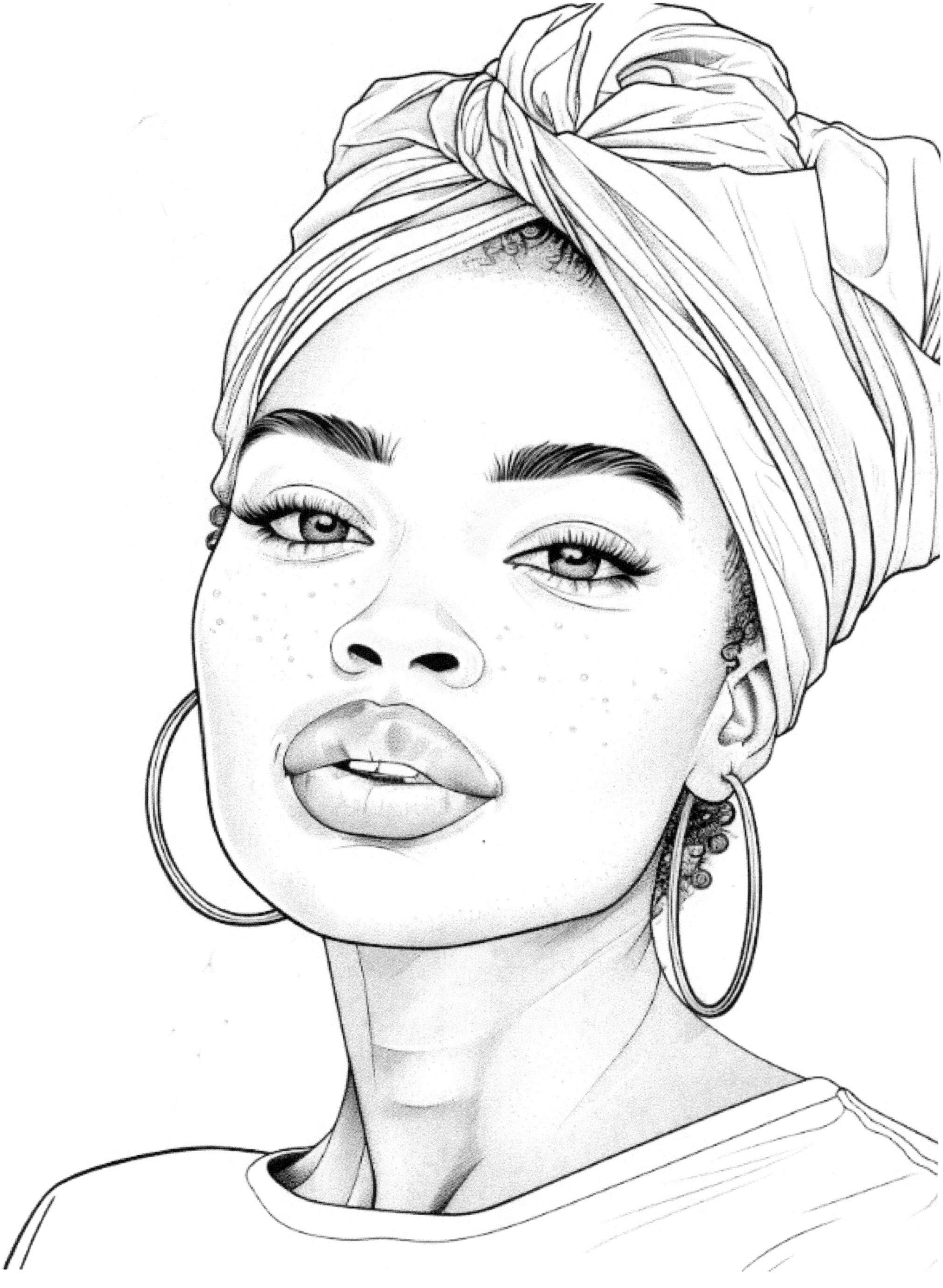

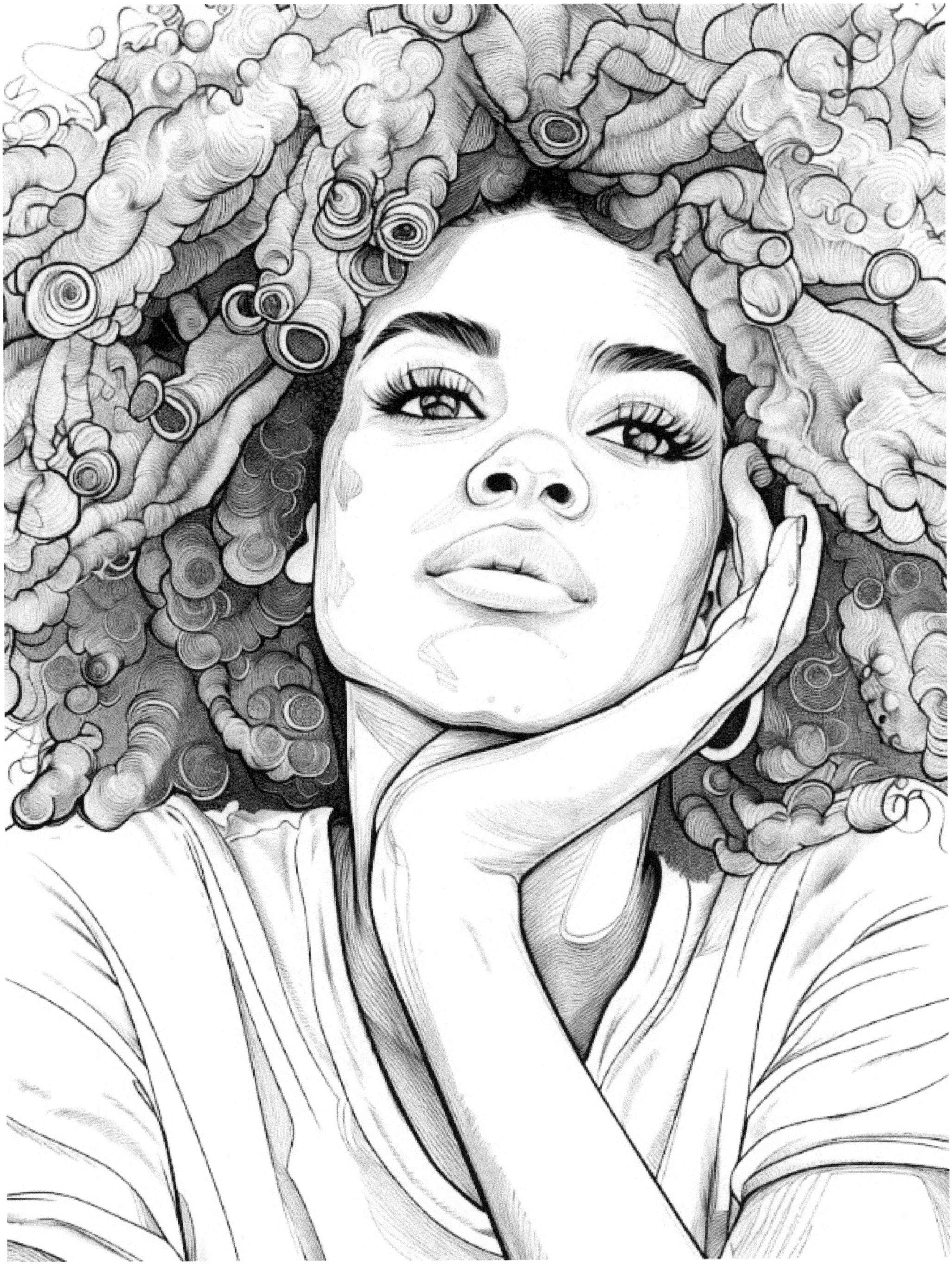

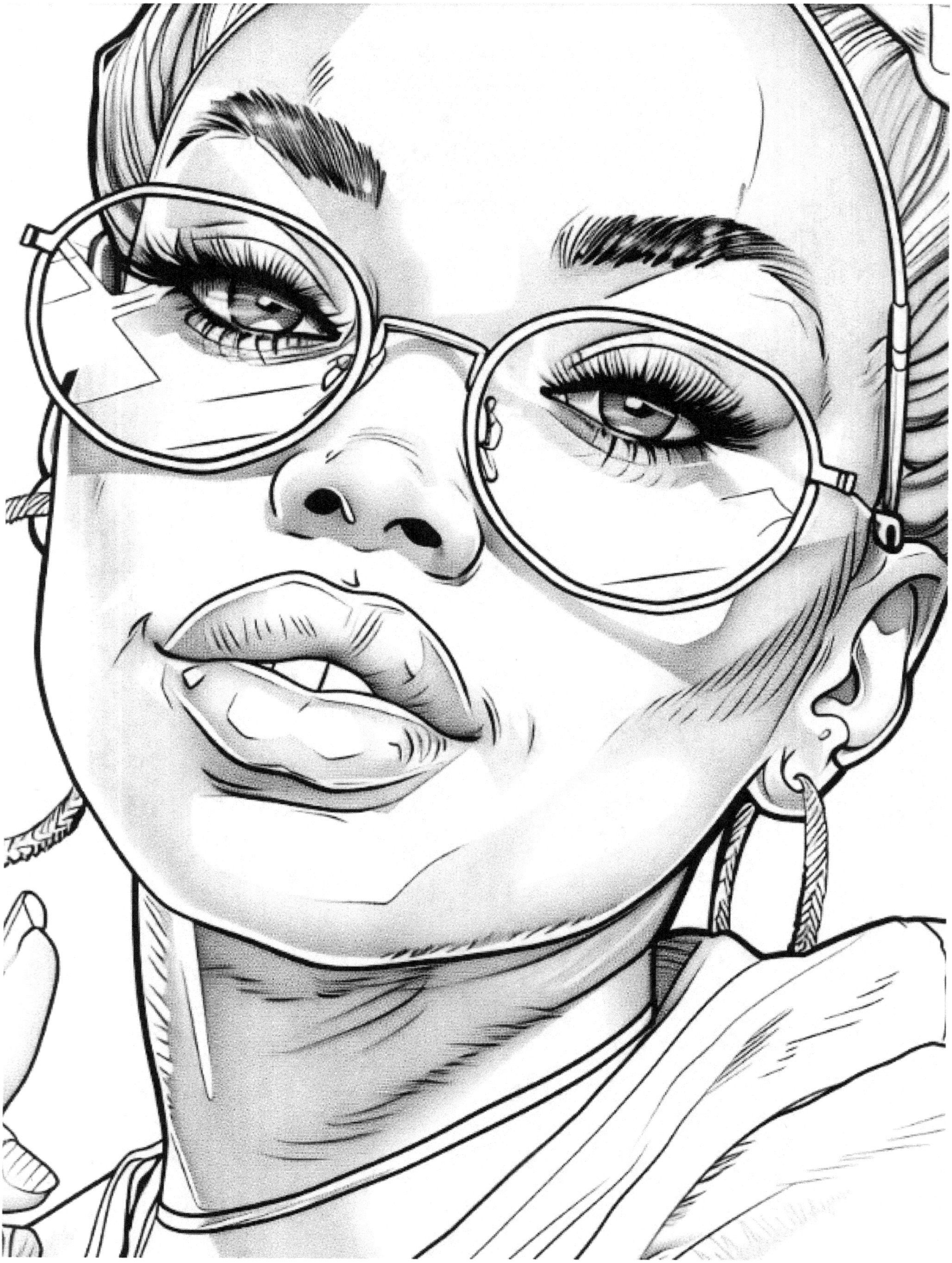

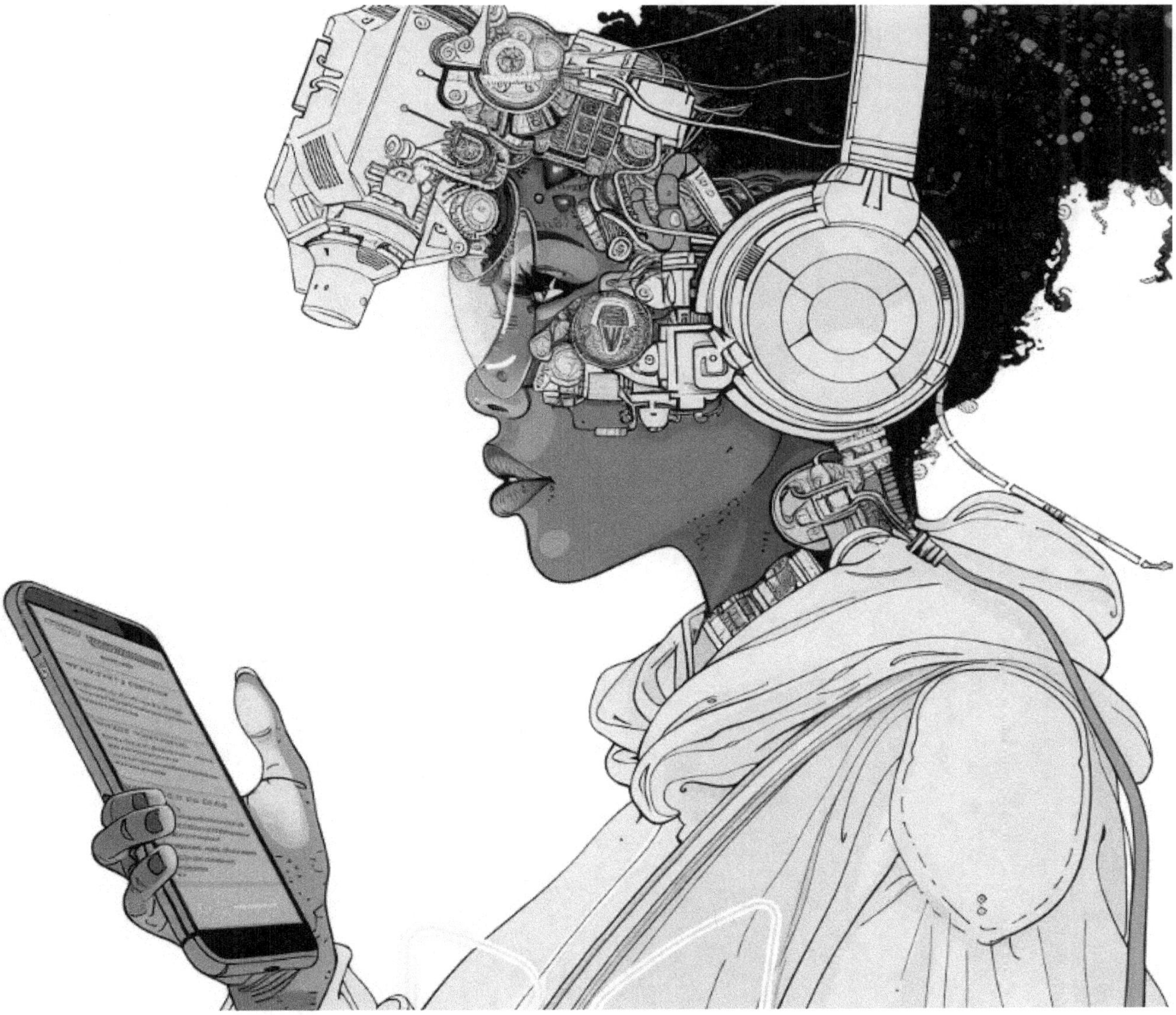

THANK YOU FOR YOUR ORDER

www.ingramcontent.com/pod-product-compliance
Lightning Source LLC
Chambersburg PA
CBHW062101220526
45471CB00010B/3565
* 9 7 9 8 3 2 1 1 3 5 3 5 8 *